STUDENTS, PROFESSORS, AND COUNSELORS AGREE:

GETTING WHAT YOU CAME FOR IS A MUST-READ FOR GRADUATE STUDENTS

I did everything that Robert Peters said to do, and my academic progress was far ahead of schedule. You really *can* get a master's and Ph.D. in three years, and this book tells you how. It is readable, funny, and enormously useful.
>—Carole S. Fungaroli, Ph.D.
>Department of English
>University of Virginia

Not since *What Color Is Your Parachute?* have I read such thorough, comprehensive material that will directly benefit the readers as *Getting What You Came For*. Anyone even remotely contemplating graduate school should read it from cover to cover. If you are an undergraduate student who can read only two "career-related" books, *Getting What You Came For* MUST be one of them.
>—John Hannabach
>Director, Career Services
>Georgia Institute of Technology

I want to applaud you for writing this book. [It] is exactly what I needed to read to realize that a lot of the problems I'm encountering really aren't that extraordinary.
>—Katherine Almquist
>M.A. candidate
>Department of French Literature
>Columbia University

I consider this book required reading for every undergraduate who asks me whether to pursue an advanced degree. It offers concrete advice on how to negotiate the hazards and the hassles that my profession has set up to weed out, chasten, and, we hope, also train those who seek to enter.
>—Dr. Herbert S. Lindenberger
>Director, Humanities Center
>Stanford University

I just want to thank you for your super book. I'm convinced it (and you) is responsible for much of the good fortune I had in getting into grad schools.
>—Ira Carnahan
>Department of Political Science
>Princeton University

Peters has created a valuable vade mecum for a typically bewildered population of students, telling them what they need to know but are unlikely to learn from the lips of college professors.
>—Dr. Edward O. Wilson
>Baird Professor of Science
>Harvard University

(Please turn the page for more praise)

GETTING WHAT YOU CAME FOR

GETTING WHAT YOU CAME FOR

THE SMART STUDENT'S GUIDE
TO EARNING A MASTER'S OR A PH.D.

REVISED EDITION

ROBERT L. PETERS, PH.D.

ILLUSTRATIONS BY THE AUTHOR

FARRAR, STRAUS AND GIROUX
NEW YORK

Farrar, Straus and Giroux
19 Union Square West, New York 10003

Grateful acknowledgment is made for permission to reprint the following material: Excerpts from *The Cat in the Hat* by Dr. Seuss, copyright © 1957 by Dr. Seuss, copyright renewed © 1985 by Theodor S. Geisel and Audrey S. Geisel; reprinted by permission of Random House, Inc. Excerpt from the *MLA Job Information List*, copyright © 1991, reprinted by permission of the Modern Language Association of America. Excerpt from *The Role of GRE General and Subject Test Scores in Graduate Program Admission* by Philip K. Oltman and Rodney T. Hartnott reprinted by permission of Educational Testing Service, the copyright owner. Excerpt from *Writing for Social Scientists: How to Start and Finish Your Thesis, Book, or Article* by Howard Becker, copyright © 1986 by Howard Becker, reprinted by permission of the University of Chicago Press.

The Library of Congress has cataloged the 1992 edition as follows:
Peters, Robert L., 1951–
   Getting what you came for : the smart student's guide to earning a Master's or a Ph.D. / Robert L. Peters ; illustrated by the author.— 1st ed.
      p.   cm.
   Includes bibliographical references (p.   ) and index.
   ISBN-13: 978-0-374-52361-9
   ISBN-10: 0-374-52361-4
      1. Universities and colleges—United States—Graduate work—Handbooks, manuals, etc.   2. Dissertations, Academic—United States—Handbooks, manuals, etc.   I. Title.

LB2371.4 .P48   1992
378.2'4—dc20
                                                      92027763
                                                           CIP

ISBN-13: 978-0-374-52477-7
ISBN-10: 0-374-52477-7

Designed by Fritz Metsch

www.fsgbooks.com

13   15   17   19   21   22   20   18   16   14

■ ■ ■ ■ ■ ■ ■ ■ ■ ■ ■ ■

TO ALL MY FRIENDS WHO MADE GRADUATE SCHOOL WORTHWHILE: VICKI Monks, Don Horak, Donna Celler, Melita Schaum, Linda Powell, David Weir, Pete and Sherry Seymour, John and Maria Tolan, Beth and Michael Machover, Irina Reuss and Jaime Court, Larry Griffing, and Tom Darling. To my patient adviser, Evelyn Shaw. And especially to my friend and colleague Joan Darling, whose advice and support guided me to graduation.

TO THE CHEERLEADERS WHO MADE THIS BOOK POSSIBLE: KAREN PROBERT(!), Mark Plotkin, and Liliana Madrigal, Andy Colb and Nancy Chapman, Frank and Alice Powell, Ginger Staron, and Tony Byrne. To my generous parents Bob Peters and Jean and Jack Brookhart. To my brother, Jeff, for his constant good cheer. To my sisters, Meredith, Kathy, and Tammy. To Joshua Pickering, for his computer expertise. And to Mark Frisk and my editor, Elisabeth Kallick Dyssegaard, whose gentle direction has made writing this book both possible and fun.

FINALLY, TO MY FIRST ADVISER. WITHOUT HIS UNIQUE IDEAS ON ACADEMIC guidance I would not have realized the pressing need for this book.

CONTENTS

GETTING
WHAT YOU CAME
FOR

1

THIS BOOK CAN HELP

(AND YOU PROBABLY NEED IT!)

> "I know some new tricks,"
> Said the Cat in the Hat.
> "A lot of good tricks.
> I will show them to you.
> Your mother
> Will not mind at all if I do."
>
> —Dr. Seuss, *The Cat in the Hat*

WHEN I WAS GETTING MY PH.D. IN FISH BEHAVIOR AT STANFORD DURING THE late 1970s, I did almost everything wrong. It took me eight long, painful years to get my degree, and by the time I finished I never wanted to work with fish again. I had problem professors and problem fish, and I eventually ran out of money. I spent the last year typing my thesis on an old portable typewriter in a tiny apartment in Austin, Texas, overlooking Jorge's Uptown Enchilada Bar and Grill, while working as a waiter in a fresh fish restaurant—not my idea of thesis-related employment. The bottom line is that all my thesis work, including course work, could have been completed in three years if I had known what I was doing.

In any given year there are more than 150,000 doctoral students and 1,000,000 master's students registered in graduate programs in the United States. Most of them don't know what they're doing any more than I did. While the greater simplicity and structure of master's programs makes it easier for master's students to complete their programs successfully, often even they have a terrible time finishing. One master's student described his thesis-writing experience as "twenty-four months of hell." The average doctoral student is enrolled full-time for 6.8 years and only about half of them eventually finish.

Graduate students run into problems because they do not understand how graduate school works; nor do most undergraduate counselors and graduate departments provide enough realistic guidance. Therefore, students charge off in the wrong direction or in no direction at all.

This book tells you what graduate school is really like. Instead of just listing degree requirements, reminding you to meet deadlines, or telling you to check with the counseling center if you have no idea what you are doing, I tell you how to create a comprehensive strategy that blends politics, psychology, and planning to ensure that your hard work pays off with a degree and a job. One of my friends, following the plan in this book, decided on a thesis topic in her first year, took her orals one and a half years early, and earned her Ph.D. in less than four years.

Some of my advice may surprise you. Instead of just telling you to choose a good university, I explain how important it is to concentrate on finding a good thesis adviser *before* you choose the university. Instead of telling you how to be a good teacher, I explain why too much concentration on teaching is a deadly trap that can prevent you from graduating. I tell you how to find a thesis topic with as little pain as possible (don't look for one that will win the Nobel Prize), how to minimize the chances that your thesis committee will make you rewrite your entire thesis, and how to get a start on your career while still in school. All this advice is based on extensive interviews with both successful and unsuccessful master's and Ph.D. students from many disciplines. Their experiences, both enlightening and terrifying, are scattered throughout the book.

The next two chapters are straight talk on why graduate school is hard. I want you to recognize the magnitude of the challenge you are facing, so that you can make a realistic decision about whether to enroll. Once you are in, I want you to do what is necessary to succeed. Therefore, while some of the descriptions of the nature of graduate school may seem alarming, they are merely meant to be eye-opening. Although most of the students I have interviewed in preparation for writing this book had significant difficulties in graduate school, a minority had relatively easy and enjoyable experiences. In general, these more successful students had worked prior to beginning school or for other reasons had developed traits of determination and organization that allowed them to succeed. My goal in writing this book is to teach you the strategies they used and to point out the pitfalls waiting for the unwary.

The work in graduate school is not intrinsically difficult. If you are smart enough to get in, you are smart enough to get out with a master's degree or a Ph.D. and a quality thesis. Most jobs demand more work than graduate school, so it is not the amount of work that creates the trouble. What is hard is the lack of structure, supervision, and help, both emotional and practical. With the advice in this book, you can create your own structure, enjoy the process, and, most important, finish.

NOTE TO READERS OF THE
▪ SECOND EDITION ▪

I wrote the first edition of this book in 1992 to help graduate students cope with their stressful educational experiences and a bleak job market. Many of my readers have written or even called to say that my advice helped, for which I'm glad. Unfortunately, now, in 1997, things have gotten even harder for graduate students. Therefore, more than ever, you need good advice and careful planning to be competitive. For would-be doctoral students, prospects are rough—you'll pay more for school, take longer to finish, and have less chance of getting a good job when you graduate. For many master's students, life's a little easier. You'll probably finish on time, but the competition to get into a good graduate school is likely to be tougher and you can expect to pay a lot more than even a few years ago—tuition at some schools has been rising 10 percent a year. Those of you who will be looking for jobs will be facing competition from Ph.D.s who got squeezed out of academic or research positions.

Competition to get into grad school is up. For example, the University of Indiana's English department now has nearly twice as many applicants and admits only half as many as during the 1980s (they now admit less than 10 percent of applicants into their master's and doctoral programs).

Costs are way up and graduate students get less free aid than they used to. The National Center for Education Statistics (NCES) reports that, for 1992–93, doctoral or master's students attending private universities paid an average of $21,000 annually in tuition, fees, and living expenses (financial aid would cover some of this). At public schools, total expenses were $17,000 to $18,000. As a result of rising costs and falling "no strings" financial aid, student borrowing is climbing rapidly. For example, average cumulative debt per graduate student at Indiana University soared from $16,314 in 1992–93 to $26,798 in 1994–95. The American Council on Education reports that students are "borrowing a lot more money than ever before" and indicates that in a two-year period the total volume of federal loans to students, including undergrads, jumped 47 percent. Chapter 9 of this book has been completely updated to bring you the latest strategies on getting the most financial aid possible and keeping your loan balance low.

Doctoral students are taking more time to finish than ever before. In 1963 the median number of years a graduate student needed to get his or her Ph.D. was around eight. As of 1994, a student needed nearly eleven years, an increase of three years. Median time increased four months just from 1991 to 1994. At $17,000 to $21,000 dollars per year, that's a lot of extra expense. Why is it taking so long? There are several factors, but the number-one cause is excessive teaching. As financial pressures squeeze universities, they turn to their graduate students for cheap teaching, working them so hard that it significantly extends time to completion. In the English department at the University of Illinois at Urbana–Champaign, grad students teach two-thirds of courses. Excessive teaching requirements coupled with poor pay and dismal job prospects have caused grad students at Yale and other schools to try unionizing, so far without much success (in 1996 Yale squashed a strike by 230 graduate students by threatening harsh reprisals). You can increase your chances of graduating on time with minimum debt load by using strategies discussed in this book.

The job market for Ph.D.s in most disciplines is the tightest ever, as exemplified by Philip J. Frankenfeld, poster child for unemployed Ph.D.s. He earned his doctorate in economics and spent seven years fruitlessly searching for a job while living at home. According to Frankenfeld, his mother was beginning to despair, saying, "My God, what's he going to do when he's not cute anymore?" when he suddenly landed a job with a Washington, D.C., research firm, studying the future of the automobile in American transportation.

Humanities are in the worst shape, with hundreds of applicants fighting over each teaching position, but some of the hard disciplines aren't much better off. The titles of recent articles in the journal *Academe* say it all: "Whatever Happened to the Job Boom?" and "Lessons from the Job Wars: What Is to Be Done?" In some fields, things aren't great for master's students either. For example, in 1994 nearly 8 percent of chemists with master's degrees were unemployed, and the percentage of chemists employed full-time dropped for the seventh year in a row. Chapter 3 reviews some recent statistics and helps you realistically assess whether it's worthwhile going to grad school, given the job market, and whether a master's or a Ph.D. makes most sense for you.

Don't let the above discourage you. Just be realistic about what you're up against and plan accordingly. My book gives you strategies to ensure that you'll be one of the lucky ones with a job. Good luck!

2

WHAT IS GRADUATE SCHOOL

LIKE?

"GRADUATE SCHOOL IS A RITUAL HUMILIATION IN WHICH NOVICE ACADEMICS are initiated into their respective disciplines," said one successful academic. Not exactly what you envisioned, right? For many students, this characterization is barely an exaggeration. Although graduate school need not be brutalizing, it can be very different from what you experienced as an undergraduate.

Many graduate students complain about a lack of formal orientation and guidance throughout the graduate experience. Although some master's programs are highly structured, resembling undergraduate education in that you primarily do course work, many master's and all Ph.D. programs leave most of the structure up to you. You will have to find an adviser and thesis topic, figure out how to study for your orals, and make the contacts that can help you get a job when you get out.

Instead of taking charge, many students waste time floundering, waiting in vain for someone to tell them what to do. This floundering breeds fear, which is a major curse of graduate school life. It will be easy for you to worry about the future. Can you write a thesis, pass your comprehensive exams, and be liked by the professors on your committee?

All this makes graduate school so tough that stress is a big problem. A study by Ramiro Valdez at a northeastern school of social welfare found that, on a standardized scale where 100 equaled the amount of stress experienced by someone whose spouse had just died, doctoral students in their first year scored an average of 313 points. Only 6 percent of the students were considered to be "below crisis level," and the other 94 percent were all described as experiencing "crisis" levels of stress. A second study by Robert Nelson, formerly an assistant psychiatrist at Harvard, found, not surprisingly, that graduate students had a higher percentage of "psychoneurotic" symptoms than undergraduates, and suggested that "more therapeutic hours should be available for graduate students than for undergraduates."

Although master's programs are shorter and tend to be better structured than those at the Ph.D. level, master's candidates also will face new, stressful challenges. The master's thesis in particular will present many of the same problems as a Ph.D. thesis.

▪ THE PROFESSIONAL IMAGE ▪

As an undergraduate you were treated more or less as a child. You could do anything short of burning down the administration building and still graduate if your grades were good.

Graduate school is more like adolescence. You are now judged by the standards of the adult world and in theory you are considered a junior colleague. Your clothes, your deportment, and faculty perceptions of your seriousness and eagerness to work all create an image that will help determine your future. At the same time, you have little money. You have little status. You might think of yourself as a fraternity or sorority pledge, or as a job trainee. You must be eager and obliging, for you are very much a *junior* colleague. Nonetheless, although this social situation can easily make you feel inferior, you must develop self-respect and confidence.

Making this adjustment can be difficult, especially if you are an idealist who believes that there is something wrong with a system that judges by appearances. Shouldn't the quality of your work alone determine your success? Unfortunately, it will not. You cannot hunker down in your carrel and hide out for a few years, all the while creating a brilliant thesis that will earn you awestruck respect. To start with, brilliance is not created in a vacuum and you must interact with other academics to produce good work. Even if you do write a brilliant thesis, you will also have to play a smart political game to maximize future job or academic options. If you want to be one of the select master's students that make it into a Ph.D. program, or one of the fraction of Ph.D.s that get a prestigious job, you've got to establish a reputation for focus, dedication, and brilliance.

Course grades will often be important only in the first year. Qualifying exams and theses are much bigger hurdles. For doctoral or master's candidates who want to go on in research, the real object is to become someone whom your adviser and other professors regard as "promising," as in "a promising young academic." In other words, your professors must believe when they recommend you for a job or a postdoctoral fellowship that you will reflect well on them. Your goal must be to show steady professional development from the first day in graduate school so that by the time you are looking for a job your professors are unreservedly proud of you. Among other things, you must learn to teach classes, publish papers, give departmental seminars, serve on committees, and make witty yet erudite conversation with professors at sherry hour.

Because there is so much to do, you need to start early with focused effort. Remember that you will not be competing for recognition and jobs against the same group you did as an undergraduate. You will be competing against a group who are all as smart as you, or even smarter. And the competition for jobs will be intense in many academic fields. (A recent advertisement for an assistant professor at a mid-ranked English department drew more than six hundred applications.)

▪ IS IT WORTH GOING? ▪

At this point you may be wondering whether graduate school is worth the effort. It is, provided you are going for the right reasons and are realistically prepared. The rewards are many: credentials for work, friendship and camaraderie with your fellow students, access to brilliant and original minds on a level that was unavailable when you were an undergraduate, and the development of your professional skills. Few experiences will be as fulfilling as when you give the first public presentation of your own ideas and find that they are accepted with respect. One master's student, who later went on for his Ph.D., said, "I loved graduate school. The intellectual enthusiasm was great—we talked about ideas that mattered."

Although unstructured time in graduate school can be difficult to manage, *you* decide how to use it, perhaps for the last time in your life. By developing a strong plan for progress in school, you can have ample time for a good social and leisure life.

Finally, for many careers a graduate degree is simply the sine qua non, the key necessary for advancement, opening up a life whose professional satisfactions would otherwise be unobtainable.

3

- - - - - - - - - - - - - -

DO YOU NEED

TO GO?

- - - - - - - - - - - - - -

Neither have they hearts to stay
Nor wit enough to run away

—SAMUEL BUTLER

IF YOU DECIDE TO GO TO GRADUATE SCHOOL, DON'T DO IT JUST BECAUSE YOU don't know what else to do. Grad school, particularly at the Ph.D. level, demands much more of you than undergrad. The work is harder, costs are high, and the chances of success are uncertain. Your undergraduate friends will be gone, and the social environment will probably be neither as lively nor as supportive as when you were an undergrad. Particularly for Ph.D. programs, the solitary nature of the work makes students feel isolated.

Therefore, in deciding whether to go, be realistic. Weigh the costs, both in dollars and in time, against the benefits. Even a two-year master's program can put you substantially in debt (a typical debt load upon graduation for a master's degree in international relations is $25,000). Recognize that students who enter grad programs for specific career goals are more likely to graduate than those with vague plans. If you do know which career you want, estimate how far school will advance your career compared with the same number of years gaining on-the-job experience. Will your lifetime earnings or job satisfaction be greater with a degree?

If you aren't yet certain what career you want, grad school might give you insight, but there are certainly more cost-effective ways of figuring out your life. You might be better off working for a conservation organization, teaching English overseas as a second language, or joining the Peace Corps until you're sure what you want to do.

▪ DO YOU NEED A PH.D.? ▪

WILL YOU GRADUATE?

Approximately 50 percent of doctoral students drop out of their programs. Even those students who have invested several years and made it to candidacy aren't safe—approximately one-fifth of students who attain candidacy fail to finish. Quitting is very painful. As one researcher, Lester Bodian, said, with academic understatement, when you are faced with the conflicting realizations that (a) you are not likely to finish the program and (b) the program is essential to your career goals, this conflict is "likely to arouse dissonance." No kidding.

A review of psychological studies by Bodian concluded that you are more likely to graduate if you:

- *Are married.* Married students are less likely to drop out, probably because they receive more encouragement and other support (e.g., back rubs) from their spouses.
- *Are on schedule.* People who take longer than usual to finish their master's programs tend not to finish Ph.D.s.
- *Are in the sciences.* Physical scientists and biologists are most likely to finish, social scientists lie somewhere in the middle, and students in the humanities are most likely to drop out. This pattern reflects higher levels of both collaborative research and funding in the sciences.
- *Are financially secure.* Financial support is particularly important in determining attrition, and students who must work full-time, for example, have high attrition rates.
- *Have clarity of purpose.* Studies show students have a better chance of finishing if they have concrete career goals and their future jobs depend on attaining the degree. Thus, doctoral students headed for university teaching are more apt to get their Ph.D.s than are students who want to teach on lower levels where a master's degree would suffice.
- *Have a good relationship with your adviser.*

Many of these contributing factors are discussed at greater length elsewhere in the book. Keep them in mind and weigh them in your decision about whether to attend. For example, if you have children, ask yourself if you will be able to manage them, household finances, and your thesis at the same time.

AVERAGE TIME TO COMPLETION

Doctoral programs are *very* time-consuming. Most universities optimistically "expect" that students should be able to finish in four years, given sustained effort. A look at statistics tells a different story. According to a report by the National Research Council, the median time spent as a registered student from the baccalaureate to doctoral degree in 1994 was seven years, a figure that jumped to nearly eleven years when respondents included time in which they were not registered, as in the case of students who took time off to earn money to continue their education. Some fields take longer than others: in 1994 chemistry took the least time at 6.0 registered years and 7.3 actual, while history took 8.6 registered and 11.6 actual (see Table, following).

Thus, if you receive your baccalaureate degree at twenty-two years of age, you can expect to receive a Ph.D. in history or anthropology when you are thirty-four years old. In English you would be thirty-two, and in biology or psychology a comparatively juvenile thirty-one. These figures include people who took time off before starting graduate school, so they may paint the picture a little grimmer than it really is. But note that the median age of graduation for all disciplines is thirty-four years old.

Moreover, these figures have been increasing in recent years, in large part because financial aid has become tighter and students therefore must work more during the learning period, carrying heavier teaching loads. The median registered time to achieve the Ph.D. increased in all fields from 5.5 years in 1970 to 6.3 years in 1980 and 7.2 years in 1994.

The amount of financial aid available is one of the major reasons for the differences among disciplines, humanities being the poor cousins. For example, in 1987 physical science doctoral students only had to earn 7 percent of their own support, while education students had to earn 51 percent.

Remember the saying that time is money. Every year you spend in graduate school means a year without job experience or savings. It may mean that you will put off having children, or if you have them during graduate school, the financial and emotional strains will be greater. Before starting a Ph.D., try to look ahead and think about how it will feel to be five to ten years behind your peers in terms of finances and life stability.

In 1912, Dean West of Princeton worried that graduate schools were attracting men "not because they must be scholars, but because they want

MEDIAN TIME LAPSE FROM BA TO PH.D.
(SOURCE: NATIONAL RESEARCH COUNCIL, 1994)

1994 AVERAGE FOR ALL DISCIPLINES	TOTAL TIME YRS.	REGISTERED TIME
AVERAGE FOR ALL DISCIPLINES	10.8	7.2
Physics and Astronomy	8.0	6.9
Chemistry	7.3	6.0
Earth Atmos. and Marine Sci.	10.6	7.7
Mathematics	8.9	6.8
Computer Sciences	9.7	7.2
PHYSICAL SCIENCES	8.5	6.7
ENGINEERING	9.0	6.4
Biochemistry	8.0	6.5
Other Biosciences	8.9	7.0
Biosciences Subtotal	8.7	6.9
Health Sciences	14.0	7.5
Agricultural Sciences	11.0	6.7
LIFE SCIENCES	9.5	7.0
Psychology	9.4	7.2
Economics	9.7	7.2
Anthropology and Sociology	12.4	8.7
Political Sci./ Internat'l Rel.	11.0	7.9
Other Social Sciences	13.0	7.6
SOCIAL SCI. INCL. PSYCH	10.5	7.5
TOTAL SCIENCES & ENGINEERING	9.3	6.9
History	11.6	8.6
Eng. and Amer. Lang. and Lit.	11.3	8.3
Foreign Lang. and Lit.	11.2	8.3

MEDIAN TIME LAPSE FROM BA TO PH.D.
(SOURCE: NATIONAL RESEARCH COUNCIL, 1994)

1994 AVERAGE FOR ALL DISCIPLINES	TOTAL TIME YRS.	REGISTERED TIME
Other Humanities	12.5	8.6
HUMANITIES	12.0	8.5
EDUCATION	19.7	8.1
Business and Management	12.2	7.2
TOTAL NONSCIENCES	15.9	8.0

a job." Being an idealistic man, he found this "the most sordid and dangerous thing just now in our graduate schools." My advice is the opposite: do not go to graduate school unless you need it for your career.

TOO MANY PH.D.s IN THE JOB MARKET

The majority of Ph.D.s have traditionally become academics, but now academic jobs have become hard to get in most disciplines. Before making the decision to go to graduate school, find out what the job situation is like in your field. Talk to professors, career counselors (your school should have a counseling center), and professional organizations. Is the chance of getting an academic position, if this is what you want, one out of five, or one out of fifty? Some fields, like forestry, chemical engineering, or American politics, may have jobs for nearly all Ph.D. graduates. Other fields, like English, animal behavior, or political theory, may have relatively few. If your field is crowded and competitive, think about switching to an allied field where job opportunities are better. For example, the large number of people who grew up fantasizing over Jacques Cousteau and his band of penguins makes becoming a marine biologist much more difficult than shifting slightly into fishery management, a field with a substantial nonacademic job market.

The last generation of professors got their start during the golden years of academia. The baby boomers were growing up and the number of college students jumped from 3.8 million in 1960 to 9.2 million in 1970. The huge increase in the number of college students in the 1960s resulted in a massive hiring of professors (including my dad), few of whom are yet retiring. By the 1980s, the baby boomers had passed college age and universities and colleges were faced with declining enrollments and budgets. Nonetheless, they still had to support tenure-heavy faculties hired during the boom years. More financial problems arose when federal funding for higher education fell substantially during the 1980s and 1990s, causing college enrollment to drop even lower than would have been expected for purely demographic reasons. The overall result is that there are many fewer college students to be taught and fewer jobs for new academics.

During the late 1980s the hopes of graduate students were unrealistically raised by predictions that the job market would improve dramatically during the 1990s due to massive retirement by the faculty hired in the 1950s and 1960s. Unfortunately for students who believed what they were told and rushed into graduate school, the predictions were dead wrong. The job market is now the worst ever for Ph.D.s in the history of academia. Jack Shuster,* professor of education and public policy at Claremont Graduate School in California, was one who predicted an expansion in teaching jobs. He now says: "We were blindsided by an abrupt economic downturn in 1990 and 1991. The ripple effect went everywhere and colleges and universities began to reduce budgets and to curtail faculty hiring."

But a more sinister interpretation of the glut is also possible, one based on understanding that academic institutions act out of self-interest. Because universities need an abundance of graduate students to teach their courses, it's in their best interests to have an overabundance of graduate students. I quote Cary Nelson, Jubilee Professor of Liberal Arts and Sciences at the University of Illinois: "Apprenticeship has turned into exploitation. Without a viable job market, Ph.D. programs have only one economic rationale—they are a source of cheap instructional labor for the universities." Plus, universities love having hundreds of high-quality applicants for each tenure-track job. What employer wouldn't? Not surprisingly, when the number of applicants to doctoral programs started dropping slightly in the 1980s because the poor chumps realized they were going to be exploited and cut off in mid-career without jobs, the universities got concerned and mobilized to lure in more grad students. My files from around 1990 contain articles by university deans deploring the coming shortage of graduate students and suggesting ways to increase production. And the word went forth that graduate students should attend in abundance, and they did. The number of graduate students has increased every year since 1987, and continues to increase as I write. As of 1996, there are more doctoral students than ever (see Chart), and the chances that most of these will find the jobs they are looking for are slim.

When asked to describe the direction of the current job market for

* Many of the educators quoted in this chapter were originally cited in the article "Whatever Happened to the Job Boom?" by James Michael Brodie, published in the journal *Academe*, January–February 1995.

DOCTORATE RECIPIENTS, TOTAL AND BY GENDER, 1964—94
(SOURCE: NATIONAL RESEARCH COUNCIL, SURVEY OF EARNED DOCTORATES, 1994)

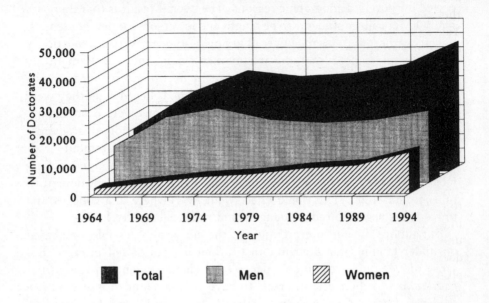

humanities, Michael Bérubé, professor of English at the University of Illinois, uses the term "implode." According to the Modern Language Association, only 51 percent of English Ph.D.s found tenure-track positions in 1991–92. This means that 49 percent of the students, who put in an average of twelve years' graduate study, aren't finding the jobs for which they were trained. According to an article in the journal *Lingua Franca*, Yale's English department, rated the best in the country, placed only two out of fifteen students in tenure-track jobs in 1994–95.

Edwin Goldin, manager of career planning and placement for the American Institute of Physics, says that, in his field, there would be only two hundred teaching positions open in 1996, compared to as many as five hundred per year in the past. Among recent Ph.D.s in physics and astronomy, the number of graduates forced to take temporary fellowships while waiting for real jobs to open up has increased more than 100 percent since 1981.

One of the effects of the tight job market is credential inflation. In order to compete, you've got to publish substantially more research while still in graduate school than was ever expected in the past. More and more undergraduates and master's students are publishing prior to applying to doctoral programs (in 1993–94, more than 32 percent of MA holders applying for direct admission to the doctoral program at Indiana University had already either presented papers at conferences or published in academic journals). In English departments, Michael Bérubé says:

> We are more or less at the point at which some entry-level jobs require a published book. . . . Our graduates who received their Ph.D.s in 1990 or 1991 and who've published substantial articles in major journals are attracting very little attention from potential employers, even when their research is considered good enough for reputable journals and prestigious university presses. My hunch is that . . . many of our current students who'll hit the market in the late 1990s will likewise have to produce a book before they'll be considered for the tenure track.

It doesn't look like the picture will improve much in the coming decade. Cary Nelson says: "For the large number of academics who believe we can ignore present conditions until better times return, it is past time to state the obvious: The good times are over." Although many professors are expected to retire, most universities and colleges are not filling these slots. Instead, they are expanding class sizes and turning increasingly to graduate-student teachers. And the competition for what jobs there are will be intense. Women and minorities are entering in larger numbers, which can make it tough for white males. After decades of privilege, the playing field is even or may in fact be tilting against them. Although possibly a statistical anomaly, it is perhaps indicative that, of the seven new Ph.D.s placed in tenure-track positions by the University of Illinois's English department in 1994, all were women. However, women are still underrepresented among faculty, particularly at the higher levels, and women faculty still receive lower pay at equivalent posts.

THE TENURE HURDLE

Webster's dictionary defines tenure as "a status granted after a trial period to a teacher protecting him from summary dismissal." Tenure review normally takes place during an assistant professor's sixth year of teaching, and if he passes review, he has virtual lifetime job security because tenured professors can only be fired for the most flagrant breaches of professional conduct. This explains why particularly bad professors aren't fired—they can't be. This mantle of invulnerability—coupled with the fact that assistant professors who fail review usually do not have their contracts renewed—is why every ambitious assistant professor sees tenure review as a life-or-death process.

You should be aware that 20 percent of graduates who obtain university teaching jobs fail to get tenure at their first job and must uproot to teach elsewhere. The budgetary considerations mentioned above mean that universities are making fewer and fewer favorable tenure decisions, because it is cheaper to work a new assistant professor hard for six years and then replace him or her with an eager new starter. For some of the more exclusive universities, the percentage of assistant professors receiving tenure may be as low as 20 percent.

Failing to get tenure doesn't mean that you won't get a job at all; what often happens is that a person failing tenure at a first-ranked school can get a tenured position at a second- or third-ranked school. Nonetheless, in many cases failure to achieve tenure makes it difficult to find subsequent jobs since the school hiring you would have to pay you more than the newly minted graduate students you would be competing with. You can find out about tenure policies by calling the departments you are interested in. Even if they do not keep formal statistics, the chairman or other faculty can give you an informal assessment.

If you don't get a tenure-track job and settle for short-term, insecure positions as an instructor or lecturer, you can expect to work year after year at approximately the same level, making relatively little money. For example, untenured lecturers in English at the University of Michigan, Dearborn, are restricted to part-time teaching and make approximately

$3,000 per quarter. In general, many of the displaced Ph.D.s—those unable to find permanent positions—eke out years of part-time, poorly paid teaching while searching in vain for tenure-track positions. A 1991 editorial by Coleman McCarthy in the Washington *Post* called these untenured teachers "academia's stoop laborers" and noted that the majority of them, 67 percent in the humanities, are female. In 1989–90 one woman who received her Ph.D. in English from Rice University taught an overload—ten courses a year—at the University of Maryland, where she was paid a total of $23,000 after fifteen years' experience. Because of budget cuts in Maryland, she is now drawing unemployment.

CAN YOU BEAT THE ODDS?

In short, for many disciplines the chance of getting a job when you get your Ph.D. is smaller than was the chance of getting into graduate school, and the chance of getting tenure is smaller still. For example, assume that 50 percent of Ph.D. candidates in your field get their degrees, which is the approximate attrition rate across disciplines, 20 percent of these Ph.D.s get academic jobs, and 80 percent of these get tenure. Then your chance of making it all the way to tenure is 8 percent. This figure is not unrealistic for many disciplines. Use such information to make a realistic assessment of whether it is worth spending four to eight years of your life at a subsistence level for a shot at what jobs are available.

■ DO YOU NEED A MASTER'S? ■

Many people start master's degree programs for the same reason they do Ph.D.s—they don't know what else to do and have blind faith that a degree will advance their career. Because master's degrees take relatively little time compared with the Ph.D., the time lost may seem insignificant, but two or three years is still a long period. A two-year master's at a private university can cost you $15,000 to $25,000, not counting living expenses, and, given that university funding of master's students is very low, you will be paying for most of this yourself, either directly or through loans. Moreover, during this time you will miss out on career experience.

Unfortunately, there is little systematized data to help master's students find out how they will fare in the job market. But you can do the necessary research yourself by interviewing people who hold jobs in the field in which you are interested. There is no substitute for talking with the people who will ultimately be hiring you or admitting you to a Ph.D. program. Call departments you are interested in and ask them for the names of recent graduates who can tell you about their experiences getting jobs. Call firms you are interested in working for and ask to speak with people in appropriate positions. Ask your friends and co-workers for contacts. Ask these people: What degrees do they hold? When they are hiring, are master's rated more highly than bachelor's degrees? What are the salary differentials? What are the financial or status rewards of master's degrees versus doctorates? Are people rewarded for graduating from more prestigious programs? Are there particular programs that are particularly well regarded? Is there an increasing emphasis on professional education in the field?

An accountant, for example, told me that she does fine without a master's degree in her firm and has risen to management level. However, she says that in larger firms a master's degree would probably be necessary, partly because the firm wants the prestige, but more practically because office politics make it difficult for the company to have a person with a bachelor's degree supervising employees with more education.

In some cases it may not pay off financially to get a master's (although you may have nonfinancial reasons for going). In physical therapy, therapists typically enter the field with two years of college and three years of professional school, and most practicing therapists do not have a master's degree. Therefore, at present, master's degrees are not required even at the supervisory level. In chemical engineering, master's degrees are rare because they do not give a significant financial advantage over a bachelor's degree (according to the American Chemical Society, in 1995 median starting salaries were $44,200 versus $40,000). After the loss of time and the cost of tuition are factored in, the difference becomes negligible. Cornell's MFA program warns incoming students that the degree "in itself is of little value in obtaining a teaching position within a college writing program; given the intense competition for such positions, a substantial body of published work is of greatest value."

For other fields the case for getting a master's degree is stronger. Many states pay primary and secondary school teachers substantially more money if they have a master's degree; also, their salary may be raised incrementally as they make progress toward the degree. MBAs are renowned for high salaries and rapid advancement, and a degree from a prestigious department is likely to be well worth the investment. However, note that the average MBA does not receive the great advantage of those graduating from the most prestigious business schools. Indeed, it has been observed that many of the business programs blossoming in the last decade are unaccredited and, according to educational consultants Howard Greene and Robert Minton, "may be a waste of time," as also has been said of many MFA programs.

As you research your field, make sure that you do not rely just on official information from the schools themselves, since they will have a vested interest in appearing indispensable. Also, recognize that the ability of a program to advance your career may be dependent upon your previous background. For example, a student in international relations noted that "investment bankers who had been making $40,000 a year in New York finished the program and immediately got jobs at $80,000 in international finance. Other people coming into the program directly from college with majors in language or political science were no more able to land a job with the master's than before. You get the real 'value added' if you come in with a marketable skill and then refine it."

Beware of trying to use a master's to teach on the college or university level. Because there is an excess of Ph.D.s, graduates of master's programs are now generally relegated to the "stoop labor" jobs described above, if they can even get these. Paul van Heuklom, a recent graduate of the University of California's master's program in English, set off to teach English composition. He says:

I was told to try metropolitan areas because there were more colleges, more opportunities. I was told to try rural campuses because no one else wanted them. At one point, I was teaching seven different courses at three campuses and commuting 600 miles a week in a Michigan blizzard . . . for about $15,000 per year and no benefits. At the same time, I was sending my curriculum vitae to every college in the country advertising openings, even temporary positions possibly leading to tenure. A few copies were dropped by airplane over Asia and the Middle East . . . I occasionally made the next-to-final cut from a field of hundreds.

He finally gave up and now says, "Since I left the teaching circuit against my will, in less than three years I've nearly doubled my salary twice doing the only other thing an unemployed English graduate can do—edit magazines. Therefore I propose a new adage: Those who can, teach; those who can't, do."

Another good reason to get a master's is simply that you want more education for its own sake. One woman pursuing a master's in communications part-time said, "I started school again because I was so bored at work." A final reason, as discussed below, is that you may need a master's degree to go on for the Ph.D.

DECIDING BETWEEN MASTER'S
▪ AND Ph.D. PROGRAMS ▪

For some of you the decision is easy because your career demands a Ph.D. or because you like the relatively high salaries paid in many fields to Ph.D.s (for example, in 1994, according to the American Chemical Society, beginning chemists with master's degrees were making $35,000, while Ph.D.s were making $50,000). For others, like public school teachers, relatively little is gained from the Ph.D. The decision becomes more complicated when there is a reasonable chance that you do want a Ph.D. and you are trying to decide whether to get a master's first.

If you're not certain whether you like research enough to struggle through the lengthy ordeal of the Ph.D., a master's program may be a good way to test your commitment. If you choose a rigorous master's program with a thesis, you will get preliminary training in research as well as further grounding in the basics of your field. One English student who earned a master's before going on to do her Ph.D. at another school said, "I had to grow up in the master's program. If I had gone directly into a Ph.D. program, I would have been in serious trouble because I really didn't have the skills to deal with people or the focus to do a Ph.D. thesis."

In some programs, like the School of Advanced International Studies at Johns Hopkins, you won't be able to choose between the master's and the Ph.D.—you must apply first for their master's program and then reapply to be one of the select few who are accepted for the Ph.D. In other departments, like Georgetown's philosophy department, there is no master's program; all students enroll for the Ph.D., and students doing mediocre work on their graduate comprehensive exams are asked to leave and given the master's degree as a parting consolation prize.

If your credentials aren't good enough to get into a competitive Ph.D. program, you can try using a master's program as a springboard. Since master's programs typically have lower entrance requirements, your chances for acceptance are better. George was one student for whom this strategy paid off. He got his master's in sociology at a school ranked thirtieth, but he excelled and moved up to the number one school for his Ph.D. One unfortunate bit of news is that many Ph.D. admissions committees do not count master's grades as heavily as undergraduate grades, under the supposition that master's grades tend to be inflated. Be aware as well that in some fields a master's degree may be of little help in gaining entrance to a Ph.D. program. For example, a recent survey of clinical psychology doctoral programs by David Hines found that, in 90 percent of the programs, having a master's degree would not increase your chance of getting in.

One good bet for getting into a Ph.D. program may be to ingratiate your way into the same department where you got your master's. If you can get involved in the research and otherwise impress a professor, he may be able to shoehorn you in. This strategy is successful enough so that some departments prohibit their own master's students from applying to their Ph.D. programs; apparently they are afraid that undeserving scoundrels might wiggle in by politicking.

There are disadvantages to being in a master's program before a Ph.D. As the American Psychological Association says, "this option is currently fraught with a number of dangers." First, it will probably cost you extra time and money, particularly if you transfer between schools. When you transfer, the Ph.D. institution ordinarily will not give you credit for all of your course work—you can expect to lose a year. Since Ph.D.s already take a very long time to earn, the last thing you need to do is retake courses or redo a master's thesis. Before committing to a master's program, call departments where you might be interested in pursuing a Ph.D. and ask them about their transfer policies.

In addition, master's students typically receive less attention from professors. A student at the Yale Forestry School noted that "with all those other master's students running around, competition for time was tough, and professors spent it with the Ph.D.s who would co-author papers with them."

Doctoral students also get the lion's share of financial aid, so it may end up costing you more to get a master's than a Ph.D. Departments prefer to give grants and fellowships to Ph.D. students, leaving the leftovers, if any, for master's students. Georgetown's chemistry and biology departments, for example, give fellowships and scholarships only to Ph.D. candidates, and the same was true of Stanford's biology department when I was there. One Stanford professor explained that the department regarded the paying master's students as a major source of financial support for the Ph.D. program. Additionally, although some government fellowships, like National Science Foundation Fellowships, are open to master's students, others favor Ph.D.s. This low level of funding for master's students means that most turn to the federal loan programs, including Perkins, and Stafford, and may accrue higher debt levels than Ph.D. students. Some departmental funding may be available for master's students, particularly in departments that do not have competing doctoral students. For example, Georgetown's English department, which gives only master's degrees, has three or four tuition scholarships available every year, and Cornell's MFA program gives teaching assistantships to second-year students.

In deciding between a master's and a Ph.D., ask the following questions: (1) What are the transfer policies of Ph.D. programs in which you are interested? (2) Within a single department, are master's students able to apply to the Ph.D. program? (3) Is it easier to get into a Ph.D. program if you are already a master's student in the program than it is if you are applying from the outside? (4) How does financial aid compare between the two degrees?

My advice is that it is better to get into a Ph.D. program if you can. If you don't like it, you can always drop out and be awarded the terminal master's degree after you finish your course work.

4

. . . .

SHOULD YOU WORK

FIRST?

. . . .

YOU SHOULD THINK SERIOUSLY ABOUT WORKING FOR A YEAR OR TWO BEFORE you go to graduate school. One student said that having worked first was "essential" for his success in graduate school. Many of the graduate advisers I interviewed said that older and more mature students who return for a graduate degree after working get through faster, have less trouble with procrastination, and have self-respect gained from real-world accomplishments that helps them deal with the insecurities of the graduate environment. One master's student said, "It was easy to tell the people who had worked first. They were the ones who knew what they were doing."

• REASONS TO WORK FIRST •

REASON A: RECHARGE YOUR BATTERIES

If you are uncertain about your commitment, or are exhausted after four years of working for the grades to get into graduate school, take a year off. Several students I talked with made it into graduate school and then hit a serious slump because they were out of energy. Wait to start graduate school until you are highly motivated so that you can begin earning yourself a good reputation from your first day.

REASON B: LEARN THE SKILLS
THEY DIDN'T TEACH YOU IN COLLEGE

In a full-time job, you are forced to make dramatic changes in the work habits you developed as an undergraduate. You have to work steadily every day, instead of in occasional frantic rushes at exam time. You learn the importance of careful planning to meet deadlines and to develop long-term projects. You realize that what seemed like a lot of work when you were an undergraduate was not a great deal when measured against the amount you can do with constant daily application. You can also acquire or improve specific work skills, like word processing and library research, and you can learn simple tricks necessary to get efficient and rapid results, like using messengers or fax machines when you are in a pinch.

REASON C: DEVELOP CONFIDENCE

The competency and confidence you gain on the job will help you break out of thinking of yourself as a lowly student and of the professors as superior beings. This adult perspective will be vital for successfully managing your committee and for getting your money's worth out of graduate school. An art history student said, "When you return to school after working for your tuition, you have much less tolerance for bad professors and bullshit work. I figure that if I'm paying for a product, it better be good."

For many of you, work will act to diminish your anxiety about finding your way in the world. Can you get a job after graduate school? Will you do well? Will you like the working world? Answering these questions by working will give you the psychological freedom to approach graduate school without feeling it is your only option. You will know that if you don't like graduate school, you can leave and still survive. Perhaps you will find that you like work so much that you don't want to go back to school after all.

REASON D: INVESTIGATE A FIELD THAT INTERESTS YOU

Working in your field can help you determine whether the area really interests you (working at Club Med doesn't help here). Perhaps you can find a job as a research or laboratory assistant. Do you like research? It would be good to find out now before you are committed to graduate school and an academic career of what amounts to writing endless term papers. If you want to be a writer, try working for a publishing house so you can learn about what gets published and how. If you are interested in art history, getting a job in a gallery or museum is an obvious step.

Taking a job related to your academic field may help you get into graduate school more easily than someone else who took an unrelated job. An economics department is more likely to take someone who has been working as a junior economist, and English departments are more likely to take people who have been working as writers or editors. Remember, in the words of one professor, that "if you take a job before applying to graduate school, you had better be able to justify it in terms of your overall academic focus. The further away from your field the job is, the tougher this will be."

While you are working, keep your eyes open for areas of thesis research. The people I know who excelled in graduate school often came ready to work on topics they had discovered on the job. A biologist worked on a wildlife refuge in Florida, where there were many introduced pests that threatened the native species, and then went on to do a master's thesis on management techniques for introduced pests. A student with a degree in art history worked in a gallery where she was exposed to the Pre-Raphaelite painters on whom she later focused her Ph.D. Another student worked as a counselor for children with emotional problems; she was also a skilled ballroom dancer and ultimately joined these two interests by doing a master's thesis on dance therapy.

REASON E: DEVELOP MOTIVATION

Many people return to school because they need the degree for further career advancement. For example, one biologist, after working as an editor for a highly respected technical journal for four years, where she made many valuable contacts in the course of working with authors, decided to return for her Ph.D. so that she could advance into more prestigious positions. The contacts she had made helped her with her graduate school career.

A historian with a master's degree taught for a number of years at a state university in Alaska and then decided to get a Ph.D. to improve his stature in the university. He used his connections to get into a good school under a professor he already knew, took a sabbatical, and completed his degree in twenty months of hard work (eight months for the thesis).

In these cases, students see graduate school as what it should be, advanced career training.

▪ DO YOU HAVE TO WORK FIRST? ▪

WORKING FIRST MAY GIVE YOU PERSPECTIVE ON WHETHER YOU REALLY WANT TO GO TO GRAD SCHOOL

Do you have to work first? Certainly not. Even though many people start graduate school without being prepared, for you it might make sense to begin immediately after getting your baccalaureate. One humanities chairman said, "If you're absolutely gung ho, go in. Any hesitation, take off one to two years." It's up to you to decide. You might know for certain that you need a master's in child psychology and want to get it as soon as possible. Or you might want to get your degree under a great professor you worked with while you were an undergraduate, so it makes sense to start right away while he remembers who you are. A student in international relations who went straight through said, "I liked going directly to graduate school because I didn't lose any momentum and I've got my master's at twenty-four. Now I'm through with school and it's not hanging over my head." A Ph.D. student in history said, "I was lucky to find my thesis topic while doing an independent study. My adviser liked it, so he asked me to stay on as his grad student. It was the safest route because I already knew I liked the guy and I was already into my thesis work."

▪ HOW LONG CAN YOU POSTPONE? ▪

This differs from field to field. In English, where Ph.D.s are almost exclusively headed for academic jobs, it was once dangerous to take off even a year between your bachelor's and entrance into graduate school. Admissions committees would look askance at such a student, believing that he demonstrated inadequate commitment to finding the academic grail.

Because every admissions committee is different, some departments may still apply this standard, but, in general, stopping out for a short period is acceptable. According to the chairman of a top English department: "Now about half the people we accept have stopped out for between one and three years, and we actually find that these students are better focused and motivated, on the whole, than those coming straight from undergrad." However, he also cautions that stopping out for more than a couple of years is risky, and that most English departments would be unlikely to take someone who was applying ten years after receiving a bachelor's degree.

In other fields, particularly in applied fields where students may be returning for additional training or credentials, on either the master's or the Ph.D. level, students who have worked for a significant period of time may have little or no handicap. Given this disparity between fields, check with professors or graduate school departments about their admissions policies *before* you stay away too long. For those of you who are considering going back after a long hiatus, look carefully for schools that have flexible admissions policies—some are more daring than others. For example, the top English department mentioned above recently accepted a well-published poet in his mid-40s who had spent the 1970s and 1980s living a hippie's existence in San Francisco. The chairman said, "Most departments wouldn't touch him, but our department was willing to take a chance."

If you do plan to take time off, you still need to ask your professors to write recommendations before or shortly after you graduate, before they have forgotten you. Set up a recommendation file with your placement center, where the letters will be safe and confidential copies can easily be requested.

5

CHOOSING A SCHOOL:

THE THESIS ADVISER

MOST GRADUATE STUDENTS MAKE THEIR DECISION ABOUT WHICH SCHOOL TO attend based on some combination of the school's reputation, location, financial aid, and the other factors discussed in the following chapter. Once admitted, they arrive on campus and belatedly start looking around for an adviser, hoping to find someone good. If you are a would-be doctoral student, this is the wrong approach. Because your doctoral adviser will have such tremendous influence on whether you get your degree and a good job, you should identify and contact potential advisers *before* you apply to graduate school, and then weigh the presence of a good adviser *heavily* with the other selection criteria.

For master's students, the importance of the adviser will differ from program to program, and therefore you need to weigh the importance of making prior contact with advisers accordingly. Some master's programs are like modest Ph.D. programs: even though they don't last as long, they may still include a substantial thesis requiring close work with a professor whose approval and guidance will be critical for success. In such cases, a bad choice can easily add an extra year to your stay in school. At the other extreme, for a master's program based largely on course work that doesn't require a thesis at all, the advising professor may be no more important than was your undergraduate adviser.

• WHAT IS A THESIS ADVISER? •

The ideal thesis adviser would advise you from your first tentative steps on campus, help you find a thesis topic, or even find one for you, help

you choose your thesis committee, read your thesis drafts, and edit the
as needed. He would give you moral support, champion you against your
detractors within the department, help you get your first papers published,
let you co-author papers with him, cheer for you as you defend your thesis
in oral examination, and pull the strings necessary to get you a job. Ideally,
he or she should be a mentor, that rare being who is part confidant, part
parent, spiritual and temporal guide. You will never find such a paragon,
but the closer you can get, the better.

▪ THE PH.D. AS PROTÉGÉ ▪

LOOK FOR AN ADVISER WHO WILL INITIATE
YOU INTO THE MYSTERIES OF HIS ART

You don't usually hear academics saying about a bright young prospect, "He is from Harvard." Instead, they say, "He is one of Theodore Vlasinsky's students." They will call you "one of Vlasinsky's students" for most of your professional life, long after Vlasinsky has died. If Vlasinsky is well respected and well connected, and if he thinks highly of you, he can use his influence to help you find a good job. A simple "Margaret, I have a brilliant prospect here for the opening you've got in twentieth-century criticism" is worth more from someone important than hours of praise coming from Joe Schmoe, a kindly but obscure professor. Ideally, you would have the best of both worlds—a top professor in a top department. But the adviser comes first.

On a lesser scale the same "protégé effect" works for master's students. If you are trying to use the master's program as a springboard to a high-quality doctoral program, for example, the more impressive your adviser's credentials and connections, the better.

For those students who don't end up in academia after they graduate but find themselves in some related field, the school's reputation may be more important than which adviser they worked under. For example, if you get a Ph.D. in ecology and then work in a zoo, or if you get a Ph.D. in art and work in a foundation to support artists, the people who hire you won't know much about your specialty, and they will be impressed by the school's name. So a rule of thumb is that the further you end up from academia, the less the adviser matters and the more the reputation of the school. But remember, even if you are not heading for an academic job, the adviser is still important because he or she can help you get a job and determine whether you finish your degree on time.

■ BAD ADVISERS ■

If you get a really bad adviser, he or she may actively try to prevent you from succeeding. Even a nice person may believe that his or her duty lies in ensuring that unworthy candidates do not succeed in graduating, and he or she may honestly believe that this unworthy person is *you*. (More common than the vindictive adviser is one who is indifferent and gives you scant direction.)

Problems with advisers run the gamut, from sexual harassment to academic sabotage. The following experiences all happened to friends of mine:

• An adviser took data representing six months' work from a student's desk and published it under his own name without telling the student. He later transferred the National Science Foundation grant the student had won to a female graduate student with whom the adviser was sleeping.
• A master's student in computer science had an insecure adviser who was up for tenure review and needed publications. The student wrote a paper for publication and asked her adviser to review it before sending it to a journal. He reviewed it and sent it off—with his own name as first author.
• A lizard ecologist put off reading his student's thesis proposal for fourteen months, so that the deadline for approval was missed. Two years later the same professor used the missed deadline as justification for asking the departmental senate to turn down the student's request for financial support.
• Another student of ecology began research in the Arctic. When he was told to run an errand in the field station's truck, he started it up, not knowing that in such cold weather the engine first had to be heated. Because the engine was frozen, it was damaged. The director of the lab took away the student's teaching assistantship on the grounds that he was irresponsible and therefore was not graduate school material. Because

he lacked money, the student dropped out of school. Fortunately, this story had a happy ending. The student went to work for four years as a research flunky on an ecology project in Asia. He figured out what he wanted to do his thesis on, collected data while in Asia, got into a graduate program in the United States, and finished his Ph.D. in under two years.

These horror stories aren't the rule, but they are also not rare exceptions. Many, many graduate students have fallings-out with their advisers or other thesis committee members. Sometimes it is the student's fault, sometimes the adviser's, and sometimes there are just problems with communication. But whoever is at fault, it is the student who suffers. In a highly competitive job market, a graduate student's reputation must be blemish-free, and anything less than enthusiastic endorsement by your adviser may prevent you from getting a good academic job.

You can change advisers, but this might be costly in terms of time. Likewise, changing to another school can be difficult if you have a cloud hanging over your head. Therefore, it is much wiser to avoid such troubles ahead of time by thoroughly investigating any adviser you are considering. *To maximize your chance of success in graduate school, you must choose an adviser with whom you can maintain an excellent personal and professional relationship.*

■ ATTRIBUTES OF A GOOD ADVISER ■

In most departments the thesis adviser's formal obligations don't extend much beyond reading your thesis, approving it or sending it back for revision, and chairing the committee that hears the oral defense of your thesis. But the ideal professor will also help and advise you, passing on his or her intellectual tradition. You need someone who will train you to think—how to approach problems, plan experiments, carry out research —so that your few years with him will enable you to make original and important contributions to your field. Traits your adviser should have include:

• *Career maturity.* Your adviser should be sufficiently advanced in his career so that he is not desperately struggling. An adviser who is secure in his field is less likely to steal your ideas and more likely to give you credit and authorship. He will be better able to protect his turf in internecine academic squabbles, and thus better able to protect you and your financial support. This can mean more money, more fieldwork, less teaching, more lab space, more computer time, and some of his secretary's time (particularly if your work will result in advancement of the professor's own). A professor who is not struggling for his own survival is likely to have more time and concern for yours.

- *Tenure.* If you are a Ph.D. student, or a master's student contemplating an ambitious thesis, *don't* take a nontenured professor no matter how much you admire his work. A nontenured adviser may depart anytime, leaving you to find a new professor, who may not like your thesis. This happened to a religious studies Ph.D. student who agreed to attend the University of Virginia, only to have her adviser leave before she even got there. She ended up staying for only a year before leaving for another school.

I do know of one case where a very motivated student at Harvard started his Ph.D. work under a nontenured professor knowing that the professor would probably leave within a couple of years. Because the student badly wanted to learn what this professor had to teach, he took the risk, but he wisely spent time working with a backup who was willing to take over when his first professor left. My own experience is more typical: when my untenured professor left the department two years before I finished, I had no source of regular advising or financial support.

- *Vigor.* Although you don't want an untenured professor, you also don't want to go to the other extreme and get one who is over the hill. Someone who is tired and jaded may not be up to date on the latest literature. He may not have enough brilliant thesis ideas stored away to give you one that's good enough to land a job when you graduate. He may not have the contacts or political pull to get you a job.
- *Rigor.* You may have an easier time finding a job if you learn from an adviser who is seen by his colleagues as "rigorous"—that is, his research is well buttressed by good knowledge of experimental design, statistics, or theory appropriate to the field. In general, departments prefer to hire assistant professors who have strong theoretical or "hard" backgrounds over those who are "soft."

In summary, look for a vigorous, active, well-respected, and kind academic. Find someone with tenure, academic eminence, and political clout, yet not so busy with politics that he or she has no time for you. You want someone old enough to feel paternal or maternal, or at least big-brotherly, yet not so advanced in years or attitude that you can't relate well.

DIFFERENCES BETWEEN ADVISER-STUDENT RELATIONSHIPS IN THE SCIENCES · AND HUMANITIES ·

One humanities dean said, "On our interdepartmental task force, one of the greatest stumbling blocks was getting people in the humanities and sciences to realize how differently the two areas view graduate students. In the sciences, students are seen as apprentices, which is not really true in the humanities."

In the sciences and some of the social sciences, faculty see you as a potential disciple who will help them carry out research and publish, so that their own productivity depends in part on the quality of their graduate students. The more papers a professor's research factory can crank out, the more his reputation will soar. This provides science faculty with a strong motivation for identifying and recruiting top students to work for them. One physics professor said, "If you don't move quickly, the best students are snapped up." To the extent that this motivation exists in most humanities disciplines, it is much weaker because in the humanities graduate students often work in areas not closely connected to their professors' research and joint publication is rare. However, the degree of professor-student collaboration may be greater in some of the humanities than others: a linguistics professor notes that in sociolinguistics joint publication is common but in English literature it is almost unknown.

The apprenticeship nature of graduate school in the collaborative disciplines makes it common for students in these fields to find advisers early. They often enter the department knowing exactly the area in which they want to work, and with whom, which gives them a big head start. They may even decide to attend a particular university because they want to work with a specific professor there, and the professor may help them get into the department. In the humanities, on the other hand, contact between professors and students before admission is rare and Ph.D. students usually face a general course of study that may last two or three years, during which time they gradually narrow their interests while deciding on an adviser, often changing fields in the process. Such prolonged deliberation tends to decrease the degree to which personal contacts can grease the way for you into a department, but some influence may still be possible.

I believe that this relatively slow focusing process by humanities Ph.D.s is one reason why they typically take several years longer to finish their degrees than those in the sciences. Moreover, science students who follow the humanities model, entering school without much idea of their thesis topic or adviser, take longer to finish than those who are better focused.

EVALUATING POTENTIAL
▪ THESIS ADVISERS ▪

Would you take a job for a minimum of four years without knowing who your boss would be? That's what it will be like if you choose a school without previously evaluating the professors you might work under. You might be lucky and find that there are good professors to choose from once you arrive at school, but then again you might end up with one of the monsters who turn their students into serfs and steal their research.

In this section I have sketched out a strategy to increase your chances of ending up with a good adviser, while at the same time increasing your chances of getting into a good department. The twin pillars of this strategy are (1) early evaluation of the "adviser potential" of professors at departments where you might apply and (2) making contact with professors so that they will use their influence to get you into their departments. By learning as much as you can about potential advisers before accepting an admission offer you avoid the worst-case scenario, encountered by many students, of entering a department only to find that the one respected person active in your field either is about to leave for another school or has a reputation for being brutal to his graduate students.

The differences between the sciences and humanities might affect how you can use this early evaluation strategy. In the humanities, for example, you might find it difficult to use the tactic of working as a research assistant to learn about a professor, because few humanities professors use research assistants. Nonetheless, the basic strategy of making early contact with potential advisers will increase your chances of success in any field.

The process of hunting for an adviser can be divided into three independent tasks. You can choose to complete all three tasks, or only one or two. The first task is to identify a small number of potential advisers who are at schools where you might apply (your "short list") and become familiar with their work. The second is to establish personal contact with professors on your short list. Third, play detective by interviewing the professors and their graduate students to find out what the professors are really like. Although my discussion assumes that you have not yet applied to graduate school, you can also adopt this strategy to choose the best adviser possible if you are already in grad school.

Because your goal is to get to know as much as possible about your possible advisers and to ingratiate yourself with them, you should begin the selection process early. Because grad school application deadlines typically come at least six months before admission (generally December–February for fall admission if you want to be considered for fellowships),

I suggest that you *start evaluating potential advisers at least one and a half years before the fall term in which you plan to start graduate school*. This will allow you a full year to build relationships. If you plan to go on to graduate school directly after getting your baccalaureate, you should begin researching schools and professors during fall and spring of your junior year. If you don't have that much time left, you can still use the following selection procedure; you will just have less time to butter up potential advisers.

Step 1: Putting together your "short list"

The first step is to identify a pool of potential advisers who are important in your area of interest. Then narrow this pool down to a short list of candidates whom you will evaluate more closely. For example, by the time I was a junior I knew I wanted to study lizard ecology, so I tried to identify good lizard ecologists as potential advisers, and ended up with three or four possibilities. Start by collecting as many names of top workers in your field as you can. There are several places to get names:

- Ask your undergraduate teachers for the names of important researchers and good university departments in the area you want to study. If a teacher tells you that a department is strong but can't recommend a specific professor, find out who at the department does relevant research by calling or writing the department itself for descriptions of faculty research. (You can get departmental addresses from the *GRE/CGS Directory of Graduate Programs*, published by the Educational Testing Service in conjunction with the Council of Graduate Schools, or from other sourcebooks in the library.)
- Add names of researchers whose work you admired when you learned about them in class or heard them speak at conferences.
- Read through the catalogue collection at your counseling center or library for descriptions of programs—many catalogues have descriptions of the work of individual professors.
- Use the library to research topics in your field, find papers that interest you, and add the names of their authors to your list.

Now you can begin paring your list down to the most serious contenders, who will then be investigated in greater depth. First, assess the type, quality, and quantity of their research. To do this, read their published articles and books carefully, and decide whose research is exciting to you and respected by other researchers. Remember that you may be spending years of your life learning to do the same type of research, and if you are not *very* interested, it will be a *very* long haul.

If you don't know how to find papers in the library, your librarian can help. There are reference books that list the articles published by each author in a given year. For example, *Biological Abstracts* contains summaries of nearly all articles published in biological journals; if you look in the volume for 1996, under the author I. M. Prolific, you will find listed all of the articles he published during that year. The abstracts also will list the journal citation so that you can find, photocopy, and read the original article. Look through several years' volumes under a particular author's name and note how many publications he has and in what journals. If the author publishes little, or publishes only in journals with names like *Occasional Papers of the Little River Fish Hatchery and Grill*, he's probably not someone it would help your career to work under. The number of publications in respected journals is the best indication you can get of a professor's status.

Another excellent way to get information about authors is to use citation indexes. Citation indexes, like the *Science Citations Index* and *Social Sciences Citation Index*, will list the number of times an author is cited by his peers, and again will tell you in what journals he or she has published. The more he or she is cited by other authors, the more influential the academic. Also, citation indexes often have sections called corporate indexes, which list together all publications produced in a given year by a specific university department. So you can look up one of your target departments and find listed all of the professors in the department who have published during a particular year, along with citations of their work. This will quickly give you an idea of the productivity of the department.

Once you have found papers by prospective advisers, you should read them carefully and try to imagine if you would like to do the same type of research. Also, get a feeling for the mind behind the writing. You are looking for clues that will lead you to an adviser who is thoughtful, well organized, and skilled at explaining difficult points clearly.

At this preliminary stage you can also begin finding out whether the people on your list have reputations for treating their students particularly well or badly. Your undergraduate professors may know some of the people on the list personally or by reputation, so ask them who would make particularly good advisers. Also, do any of your teachers know graduate students who are studying under academics on your list? If so, call the students and speak to them.

This may sound unnecessary, but check that the professors you are interested in really are at the departments where they are supposed to be. It is common for departmental catalogues to continue listing professors—particularly famous ones—long after they have resigned, retired, or died. A top-ranked sociology department listed a famous professor in their catalogue while he was in a two-year coma (one nasty colleague wondered whether his students noticed), and they continued to list him for several years after he was dead. Also, check to make sure that active professors will not be on sabbatical during years that are critical for you.

When compiling your short list, weigh the quality of the professors, but also be realistic about your own potential. Avoid wasting time on advisers at schools where you have no chance of admission because you had trouble mastering Russian or macroeconomics.

STEP 2: BUILDING RELATIONSHIPS WITH POTENTIAL ADVISERS

The better you can get to know any of the people on your short list, the better you can (a) evaluate them and (b) convince them to use their influence to help you gain admission. I have deferred discussion of one tactic, which is to visit schools to interview potential advisers, to the next section, since it is usually the last thing you will do before applying.

You don't have to follow this "getting to know them" strategy—the vast majority of students don't, and many of them get into top schools. Instead, they take the normal route of applying cold to schools on the basis of their GREs, GPAs, and references, with no personal contact. However, if you do use this strategy, it may boost you into a better school or match you more wisely with an adviser. Because customs on whether and how a prospective student may contact a professor differ from field to field, check with your wisest undergraduate professor about any strategy you want to try.

IDENTIFY POTENTIAL ADVISERS AND CULTIVATE THEIR GOOD WILL

It's obvious that the more time you spend with a potential professor, the better you can judge whether you want to work with him. The following stories may convince you that contacting professors before application can help you gain admission.

• A science professor at a top university with tens of applications for each spot told me,

"When I accept a doctoral student, it's always someone who has worked with me, usually as an undergraduate, intern, or master's student. This means I often take students with lower credentials than many of the other applicants. The graduate school yells at me for doing this—they think we should accept only the very cream of the crop based on applications. But I tell them, no way I'm going to take someone I've never worked with."

- A humanities professor said, "I had top grades and GREs, so I was accepted by a number of good grad schools. Nonetheless, personal contacts helped. I ended up attending the same school where I had done my undergrad, so the admissions committee there knew me. It turned out that I had missed the deadline for application, but the dean of the graduate school was one of my old professors, and when I called he slipped me into the applicant pool."

- Joan took two years off after her bachelor's to work as an administrative assistant in the graduate school where she later did her master's in international affairs. While she worked, she took master's-level classes in the department as a nonmatriculated student. She says, "Taking those courses definitely helped me at admissions time because the professors already knew what I was capable of."

- Ron spent five years after his BA working at a conservation organization and then was accepted by a good master's program in zoology. He said, "I found someone whose work I liked and met with her several times to convince her that I'd be a good student. The husband of one of the people I knew at work also taught at the university, and he gave me a lot of advice and kept me up to date on how my application was doing." When I asked Ron whether the support of these two professors helped him get into their zoology department, he said, "Are you kidding? My undergraduate major was *history*."

As these anecdotes demonstrate, your chances of admission *are* greater if you have already made an ally or two among the faculty. While influence won't get you in if you aren't qualified, it can make a big difference in a close contest. Basically, your plan is to get recommendations from the most influential source possible—the faculty where you are applying. If you are lucky, some of these people may also be on the admissions committee. Since most would-be students won't bother to make these initial contacts, you will have an advantage over the majority of applicants.

The best tactics to use are those where you can spend enough time with a potential adviser so you really get to know each other. Particularly if you have been out of school for a while and may be lacking recent undergraduate recommendations, you may need to take classes or otherwise spend considerable time with professors to earn updated recommendations. Some tactics are:

- *Take classes.* One of the best ways to impress professors in a department you apply to is to take courses. If you are now an undergraduate, you might be able to take a course or two at another institution during the summer under a professor you have identified as a likely adviser. If you are working, you may be able to worm your way into a nearby university by taking courses part-time.
- *Help with research.* Look for research assistantships, fellowships, summer research jobs, or even volunteer to do research if you can afford to work without pay. If you are presently working, you may be able to help with research part-time. Even a few weeks volunteered during the summer may be enough to impress a professor.
- *Pursue independent study.* If there is a professor at a nearby university whom you want to get to know, it may be possible to arrange an independent study with him. Usually, one of your undergraduate professors must be responsible for overseeing the independent study—check with your department.
- *Attend conferences.* In some fields this is a good way to meet professors. It will help if you can enlist one of your undergraduate professors to introduce you. At one English department two professors hold a small professional conference every two years to which they invite their best undergraduate students so they can interact with the visiting professors in a professional environment. If you have an opportunity like this, use it.
- *Visit prospective universities.* As described below, you can set up interviews with professors and students at departments that interest you.
- *Write letters.* This method is discussed below.
- *Solicit introductions.* This is also discussed below.

Some of these tactics may be difficult for you to use. For example, it is hard to convince a professor at a distant school that he needs your help with research if he has never heard of you. Likewise, it will be tough in a field that rarely uses research assistants. However, you don't have to employ every tactic. Just use the ones you can to make contacts and follow up whatever leads result. Remember, it only takes one good contact to help you into graduate school. In my own case, when I was a junior at UC Santa Cruz, my teacher in animal ecology was impressed by my knowledge of lizards; on my behalf he called a colleague at Stanford, a lizard ecologist, to see if he knew of research openings. By chance, the lizard ecologist had just received funding from the National Science Foundation to support an undergraduate research assistant during the summer, and I got the job. When it came time to apply to graduate school, this professor shoehorned me into the Stanford biology department as his student.

Use anyone you know who will make unobtrusive introductions for you. If you know friends of professors, ask them for introductions. The best bet for introductions are your undergraduate professors. Be frank with them about your interest in graduate school and your desire to get to know potential thesis advisers. Ask them if they know anyone in your field who might have openings for a research assistant or if they might help you do an independent study with someone whose work excites you. Ask them to introduce you to professors at conferences or those who are visiting your department. One professor says, "Conferences are one of the very best ways of meeting important people. Have your adviser introduce you, tell the important people how much you liked their presentations, tell them you're interested in their grad schools, and ask if they'd be willing to talk about their departments. You can follow up with a letter or phone call." Even if you can't get an introduction through someone you know, you can still bravely contact professors directly by letter and with follow-up phone calls or by setting up interviews through the department or the dean's office.

If you start contacting professors well in advance of when you apply, you will have time to gradually build relationships. Inquire about summer courses the professor will teach, the possibility of volunteering in his laboratory, or aspects of the departmental program *that cannot be obtained from the departmental office*. I emphasized this last point to stress that you shouldn't irritate a professor by asking for general admissions information that is available elsewhere. Eventually, you may be able to parlay these initial contacts into more extended access, such as taking courses or assisting him.

One cranky English professor warns that she personally would find it irritatingly presumptuous for an undergrad to contact her about either her own research or advice on graduate school. Given this warning, check with your undergraduate professors about the advisability of making cold contacts in *your* field. My own gut feeling is that you've got little to lose and much to gain by writing a respectful letter or making a pleasant phone call. The worst that can happen, provided you don't come off as a complete dolt, is that the professor won't be helpful. Indeed, the professor's response, or lack of one, can tell you something about whether or not he has the time or temperament to be a good adviser. If a professor has not answered your letter, maybe it got lost, maybe he's swamped with work. Write again or call—because professors are so busy, often they would rather talk on the phone for a few minutes than write a letter.

What excuse do you use for your first call or letter? One is to ask the professor's advice about a research paper or project, if your project is *directly* related to his work. Another is to ask questions about a paper he has recently published. Perhaps the easiest approach is to introduce yourself as a prospective graduate student and ask directly for information about the department or the professor's work (a phone call is best in this case—don't expect the professor to write a detailed letter to you about the department or his research).

Whether you write or phone, try to establish your credentials so that you are taken seriously. If one of your undergraduate professors suggested you call, say so. If you are an honors student, try to fit that in. Also, don't be afraid to directly but succinctly praise the professor's work. If you think his most recent paper is exciting, tell him.

Whenever you write to a professor, be meticulous with the letter's tone and content. For goodness' sake, *don't have spelling errors or other typos in your correspondence*. Proofread your letters, and, if you can, write them on a word processor so you can use a spell-check program. Also, because it is hard to get the tone right in this kind of letter, have an adviser or astute friend read it to make sure you don't sound pompous or ingratiating.

Most of the professors you contact will realize that you are trying to get to know them, but don't be ashamed of it. You are admirable for trying to plan ahead, and that alone might make you stand out. A humanities chairman said, "No one has ever contacted us before admission, and when students get here, I'm amazed they don't know anything about our work." If you write or call every few months for legitimate reasons, such as to request papers, inform them you are applying, or ask questions about research opportunities, most professors will feel at worst a grudging admiration for your savvy and dedication (unless they're confirmed curmudgeons like the English professor above). Repeated contacts show that you have a sustained interest in them and their work. This said, it's still good to start the process as early as possible (ideally at least a year before application), because you can be less obvious about your ulterior motives. You want to give the impression that your interest in their work has gradually flowered.

Even though you should be persistent, be sensitive about overdoing it, particularly if you have a naturally aggressive personality. Being perceived as a potential pest undermines your chances. One professor put it succinctly, "If you have poor personal hygiene and hang around at conferences interrupting the professors' conversations, you'll blow it."

ve managed to develop a good relationship with a professor, ing whether he would take you as a student, provided you ion. Tread carefully here, particularly in the humanities, where be usual for a grad student to choose his adviser until several yea. the program. Nonetheless, if you are genuinely enthused about a professor's work—and you should be if you are considering working under him—you have little to lose and much to gain by asking. Be careful not to put him on the spot by asking for a quick decision, especially if he barely knows you—don't ask unless you're fairly sure the answer will be yes. To help him make up his mind, give him copies of your résumé, grades, and test scores (if available). He needs to be convinced that your credentials are good enough to be competitive with those of other applicants, so he won't embarrass himself by speaking up for you. As I said before, even with a professor's help, you probably can't compensate for substandard qualifications, but it can be decisive if you are marginal or one of many possible admittees with equivalent credentials. If the professor's response *is* yes, ask whether he would be willing to write a letter to the admissions committee expressing his interest in having you for a student. This is very important. If he's not a member of the committee, you need a letter in your file to ensure that his interest in you is taken into consideration, and if he is a member, to ensure that in the confusion of the committee meetings he doesn't forget you.

Finally, if the department at your undergraduate school has a good reputation, don't overlook applying there. It is one place where you and the faculty already know each other, so if they think well of you, you may have an edge. For example, one political scientist who had gone to Harvard as an undergrad and had a high-placed patron in the department was told by the dean's office, "If Dr. X wants you in, you're in." In other cases, departmental regulations specifically forbid accepting undergrads from the same university in order to prevent such influence.

STEP 3: INTERVIEWING PROFESSORS AND THEIR GRADUATE STUDENTS

As the time to apply approaches, you should have reduced your initial pool of adviser candidates to a handful of well-researched names, some of whom you may have previously contacted by letter or phone or spoken to in person. Now—shortly before applying—is the best time to visit these professors for interviews. If you have previously contacted some of them, you can reinforce positive impressions you have made with a well-prepared visit. For any professors not previously contacted, a visit and interview is the best way to make a memorable impression late in the game.

In addition to using your visit to assess and impress potential advisers, you can also interview other faculty and graduate students, sit in on classes, evaluate housing, academic facilities, and social environment, and in general get a feel for how well the school suits you. One student said, "Visiting the schools was really important—I only seriously considered ones I had already visited because they were known quantities."

Here's what one biology chair had to say about how important it is to interview when applying to his department:

> On our departmental brochure, we list phone numbers of professors so a prospective applicant can contact us directly to talk or set up an appointment. We like to be able to talk to an applicant, to judge their personal skills, and most important, how they would get along with others in the lab. Therefore, we look very positively at someone who interviews, and even a phone call increases their chances of admission quite a bit. However, even though it's such a big advantage, only about 10 percent of our applicants make prior contact by phone or interview.

You should be one of these 10 percent. You need sound information about potential advisers and the extra edge with the admissions committee that you can only get by visiting. Considering the heavy investment you are about to make in time and money, it would be foolish to jeopardize your future by scrimping now. Therefore, although it will be expensive to visit several schools, you should beg or borrow the money somehow.

Set up your interviews for *before* schools start evaluating applications and before the schools are swamped with other requests for interviews. But don't visit so early that your key professors will have forgotten who you are by the time they review applications. You should check with individual departments and professors about best times for visiting—final-exam week is obviously bad—but figure on arriving between a month and a couple months before the application deadline.

As a first step, check with the department or graduate school to see if they will set up appointments with both professors and exemplary grad students—many schools do this as a regular service. Even if they do schedule the appointments for you, you should still personally write the professors to (a) double-check that they will be available at the scheduled times, (b) let them know about your enthusiasm for working with them, and (c) so you have another opportunity to make them notice your existence. If the department or school doesn't schedule interviews, write or

e candidates directly to ask whether they will meet with you. The
st and most efficient tactic is to write a letter, explaining that you
want to visit and telling them that you will follow up by telephone to (a)
find out if they have time to talk with you and (b) if so, when it would
be convenient. A letter alone may be ignored and an unexpected phone
call may seem impolite, but the two together are a good combination. In
both cases make sure that you do not sound as though you are taking it
for granted that they will spend time with you—be grateful.

Given that you have limited funds, be as cost-efficient as possible and
work out a careful itinerary for your trip. One student hit all the schools
he was considering by driving a VW van across the country from UC
Berkeley to Yale. Don't waste time visiting schools where you have little
chance of being accepted.

Although there is some advantage to meeting *any* of the professors who
may be on the admissions committee or who may put in a good word for
you, the most important professors to interview are the people on your
short list because (a) you need to assess whether you want to work with
them and (b) they are the ones that have the greatest incentive to help
you get in. The more convinced they are that you are a brilliant young
student who wants to work with them directly, the more likely they are
to push for you. Here is what a professor of government said:

> Our department is highly competitive, with three hundred applicants
> last year for four positions. Forty of these students requested inter-
> views with me because I'm the head of the admissions committee—
> and the interviews didn't do them any good at all, a total waste of
> time for both of us. First of all, they annoyed me by primarily asking
> for information that they could have gotten from our printed material,
> and second, by the time we evaluated applications, I'd spoken to so
> many students I couldn't remember who any of them were. What
> *can* help is if you identify someone who would be your mentor and
> talk with him. If the faculty member tells the admissions committee
> "Gosh, this guy is good," then we take a special look at him.

When you do visit, it's important to present yourself well; otherwise
the interviewing process can actually hurt you. The biology chairman
quoted above noted:

> One prospective student came by several times last year and made a
> very favorable impression—she came across as friendly, confident,
> and well focused. She seemed to know exactly what she wanted to
> do, which was to work in neurobiology, and she had even narrowed

Don't ask for obvious info.

down her choice of adviser to three candidates. She also made it very clear to us that our department was her first choice—so we were confident that we weren't wasting our time by admitting her.

On the other hand, a few people have really bad personal skills, and the interview hurts them. For example, there was one man who dropped by several times last year whom we probably would have admitted based on paper credentials alone. However, he came across as paranoid and made everyone who talked with him uneasy. He wouldn't make eye contact and refused to answer even the most innocuous personal questions, such as why his leg was in a cast.

You can increase the chances that your interviews will go well by preparing carefully. First off, it can help immensely to ask your counseling center for training using mock interviews. Have yourself videotaped so you can spot potential problems with body language or diction. Ask your friends to interview you too—you can't get too much practice. When you do go to an interview, make sure to dress appropriately. Also, the Modern Language Association of America (MLA) warns you not to

slouch, mumble, be loquacious or laconic, use terms such as "you know" or "like," be either apologetic or arrogant, chew gum, smoke without permission, appear opinionated or contentious, argue with the interviewer, let yourself be intimidated, volunteer negative information, downgrade other candidates, jobs, or institutions, get off the track or ramble, ask questions for which answers may be found in the catalogue, or overstay your welcome.

Got all that? In preparing, review the professors' papers and those of related researchers so that you can talk about them intelligently. Know the names and specialties of the other faculty and familiarize yourself with the departmental catalogue. Ahead of time, compose a list of questions to ask the professors. Topics might include the nature of their current research, the focus of other graduate students, potential topics you might work on, whether departmental funding is generous, and whether their students finish on time with good publication records.

In addition, when talking with a professor you will be asking yourself: Do you like the way his mind works? Do you want to do the kind of work he does? Do you have rapport? Do you feel that he is generous? The two of you will have a close and important relationship that most likely will be ambivalent at best. Given the strains that are present in student-adviser relationships, it will help tremendously if you start out with someone you genuinely like. *Remember: don't choose someone who makes you feel 'ortable or afraid, no matter how important he or she is in the field.*

After you have made your own evaluation, talk to his or her graduate students. *This is essential.* Lure them away from their offices if you can, ply them with beer, and pump them for information. They will be your most reliable source for finding out if an adviser is an ogre, a bumbler, or someone you would be lucky to work with. Remember, however, that graduate students are stressed and tend to resent their advisers as a matter of course, so weight their comments accordingly.

Here are some important questions to ask the students:

- Most important, do his students get good jobs? You can get additional information from data published by some professional associations. For example, the *American Association of Sociology Guide to Graduate Departments* lists every sociology professor by department, tells who his recent students were and where they now work.
- Does the adviser give students enough time? Some professors may be so busy with their own careers, writing the "big book," serving on committees, doing field research, getting divorced, that you will rarely see them, which is, needless to say, not good. Not only will you get too little help, but it will be difficult to develop a natural, friendly relationship with someone whom you only see once a month for an hour. One student's adviser traveled so much that in order to get any help at all she had to intercept him for short meetings in between flights at Kennedy International Airport.
- Do his students finish quickly? One student said of a big-name psychologist, "He wasn't interested in getting students out, only in having them complete *his* research." Advisers may slow their students down by ignoring them, overworking them on extraneous projects, or torturing them psychologically. Even the friendliest adviser, liked by all his students, may fail to direct his students adequately. The bottom line is that it doesn't matter why an adviser's students don't finish on time. Wasted time is wasted time.
- Does the adviser give credit for work? Let's say that you write a paper under his or her direction and it gets published. Who gets first authorship? Remember that first authorship is more prestigious than second and can help you get jobs and fellowships. It is not bad or out of the ordinary for the professor to want first authorship, even if you did all the work except for the idea. But some professors can be generous about giving you credit, particularly if they are already well established and don't need more papers hanging from their belts.

- Is he or she consistent in what he or she demands? Will he or she tell his or her students to do one thing with their research at the beginning of a project and two months later angrily demand to know why they did it that way? While this may sound ludicrous, unfortunately it is a common occurrence. One master's student who had a terrible time with her adviser said, "I seriously considered smuggling in a tape recorder so I could have proof when he contradicted himself." Sometimes professors genuinely seem to forget what they told you the first time, some professors change their minds a lot, and a minority are just plain sadistic.
- Is he reasonable about the amount of work expected? Although times have changed since the third century B.C. when the Greek philosopher Bion was sold as a slave to his rhetoric professor, many advisers still believe in serfdom. One physics student at MIT argued strenuously that his professor expected him to spend too much time in the lab working on their joint experiments. They finally compromised and the student's lab time was cut to ninety-five hours per week.
- Do students respect him intellectually? Some professors have gained fame for a small amount of top work, but, all in all, may not be very bright. Other professors may have made major contributions in the distant past and are now not as sharp as they once were. Or they may be very good at some things and not good at others, like writing. It is extremely rare to find someone who will admit to being a bad writer—certainly not an academic. Yet many are. And, as adviser, he will have ultimate say over anything you write, including your thesis. If you are so unlucky as to find yourself laboring to fulfill the stylistic and structural demands of a literary dunce, who may destroy the writing you have labored over, you will become a candidate for therapy.

6

• • • • • • • • • • • • • •

CHOOSING A SCHOOL:

SECONDARY ASPECTS

• • • • • • • • • • • • •

IN ADDITION TO A GOOD THESIS ADVISER, THERE ARE OTHER CRITERIA TO
consider when choosing a school, including the department's prestige, area
of emphasis, and emotional tone; rates of attrition, completion, and job
placement; requirements for teaching and languages; and types of financial
and logistical support. Obviously, the degree to which you weight the
various criteria depends on your academic and career plans. If you are
headed for a Ph.D. program to become a college professor, then finding a
good thesis adviser is paramount. Alternatively, if you are headed for a
nonthesis master's degree, the thesis adviser is relatively unimportant and
you should weight the criteria in this chapter most heavily.

• PRESTIGE OF THE DEPARTMENT •

For master's students in certain fields the prestige of the department may
determine the quality of the job you get upon graduation. MBAs from
the top-ranked schools earn significantly more money than those graduating from lower-ranked schools. And the quality of your first job will
determine whether you are given the opportunity to develop responsibility
and experience that will translate into later career advances. On the other
hand, for some master's students the quality of the adviser and the prestige
of the school are less important. For example, if you are a primary school
teacher who needs a master's degree for the next step on the salary ladder
and you will receive the bonus regardless of the rigor or reputation of the
program, it may make sense to choose an easy program with few requirements, dodging the thesis. Or if you want practical training in computer

programming and you know you can get it economically and adequately at a local college, there may be little to gain careerwise by attending a more prestigious program.

For Ph.D.s there is a high correlation between departmental prestige and job quality. Newly minted Ph.D.s from prestigious departments are more apt to land prestigious jobs than their less illustrious colleagues, and they are also more likely to get coveted research-track jobs. Whether or not you teach or do research in your first job is important, because once you are marked as a teacher, it will be hard to move up to research, in part because people carrying heavy teaching loads rarely have the resources or time to do research.

When it comes to academic hiring, high competition for jobs creates a cascade effect. Ph.D.s from prestigious institutions who fail to land jobs at top-rank schools take jobs at second-rank schools, thereby displacing graduates of second-rank schools to those still further down the line. Because of this displacement, many second-rank schools rarely hire their own graduates, preferring to fill their teaching positions with graduates of the schools above them.

There are two primary reasons that departmental prestige translates into job prestige. The first is that the department's reputation itself may impress a hiring officer or committee. Often people judge work by academics from prestigious backgrounds more highly than identical work by less prestigious people.

A second, more important effect is that students attending prestigious departments tend to have advisers and other committee members with large reputations and good connections. These powerful people can write influential letters of recommendation, lend authority to a student's thesis and co-authored papers, and pull strings during his job search. Their string pulling is effective because many have old classmates, colleagues, and past students sitting on the search committees of prestigious universities. Research, such as that reported by David Breneman and Ted Youn, shows these old-boy connections outweigh more objective measures of how good a graduate student is—such as the number of papers he has published in graduate school—in part because it is difficult to evenly assess the quality of students who do not have a long track record of publication. These old-boy connections work outside academia as well; for example, one computer science professor, who worked extensively in industry before taking his teaching position, regularly finds his master's students high-quality jobs in industry through his professional connections.

This association between sponsorship and job placement suggests two things. The first is that if you are not at a high-ranked school, you still have a good shot at prestigious jobs if your adviser is well respected (hence the importance of choosing advisers carefully). The second is that you can be in a top department and still fail to get a good job if you neglect to make the necessary connections with powerful faculty.

■ EMPHASIS OF THE DEPARTMENT ■

Different departments that nominally cover the same area may have very different emphases. By emphasis I mean a strong faculty and curriculum in the area you like. For example, if you are interested in field ecology, you might consider the biology department of the University of Florida at Gainesville, as opposed to Stanford's biology department, which focuses heavily on population genetics. The Johns Hopkins School of Advanced International Studies prepares students for nonacademic careers in international economics and relatively few of their Ph.D.s take academic jobs, whereas Princeton's international studies program emphasizes preparation for an academic career. (See pages 66–67 for sourcebooks that evaluate the strengths of departments.)

There are several advantages if the department is strong in your area. First, there are apt to be more faculty with good political connections who can help you get a job. Second, you have a wider choice of thesis committee members. Third, if things do not work out with your thesis adviser after you have started school, you are more likely to find a good replacement. Fourth, strong departments are more likely to have large endowments and therefore more money to support graduate students.

A final warning is to be aware that the fact that a department has a good reputation based on past performance does not necessarily mean it is still strong. Key professors may have recently left or died, vicious political battles arisen, or funding been cut back. It sounds unlikely, but more than one student has blithely set off to graduate school only to have the department collapse around him. A doctoral student in a new interdisciplinary program in art and anthropology went off to do two years of fieldwork in Papua New Guinea. When she returned, filled with malaria and other parasites, she received unexpected news. Not only had her professor moved to another country but the art and anthropology program had been disbanded. No Ph.D. for her. Please check that any programs *you* are considering are secure, particularly if they are interdisciplinary programs, which are commonly weak, or if they are newly founded or nontraditional departments. Because of shortfalls in academic funding, many universities are either scaling back departments or cutting them out completely.

• ATTRITION POLICY •

MANY DEPARTMENTS BELIEVE THAT
GRADUATE STUDENTS WILL
OVERPOPULATE UNLESS THE HERD IS
THINNED ONCE A YEAR

With attrition rates for doctoral students standing at nearly 50 percent, you don't need to stack the deck against yourself. Find out from the departments what their attrition rates are. Many can tell you how many students drop out at each stage. Princeton, for example, loses 15 percent of its doctoral students by the end of the first year, an additional 27 percent by the end of the second year (when qualifying exams are held), and an additional 9 percent by the end of the third year, for a total of 51 percent. Departments may have substantially different attrition policies. Some, like Stanford's biology department, admit a relatively few highly qualified doctoral students and attrition rates are low. Other departments may admit many more students than they can cope with, using comprehensive exams or other means to weed out the riffraff. The English department at the University of Virginia uses what its students describe as the "bloodbath" method: its policy has been to cut the number of would-be Ph.D. students by nearly two-thirds at the end of the first year, largely on the basis of grades. Such high-attrition policies may help the department end up with the most competitive students, but they are traumatic for the graduate students who have spent a year or more earning at best a consolation master's degree upon termination.

• TIME TO COMPLETION •

Master's students typically finish close to the planned one or two years, although students who fail their exams the first time around, or whose theses become problematic, may take longer. One electrical engineering master's student had both of these problems: the master's exam was graded very strictly the year she took it, and she failed along with 35 percent of the class. Rather than restudy for the exam, she decided to do a thesis, which took longer than expected, so that her total time in the master's program ran slightly over three years. Some programs commonly take longer than others: I know one excellent, rigorous biology program in which students doing a master's thesis regularly take three years.

Average Ph.D. completion times can differ dramatically among departments in the same field. For example, a psychologist received her Ph.D. from Ohio State, where a tightly run program with excellent guidance got nearly all students finished in four years, including herself. She then did postdoctoral work at a big-name department where the doctoral program was poorly coordinated and most students floundered for six or more years. She said, "I hadn't realized how good Ohio State was until I saw how shitty C—— was." Ask departments for their average time to completion.

▪ PLACEMENT SUCCESS ▪

You can also contact departments to get information about how successful they are in placing their students in jobs. For example, Duke's English department reports that more than two-thirds of the approximately seventy Ph.D.s to graduate from their department during the 1990s are teaching at major colleges and universities. Departments vary in how actively they prepare students for the job market. Good departments hold mock interviews and job seminars, teach courses in job hunting, and orchestrate active efforts by the faculty to find jobs for their students.

EMOTIONAL QUALITY ▪ OF THE DEPARTMENT ▪

Another consideration is the tone of the school. Is it formal or informal? Do graduate students call the professors "Dr. So-and-so" or do they call them by their first names?

Some schools will have an intensely competitive "we are serious academics" tone. Highly competitive schools will hire big-name professors (Nobel Prize winners are particularly coveted) even if they are eccentric, nasty, and can't teach. Such schools are likely to have value systems that put being nice to graduate students low on the list of priorities. Other schools are warmer and more casual, and professors may socialize freely with graduate students, so that bonds of genuine affection form.

When I was in graduate school, I regularly attended seminars in the biology departments of Stanford and Berkeley. At Stanford, graduate students rarely asked questions. They were not expressly forbidden to do so, but the students were cowed by the professors, and any question was likely to be met with condescension and belittlement. At Berkeley, graduate students could ask questions freely and there was a feeling of camaraderie. Not surprisingly, attendance was greater at seminars in the kinder department, and the graduate students were happier.

When you are interviewing prospective advisers and their current graduate students, talk with other professors as well and pay attention to the tone of the department. You can also ask to sit in on classes. Try to sense whether the ambience matches your personality. Is it too dry and competitive for you? Or does excessive informality suggest to you that there will not be sufficient intellectual rigor?

Also, keep your ears open for information on the tenor of departmental politics. Just like other organizations, academic departments will go through periods of bad morale and dissension. Avoid getting into a department where major turf or personal battles are being fought. You may well end up a casualty, since you will be seen as an extension of a particular professor's forces.

▪ LOGISTICAL RESOURCES ▪

A school's resources will be important in determining how quickly, cheaply, and well you can get your work done. Is there enough support so that you can get out of school on time with ease?

- Will you have easy access to a word processor? Word-processing capability is crucial for writing your thesis.
- Is there free or cheap computer time? Is there equipment, preferably personal computers and laser printers, for producing graphs and figures, or will you have to draw them by hand? The time differential here is hours versus days or weeks.
- Is there money for travel to conferences?
- Is there money to do fieldwork?
- Is there fifth- and sixth-year support, in case you don't finish on time?
- Is there adequate lab space?

▪ TEACHING REQUIREMENTS ▪

Graduate students have identified excessive teaching requirements as the number one reason they are late in graduating. Therefore, the amount of teaching-free financial aid you are offered by different schools should be a major factor in deciding which school to attend—*the less teaching, the better*. Remember that every quarter you teach a full load is an extra quarter you will spend in school.

When you do have to teach, put in the minimum amount of time and effort to do it competently. It will be tempting to overinvest in the classroom because the students will be eager to learn and you will feel important in your role as teacher. Unfortunately, the academic system won't reward you for being a good teacher. It will only reward you for doing research, which in your case means writing a good thesis. Don't get distracted.

▪ FINANCIAL SUPPORT ▪

The amount of financial support available may determine whether you can afford to attend a school. It will certainly help determine how long it takes you to finish your thesis.

The best thing to get is free money—a scholarship or grant. Not only is there nothing to pay back, but this "no strings attached" money makes you much more attractive to potential advisers because they will not have to worry about your support. The worst is work unassociated with your academic career, since even part-time work can substantially increase the length of time it takes you to get your degree. Instead of working, if nothing else is available, take out a loan. Because you will make so much more per hour when you are working after graduation, it is cost-effective to borrow now and pay back later.

Research assistantships (RAs) and teaching assistantships also have the disadvantage of slowing you down, but at least there may be career benefits. RAs can be very good as a means of training in research, getting to know faculty, and deciding whether you enjoy a particular type of research. Teaching assistantships are less desirable, for the reasons given above—although you may have contact with professors, teaching doesn't help your career that much and it slows you down a lot.

It is not uncommon for financial aid to suddenly disappear or be reduced. Take the case of Kathy, who flew from her home in England to enter a prestigious philosophy program in the United States only to find that her department had overspent the previous year, leaving no money for her fellowship—she didn't even have money for rent. She finally got her money by threatening to sue. Even though it won't protect you 100 percent, make sure to get any promises of financial aid in writing before attending the school.

Consider taking out the cheap, deferred-interest student loans (Perkins and subsidized Stafford Loans) every year in which you qualify, even years in which you don't need the money. If you don't borrow the money when you can, you may regret it later: most Ph.D. students find that in their last year or two they are working on their theses full-time, but they aren't allowed to register as full-time students and are therefore ineligible for the best student aid at the very time they need it the most. They get stuck working or taking out relatively expensive unsubsidized loans. It doesn't cost you much to take out subsidized student loans—interest rates are considerably lower than market rates and you don't start incurring interest until you graduate. Stafford loans do have loan fees of 4 percent. If you choose not to use the money during school, you can either pay it back after you graduate or keep it in an interest-bearing account and come out ahead if the interest you pay is less than you earn. Note, however, that you may have to start repaying once you are no longer enrolled as a full-time student, even if you are still in graduate school.

▪ EXTRA-YEARS SUPPORT ▪

You would be wise to find out whether a school offers support past the fourth, fifth, or sixth year, and how this compares with the number of years it takes an average student to complete his dissertation. If a school cuts off financial aid after the fourth year, and you end up taking seven years to finish, that's three years to spend waiting tables while trying to type your thesis. Or you may end up as a "freeway flyer," a graduate student who drives from campus to campus in a frantic race to teach enough classes to support himself. When I was in the biology department at Stanford, the average time to completion was over five years, yet financial aid officially ended after four years. It was possible to petition for fifth-year support, to be voted upon by the departmental faculty, but this was a terrifying ordeal if you had not played a good political game and were uncertain whether you were still considered "promising."

▪ LANGUAGE REQUIREMENTS ▪

Language requirements can add a year or more to your stay in graduate school. In a survey of recent Ph.D.s, language requirements were one of the most common reasons given for tardy completion of the degree. Therefore, when choosing a school, avoid those that require languages, unless you really need one for your future work. You would need Spanish, for example, if you wished to do conservation or social work in Latin America.

However, in most cases, unless you plan to do your work in a foreign country or are getting your degree in language study, a language will make relatively little contribution to your professional success. In science, for example, the international language is English and command of it, or what passes for English among scientists, generally will be adequate.

▪ SOCIAL CLIMATE ▪

The social climate of the university may help to determine whether your years in graduate school are happy or not. If you are a returning student, a woman, a minority student, or a foreign student, you need to check how welcoming the institution will be (see Chapter 23). Note, also, if you are single, five years is a long time to be celibate. Having been suitably warned, you should ask other graduate students about the campus social life. Are there well-located graduate dorms? Do graduates and undergraduates socialize? Do they share dormitories? Is there an active graduate student association? Is there a reasonably balanced sex ratio? Are there adequate resources for the types of athletic and cultural activities you enjoy?

7

. . . .

APPLICATION AND

ADMISSION

. . . .

· THE ADMISSIONS COMMITTEE ·

Graduate admissions committees are small groups of overworked faculty (and sometimes graduate students) whose task is to process hundreds of applications within a few weeks, whittling them down to the tiny fraction that are admitted. The committee's decisions not only are based on academic guidelines for acceptable grades, GREs, and recommendations but also reflect political forces within the department, needs for balancing the student mix, and the personal biases of the faculty for certain types of research or intellectual orientation.

Here's a description of the process by a recent member of the admissions committee of Stanford University's English department, where the committee's goal was to boil down 600 applications to 18 acceptances:

First we divide the 600 applications into 12 stacks of 50 applications and give each stack to a different two-person team for evaluation. Each of a team's two reviewers reads all 50 applications and independently rates each one as deserving either a 1, 2, or 3. If both reviewers rate your application as a 1, you get passed on to the next level, but if they give it two 2s or 3s, you're out of contention. If your application gets a split decision with both a 1 and a 2, then the director of admissions takes a look at the application and decides whether or not you make the cut. This process whittles the initial 600 down to approximately 90.

Next, we hold a meeting of all 24 committee members, which lasts two and a half days, at 8 hours per day. It's brutal. During the first day, each team presents a briefing on their top 3 or 4 candidates, explaining why each candidate is good enough to be admitted. At this point we are trying desperately to eliminate people, to whittle the 90 applications down to 35, so any blemish means "Out they go." For example, if the presenting team says, "This student wants to study Wordsworth and has submitted a paper he's written," then our resident Wordsworth scholar says, "Let me look at that." He skims a couple of pages and says, "This is crap, totally unoriginal." So that guy's out. Or, about another application, someone else will say, "Let me look at that one." After they've read a few lines they say, "My God, this is a male chauvinist." And he's out.

Basically, because the process is so political, the student has the luck of the draw. You don't know what types of people are on the committee or who will take a special interest in your application. That's why one person may get a huge fellowship at Cornell and be rejected by Johns Hopkins.

By the second day, everyone is exhausted. We're down to about 35 applications, strewn over all the tables and chairs. We have some sandwiches delivered, and take an hour to eat while we look over all 35 applications. This gives you roughly two minutes to review each application, between bites of your sandwich. When we reconvene, we vote on each application in order to cut the 35 finalists to approximately 18 winners. Because we base our votes on only a couple of minutes' review of each application, plus whatever we can remember about the presentations from the previous day, the voting can be pretty uninformed. The students would be terrified if they knew the degree of chance involved, although it's better than throwing darts.

We only have about 12 fellowships to offer, but we make 18 offers because we assume that at least 6 of our 18 will turn us down. An additional 15 or so are put on a waiting list. Because our top 10 choices are also likely to be top 10 choices at other institutions, we only expect maybe 3 of these to accept our offer. The fact that our top choices are also the top choices at other schools is one of the things that make us confident that our selection method works fairly well, despite appearing haphazard.

For comparison, the chairman of a biology department comments:

We need to cut 60 applications down to about 5 fellowship offers. As soon as 20 completed applications come in, we circulate them to all four members of the admissions committee to read over a two-week period. Then we have a meeting to talk over our individual judgments.

Each committee member comes to the meeting having decided how to vote on a particular student. As each applicant's name comes up, we tally the votes. Four votes to reject is an easy decision; so is four votes to accept. However, the decision is harder if the vote is tied two to two. Ties are where it makes a big difference if you've made prior contact with a faculty member—on a split vote, we usually accept the judgment of whoever knows the student.

WHAT ARE COMMITTEES ▪ LOOKING FOR? ▪

In a doctoral program, the faculty is trying to decide if you have the brilliance and dedication necessary to become an important researcher in your specialized field. In a master's program, there is more focus on whether you will be a credit to the field you wish to work in. In either case, the school has an incentive to choose promising students because its reputation is affected by the quality of students it produces.

Faculty also have personal incentives for choosing students with certain qualities. Some professors, particularly in the hard and social sciences, need capable students who will help them with research or teaching. In such cases, a professor may push hard to admit a student he has already judged to be capable. His influence may be decisive in departments where faculty are allowed to draft candidates from the applicant pool: "This year it is Joe's turn to have a new graduate student."

Both the department and the individual faculty members want to avoid students who need a lot of guidance or who have difficult personalities. Therefore, the committee favors students who appear well adjusted and whose research goals are well focused. Advisers regularly say that their favorite type of student is one who comes in knowing just what thesis topic he wants to work on. As one professor said, "You need a student who's quick to learn, self-motivated, technically good, and a real self-starter—and most students are not."

If there are students on the admissions committee, you may have special problems. Several faculty members who serve regularly on committees told me that students judge the applicants more severely than the professors. For example, students tend to like fields that are "hot," and they are more likely than faculty to disapprove if you want to study something solid but unexciting. Also, one faculty member noted that students look for "political correctness," weeding out those who appear to hold improper views on feminism or equal opportunity. Finally, students may not have the experience to realize that schools differ substantially in the toughness of their grading, not recognizing that a B-plus average from Swarthmore might actually indicate a better student than an A average from another school.

HOW DOES THE COMMITTEE
▪ WEIGH YOUR CREDENTIALS? ▪

Many departments have formal or informal cutoff points based on either GPA or GRE scores—if you don't pass the minimum requirement, you're out. Once you've made that cut and are part of the pool of acceptable applicants, most departments use no set formula, but look at the whole package. The chairman of a biology department said:

> We look at the Graduate Record Exam (GRE) scores first. If they're way off, they don't totally disqualify someone, but they set the tone. Grades come next, with recommendations less important. But even though this is the general pattern, it varies a lot from case to case, and we really look at the total package. One person might not have top GREs or grades, but we let them in because they have a very focused statement of research goals and do an impressive interview.

It's not all about the GRE [handwritten marginal note]

The process also reflects the biases of the individual committee members. The chairman of a history department said:

> We don't have formal criteria, and each person on the committee emphasizes somewhat different things. Some think the GREs matter more, others emphasize grades, and some give most weight to the statement of purpose. When we're reviewing applications, the grade person might say, "Yeah, he's okay, but look at the grades, they're a little low," and the GRE person answers, "Yes, but his GRE scores are great."

Despite these faculty biases and variability among departments, comprehensive surveys can sum up trends over many departments and academic disciplines. One such large-scale study by Philip Oltman and Rodney Hartnett for the Educational Testing Service (ETS), which administers the GRE, surveyed how twelve disciplines judged admissions criteria. Of those departments that required submission of GRE results, 151 responded, rating the admissions criteria from 1 (not used) to 5 (extremely important). Although this is only one study, it is comprehensive enough so that you can use it as a rough guide for how much weight you should give to y_ credentials:

3.9 Undergraduate grade point average in major field
3.8 Recommendations from faculty known by members of department
3.7 Undergraduate grade point average in junior and senior years
3.6 GRE General Aptitude Test verbal score
3.6 Undergraduate major related to field of graduate study
3.5 Undergraduate grade point average overall
3.0 Educational or career aspirations of applicant
3.0 Recommendations from faculty not known by department members
3.0 Applicant known to department faculty
2.9 Other academic achievements (papers, projects)
2.9 Quality of undergraduate institution
2.7 Personal statement on application form
2.7 Impression made in personal interview
2.6 Work experience
2.6 GRE General Aptitude Test analytical score
2.5 Other nonfaculty recommendations
2.5 GRE Subject (Advanced) Test score appropriate to program
1.9 Other test scores
1.9 GRE Subject (Advanced) Test score appropriate to applicant's undergraduate major
1.6 Particular subscores on the appropriate GRE Subject (Advanced) Test

ETS also surveyed an additional eighty departments that did not require or recommend GRE scores. As expected, these departments weighed GRE scores less strongly, giving all subscores values between 1.3 and 1.6. These departments gave the other variables, including grades and recommendations, weights similar to those given by departments that required GRE scores.

Different subfields within disciplines may weigh admissions criteria differently. For example, in the ETS study, 78 percent of zoology departments required the GRE subject test, whereas only 21 percent of environmental study departments did. Likewise, within the humanities, 61 percent of Romance language departments required the GRE Subject Test, whereas only 9 percent of religion departments did so.

Other studies and informal assessments back up the ETS finding that grades and recommendations (from people known to the faculty) are most important, with GRE results equally important for some fields and departments.

Grades are so important to most admissions committees because they not only reflect aptitude but also provide a track record that indicates your ability to do consistently good (or bad) work. The committees also know that undergraduate GPA is the variable most highly correlated with later graduate school success.

Generally, students with lower than a 2.5 GPA will find it almost impossible to get into a graduate school, and those below 3.0 will find it difficult. (Both GPA and GRE requirements are often somewhat lower for master's than for Ph.D. programs.) In psychology doctoral programs, the most selective schools require a GPA of at least 3.5 and a total GRE score (verbal plus quantitative) of at least 1300, second-rank schools require a GPA of at least 3.3 and a GRE of 1200, and lesser-known schools require GPAs greater than 3.0 and GRE scores of 1100.

Understand that your GPA isn't just a number—it is usually interpreted by admissions committees in light of which courses were taken. For example, two psychology applicants with the same GPA might be judged very differently if one had taken only university-required breadth courses, nonmajor electives, and a wide variety of psychology courses, while a wiser student had added courses in English composition, math, and statistics, all courses that would help a student meet the graduate demands of writing, analysis, and statistical interpretation.

GRE scores may be used differently by different departments: Some only use them as minimum cutoffs. Other departments pay attention to scores only if they are either extraordinarily good or bad. Still others give them equal weight with GPAs in deciding between the more competitive students. Another frequent use of GRE scores is to offset weak GPAs. The admissions committee may feel that good GRE scores show potential for excellent work even though the student didn't apply himself well in the past. This analysis would be most likely to work in the student's favor if he showed recent signs of serious endeavor, like excellent grades in his latest courses. Finally, 50 percent of departments requiring GRE scores in the ETS study reported using them to help determine financial awards because they are helpful in distinguishing between a number of students who have excellent academic records.

In your enthusiasm for improving the big three—grades, recommendations, and GREs—do not neglect the remaining criteria, which the ETS study ranked as only *slightly* less important. Remember, the committee will be looking at the "total package." And when the big three are essentially equal, the committee has to turn to other criteria, such as the strength of the personal statement, to decide. These other important criteria include: personal contacts with the faculty, other academic achievements such as

papers or research projects, work experience, quality of undergr
institution, career goals, and personal interviews.

• WHERE CAN YOU GET IN? •

You obviously want to get into the best school possible, but it doesn't
make sense to waste your money applying to schools where there is no
realistic chance you will get in.

The facts are that even the best students may not be able to get into
their first-choice school, most students have to settle for schools below the
top rank, and many aren't accepted at all. In one study, of thousands of
students who applied to three doctoral programs apiece, nearly 45 percent
were not admitted to even one of their chosen programs. Many were
unrealistic and aimed too high. Assess your credentials accurately and
match them to the schools' admission requirements.

It's fairly easy to check out your own competitiveness—you know your
own GPA, GRE scores, and the potential quality of your letters of recommendation. How do you find out the level of qualification a particular
department demands? First, if you are interested in a specific school, *the
best source of information is the department itself*: you can contact the
department or the dean's office of the graduate school directly by phone
or letter and ask them for data *on percentage of students admitted and
on minimum and average admission qualifications*. Georgetown's economics department, for example, tells prospective Ph.D. students that
admission usually requires GRE scores above the 80th percentile on the
quantitative aptitude section and above the 70th percentile on the economics advanced test. It is wise to inquire if a particular subfield you are
interested in—say population biology within the biology department—
has more stringent minimum requirements than the departmental requirements. Even if it isn't possible to locate comprehensive data on a
particular department or subfield, a department's graduate adviser or an
admissions committee member can give you his informal assessment of
average qualifications. Likewise, if you want more detail on the admission
procedure than is officially available from the department's office, or you
want to discuss your individual case, ask to speak with a member of the
admissions committee.

You can get information rapidly about a large number of schools by
consulting library sources. These sources won't give you as much information as the departments themselves, but you can use them for identi-

fying possibilities that you can follow up by direct contact. Here are six sources:

- *Educational Rankings Annual*, edited by Lynn Hattendorf, is a digest of more than 1,500 different rankings and lists on education, compiled from a wide variety of published sources.
- *Peterson's Guides to Graduate and Professional Programs* contain much information on, among other things, the number of graduate assistantships and fellowships awarded and the percentage of applicants accepted, giving you a measure of exclusivity.
- The *National Academic Advisor's Association Journal* (*NACADA Journal*) in spring 1991 published a comprehensive report by David Webster, of Oklahoma State University at Stillwater, called "The Academic Advisor's Guide to Quality Rankings in Various Fields of Study," which discusses more than 100 academic quality rankings. He describes the 100 studies and gives you the citations necessary to find them. Although tracking down the studies relevant to you will take library research, they will be more useful than general college guides.
- The *Graduate Programs and Admissions Manual* includes statistics on numbers of degrees awarded, faculty-staff ratios, and school size, and it lists phone numbers and addresses for the departments you will wish to contact.
- For psychology, the American Psychological Association publishes *Graduate Study in Psychology*, which lists the minimum grade point average necessary for admission to each school. Check with your school's reference librarian or career counseling librarian for sources in your field that might have similar information.
- Finally, good sources for rankings are the periodic surveys published in the *Chronicle of Higher Education*.

▪ MAXIMIZING YOUR CHANCES ▪

You can maximize your chances of admission through a combination of strategies, including improving your academic credentials, slanting your essays and interviews to meet the committees' biases, and personal contact. Here are some useful strategies:

- *Project the right image in your essays and interviews.* Since the committee is looking for dedicated scholars, present yourself differently from the way you did as a college applicant. Do not advertise yourself as a Renaissance person, one who is likely to spend time running student government, playing theatrical leads, or dividing energy between a study of pre-Socratic philosophy and physics. A lengthy list of extracurricular activities unrelated to your field can actually hurt your chances of admission by bringing your dedication into question. Instead, you must appear to be a dedicated scholar whose burning desire to specialize will lead you to focus on nothing but research.

• *Research the department's current emphasis.* Given that the emphasis and philosophy of the department will always be changing, talk to graduate students and professors at the school about what types of students are most likely to be admitted. If the department is moving away from research toward theory, or emphasizing a new area, you should find this out and reflect it in your personal statement.

• *Choose a less competitive field or subfield.* If your chosen field is highly competitive, look carefully at related fields that might be less so. For example, your chance of admission to one prestigious university's comparative literature department is three times better than your chance in the same university's English department. Also, even within a single department, you may increase your chances by specifying a relatively unpopular subfield. For example, within one highly regarded political science department many fewer applicants wish to study American politics than international relations, and the caliber of the American politics applicants is lower. A professor in the department says:

> If we based our decisions solely on quality, we would probably admit only students who wanted to work on international relations, because their qualifications are so outstanding. However, because we want a balance, we accept lower-ranked students who want to study American politics.

Clearly, if you wanted to get into this highly competitive department, you should apply in American politics, and then, if necessary, change your specialization after you're in.

However, you can eliminate yourself if you specify a subfield that no one is teaching. For example, if you were to apply to the political science department above, happily telling them about your burning interest in the international relations of sub-Saharan Africa, your chances of admission would be slim because they don't have an expert in sub-Saharan politics. A member of the admissions committee said, "If the student is truly outstanding, we might call and ask whether he insists on studying Africa. If he's not outstanding or is unwilling to change areas, forget it."

- *Look for up-and-coming departments.* One of your best bets is to identify departments that have just strengthened themselves by expanding, increasing funding, or hiring new top-rank faculty. Such a newly improved department's reputation may not yet reflect its new excellence, so competition for admission may still be relatively low. Nonetheless, the improvements will cause its reputation to grow, so it may be high by the time you graduate—which is what counts when you're looking for a job.
- *Use personal contacts and interviews.* This is your greatest chance to outshine the competition. If you make no other early contact, do visit the schools to which you apply.
- *Improve your academic credentials.*
- *Write strong essays and personal statements.*

▪ THE APPLICATION PROCESS ▪

WHICH SCHOOLS SHOULD YOU APPLY TO?

Because it costs at least $25 to apply to each school, you don't want to apply to more schools than necessary. At the same time, you would be foolish to stake all your hopes on only one or two schools. Therefore, a sensible strategy is to apply to approximately ten schools of varying competitiveness. Choose several schools where you have a good chance of getting in, several whose admission standards are a bit higher but where you might get in with a bit of luck, and a couple with lower standards where you are almost certain to get in.

If you have to do a thesis, you should give top priority to schools where you have identified likely advisers. The better you know these advisers, and the more you like them personally and admire their work, the greater priority you should give that school. You also need to factor in other attributes, including, most importantly, the department's reputation, which will directly affect your ability to get a job. You will also weigh average completion times, attrition rates, teaching requirements, language requirements, and so on. Geographic location and social climate should be least important. If you are applying to master's programs and do not intend to do a thesis, these attributes are more important than the adviser (although prior contact can still help your chances of admission). One extra thing to check about master's programs is whether, within a certain department, master's students are given adequate attention, compared with the Ph.D.s. One professor said, "We still admit twenty master's students a year, but we are trying to phase them out because we believe they detract from the academic focus of the department." His department is unlikely to take good care of their master's students.

Never decide against schools ahead of time on the grounds that they are too expensive. Private schools with high tuition often have large endowments and therefore are generous with financial aid. Apply first. You can always turn a school down if you don't get enough financial help. Once you have been accepted on academic grounds, many schools will work with you to find funding.

Apply early

Start the application process early using a well-organized timetable. It won't do to run around frantically at the last minute trying to collect letters of recommendation and deciding where to apply. It takes time to build relationships with professors, to study carefully for the standardized tests, and to write clear, well-organized personal essays. You need to start preparing to apply one and a half years before you attend graduate school. If you are in college, this means midway through your junior year. By this time you should make a two-year timetable, like the one on page 68 and following, to plan the steps in your application process.

Submit your applications early rather than at the last-minute deadline. Some schools have rolling admissions, in which even if you meet the official deadline, later applicants have less chance of getting in than early ones. Also, *financial aid applications may be due months earlier than the actual admission deadlines.*

Make requests for interviews early because the department may not have time to interview all people who request them. For example, the Johns Hopkins School of Advanced International Studies cuts off applications for interviews a month before the application deadline. Note that interviews requested by the department are not substantially different from those you set up for yourself, as described in Chapter 5.

Your school may have an annual graduate career fair, in which representatives from a large number of graduate schools provide information to prospective students. In the Washington, D.C., area, for example, several schools join together to hold a fair at George Washington University,

START YOUR APPLICATION PROCESS EARLY

where representatives from more than a hundred schools set up booths. You aren't likely to get much information about specific departments from these fairs, since each school will send only one or two people, who obviously can't cover all areas in depth, but fairs are an easy way to pick up catalogues, get on mailing lists, and find out about social life, cost of living, and other general qualities of the schools you are interested in. A well-organized fair will have lectures to give overviews of graduate study and career opportunities in various disciplines, and may also review strategies for getting financial aid and taking the GREs. Don't rely only on your own school, but check with other schools in your area to see whether they have fairs. Because the quality of fairs and the number of schools represented at them vary considerably, call beforehand to find out whether schools you are interested in will be represented.

TIMETABLE FOR THE APPLICATION PROCESS

This timetable schedules the tasks as though you were in college. If you are out of school, take "spring of junior year" to mean approximately one and a half years before you plan to attend graduate school.

Spring of Junior Year

1. Get catalogues.
2. Get GRE Information Bulletin and purchase sample tests. You can take these tests in the spring of your junior year if you are ready, or wait until late summer or early fall. One strategy is to take the general aptitude test in the spring and the advanced test the following fall, when you have completed more classes.
3. Begin talking with your adviser and other sympathetic professors about your graduate school goals. Ask them for advice pertinent to identifying good departments, contacting potential graduate advisers, and getting honors.
4. Begin identifying and contacting potential graduate supervisors at a variety of schools, as a first step toward choosing the schools you will apply to.
5. Begin soliciting letters of recommendation while you are fresh in your teachers' minds. Set up a file with your school's counseling center to hold these letters. You can ask professors to update these letters later as needed.
6. Become involved in a research project.

Summer Before Senior Year

1. Accelerate process of choosing which schools to apply to.
2. Write or phone for applications and catalogues. Order two copies of each application so you have an extra if you spoil one.
3. As applications come in, read each carefully, note all documents and other supporting material you are required to provide, and make a master checklist of deadlines which you can use to note whether you have sent applications, transcripts, letters of recommendation, and other necessary material. Note that many schools have two deadlines—an earlier one for financial aid.
4. Verify that your official transcript is correct and complete. Look at it carefully, since there are often errors, which take time to correct.
5. Draft a general statement of purpose outlining reasons you wish to attend graduate school. You will use some version of this in most applications.
6. Prepare a résumé.
7. Begin taking practice GRE exams at least by the beginning of the summer and study to improve your final scores.
8. Consider taking the real GRE exam during the summer or early fall, as a dry run, and canceling the results.
9. Enroll in Kaplan, Princeton Review, or another GRE study course as needed.
10. Continue correspondence and otherwise build relationships with potential advisers.
11. Visit possible advisers and graduate students at their schools. You can also put these visits off until early fall.

Fall of Senior Year

1. Complete your list of application deadlines and supporting documents.
2. Get and file financial aid applications for institutions like the National Science Foundation. These deadlines are often earlier than the admissions applications.
3. Start filling out applications at least two months before deadlines.
4. Your personal statements will give you the most trouble, so start these first, at least by November.
5. Make sure you have enough money for the application process. You will probably need $300.
6. By *early* in the fall, at least two months before deadlines, ask your professors for those letters of recommendation that you still need.
7. Take the GRE or other standard exams (e.g., the Miller Analogies Test)

if not yet taken. As soon as you have decided which schools to apply to, request that the ETS send GRE scores to these schools.
8. Mail application forms to each school at least a month before the stated deadline. This gives you a margin of error for emergencies and will save you spending money for overnight mail at the last minute. Photocopy each application before mailing it. This way, if an application gets lost in the mail, you can rapidly send them a copy. If you are mailing an application close to the deadline, send it registered mail so that if it is lost you have proof it was mailed on time.
9. Before the deadline, call each school to double-check that all your applications have been received, including:
   a) all letters of recommendation
   b) GRE results
   c) transcripts

Be prepared to send photocopies of any missing material (an unofficial photocopy of a transcript or GRE scores may allow the school to process your application, pending official verification).

▪ DECIDING AMONG OFFERS ▪

If all goes well, you should face what can be the most stressful part of the whole process, deciding among competing offers. Not only will the offers come in from different schools at different times, so that you may have to decide whether to accept some offers before you have even heard from other schools, but each school will complicate things by offering you a different financial aid package, ranging from a free ride to heavy teaching loads.

Now that the schools have decided whom they want, they are in the role of suitor, trying to convince their top applicants to attend. If you are a top choice, faculty members may call to convince you, describing the glories of their school. Even if you're not a first choice, a school still may try to keep you on the hook as a backup in case their first choices don't come through. One department chairman said:

If there's someone really good, we phone and tell him that the official offer's in the mail. Sometimes he'll agree to accept right away, but sometimes he'll want time to make up his mind. If one of our first choices wants time to think about it, we may phone the next person down the list and say, "We'd like you, but we haven't freed up a fellowship yet. Please wait and call us before you accept another school's offer." Hopefully, this person will hang around until we hear from our first choice.

Unless you are one of the very best applicants in the country, you are likely to find yourself in the difficult position of choosing between a top school with poor financial support and a lesser school with better support. Make no mistake about it, the more aid you receive, the easier your life will be and the faster you will finish. Balanced against this is that a more prestigious department is better for your career. If you have to make this choice, inquire what the chances are of getting good funding at the prestigious department beginning in your second year. If the chances are high, it may be worth the sacrifice of assuming loans for the first year in order to get into the better department. One biology professor said:

> If you come into our Ph.D. program without funding for the first year, it can happen that you get picked up the next year. You have to compete with the new crop of students for funding, but you have a big advantage. If you're established with a lab, doing productive things, and your adviser feels strongly about keeping you, the committee would be very hard pressed not to accept his recommendation for funding just to keep it collegial.

If you get multiple offers, you may be able to use them as leverage to negotiate some of the terms. If you have two offers, and one is for less financial support, you can be frank but polite about your considerations. You can tell School A that you are very interested but School B is giving you a significantly larger grant. Might A be able to improve their offer? Although many departments cannot bargain, others have excess funds that they can give to a student they particularly want, or they can shift awards around among students, so you might be able to get some unfortunate student's grant, while he gets your work-study. One student said:

> I received $10,000 in support from my second-choice school and only $3,000 from my first choice. So I went to my first choice and told them that I would be forced to take the second school's offer unless they could do better. They did. I got another fellowship for $9,000 a year.

Life gets complicated when the timing of the offers is off. Suppose School A gives you an offer of acceptance good for only ten days, while School B, which you are more interested in, keeps you waiting. Should you take a risk and say no to A, hoping B takes you? It may help to phone your faculty contacts at school B, the one that has not responded, and explain your predicament. They may be able to speed up the decision process to avoid losing you. The obvious strategy is to play it safe by accepting A's offer, and then change your mind if you later hear positively from B. You can do this without risk up until April 15, which is the deadline decreed by the Council of Graduate Schools in the United States. After April 15 you are committed "not to accept another offer without first obtaining a written release from the institution to which a commitment has been made. Similarly, an offer by an institution after April 15 is conditional on presentation by the student of the written release from any previously accepted offer." Most schools will release you after this date—they don't want unhappy graduate students—but make sure you discuss this with them before making a unilateral decision.

Finally, make sure that you have given all the schools a phone number where you can be reached easily during the summer. It is critical that they be able to reach you because offers of admission only last for a short time. If you don't respond to their letter by the deadline, and they can't reach you by phone, you lose.

8

IMPROVING YOUR
CREDENTIALS FOR
ADMISSION

▪ GRADES ▪

Fortunately for late starters, admissions committees tend to weigh grade point average in your junior and senior years more heavily than previous grades, so a strong finish can help. Therefore, if you are still in school, you can strengthen your transcript in the time remaining by getting all A's and by taking additional courses to make up for weaknesses. If you previously received a low grade in a course that is important to your graduate field, repeat the course and get an A. Even if the admissions committee averages the two grades, the fact that you took the course again will show that you are dedicated. If you will be attending graduate school in a field in which mathematics, statistics, or computing skills are important—areas where many applicants are weak—improve your competitiveness by taking a couple of advanced courses and doing well. A good course in English composition may be helpful since you are headed for extensive writing on your thesis or other reports. In your application essays, bring the higher grades reflecting your increased determination and focus to the attention of the admissions committee.

It is also possible to make up for a weak start by deferring graduation so you can take extra courses. In my own junior year I changed majors from art to biology and deferred graduation for a year so I could take more biology courses. The extra year changed me from an average to a strong grad school applicant.

Even if you have already graduated from college, you can still improve your record by going back to school full-time for a term or two or by taking courses part-time while working.

If you are seriously interested in a graduate program, but lack course requirements, some universities will allow you to enroll long enough to complete the classes you need for full consideration. At Princeton, for example, students who meet the standards for admission to graduate school except for course requirements may register as "qualifying students" while they take remedial courses. After completing the missing courses, they must reapply to the graduate program, where they will be judged on their total record, including the new courses. One drawback to this procedure is that students are not eligible for financial aid while they are qualifying students.

Here are some tips that will help you get the grades you need for graduate school entrance and to do well once you're in. The key for doing well in classes is very similar to that for writing—don't procrastinate and stay immersed. Therefore:

• *Sit in the front of the class.* This way you can't fall asleep and can get the full benefit of the teacher's attention.
• *Go to the teacher's posted office hours.* Do this regularly, even if you are doing well in the class. You can get extra help, the teacher will be likely to give you the benefit of the doubt on close grading decisions, and you will be motivated by your very conspicuousness to do well. Also, you can develop a relationship with the professor that may pay off with work-study jobs, research opportunities, or recommendations. Remember that recommendations from your teachers are one of the most important criteria for graduate school admission. *If they don't know who you are, they can't give you meaningful recommendations.*
• *Read your course text before going to lectures.* This will help you understand lectures, take good notes, and ask insightful questions in class.
• *Ask questions in class.* If you are shy or have trouble thinking up questions during class, read ahead and prepare them the day before. The point is not just to get information; it is also to keep you interested in the class and help you be noticed in a positive way.
• *Start large assignments early.* Talk early with your teacher about term papers and other large projects before everyone else does. You can get a tremendous amount of help from the teacher if you ask for it a month before all the other students surround him in a last-minute panic.

■ HONORS ■

Honors can help you stand out to an admissions committee, and writing an honors thesis under a particular teacher's guidance is an especially good way to get his recommendation for grad school.

The key to getting honors is to plan a campaign. First, find out ahead of time exactly what you have to do to earn them—often a university has several types of honors, each earned in different ways. Second, early in your college career talk with your adviser and other teachers to ask their advice and to put them on notice that you will be working for honors. Then they can start thinking of you as honors material and guiding you appropriately. Finally, when it comes time for teachers to nominate students, don't be shy about asking the teachers with whom you did exceptionally well to nominate you. Many students who deserve honors are passed over because their advisers overlooked them.

■ GRADUATE RECORD EXAMINATION ■

Most applicants need to take the general GRE, which is divided into quantitative, verbal, and analytic sections. You can find out from the departments you are interested in how heavily they weigh each section. Many departments will also require you to take the special subject test in your area, and some departments may weight it heavily, since it focuses on the area in which you wish to specialize.

There are a number of things you can do to substantially raise your scores. I used the following strategy myself and scored a 930 on the biology advanced test, 80 points above the 99th percentile:

- *Get exam materials early.* Get the GRE materials no later than early spring before the fall in which you will take the exam. This will give you six months to prepare. Write or phone Graduate Record Examinations, Educational Testing Service, PO Box 6000, Princeton, NJ 08541-6000, phone: 609 771-7670, fax: 609 771-7906.
- *Take the appropriate examinations early.* If you take the exam early in the year, you will have time to cancel the scores and retake the exam if you feel you didn't do as well as you could. The possible GRE testing dates are in June, October, December, and April. You should plan to take the exams either in the summer of your junior year or at the October testing date of your senior year. The December exam should be considered a fallback. Some schools will allow you to take the test up until

April, but this is cutting it very short and will not allow you to retake the test in case you have problems with it. The ideal procedure, as described below, is to take the June exam to familiarize yourself with the test, cancel the results within five days, study some more, and then take the October exam when you are fresh from studying over the summer.

- *Master your course material.* If you are still in school, master thoroughly all material in future classes up until the time you take the test. Don't just do the minimum necessary for an A.
- *Review thoroughly for the exam itself.* If you are still in school, the ideal time to study is during the summer break between your junior and senior years. Even studying as little as two hours a day over the summer can make a huge difference in your score. If you have been out of school and are reentering academia, you will be rusty and need extensive review.

To figure out how much to review, look at practice tests or actual old GRE exams (see below). Many people have particular trouble with either the verbal or the quantitative portion of the GRE. You can find help either through the GRE preparation courses described below or through any of the various GRE preparation books (check your college bookstore).

For GRE subject tests you don't need great depth of knowledge; you need broad knowledge at approximately the level of a lower-division introductory college course. You can use your old texts to review—make sure you know everything in them. Also, you can fill in knowledge gaps by buying additional introductory texts on topics you haven't covered—advanced texts are likely to be more detailed than you need.

To help you prepare, Princeton Review publishes a good book called *Cracking the GRE*, which contains strategies on scoring well on the general GRE and includes a CD-ROM containing seven computerized diagnostic exams. The program has a user-friendly interface for Windows or Macintosh. The same company also makes a CD-ROM for Windows 3.1, Windows 95, and Macintosh called *Inside the GRE* with lots of drills and clear explanations of questions. Princeton also has good strategy and review books for a number of advanced tests, including psychology, biology, and English, but these do not come with software.

Cliffs Studyware also sells a line of computer programs to study for the biology, calculus, chemistry, economics, physics, and statistics advanced tests, and for the GRE, LSAT, and GMAT. The GRE version lets you take timed full-length practice tests. If you've got a choice between Cliffs and Princeton Review, go with Princeton. Cliffs hasn't really caught up with the rest of the computer age, and their programs look and act like shareware from ten years ago—DOS-based, terrible graphics, and not user-friendly.

• *Take practice tests.* The Educational Testing Service will provide you with one practice general test contained in the GRE Information Bulletin, available at no charge. You can also order larger books containing previously administered general tests from Educational Testing Service Publications (800 537-3161). A book of six tests costs $15, and, for those with a masochistic bent, there is a book containing over 5,000 questions from seventeen past tests for $30. The same source can also sell you specialized study guides containing practice tests for each of sixteen different subject areas, including biology and psychology, for varying prices (approximately $10 each). I *strongly* recommend that you order practice tests and use them beginning in your junior year so that you can identify areas for study and special concentration. If you find yourself procrastinating because it seems too difficult to write the GRE Board a letter, you can order these books by phone with a credit card.

Take your first practice test at least several months before you face the real exam. This means you should take the first practice test no later than the beginning of the summer between your junior and senior years. Then study some more, take the next practice exam, and so on. If you order both books of practice exams for the general GRE from the GRE Board, giving you six tests, you can take one every two weeks.

Take the practice exams under actual test conditions. Make sure that you will not be interrupted. Use an alarm clock to let you know when your time is up. This way you become familiar with actual test-taking conditions.

• *Take a GRE preparation course.* These aren't a magic cure, but they spoon-feed you the material and keep you from procrastinating. First, check with the universities near you; some offer good courses at lower prices than the commercial review companies. For example, George Washington University offers an intensive preparation for the GRE general test for $295, and you can retake the course for $50. Both the Princeton Review and Stanley H. Kaplan Educational Center Ltd. offer commercial courses on the GRE general test throughout the country for roughly $700. Once you've taken a basic course, both companies offer brush-up courses, either free or at lower cost. Training is available for only one advanced test, psychology, from Kaplan, which offers audiotapes and a home-study kit for $495. Kaplan's address is 810 Seventh Ave., New York, NY 10019-5890, phone: 800 Kaptest. Princeton Review can be reached at 2315 Broadway, New York, NY 10024, phone: 800 273-8439. Both Kaplan and Princeton Review offer some tuition assistance, based on financial need.

• *Retake the actual test.* This advice helped me. Although it might sound like a hassle, people who retake a GRE test score 25 to 30 points higher on average than they did the first time. This is not a huge amount, but it indicates that familiarity increases your competency. If you take the exam once, identify your weak points, study hard, and take the exam again, you should be able to raise your score significantly. Some graduate schools look at only your most recent scores, which is great, but many schools average repeat scores because they know that scores improve with retesting. Fortunately, you can get around this with a loophole: to accommodate people who were ill or for other reasons suspect they bombed the exam, the GRE Board lets you cancel test scores either on the day of the exam or by mailing in a score cancellation form, which they must receive within seven days. *Note that this does not mean "mailed within seven days." They must actually receive your notification within seven days. If for any reason the cancellation form does not reach the GRE Board within seven days, you are stuck with your scores.* I suggest that you send your cancellation notice by certified mail and call to confirm receipt so that there are no misunderstandings. If you cancel, your scores are not reported to the schools you later apply to; nor are the schools notified that you even took the test. Also, *you cannot examine your own scores.* Even though you don't find out what your scores are, I think it is a good investment to have a no-risk chance to take the real test under actual conditions. This way you can take the test, cancel the results, study for another month, and then take the test whose results will stand. This plan is particularly good if you are nervous about test taking, because you can desensitize yourself by going through the real experience at no risk. Note that if you take the electronic version of the GRE, you cannot cancel the results once you have asked the computer to tabulate your score!

▪ OTHER STANDARDIZED TESTS ▪

In addition to the GRE, some fields and departments may require other standardized tests. For example, many psychology departments require the Miller Analogies Test (MAT), and business schools require the Graduate Management Admissions Test (GMAT). The same rules apply as for the GRE. There are how-to books for all the tests. Get them and start studying early while there is a chance to correct deficiencies. You may want to take preparation courses, like the Kaplan course for the GMAT. You can find out about helpful books and courses from your college counseling center, library, or college bookstore.

· RECOMMENDATIONS ·

WHAT MAKES A GOOD LETTER?

Recommendations are particularly valuable if the person writing the letter is known to the committee, either personally or by reputation. A big name in the field, someone famous for top work, is much more valuable to you than an obscure teacher. However, don't panic if you can't get a big-name recommendation—a praiseful, well-written letter from a lesser light who knows you well can still be a tremendous asset. A detailed letter from a less well-known teacher is better than a perfunctory letter from a big name who doesn't really know your work. Moreover, the faculty on admissions committees know that it is often difficult for students to meet the big names. One professor said, "Eminent persons from Harvard or Yale rarely write because they don't teach undergraduates. At Princeton and Stanford it does happen."

The ideal letter of recommendation speaks specifically to your strengths and describes enthusiastically what sets you above the pack. Valuable letters praise your quickness of mind, maturity, self-direction, organizational ability, speaking skills, determination, and research ability, and use specific examples of your successes rather than vague generalities.

Some schools give you the option of "open" or "closed" letters, "open" meaning that you can see them before they are sent out. I recommend that you take the "closed" option. Studies have shown that letters of recommendation are more flattering when they are open to the student, and admissions committees know this. Therefore, committees devalue an open letter. If you worked hard to deserve a good recommendation from a teacher, then you don't want a committee doubting the letter because you have had an opportunity to see it. If you doubt the quality of the letter you will get from a teacher, you shouldn't be asking him for it anyway.

HOW TO EARN OUTSTANDING RECOMMENDATIONS

In order to get outstanding recommendation letters, it's not enough just to get good grades. You must develop long-term relationships with your best professors. They need to have enough interaction with you to see that your work is consistently excellent and that you possess traits of brilliance, maturity, and perseverance that will help you excel in graduate school. Put yourself in the place of a professor who taught a class with one hundred students, twenty of whom received As. A year later one of the A students comes to you at application time and asks for a recommendation. What more could you say than "Mary Jones was in my upper-division twentieth-century European history course, did excellent work, and received an A"? This recommendation won't hurt you, but it won't help either.

Therefore, take every opportunity to get to know your teachers. Go to office hours, ask questions in class, take additional classes from your favorite professors, do independent studies, and attend all the departmental seminars and other functions you can. Talk with professors whenever possible, asking their opinions, for example, on seminars you attend together. If you can get to be personal friends with some of your teachers, so much the better.

The easiest teacher to approach will be your academic adviser, because it's his job to talk with you. If your adviser isn't suitable because of personality or academic emphasis, get a new one. Once you have a good adviser, make regular appointments so that you visit him at least once a quarter, and more often during critical periods. Use your adviser in the same way that you will use your graduate school adviser, as a *regular* source of advice. Your adviser should become a friend who will give you a good, knowledgeable letter of recommendation.

One way of getting a good letter of recommendation is to do independent study or research with a teacher whose recommendation you want. Remember that the stature of your recommenders is crucial, so target a couple of the biggest names at your school as people you want to work with. Your research should focus on the field you want to concentrate on in graduate school, so that it will indicate to the admissions committee that you have a constant focused interest in your chosen area.

There are several ways of undertaking research. One route is to develop your own research plan and then find a faculty member willing to oversee your work. You may need to do it this way if you are proposing an honors project. Another method with several advantages is to find a teacher whose ongoing research interests you and then ask if you can assist in the research—he may be glad to have an extra pair of hands. The first advantage to this method is that the teacher may be able to pay for your assistance out of his research budget. The second is that, because supervising research is time-consuming, your offer of assistance on a project may be more welcome than a request that he supervise an entirely new project. Last, as a first-time researcher, it makes sense for you to work on a well-conceived, ongoing project so that you learn how research works. Your next step might be a small self-planned research project as an outgrowth of the work you have undertaken with your supervisor.

Don't overlook the possibility of using work-study funds to work on research for a professor. It will help your career a lot more to a[...] possible recommender than to work in the library. If you have work-stud[y] funds that can be used to assist research, make the rounds of the professors in your department to ask if they can use you. My own work-study experience included boiling bees' genitals in potassium hydroxide to prepare them for microphotography. The work was incredibly boring but helped me get to know the teacher who was later instrumental in getting me into Stanford.

What if you don't have anyone to recommend you?

If you find yourself in the difficult position of not having anyone to ask for recommendations, perhaps because you didn't do well in previous courses or were too shy to be noticed, try to rectify this now. If you are in your junior year in college, follow the suggestions above. If you are in your senior year it will probably be too late to do research, but you may be able to do outstandingly in a couple of important courses and cultivate your adviser. If you are already out of school, think about enrolling in enough classes to earn recommendations.

If you are applying to graduate school some years after having received your bachelor's, professors may have forgotten who you are. Letters from employers will carry relatively little weight with admissions committees except in applied fields with close links to the working world. The least costly response to this problem is to recontact undergraduate teachers and remind them who you are. You could start by writing a letter describing who you are, why you are applying to graduate school, and reminding them of your outstanding accomplishments. Send copies of recent work you have done in the field, if any, and mention other recent accomplishments in the letter. Try to give each professor the feeling that he will be writing a recommendation for someone who has been moving forward since he last saw you. You could follow up this letter with a meeting to become reacquainted, using the excuse that you want his advice on applying to graduate school. During the meeting you can bring him up to date on what you have been doing and impress him with your determination. When someone spends time with you in person they are more likely to feel positive about you and wish to help you succeed. If you can make a good impression the teacher may feel more comfortable about writing a strong letter.

GETTING THE LETTERS OUT

When it comes to actually asking teachers for letters, don't be shy. No one is thrilled about writing them, but it is your teachers' job, and they wouldn't be where they are today unless *their* teachers had written *them* letters. Ask for the letters about two months before the deadline since it might take a month for a teacher to actually get your letter written and in the mail. Also, the later in the term you ask, the more likely it is that a teacher will hesitate to write a letter because of other time constraints.

It's important to have a good feel for whether a teacher will write you a genuinely enthusiastic letter. A mediocre letter won't help and can hurt. Most professors are good about declining to write if they don't think well of you—few are vindictive enough to want to write a negative letter. But it has happened: a master's student was applying to a Ph.D. program and one of her teachers *volunteered* to write a letter. The letter was so bad, saying the student would be incapable of doing even the poorest research, that a sympathetic secretary warned the student so she could remove it from her file. Therefore, if you have doubts, it doesn't hurt to ask point-blank whether the teacher feels he can write you an outstanding evaluation. You can phrase it diplomatically by asking something like "Do you feel you know enough about me to write a good letter?" Try to find out whether professors have a reputation for writing good or bad letters by asking other students.

If a professor knows someone at a school you are applying to, check tactfully to see if he is comfortable about calling or writing the person there. It can help substantially if your favorite literature teacher, who has encouraged you to apply to graduate school, calls up a friend and speaks highly of you. Note that a professor will probably be willing to do this only if you are outstanding (it is a tremendous favor). But if you have a good relationship with a teacher, it's not unusual. One professor said, "I always call to follow up for my best students if I know someone in the department where they're applying. My recommendation carries a lot of weight in the department where I got my Ph.D., and the admissions committee there gives special consideration to my students."

Some schools will provide you with standard forms for the letter of recommendation. If the school doesn't provide a special form, your counseling center may have standard forms that will make it easier for your teacher to complete his recommendations. When you ask your teachers for recommendations, give each a stack of all the forms you will be needing for all the graduate schools you are applying to. This way they can get them all done at once. If you keep going back every few days with a new request for a different school, the odds are that your recommenders won't praise your organizational skills.

When you give the forms to your recommenders, also give them (1) a postage-paid envelope to each school, (2) an unofficial transcript of your courses, which you can obtain from the registrar and then photocopy as necessary (note that the graduate schools need *official* copies), and (3) a copy of your résumé. Also vital is (4) a memo from you to your teacher reminding him about things to put in the letter. *This is very important* because the teacher may forget some of your accomplishments. Also, because writing these letters is a nuisance, if you word your memo so that phrases can easily be lifted out and put into the letter, the teacher may quote you verbatim and you may be able in effect to write parts of your own letter. Some teachers may even ask you to draft a letter for them, something I have always hated to do. It is hard to strike the right note when writing about yourself. In the memo to the teacher, put in all the relevant things you want him to remember—don't just put in empty generalizations like "a superlative student." Give him the specifics. If you scored in the top 5 percent on both the midterm and the final, say so. If you showed unusual dedication by attending most office hours, say so. If you were one of five students chosen to give a special report, say so. Don't assume that the teacher will remember anything, so briefly put *all* your strong points in the memo for him to choose from.

A final important thing to include is a stamped postcard *addressed to you* saying that the University of Sasquatch has received the letter of recommendation from Dr. Bigfoot. Give each professor a postcard like this that he should enclose with his letter of recommendation. When a school receives his letter, they will mail back the postcard to you so that you will know they received the letter. Teachers are notoriously slow about sending in letters of recommendation and many application files approach deadline complete except for recommendations. This way, if you don't get a postcard back within a couple of weeks you can call the school, find out if they received the recommendation, and if they haven't, nicely remind your teacher to get cracking.

Some universities try to make the process of sending out letters simpler for both students and teachers by having each of your recommenders put a single letter in a central file, either in your department or in the career placement office. You can then request that the office send out official copies of these letters to any schools you are applying to, much as transcripts are sent. The disadvantage of this system is that each letter sent out is identical and not tailored to the particular departments to which you are applying. There are also advantages. One is that you can get the letters sent out rapidly to a number of schools and not have to worry that your teacher will mail them late. Another is that, even though you can't read the file letters yourself, some schools allow your adviser or someone at the career placement office to read them. They can then alert you to potentially damaging letters so you can have them removed. Try for the best of both worlds—have letters placed in the school's file as a backup in case you can't get a professor to write a letter in time, but also ask your teachers to write personalized letters whenever possible. Especially if one of your recommenders has contacts at a school to which you are applying, his letter should be personalized and reflect his knowledge of the department and your special appropriateness.

ESSAYS/AUTOBIOGRAPHICAL
▪ STATEMENT ▪

Most departments will want you to write one or more short essays as part of your application. One is usually an autobiographical statement in which you describe the development of your career goals, and a second often addresses the question of why you have chosen the particular department to which you are applying. It is important that these essays be excellent because, although a good essay probably won't do much to compensate for otherwise weak credentials, a bad essay can seriously hurt you. One department chairman said:

> Admission to our department is very competitive, and essays make a big difference. After two days of deliberation we'll be trying to cut the top ninety students down to fifteen. They all have straight-A averages, high GREs, and all the recommendations say, "This is the best student I've had in twenty-five years." All we've got left to go on is the statement of purpose and papers they've written. That's why the statement of purpose is so important—it's where the student has a chance to establish a personal voice, to appear unique in a situation where everyone looks the same.

These essays often seem the most terrifying part of the application process, but they are fairly straightforward if you avoid a few obvious pitfalls. First, recognize that graduate schools don't want romantic dreamers who state in poetic and emotional terms their undying consecration to enlightening their fellow beings. On the contrary, given the great difficulty graduate students have in finishing their degrees, one of the prime characteristics that admissions committees look for is focus. They want to

Essays

know if the student is practical and determined. Is the student clear why he wishes to go to graduate school? Is his area of research well defined? Has she made previous contact with teachers at the university? Has she done previous research that indicates familiarity with her field? You want an essay that clearly answers yes to all of these.

Because different departments may ask different questions, and because the essays should be adapted somewhat to each department to which you are applying (see below), you will be generating many different essays. Nonetheless, most will be slight adaptations of each other, and you can usually write one or two master essays which you then change slightly for each department (thank goodness for word processors!). When you adapt an essay for a particular school, proofread carefully—in her personal statement to Johns Hopkins, one student discussed throughout how much she wanted to attend the University of Virginia! Even if a school doesn't require an essay, I suggest that you still send them a version of your master essay, which talks about your academic development and research goals, answering the questions above. This may help you stand out from the crowd.

Here are the three essay questions asked by the Johns Hopkins School of Advanced International Studies:

(1) Describe your past and present interest in international relations and why you are applying to SAIS. Explain why the background and experience you have outlined in this application show how you are qualified for study at SAIS, what you can contribute to the school, and what you hope to gain from it. (2) Building upon your answer to Question 1, describe your professional and career goals and how you hope to further prepare yourself to achieve them by studying at SAIS. (3) Imagine you are a member of the SAIS Admissions Committee. The Committee needs an additional essay question for the application by which to learn more about the personality and motivation of applicants. What new question would you propose? As an applicant to SAIS, please answer it.

The last question is a bit of a curve, but otherwise these are fairly standard examples of what you can expect. Although these questions undoubtedly fill you with an urge to say, "You boneheads, admit me at once or I'll fustigate you to within an inch of your life," in most cases this will probably fail to gain you admittance.

Instead, write your essays in a straightforward style. Avoid stylistic flourishes, slang, and the temptation to make yourself sound more sensitive than everyone else. Avoid references to childhood formative experiences, such as "My interest in international relations was first stimulated by a high school trip to Sweden." Avoid attempts at the profound, such as "The reason I want to study ecology is that I have a deep reverence for all life on earth." Avoid humor—it is too easy to sound sophomoric. Avoid any mention of problems you have had. Don't, for example, reveal that your desire to study psychology is based upon your own experiences with mental breakdown and drug addiction. Keep the tone positive. If you must explain to the committee some weakness in your history, such as a period of bad grades, don't destroy a strong essay by discussing it here. Instead, attach a short addendum to your application in which you *very briefly* explain the mitigating circumstances.

Your essay will be most readable if you answer essay questions truthfully and simply, without trying to impress the committee. If you want to become a college professor because you like teaching, say so simply instead of trying to cloak this fact in fancy language about the "didactic process" or the "transmittal of knowledge." It is more effective to say, "Like the best teachers I had in college, I want to become a good researcher and an effective teacher, responsive to my students."

Make sure your essays have a good lead—just as with a news story, you should be able to grab the reader from the first sentence. Do not begin with the formulaic "The reason I want to go to graduate school is . . ." Instead, try starting with an interesting anecdote, an intellectual problem that particularly interests you, or a clear statement of why you want to attend the particular department you are applying to. End your essays cleanly. Don't conclude: "If accepted, I will work for the betterment of humankind."

Because it is difficult even for advanced writers to avoid sounding fatuous in an autobiography, it is *vital* that you get drafts of your essay reviewed by your adviser or other competent readers before sending it. They can help you weed out your natural tendency toward the pompous, naïve, and self-congratulatory.

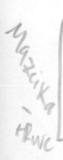

Your essays should unobtrusively but noticeably mention important people who have influenced you. For example, if you are discussing why you want to attend the school in question, talk about specific researchers at the school whose work you admire. One or more of these should be possible advisers whom you have already contacted. Don't overdo it by citing their papers by name, and don't quote from papers, but do mention their expertise.

If you have been successful in establishing previous contact with a potential adviser, tell the committee that you have a preferred adviser already selected. Some departments will actually have a place on their application form for this name, but even so, you can repeat it here to make sure it's noticed.

Your essays are also the place to mention important research experience you have had, papers you have published, and *academic relationships you have had with big names* who have influenced you. If you have special computer, statistical, language, photographic, or other skills that could make you of particular use to a future adviser, make sure you stress these. Remember that the committee will be looking at you as someone to help them teach and do research.

Start early on your essays so that you have time for extensive rewriting, review by others, and more rewriting. Most people write their essays at the last minute and, at best, send in a second draft unread by others. *You* should write several drafts. Count on taking at least a couple of days to write your basic essays, but I would recommend working on them over a couple of weeks.

Make sure your final essays are typed cleanly. Send no carbons—original forms or clean photocopies only. It goes without saying that the grammar and spelling should be impeccable.

If you want to read more about good application essays, try *On Writing the College Application Essay*, by Harry Bauld, or *Graduate Admissions Essays: What Works, What Doesn't, and Why* by Donald Asher.

• PUBLICATIONS •

Many of the best undergraduates are able to publish papers in academic journals while still in college. If you helped a professor with his research, you may be able to be a second or third author on his paper. If you are able to do your own research project under a professor's guidance, then you might publish it under your own name, or perhaps in collaboration with him.

Be forthright about your interest in publication and discuss it with your professor before you begin research. He should be impressed with your ambition and understanding of the critical importance of publishing to an academic career. Ask him to help you plan your research in such a way that it will be of publishable quality. If he feels that your first idea isn't good enough, ask him to work with you until you come up with a plan that will yield a publishable paper.

Publishing a paper is a lengthy process, often involving numerous revisions. Work closely with your supervisor to ensure that your paper is suitably written and follows style guidelines for the journal you decide to submit to. The average length of time from submission of a paper to publication is usually more than a year, so you may not see actual publication until after you have applied to graduate school. Nonetheless, you can list the publication on your résumé as "in press" if it has been accepted, "submitted" to a certain journal if it has been submitted but not yet accepted, or "in preparation" if you are still writing it. Another way to get credit for your research is to present the paper orally at a conference in your field. Your adviser or other professors can help you join professional societies in your field as a student member and find out about conferences where you can present your paper.

9

. . . .

FINANCIAL AID

. . . .

AS ONE SUCCESSFUL PH.D. PUT IT, "MONEY IS TIME." THE BETTER FUNDING you have, the more time you will have for study and research and the sooner you can finish. One graduate student had all his expenses paid by a National Science Foundation Fellowship and therefore did not have to teach to support himself. While the other students who would eventually compete with him for jobs were teaching, he was doing research and writing papers, so that at graduation he had published twenty academic articles.

Master's and doctoral students are treated differently when it comes to financial aid, and this can affect your decision about which type of program to apply for. Many doctoral programs try to support all Ph.D. students with fellowships or assistantships during the four or five years the school believes necessary. On the other hand, master's students often get little or no financial aid from the school and depend heavily on earned income or government loans. Harvard's School of Education, for example, reserves grants, fellowships, and teaching assistantships for doctoral students. Other schools may have more money for master's students, so be sure to inquire.

As costs rise, it is increasingly common for doctoral programs to offer support only *after* the first year, so that only serious students who have been judged likely to succeed in getting their degree receive aid. Conversely, some schools only guarantee aid for the first year, but this should not scare you off. Investigate what the standard practice is at the school, and you will find that most schools enable continuing students in good standing to get adequate funds.

Because applying for financial aid is a perplexing process, I've devoted this chapter to giving you what I hope is a clear overview rather than present a detailed compendium of all sources of aid. For such detailed

information, ask your librarian or counseling center to refer you to specialized books on financial aid, like Peterson's *Financial Aid for College*,
or *Don't Miss Out* by Anna and Robert Leider, from which I drew information for this chapter. The Leiders' book is particularly clear, and packed
with sensible advice. Other useful books include *Grants for Graduate
Students* by Peterson's Guides (which is boring), *The Graduate Scholarship
Book* by Daniel Cassidy, and Harvard University's *Graduate Guide to
Grants* (to purchase a copy for $25, including postage, contact the Office
of Student Affairs, Byerly Hall, 2nd floor, 8 Garden Street, Cambridge,
MA 02138, phone: 617 495-1816).

▪ THE FINANCIAL AID PROCESS ▪

At a typical school, financial aid for graduate students involves three separate processes. At the department level, the same committee that decides
admissions also decides who gets fellowships, scholarships, and research
and teaching assistantships. At the level of the graduate school, additional
merit-based awards may be given—typically, these are awards that go to
students within specific programs or even university-wide. For example,
at George Washington University, the Office of Fellowships and Graduate
Student Support awards special fellowships for policy studies, which may
be given to students in various policy programs throughout the university,
including education policy, security policy studies, and health services
management and policy. Finally, decisions about federal loans and other
need-based funds are made by the school's financial aid office.

In most schools, it works something like this: First, the departmental
admissions committee ranks all applicants on the basis of academic excellence to create a pool of students the department would like to admit.
Next, the committee decides on the basis of academic qualifications who
gets merit-based aid, including fellowships and teaching assistantships.
Top students may receive funds for full tuition and living expenses. Usually, these decisions are made without consideration of financial need, and
the department probably does not even have access to the students' financial
aid applications.

If you are one of the people the department wants to give merit-based
aid to, you will receive an award letter describing the offer. Particularly
if you are a top student, you may be able to negotiate with the department
if you feel the amount of offered aid is too little. If you've previously
made contact with one or more committee members, or with a potential
adviser, it can help to discuss with them tactfully any offers you've had
from other schools—the department may offer you more money to prevent

you going elsewhere. Jeri Rypkema, director of George Washington University's Office of Fellowships and Graduate Student Support, says, "When one department offers half tuition and the other offers full tuition, it absolutely makes sense to call and explain the situation. Maybe more students than expected will have declined, so some money is freed up." In trying to negotiate, just remember that you're not playing corporate hardball—if you come across as a hard-nosed jerk, you're likely to hurt yourself. One victim of graduate student abuse says, "This year a student made himself so obnoxious by repeatedly calling me and the dean to hold us up for more money that he ended up losing the fellowship we'd already offered him."

At roughly the same time the department is measuring your academic merit, you may be evaluated at the graduate school level for special awards, like George Washington's policy fellowships. Typically, the department nominates their top applicants and/or present grad students for awards, in competition with students from other departments. As soon as the departmental committee reviews the applications and can identify the outstanding students, they send nominating letters and copies of the students' admission materials to the fellowship office for judging. If you are selected, you will receive either an award letter from the graduate school or a letter from the department containing both departmental and school awards.

What if the department wants to admit you but neither they nor the graduate school can offer you complete support? Depending on your financial need, you may receive funds—primarily loans—from a third source, the school's financial aid office. For the purpose of figuring out how much aid you need, the financial aid office compares your available funds, including your savings and merit-based aid, with their estimated cost of attending school for a year. In the case of American University, a graduate student was allotted $24,820 for the 1996–97 school year, an amount that included full-time tuition, full-time fees, and $13,383 in living expenses.

If you were applying to the history department at American University, the complete process would look like this: Even though departmental admissions do not close until March 1, you've got to get your application in much earlier, by February 1, if you want a shot at merit-based aid. The department makes their decisions about whom to admit in the next month or so, and if you're accepted they send you an offer of admission. If you're one of the top students they may also send your application to the Office of Graduate International Admissions for a crack at university-wide fellowships. After further deliberation, the department allocates merit-based aid and sends you another letter telling you what fellowships, research assistantships, or other merit-based aid, if any, you're going to get from the department and the Office of Fellowships and Graduate Student Support. After all students have accepted or rejected their offers, the department puts together a final student roster listing each student's awards and sends this roster to the financial aid office by May 1. At this point the financial aid office looks at your total costs to attend school, subtracts departmental aid and other merit-based aid, subtracts the money you are expected to contribute, and—assuming you are broke enough to qualify—mails you a financial aid package of need-based aid (primarily federal loans) to cover your remaining need.

At this point, if you still haven't been given enough support to cover your needs, your ace-in-the-hole is unsubsidized Stafford Loans. All graduate students, regardless of need, can borrow up to $18,500 per year from this program, to a maximum of (gulp) $138,500, including money borrowed as an undergraduate. The disadvantage to this program is cost—interest starts accruing as soon as you take out the loan.

■ APPLYING FOR NEED-BASED FUNDS ■

You can increase your chances of receiving the best need-based loans or grants from the office of financial aid if you apply early, fill the forms out carefully, and manage your money in ways that minimize your apparent wealth.

The first rule is, *Apply early*. As at American University, financial aid deadlines usually beat admission deadlines by a couple of months (aid applications are often due in January), so make sure you're paying attention. You've got to make the deadlines if you want the money (see Chapter 12 for hints on organizing yourself).

Don't just make a deadline, beat it. Ideally, have your applications in the mail on *January 2*, the earliest date at which federal law allows submission. Your chance of getting grants or lower-interest loans depends in part on whether there is still money in the pot when you apply. So the earlier the better.

The second rule is to start figuring out your finances at least a year ahead of time. It's analogous to doing financial planning to minimize your IRS taxes. By understanding how financial aid formulas interpret the information on your FAFSA and PROFILE forms, you can make your pressing need for financial assistance more compelling.

The application process for need-based aid has been simplified—somewhat. The old GAPFAS and FAF forms have disappeared, and grad students now fill out the same two forms used by undergrads. The first is the Free Application for Federal Student Aid (FAFSA) to qualify for federal aid.

Obtain it from the Federal Student Aid Information Center (800 433-3243), from your school, or from libraries. You can also download and electronically file a FAFSA if you have a PC and modem. The address is http://www.ed.gov/offices/OPE/express.html. As the name of the form suggests, there is no fee for application and no charge to forward your processed application to the schools to which you are applying.

For many schools you will also have to fill out a PROFILE form from the College Scholarship Service (CSS), a private service. Order the form by phone (609 771-7725) or via the Internet at http://www.collegeboard. org./css/html/proform.html. CSS charges you a $5 application fee and $14.50 per school to which you want a PROFILE report sent. This form is required by schools that feel the FAFSA does not reveal enough hidden financial resources, so expect the questions to dig deep. Generally, the PROFILE schools are relatively expensive private schools, where there is likely to be a gap between your federal student aid and what you need. Because they're going to make up some of the difference from their own funds—from endowment or other students' tuition—they want to make sure you really need it.

In addition to FAFSA and PROFILE, you may have to fill out special applications if you're applying for state aid or for assistance at some private schools that have designed their own forms in an effort to gather even more information. Schools will also require Financial Aid Transfer Records from schools you attended in the past to make sure you aren't in default on past loans.

Be careful in filling out your financial aid forms, since a mistake may cause the form to be rejected and a delay can cause you to lose out on limited aid. The authors of *Don't Miss Out* list common mistakes:

• Omitting your social security number
• Forgetting to sign the form
• Entering a range of figures, such as $200 to $300, when one figure is wanted
• Giving monthly amounts instead of yearly amounts or vice versa
• Leaving spaces blank instead of entering zero
• Entering cents
• Using a felt-tip pen
• Writing illegibly

If a figure is asked for that you do not yet have, such as income for the present year, you can estimate it and notify the processing centers of later changes if necessary.

If you ultimately decide to accept admission at a school offering loans, you will need to fill out separate applications for the loans themselves, which may include federal Stafford or Perkins Loans. Graduate students are not eligible for Pell Grants, Supplemental Educational Opportunity Grants (SEOGs), or Parent Loans for Undergraduate Students (PLUS). Perkins Loans are handled by the school, as are Stafford Loans at schools with direct-lending programs. Many schools do not have direct lending, and in this case Stafford Loans are made to you by commercial lenders like banks, savings and loans, and credit unions. You get the application from the lender, the school certifies on the application that you are a student, and then—provided your credit is good—the lender approves the loan. It can take weeks or months before you get the money, so make sure you plan ahead. One financial aid officer tells a story about what not to do:

> This woman showed up from Arizona right at the start of school without having registered for classes or filing a financial aid form. She installed a giant moving van in front of the building and camped out in our office for a couple of days with four children and a dog. She demanded money immediately because she and her kids had no cash, nowhere to stay, and no friends.

▪ HOW SCHOOLS ASSESS NEED ▪

Once you have sent in your financial aid application to the processing center (the federal center for FAFSA or CSS for PROFILE), the center calculates your Expected Family Contribution, which is how much you will be required to contribute toward your education in the next school year. Your expected contribution will vary depending on whether it is calculated using FAFSA or PROFILE. In most cases, your expected contribution will be higher at schools using PROFILE because, unlike with FAFSA, they consider how much money you have socked away in home equity, they may consider retirement funds as assets, and they require a minimum student contribution, regardless of how broke you are.

After the processing center for FAFSA or CSS has finished with your form, it sends a financial report, including your Expected Family Contribution, to the schools where you are requesting aid. Request that a copy of both the FAFSA and the CSS report be sent to you—in the case of PROFILE, this will cost you $5.50. Scrutinize the reports carefully for errors.

Once a school's financial aid office receives a report, it uses your Expected

Family Contribution to calculate how much need-based aid you require, using roughly the following formula:

$$\text{Costs} - \text{Merit Aid} - \text{Expected Family Contribution} = \text{Need}$$

Depending on the school, the figure used for your Expected Family Contribution may be based on FAFSA, PROFILE, or the school's own financial aid form. Note that your "family" consists of yourself alone if you are single, you and your spouse if married, plus any children.

Here's an example of how need is calculated: if the projected costs of tuition and expenses total $24,000, and you receive a fellowship for $10,000, and the financial aid office judges your Expected Family Contribution to be $3,000, then your need will be $24,000 − $10,000 − $3,000 = $11,000. The financial aid office will then try to put together a package of loans or grants totaling your need, in this case $11,000. If your calculated need is zero or negative, you will receive no need-based aid.

When you are an undergraduate, whether you are financially independent from your parents is a critical factor in determining the Expected Family Contribution, and therefore the amount of need. Independent students typically receive more aid because their parents are not expected to contribute and Expected Family Contribution is based solely on the student's income. With the FAFSA form, all graduate students are automatically considered independent, and parents' income and assets should not affect your federal aid. In the case of PROFILE users, some schools may take into account parents' ability to contribute—for example, George Washington University Law School considers parental income and assets for students under thirty years of age. In such cases, strategies to minimize parents' available assets and income prior to application may make sense (see below and *Don't Miss Out* for suggestions).

HOW BIG WILL YOUR EXPECTED FINANCIAL CONTRIBUTION BE?

Generally, the more assets you and your spouse own and the more income you make in the tax year prior to applying, the more you will have to fork over. But because most schools base their assessment of need on the Expected Family Contribution from your FAFSA or PROFILE form, you can maximize aid and minimize your contribution by understanding how the financial aid services calculate your Expected Family Contribution and by planning ahead of time to minimize your apparent income and assets.

Filling out FAFSA and PROFILE will remind you of filling out income-tax forms, and you will need to have on hand figures for your taxes and income for the previous tax year (1997 if you are applying for the

1998–99 school year). You will also need complete data on assets at the time of application, including real estate, stocks, bonds, and savings. For some schools that use their own application forms, you may also need your parents' income and assets information.

No matter which form is used, the processing center starts with your Adjusted Gross Income from your IRS tax form (1997 tax form for school year 1998–99), then deducts certain allowances. This is analogous to how the IRS lets you deduct some expenses from your income before figuring taxes. Deductible expenses for either FAFSA or PROFILE include state and federal income taxes and social security taxes.

Other deductions differ from form to form. FAFSA, for example, lets you deduct $3,000 of your income if you are single.* PROFILE, instead of a flat $3,000 deduction, lets you deduct amounts tied to living expenses during the summer or other months when you are not in school. Once deductions have been taken out, 50 percent of your remaining Adjusted Gross Income goes toward your Expected Family Contribution. For example, if your Adjusted Gross Income for 1996 was $20,000, and you paid $10,000 in taxes, then you would be expected to contribute $3,500 toward school from your income using the FAFSA method:

$$(\$20,000 - \$10,000 - \$3,000)/2 = \$3,500$$

But that's not all. Depending on your income, you may have to contribute a portion of your assets in the year for which you're applying. Luckily, you don't have to contribute anything from your assets if family income is less than $50,000 and you are eligible to file a 1040A or 1040EZ—you use a simplified methodology that doesn't count assets. If you make more than $50,000 or you must file a standard 1040, you'll have to contribute somewhat less than 35 percent of your assets, which include stocks, bonds, and savings accounts (in the case of FAFSA, home equity is excluded). This calculation is done by totalling all assets, deducting an Asset Protection Allowance, and then subtracting 65 percent. The Asset Protection Allowance (APA) was devised to prevent students from spending all their retirement income on education. Because older students have less time to save before retirement, more of their savings are protected than for younger students. Therefore, the APA slides from zero for a student under twenty-five years of age, to $16,300 for a student of thirty-five, to $45,000 for a student of sixty-five.

For example, assume that you are twenty-nine years old and have

---

* For simplicity, the following overview assumes the reader is single. Deductions and exemptions differ for married students. Refer to *Don't Miss Out*, or request literature describing calculation methods from the Federal Student Aid Information Center (800 433-3243).

$10,000 in a savings account. Your Asset Protection Allowance at age twenty-nine is $6,500, so your unprotected assets are $10,000 − $6,500 = $3,500. Thirty-five percent of $3,500 is $1,225, which is added to your Expected Family Contribution if you and your spouse made more than $50,000 during the year prior to applying or you had to file a 1040. If you reapplied for aid the following year, you would be expected to contribute 35 percent of your remaining $2,275 in unprotected assets. (For a more detailed explanation, see Appendix 3 of *Don't Miss Out* and the reference tables at the back of that book.)

Schools that use PROFILE will make life tougher for you. First, no assets are excluded, no matter how little you make or what tax form you filed. If you've got it, it's at risk. Second, PROFILE lumps your home equity into the assets pot, so this money isn't sheltered as it is under FAFSA. According to *Don't Miss Out*, this is likely to bump your family contribution by 5 to 6 percent of equity. On the plus side, PROFILE will give you credit for unusually high medical or dental expenses (totalling more than 4 percent of income), which FAFSA will not, so one strategy for PROFILE applicants is to defer medical bills to the year for which you'll be reporting income.

One result of the above need formula is that if you are successful in finding an outside source of money, such as a scholarship, it usually does not reduce your own Expected Family Contribution; it merely substitutes for need-based aid. For example, consider again the student with expected costs of $24,000, a fellowship for $10,000, an Expected Family Contribution of $3,000, and a calculated need of $11,000:

$$\$24,000 - \$10,000 - \$3,000 = \$11,000$$

The need of $11,000 could be supplied as a subsidized Stafford Loan or work-study. If the student then receives an additional $2,000 scholarship, her need decreases to $9,000, but her Expected Family Contribution of $3,000 remains the same:

$$\$24,000 - \$10,000 - \$3,000 - \$2,000 = \$9,000$$

Either the work-study or loan funds would be replaced by the scholarship money, and the work-study or loan funds would be freed for other students.

However, don't let this apparent lack of incentive prevent you from applying for scholarships and fellowships for three reasons:

- You will be better off replacing loans or work-study money with funds you don't have to repay.
- A fellowship or scholarship will give you prestige in your department and can give you freedom in choosing departments or advisers to work with—it's hard for them to turn down a student who comes with solid outside funding.
- Finding additional money will not affect the merit-based awards you receive from the department. For example, let's say your total school costs are $24,000, of which $10,000 is paid by the department through a fellowship. Assume also that your Expected Family Contribution is $20,000, so that the balance of costs after applying your fellowship is paid by you. In this case, if you receive an additional scholarship for $1,000, the $1,000 goes to you and not to the department.

How to pay less

I suggest that you get FAFSA and PROFILE forms at least a couple of years before applications are due and use them to estimate your Expected Family Contribution for your first year in grad school. The sooner you know how much money you'll have to come up with, the sooner you can work out realistic strategies for getting the money, cutting school costs, or taking advantage of some of the ways mentioned below to decrease Expected Family Contribution.

One place to focus is on the income you earn in the year you apply, because this has a large impact on your Expected Family Contribution. If you are earning a substantial salary at application time, it is unlikely that you will be able to qualify for Perkins or subsidized Stafford Loans. This may be a particular problem if you work between undergraduate and graduate school and therefore have a substantial income at the time you apply. Given this "first-year-penalty," you might consider ways to reduce your income in the application year—if you have always wanted to spend a year doing something romantic and poorly paid, such as volunteering for an archaeological dig, this might be the year to do it. In subsequent years, when you are a full-time student, your income is likely to be too small to be a problem.

There are other ways to reduce reportable income or assets. *Don't Miss Out* lists at least eleven methods of reducing the Expected Family Contribution, including:

- Accelerating or postponing gains and losses in stocks or real estate.
- Decreasing cash reserves by purchasing an automobile, clothes, and other

property that will not be reportable as assets. If you are going to need a new car while in school, buy it before you apply for aid!

- Hiding money as home equity by paying down your home mortgage. This won't work for PROFILE, but FAFSA doesn't count home equity as assets, so the more money you can shift to your home, the less will count toward your Expected Family Contribution.
- Putting as much money as you can into an IRA or 401(k) plan in the years prior to attending grad school. Retirement accounts don't have to be reported as assets on FAFSA or PROFILE, and you need only report the amount contributed in the year before application as income. (Note that PROFILE gives schools an option of including retirement income, so some schools might count it, as may schools that use a self-designed financial aid form.)

One thing to avoid is marriage. Both FAFSA and PROFILE add together salary and assets for spouses, which could bump up your Expected Family Contribution substantially. Better to put off marriage until after grad school, unless you're both attending school at the same time. If both husband and wife are attending, your Expected Family Contribution will drop greatly because it is divided by the number of students in your family attending school at least half-time. This includes your spouse and children. It does not include your parents—as a graduate student, you're considered independent, so your Mom and Dad don't count, no matter how studious they are. Bottom line is if your husband, wife, or children will be going to college or grad school in the near future, you'll save a tremendous amount of money if you synchronize attendance.

Another mistake, for those people who are accepted but defer admission for a year, is to assume that equal financial aid will be offered when you finally get around to attending. In fact, the offer you receive the first year is usually not guaranteed for deferred students. For example, in 1994, Jennifer applied to several top master's programs and was offered a full-tuition fellowship by Duke and $5,000 by George Washington. Because of other obligations, she could not accept these offers. Duke did not allow deferral, so she accepted GW's offer and deferred admission for one year. The following year she reapplied at Duke, and was offered only half tuition, while at GW she was offered $3,000 instead of the original $5,000. Reasons for such decreases can include a change in the department's finances, better-quality applicants and hence greater competition for awards in the second year, and decreased incentive for a school to bribe you to come if you are already committed.

If all this is too confusing, you can find professional services that will counsel you on financial strategies. One is run by the firm that publishes

Don't Miss Out. For a brochure describing their services, write Octameron, PO Box 2748, Alexandria, VA 22301; phone: 703 836-5480.

STAY IN TOUCH

One thing that can help you in getting aid is to develop good relationships and stay in touch with the people who dole out the money. Financial aid people are working in the field because they like to help, so let them. One financial aid officer says, "Absolutely, it helps students to know the financial aid people. I know many of my students by name and face, and for the ones I know I always go the extra mile. But some people hurt themselves by being nasty or throwing a tantrum when their aid hasn't come through on time. Let's say someone's aid is held up because their undergraduate school hasn't sent a transcript. I can do the student a favor by calling the school and telling them I need the transcript immediately. Or, if they've been yelling at me, I can just let it sit."

You can start getting acquainted even before you apply for aid. In Chapter 5, I recommend that you visit campuses before applying, to get to know professors and learn about the department. At the same time, you should visit the financial aid office. Set up an appointment to discuss the application process and start building rapport.

Getting to know the financial aid folks could be especially beneficial at expensive schools where the gap between costs and available federal funds may be made up in part from the school's own funds (these schools likely will be using PROFILE or their own forms). At these schools, financial aid officers may have more discretion about how to interpret your finances—for example, do they or don't they consider the $100,000 your father makes, given that you're now twenty-nine years old? It could depend on whether the financial aid officer believes that you're really estranged from your dad and that there's no way the old man will give you a penny.

Contact can also help in the contest for merit-based departmental money. Because this money is awarded based on the professors' partly subjective impression of your professional merit, you may be able to influence the amount you receive by letting them know and appreciate you. In the sciences, some professors hold grants from the National Science Foundation or other sources that support students helping with the grant-funded research—in such cases the professor decides who gets the fellowship, so an "in" with the professor is obviously a good thing.

Don't stop cultivating those who dole out the money once you've gotten your award for the year. Not only should you be thinking about improving your chances for next year, but frequently it's even possible to find additional money after the award process is officially closed. Departmental or graduate school funds often have been held in reserve or become available for other reasons; for example, because someone less tenacious than you drops out of the program.

Throughout the year, continue to meet regularly with your financial aid officers to talk over finances—you're more likely to get vital information or find new ways to qualify for money. American University's Janet Pearlman says, "What if your income changes unexpectedly—say, you make less money and therefore become eligible for more aid? I don't have time to monitor everyone's 1040 form, but if the person is visiting me to discuss how things are going financially, we're going to pick up the change."

So be persistent. A Ph.D. student in foreign affairs says, "I was told by my department that no funds existed. It's true, there weren't any *departmental* funds, but because I was stubborn and continued nosing around, I found out that there was money I could get through the *graduate school*." A second student, working toward a master's in German studies, received minimal aid her first year and supported herself by working in the university administration. After realizing that it would take her ten years to get her degree if she had to keep working full-time, she went to the financial aid officer, whom by this time she knew well, to plead her case. He was able to put together a good aid package for her second year so she could stop working full-time and finish her degree.

• TYPES OF AID •

Aid may come from federal or state governments, the school itself, philanthropic foundations, professional organizations, and eccentric millionaires. Of these, the federal government lends the most money and eccentric millionaires the least.

Most financial aid comes from a few sources—in graduate school, about 70 percent comes from major federal government programs, 12 percent from departmental or school funds, 3 percent from states, and the remaining 15 percent from a hodgepodge of military, private foundation, business, and federal agency programs. A large percentage of doctoral students are funded directly by departments and federal research grants, while many master's students receive funding from their employers for continuing education.

▪ DEPARTMENTAL AID ▪

Although direct support from the university accounts for only about one-tenth of all graduate support, this misrepresents its importance to Ph.D.s, who derive most of their support from this source, while master's students receive proportionately less. Scholarships, grants, and fellowships are the most advantageous forms of aid because they usually require no work or financial payback. Moreover, although money earned through assistantships or used for room and board is taxable, scholarship funds used for books, tuition, fees, or supplies are not taxable. Additionally, the fellowships and scholarships may confer prestige if they are based on academic excellence.

Teaching and research assistantships are the most common source of Ph.D. support. In part this is because Ph.D.s are seen, as the Duke catalogue puts it, as "apprentice member(s) of the research and teaching faculty" and are extensively used to fill research and teaching needs inexpensively. Research assistantships are often funded through outside grants that support both a professor's research and the students necessary to help carry it out. Duke, for example, has "over three hundred traineeships and assistantships available in the biological, physical, and social sciences under grants from the National Institutes of Health, the National Institute of Mental Health, the National Science Foundation, research agencies in the Department of Defense, and other government agencies." Master's students may also find employment through professors' grants, either as assistants or through work-study.

Departments recognize that the obligations of a teaching or research assistantship can interfere with graduating on time, so they often restrict the number of years assistantships can be held. At Harvard, for example, many departments do not allow students to hold teaching or research assistantships during the first or second year. Assistants are often allowed to reduce the number of units they register for in a given term to accommodate the demands of teaching or research, but may then be expected to make up lost ground during the summer—another reason to try for fellowships instead!

Ask your undergraduate adviser or other professors whether there are journals or other sources in your field that advertise for research assistants. For example, the *Ornithological Newsletter of North America* regularly advertises paid research positions. Many of these request that you enroll as a graduate student, often in a master's program, and the work you do functions as your thesis. If you can obtain such a position on a project that interests you, then you can solve all at once the three problems of admission, financial support, and finding a thesis topic.

• FEDERAL LOANS •

By far the largest source of graduate financial aid is the federal government, which either makes money available through the schools or guarantees loans that are made through private lenders. Unfortunately, the free-money grant system, consisting of Pell Grants and Supplemental Educational Opportunity Grants, which are mainstays of *undergraduate* financial aid, is not available to graduate students. This means that federal aid available to you is in the form of loans, which greatly increases the chance that *you* will pay for your education. There are two main types of federal loans important to graduate students: Perkins Loans and Stafford Loans, the latter of which come in both subsidized (good) and unsubsidized (not so good) varieties. These loans are particularly important to master's students and doctoral students who got their applications in late, because relatively few departmental fellowship, assistantship, or other merit-based aid will be available for them. For information about these loans, check the government's electronic student aid guide at http://www.ed.gov/money.html, or phone the Federal Student Aid Information Center (800 433-3243). The counselors are knowledgeable and helpful. You can also request the free pamphlet *The Student Guide: Financial Aid from the US Department of Education* by calling the above number or writing to the information center at PO Box 84, Washington, DC 20044.

Perkins Loans have great terms—you won't start accruing interest until nine months after you graduate, so you don't have to start worrying until you're out of school and have a job. The interest rate is lower than on the other loans—currently, a fixed 5 percent. The only bad thing about Perkins Loans is that they're hard to get—they go to students with the greatest financial need and there are relatively few funds available, so apply early.

The money for Perkins Loans comes from a federal fund and is lent to the school, which in turn lends it to you. When irresponsible students in some schools create high default rates, the federal government cuts back on the amount of Perkins money it gives to these schools, and some schools do not participate in the program at all. At others, Perkins funds are restricted to certain fields. For example, at George Washington University, Perkins funds for graduate students are restricted to nursing and other medical fields. You can check with the financial aid office of a school you are interested in about the availability of Perkins funds at that particular school.

Under the Perkins system you can borrow $5,000 per year up to a total of $30,000, less what you borrowed as an undergraduate. Certain schools with low default rates belong to the federal Expanded Lending Option program, which allows you to borrow $6,000 per year up to $40,000.

Subsidized Stafford Loans are the next best. As in the case of Perkins, interest is paid by the government while you're in school. You start being responsible for the interest slightly sooner than for Perkins—at six months versus nine months. The interest rate is variable, reset every year, with an 8.25 percent cap. In 1996, it was at 8.25 percent. In addition, the lender subtracts a 3 percent loan origination fee and a 1 percent insurance fee (to cover defaulters), so that your nice round $5,000 loan will immediately become $4,800. You start repaying the loan at the same time interest starts accruing six months after graduation (or after you drop below half-time student status).

At most schools the subsidized Stafford Loans will be made to you by private sources—primarily banks and savings and loans, which you apply at the financial institution for as described above. At schools that participate in the federal direct-lending program, the money is federal money loaned to you directly by the school.

You can borrow up to $8,500 per year in subsidized Stafford funds for a lifetime total of $65,000. Financial aid expert Anna Leider warns that these subsidized Staffords may not be available to grad students for long —they're a target of budget cutting in Congress. As of this writing (April 1996), the fate of next year's Staffords had still not been decided.

Unsubsidized Stafford Loans are least desirable. They have the same variable interest and fees as the subsidized Staffords, but Uncle Sam doesn't pay your interest while you're in school, so it starts mounting up as soon as you sign the papers. However, as for subsidized Staffords, you don't start making payments until six months after graduation. The advantage of unsubsidized Staffords is that they aren't need-based, meaning that you can apply for one if you want supplemental money for any reason.

You can borrow up to an annual limit of $18,500, less what you receive from the subsidized Stafford program. Your lifetime limit is a terrifying $138,500, less your subsidized Stafford Loans and Stafford Loans you took out as an undergrad. For unsubsidized Staffords you apply to either private sources or your school if it participates in direct lending, just as for subsidized Staffords.

If you take out additional federally insured loans, of whatever type, try to borrow from the same lender from whom you received any previous loans. This will decrease the chance that after graduation you will find yourself having to pay off on multiple loans from multiple lenders, each of which requires a substantial monthly payment. By getting your loans from the same lender, you may avoid the expense and nuisance of trying to consolidate your loans.

▪ PRIVATE LOANS ▪

For those of you who find that $18,500 per year in Stafford Loans isn't enough, American enterprise has stepped in to fill the gap. Some private lenders, like the giant Nellie Mae (New England Loan Marketing Association), will lend you more money. When I first talked to the loan counselor at Nellie Mae about their new private loan program, I started laughing. I asked, "Who in his right mind would have already maxed out his $18,500 per year and is now looking for more while in school with no job security ahead?" So she pointed out to me that attending med school or some other programs at Harvard or Stanford could cost you $35,000 to $40,000 per year, and $18,500 isn't even half of that. Yikes. Lucky these guys are waiting around to be Good Samaritans.

Nellie Mae has what are called "share programs" with certain schools. If you're fortunate enough to attend such a school—there are thirty-two of them—you can borrow a bunch of money on just your signature (sounds like the way Grandpaw lost the farm). Nellie Mae figures that someone in Harvard Medical School is going to be good for it, so they'll lend you up to $20,000 per year via Medical and Dental Share. Someone in medieval history at Harvard would be part of the Grad Share Program, and can only borrow $12,000 per year (you can get more with a co-signer). Personally, I can't see how the average humanities grad student is ever going to be able to even pay off the Stafford maximum of $138,500, let alone more, but we live in wondrous times. Interest rates for the Grad Share Program are variable and pegged to the prime rate—for academic year 1996–97 the rate is 8.25 percent for a monthly variable loan. Take warning that at present there is no loan consolidation for share loans to help you if you get into financial trouble.

▪ LOAN CONSOLIDATION ▪

You may find yourself in financial trouble after graduation when you try to set up housekeeping while paying off the $138,500 debt you incurred because you spent the last fourteen years studying the impact of sheep-shearing contests on the social development of Australia. Fortunately, you won't have to declare bankruptcy or flee the country, because—provided you got your loans in participating states—you can consolidate most federal loans into one new loan with lower payments. You can also arrange to start the payments small and have them gradually rise through time, for your increasing earning power should be able to keep up. You can consolidate graduate Stafford and Perkins Loans, as well as undergraduate federal loans, such as PLUS loans. Consolidation is offered by both the federal government and by Sallie Mae, Nellie Mae, and other commercial institutions. Rates are comparable for both federal and private consolidation.

You can find out about consolidation through your school financial aid office, or you can contact the federal or private programs directly. Both the federal government and the private associations want your business, so they will give you information over the phone and send you an application. After you have applied, they will contact your original lenders to arrange the consolidation. To contact the federal consolidation program, call the Direct Loan Servicing Center's Consolidation Department at 800 848-0982. For private consolidation, you can ask for referral by the commercial financial institutions that gave you the original loans, or you can contact consolidating lenders directly. Contact Sallie Mae (Student Loan Marketing Association) at the SMART Loan Originations Center, PO Box 1304, Merrifield, VA 22116-1304, phone: 800 524-9100. For Nellie Mae try Loan Consolidation Department, 50 Braintree Hill Park, Suite 300, Braintree, MA 02184, phone: 800 634-9308.

The way consolidation works is that the institution giving you the consolidation loan buys up all your old loans and lumps them together. The lender then calculates a weighted average of your old interest rates, and rounds up to the nearest whole percent to give themselves a little profit. This is the new, higher interest rate for your new loan. You may be wondering how paying higher interest benefits you. By consolidating, you get to drop your monthly payments by stretching repayment out over time. For example, most of your original loans had to be paid back over ten years, but a consolidated loan may have a twenty-five-year schedule. The total number of payments is much higher, the interest is higher, the total amount you will pay is higher, but monthly payments are lower because you are paying back less of the principal each month. If you are really having financial difficulties, the association can even arrange for you to pay only interest for a limited time. You may also save yourself money by paying on time—Nellie Mae, for example, drops your interest a full percentage point if you make payments on time for forty-eight months. Most lenders have a similar incentive program.

One thing to be aware of is that while you may be able to defer payment on consolidated loans if you return to school, interest will keep accruing while you attend. Therefore, before consolidating Perkins or subsidized Stafford Loans, make sure you're not going back to school. Otherwise, your new consolidated loan will accrue interest during that time.

• FEDERAL WORK-STUDY •

Federal work-study funds are available for graduate students at some schools, but many restrict the funds to undergraduates, as is the case at George Washington University. At American University, work-study is not normally granted to graduate students but can be if the students request it. Whether or not work-study goes to grad students is not a federal decision. It's up to the school, and one financial aid officer told me he believes the reason schools don't offer work-study to grad students is that they're not as well organized a pressure group as undergrads and their parents.

If available, work-study may or may not be better than loans, depending on whether you get paid to work in your field of study or whether you're a dishwashing cafeteria drudge. Under this need-based program, the government pays up to 75 percent of your wages and the employer provides the remainder. This makes students with financial aid awards a hot commodity in the job market because employers can hire them cheap. Use this leverage to try for work in your field—professors love to stretch their research grants by hiring work-study students. *You must have your job placement approved by your school's financial aid office.*

You'll be given an award of work-study money, say $2,000 for the year, and you'll have to work the number of hours necessary to earn it. The more you earn per hour, the fewer hours you have to work to receive your entire award. Hourly work-study rates vary widely, from the federal minimum wage to as much as $15 to $20 per hour. Work-study jobs pay more if the going rate on the open market is high. At George Washington University, for example, some of the best-paid work-study students, earning over $15 per hour, are computer specialists and aerobics instructors!

• MISCELLANEOUS SOURCES •

STATES

States contribute relatively little to graduate education compared with the federal government, only 3 percent of total aid. Further, this aid is usually only for state residents attending school within the state, but that might be you. One example of state aid is the California State Graduate Fellowships offered through the California Student Aid Commission (phone: 916 323-0435). You must be a resident of California for at least one year before applying. These are highly competitive fellowships—only five hundred in all—based on need plus academic merit as reflected in GRE scores. You can find out about state sources by querying the education agencies of states where you want to go to school. For the names of state agencies, call the Federal Student Aid Information Center or consult *Don't Miss Out*, which lists state education agencies for the fifty states plus the District of Columbia, Guam, Puerto Rico, and the Virgin Islands.

FOUNDATIONS AND AGENCIES

Foundations and agencies give a small amount of aid to specialized recipients. Examples include the Mellon Fellowships in the Humanities (write Woodrow Wilson National Fellowship Foundation, CN 5329, Princeton, NJ 08543-5329, phone: 609 452-7007, e-mail: Jacquie@woodrow.org); National Science Foundation Fellowships for science, mathematics, engineering, and social sciences (write Fellowship Office, National Research Council, POB 3010, Oakridge, TN 37831-3010, phone: 423 483-3344); and Jacob Javits Fellowship Program for arts, humanities, and social sciences (Division of Higher Education, Incentive Programs, U.S. Department of Education, Room 3514-ROB-3, 400 Maryland Ave., SW, Washington, DC 20202-5251, phone: 202 554-7699).

You can start researching these sources by asking for the appropriate publications at your library or financial aid office. These include *The Foundation Directory* and *Foundation Grants to Individuals*, both published by the Foundation Center; *Don't Miss Out*; and the *Selected List of Fellowship Opportunities and Aids to Advanced Education*, available from the Publications Office, National Science Foundation, 4201 Wilson Blvd., Arlington, VA 22230, phone: 703 306-1234. A more efficient way to get information is to check out the Internet. A good place to start is the Financial Aid Information page at http://www.cs.cmu.edu/~finaid/finaid.html. They offer links to other sites and a free database of more than 180,000 private-sector scholarships, fellowships, grants, and loans. The page also runs an "Ask the Aid Advisor" service, in which sixty financial aid administrators and professionals answer questions submitted by students.

Be aware that there are many scam artists offering "scholarships" in exchange for application fees that may exceed $100. Legitimate nonprofits that offer scholarships do not charge fees. For some fascinating case studies of imaginative scams described by Mark Kantrowitz, see http://www. finaid.org. One of the dubious scholarship offers described by Mark comes from the National Academy of American Scholars, also known as the R. C. Easley Foundation. According to Mark, this "foundation" collects hefty application fees for scholarships that commemorate an apparently nonexistent R. C. Easley "for his outstanding accomplishments and his contributions to the advancement of humanity." One Harvard medical student did indeed win an R. C. Easley award for $5,000, of which he eventually collected only $1,004, in ninety-five payments! When the student requested the balance, he received a thirteen-page document detailing further achievements he would have to attain in order to continue receiving payments, and a letter "personally and professionally attacking both the student and the university." Mark contacted the Better Business Bureau (BBB) and reports: "According to the BBB, this organization is a private for-profit organization and is not tax-exempt. . . . The BBB report adds that this organization declined to provide substantiation that the scholarships are actually awarded."

WORK FOR A UNIVERSITY

Many students take full-time jobs with universities specifically because at some schools full-time employees may get partial or often complete tuition waivers. This happens so frequently that one student, also a full-time employee at her university's career-counseling center, said: "It is so common for people to take relatively humdrum jobs at this school in order to get free tuition that it's almost expected you'll take classes part-time. The people hiring you are glad if you want the free tuition, because then they know you have a strong incentive to stay with the job for a few years."

Note that getting a degree part-time is a slow and often discouraging process. However, once you have been working at a college or university, you may be able to use your contacts to grease your way. A master's student, after working for two years in the financial aid office, was able to convince her colleagues that she deserved a full-time scholarship so she could finish school. A doctoral student in education who was working full-time as a high-level college administrator convinced the university president to let her have a paid sabbatical in order to complete her dissertation. She successfully argued that if she obtained her degree, it would reflect well on the university.

RENT A HOUSE

Finally, one of the best ways to help support yourself while in graduate school is to set up a group house. The strategy is either to buy or get your parents to buy or lease a house and then rent rooms to other students. In many college towns the large number of students looking for housing makes rooms easy to fill, and in many cases you will be able to charge rents that are reasonable enough so that you don't feel like Simon Legree, while still bringing in enough money to pay your mortgage or rent. I did this in graduate school and earned free rent plus some spending money every month. Although it takes some effort to set up and manage a house, the free rent is likely to outweigh what you could earn in a part-time job.

▪ A SUMMARY OF TIPS ▪

1. Apply early to have the greatest chance of getting aid from the limited supply of funds.
2. Fill out your application *carefully*.
3. Fill out a FAFSA or PROFILE form at least a year ahead of application, so you can plan financial strategies.
4. Look for ways to decrease your financial contribution by decreasing reportable income or assets.
5. If you have a choice between master's and doctoral programs, remember that doctoral programs come with better aid.
6. Because departments offer the best aid to the best students, apply to a number of schools of different quality levels so that you have a chance at being a "best student" at some.
7. Use multiple offers of aid from different schools to bargain politely for the best deal.
8. Target schools that have large endowments in your field or otherwise have large numbers of fellowships and grants.
9. Avoid accepting too much aid with teaching or other work requirements—it may be better to run up some loan debt and finish early than work more and finish late.
10. Don't lie on your financial forms—the government checks many IRS and financial aid forms to make sure the same information appears on both.

10

· · · · · · · · · · · · · · ·

THE MASTER'S DEGREE:

HISTORY AND HURDLES

· · · · · · · · · · · · · ·

· A DIVERSITY OF DEGREES ·

U.S. master's degrees began in the seventeenth century as fund-raising devices that catered to people who liked titles after their names. Any student who successfully completed the bachelor's and refrained from ungentlemanly activities for three years while paying college fees was automatically awarded a master's degree. Before you get too excited, you should know that the University of Michigan changed the rules by awarding the first "earned" degree in 1859, so you will have to work for yours. The amount of work can differ greatly from program to program. The master's student getting a degree in holistic healing and parapsychology from a small California college faces very different hurdles from one getting a physical therapy degree from rigorous Northwestern University.

Compared with bachelor's and Ph.D. degrees, the status of master's degrees is confusing and poorly standardized. The number of different types of master's degrees is overwhelming, with literally hundreds of different letter designations, including MBA, MCE, MSW, M.Phil., and the standard MA (Master of Arts) followed by "in physics," "in history," et cetera. Master's degree programs may last for one, two, and more rarely three years. This diversity has led to the master's degree being called the "jack-of-all-trades." Approximately 300,000 master's degrees at more than one thousand institutions are given every year, many times the number of Ph.D. degrees.

Because of the proliferation in number and type of master's degrees awarded in recent years, august bodies of higher education, such as the Association for the Study of Higher Education and the State Higher Education Officers, have expressed concern over lack of quality control and resultant devaluation of the degree. When anyone can get a master's degree somewhere, and when standardization is poor, it is difficult to judge the worth of a particular degree without knowing the specific program that awarded it. Some degrees may not be very helpful in terms of either training or getting a job.

This being said, it is also true that master's degrees in many fields are increasingly important for career advancement and training. Judith Glazer, author of a report entitled *The Master's Degree*, writes that in areas like business, engineering, education, and social work the "professional master's has become a credential providing access to the ranks of middle management." In other fields, like nursing and physical therapy, increasing professionalism is reflected in increasing numbers of master's degrees, although the overall percentage is still small—only about 5 percent of registered nurses have a master's. It is up to you to judge carefully whether a particular degree will benefit your career. Given the extreme variability in master's programs, my generalizations may not hold for a program you are interested in.

TERMINAL VERSUS NONTERMINAL ▪ MASTER'S DEGREES ▪

In view of the profusion of master's degrees, it is useful to divide them into categories. One division you will see often used by departments is between "terminal" and "nonterminal" master's. Terminal master's programs are *not* designed to feed into an associated Ph.D. program. An example is the typical MBA program. Thus, if a department says it gives only terminal master's, this means students cannot go on for the Ph.D. Conversely, if the department says you *cannot* get a terminal master's degree, this usually means that if they offer the master's at all, you can only get one after being accepted into the Ph.D. program.

Terminal master's degrees may also be given to students who drop out, or are forced out, of a joint master's-doctoral program. Such terminal master's degrees given to unsuccessful doctoral students may be acceptable as a teaching credential because transcripts don't distinguish between a "normal" terminal master's and a consolation-prize master's.

Nonterminal master's degrees are earned as a first step toward the Ph.D. In some departments students who intend to go on for the Ph.D. register for the master's program first, and after completion apply to the departmental Ph.D. program or otherwise are formally inducted if considered suitable for further graduate study. In other departments students do not enter a separate, formal master's program, but instead enter a Ph.D. program directly after the baccalaureate. It is common for such Ph.D. programs to award what are called "incidental" master's to students who successfully pass their initial Ph.D. hurdles, usually consisting of the first or second year's course work. In some departments students are automatically awarded these incidental degrees—often called Master of Arts, Master of Science, or Master of Philosophy—while in others they must petition if they wish to receive them.

PROFESSIONAL VERSUS ACADEMIC ▪ MASTER'S ▪

The most common type of terminal master's is the professional or vocational (as distinguished from academic) degree awarded for advanced technical training past the baccalaureate. A student typically gets this degree and then enters the job market without further education. Examples include Master of Business Administration (MBA), Master of Architecture (M.Arch.), Master of Physical Therapy, Master of Electrical Engineering, and Master of Education (M.Ed.). The majority of degrees are conferred in just a few areas where career rewards are perceived as high: in 1992–93, according to the Office of Educational Research and Improvement, 26 percent were in education, 24 percent in business, and 8 percent in engineering.

The second broad category of terminal master's are degrees that are considered more academic than professional. They are typically termed Master of Arts or Master of Science, usually followed by an "in biology" or "in art history." The lines between this and the professional degree are blurred, particularly since most people who take an academic degree probably have some idea of putting it to practical use, but to take an extreme example, the academic nature of a degree in Egyptian hieroglyphics compared to a degree in electrical engineering is obvious. For secondary school teachers it might be argued by hairsplitters that master's in education are professional, while master's in specific disciplines like English, history, or biology are academic.

The academic master's may qualify the recipient to teach college courses and is important for gaining entrance to Ph.D. programs. Some university departments require that students obtain a master's before admission to the Ph.D. program, while others allow direct application to the Ph.D. program without a master's. Because of increasing competition with underemployed Ph.D.s, graduates from master's programs may find it difficult to obtain college-level teaching jobs. An indication of the lack of seriousness with which they are treated is that an English department takes only about one month to hire a short-term masters-level lecturer but six months or more for a tenure-track teacher with a Ph.D.

■ THE IDEAL MASTER'S PROGRAM ■

Jules LaPidus, the president of the Council of Graduate Schools in the United States, has said that "a student must be able to understand and use . . . knowledge . . . at the master's level and make significant contributions to it at the doctoral level." A master's thesis therefore can be substantially less ambitious in size and contributory importance than a Ph.D. thesis. The average master's thesis takes a year or less to research and complete, compared with the Ph.D.'s usual three to four years, although some master's programs demand ambitious theses and students may take two years to complete them.

The master's should teach the student to think at a higher integrative and creative level than the bachelor's. Therefore, master's programs that consist simply of course work without theses or other integrative experiences have been criticized for their "additive fallacy" because they assume that simply adding more course work can magically teach students to think at a higher level. By contrast, to find a *good* master's program look for one that has two kinds of experiences that go beyond course work: First are *integrative experiences* that help the student pull together knowledge learned in courses and translate it into practice. Examples are internships, seminars, and other research or fieldwork. Second are *summative experiences* which test the student's knowledge and ability to do this integration on a higher than undergraduate level. They include theses, research projects, and/or comprehensive examinations; they are learning experiences in their own right which develop higher-level integrative skills necessary in, for example, doing further research on the Ph.D. level.

■ STRUCTURE OF PROGRAMS ■

The bulk of a master's program usually consists of course work, regularly with the addition of a comprehensive exam, a practicum (practical work experience), or a thesis. Programs may be as brief as one year, requiring approximately twenty-four semester hours of courses, or more usually require two years, including between forty-five and sixty hours of course work. Following are descriptions of some of the major hurdles involved in earning the degree.

• RESIDENCE REQUIREMENT •

Most universities require that all graduate students be enrolled full-time in residence at the campus for at least one year before becoming eligible for examinations or degrees.

• COURSE WORK •

You will be busy with courses during most of the time you are in school. Students are required to perform up to standard, often a B average being the minimum acceptable for good standing. Students expecting to go on for the Ph.D. should aim higher. In some cases, master's students take the same course work as Ph.D.s during the first year.

• MASTER'S EXAMS •

Master's students frequently take comprehensive exams at the conclusion of their studies. These may be oral or written, and are generally shorter and easier than Ph.D. qualifying exams. If you have done well in course work, you should have no problem with these exams, although you do need to review carefully for them.

• THESIS •

Master's programs requiring a thesis are generally considered stronger than those without. In Tennessee, 347 master's programs at public institutions were rated in 1983 by the Tennessee Higher Education Commission. According to Robert Appleson, director of Assessment and Program Review for the commission, 26 percent of the programs were considered "anemic" because they lacked both a thesis and a comprehensive exam, while the 41 percent with an exam but lacking a thesis were considered "marginally acceptable."

In many cases the thesis is elective and, depending upon the department, may be substituted by a research project, an internship, a comprehensive exam, or additional course work. The choice you make will depend upon which alternative you feel best able to accomplish *and your plans for the future*. If you intend to go on for a Ph.D., you should probably do a thesis, because (1) it will earn you more respect from admissions committees, (2) it is often a prerequisite for admission to Ph.D. programs, and (3) it can make your life easier in a Ph.D. program if you already know something about how to do research and write it up.

On the other hand, if you are not going on for the Ph.D., other alternatives, notably doing an internship or practicum, may be more useful for your career. One master's student in nutrition said, "I knew I didn't want a Ph.D., so instead of a thesis, I did an internship that led directly to my present job." There are also advantages to taking an exam option instead of a thesis: notably, exams take much less time and there is less opportunity for unexpected problems that will delay graduation.

▪ SELF-SET REQUIREMENTS ▪

If you intend to go on to a Ph.D. program, you should try to maximize your chances of acceptance by getting a head start on your academic career. When you are planning your thesis or other research papers, talk with your adviser about tailoring them for publication. Some departments even require a thesis that is in a form "appropriate for submission to a professional journal." Set yourself the goal of getting at least one paper accepted for publication by the time you graduate. Also, make professional contacts and develop an understanding of your field by attending conferences.

▪ PART-TIME OPTION ▪

Older students who have well-paying jobs may wish to avoid the penury of graduate school by becoming part-time master's students while remaining at work. Some students may find their employers willing to pay for MBA or other master's-level training. Part-time education can be a particularly good option if you can meld your employment with your research. For instance, workers in international conservation have done master's degrees in their field by using their ongoing research to fulfill course or thesis requirements. Drawbacks to part-time education include lack of financial aid, length of time to completion, and the absence of student camaraderie. One part-time master's student in ecology said that if she had it to do over again she would go full-time because she feels like an outsider in the department, having missed the shared experiences of classmates. Another student, after two years in a museum studies program coupled with full-time work, is quitting because she cannot stand the disruption that two more years of intense study would bring to her life. She says,

> The strain of balancing a job and school is tremendous. You need a very understanding boss, and even if you have one, you are always feeling guilty about either work or school, because you can't give either 100 percent. The professors in particular don't understand. They're used to full-time students, and they get angry if sometimes you have to put your job first. On top of that, they treat you like a child, not like an adult, and after I've been in the working world for five years, this is hard to take. I'm finally asking myself if I really need the aggravation.

11

. . . .

THE DOCTORATE:

HISTORY AND HURDLES

. . . .

And this mess is so big
And so deep and so tall
We can not pick it up.
There is no way at all!

—Dr. Seuss, *The Cat in the Hat*

THE BIGGEST MYSTERY ABOUT THE PH.D. IS WHY IT'S CALLED A DOCTOR OF
Philosophy if the field doesn't have anything to do with philosophy. Apparently, in the olden days "philosophy" not only dealt with the study
of metaphysics, epistemology, and so on but also included the physical
sciences because it wasn't clear in the minds of alchemists that there was
a distinction. If you go back to the Greek roots meaning "a lover of
wisdom," things make more sense, even though it could be argued that
getting a Ph.D. is more likely to make you a lover of minutiae.

The doctorate is the highest-level academic degree attainable and is
correspondingly more prestigious than the master's degree. As with the
master's degree, the number of doctorates awarded has grown dramatically
since the first successful doctoral program was established at Johns Hopkins
in 1876, most of this growth occurring in recent decades. The National
Research Council reports that in the three decades from 1964 to 1994 the
number of doctorates conferred yearly has increased nearly three times,
from 14,000 per year to 41,000 per year.

Compared with the master's, the doctoral degree remains relatively
undiversified. In addition to the ubiquitous Doctor of Philosophy (Ph.D.),
there are only about twenty-seven other named doctoral-level degrees,

including Doctor of Library Science (DLS), Doctor of Public Health (DPH), and Doctor of Education (Ed.D.). The recently created and rapidly growing Doctor of Arts (DA) is given to students with a focus on teaching higher education in an attempt by universities to offer an alternative to the traditional Ph.D., which emphasizes research over teaching. All doctoral-level degrees are substantially more challenging than master's and require original, contributory research presented as a thesis or similar culminating project. Because of their closely related nature, this book uses the terms "doctoral degree," "doctorate," and "Ph.D." interchangeably.

As with master's degrees, if you have the option of taking different types of degrees, investigate them closely. For example, the Doctor of Arts (DA) degree at some universities may have less prestige than a Ph.D. in the same discipline. One English professor, who has served on many hiring committees, said, "Sometimes it seems from those we interview that all the weenies who couldn't cut it in the Ph.D. program went for the DA. Some of their dissertations were ludicrous. If I were on a search committee, and had a choice, I would tend to go with a Ph.D. because Ph.D.s are supposed to know how to teach on top of doing solid research." Similar concern may exist over the Doctor of Education (Ed.D.). I'm not saying that you shouldn't do non-Ph.D. degrees. Just make sure you check out the implications ahead of time.

FORMAL STAGES
▪ OF ADVANCEMENT ▪

Graduate students earn different ranks according to whether or not they have passed hurdles like qualifying exams. The names of these ranks vary somewhat among departments; I have used the most common terminology below.

You start out and remain a *graduate student* until you get your Ph.D. During your first and second years, before you have passed your qualifying exams, you can think of yourself as a probationary recruit whose success or failure has not yet been determined. Important hurdles during this stage are adequate performance on course work and fulfilling residence and language requirements.

A few departments give the next-highest rank of *doctoral student* to show that a student has passed from master's to doctoral level but not yet become a doctoral candidate.

Doctoral candidate (also called "dissertator" by departments with no ear for euphony) is almost invariably the rank certifying that course work is completed and a student is off probation, needing only the thesis and oral defense of the thesis to finish. Most departments skip the rank of doctoral student and go right to doctoral candidate upon successful completion of requirements. Although candidates must usually have complied with language and residence requirements, and in some cases must have chosen the area of thesis concentration, the major hurdle to candidacy is the qualifying exam. It is this exam that primarily determines whether the department feels that a student is qualified to continue for the doctorate, although the overall record is usually considered and a department may terminate a student for reasons other than failing the exam. The qualifying exam typically covers the broad range of the student's field, as well as focusing on one or more specialty areas. The exam usually is taken near the end of the second year, and passing is vital for continuation of study. Generally, if you leave school after passing the qualifying exam, you can be awarded the consolation-prize master's degree.

The final phase is successful completion and defense of your thesis, whereupon you will become a *doctor of philosophy*.

▪ SELF-SET REQUIREMENTS ▪

There are three things that are not formally required by your department but are so important you should make them requirements for yourself. They will help determine whether you finish, how you are perceived in your department, and whether you get a job. Tattoo this list somewhere you won't forget to look. (1) *Publish academic papers.* (2) *Go to conferences.* (3) *Get on committees.* If you dive into the administrative pond, you can swim around with your professors and get to know them on a collegial level (a cynical colleague refers to this as "amplexus," which is the mating embrace of frogs).

▪ RESIDENCE REQUIREMENT ▪

Universities usually require that Ph.D. students reside on campus as full-time registered students for at least one year, many for two. They don't want you breezing into town, registering for a quarter, dumping a thesis on your adviser, and getting a Ph.D. unless you've been around for a while paying tuition and soaking up the academic ambience. Although many people earn their master's degrees part-time, the doctoral-level program is so time-consuming and arduous that it is very difficult to be successful on a part-time basis.

▪ COURSE WORK ▪

You will generally spend at least the first year in course work, which should be thought of as preparation for the qualifying examination. Your course of study should be decided through early consultation with your temporary or permanent adviser so as to provide a firm grounding in your field. It is usual for qualifying exams to test both a wide-ranging knowledge in the field and in-depth knowledge of your specialty area. Therefore, your selection of courses should meet both these needs. In some cases departments help students discover weaknesses early by administering prescriptive exams before or shortly after they start school, and the students then take remedial classes as indicated. These prescriptive exams may be called "qualifying" exams, but don't confuse them with the true qualifying exams for candidacy taken after the completion of course work. Departments also will set minimum requirements for the number and type of courses to be taken. If you have deficiencies in preparatory courses at the time you enter, you may be asked to make these up without having them count toward the number of graduate courses required.

It goes without saying that you should do well in your courses. Departments frequently stipulate that at minimum a B average must be maintained each term. In general, you should shoot for at least a B+ average. In many schools, anything below an A may be unsatisfactory. Avoid incompletes, which tend to be viewed poorly. In UC Irvine's English department, for example, records of incompletes remain permanently in a student's file and "can influence changes for the award of future TA-ships." Even more terrifying, the department says that failing to meet a deadline for making up an incomplete will "generate correspondence with the Dean"!

▪ MINORS ▪

Many departments require that Ph.D. students complement course work in their major area with a specified number of courses in one or more "minor fields." The minor field is typically chosen in consultation with the major professor so that it adds insight to study in the major field. Thus, for a major in history, economics would be a logical minor because it can help in historical analysis.

▪ QUALIFYING EXAMS ▪

You will generally finish course work and take qualifying exams near the end of your second year. These are lengthy, mind-numbing exams that may last for several days. Although your course work forms the base of knowledge upon which you will be tested, it is common for exams to reach deeper for theory and examples that didn't show up in class. It is this open-endedness that puts terror into students. Your department will justify these unpleasantly vague ground rules by asserting that you, as a budding academic, should *know everything important about your field*. To make matters worse, it is likely that part of your examination will be an oral grilling by the examination committee. Scared yet? Fortunately, there are good ways to figure out what you have to know and learn it. Once you pass your qualifying exam, you're a doctoral candidate, and are virtually ABD (all but dissertation).

▪ TEACHING REQUIREMENTS ▪

Some departments require you to teach as little as a single class, while others require a year or more. Because teaching will slow you down, teach as little as possible.

▪ LANGUAGE REQUIREMENTS ▪

It is common to require proficiency in one or two languages. The required level varies, but reading at a level sufficient for research is the minimum. This may be equivalent to two college-level years. Although Princeton's history department requires only a single language, specific subareas may require additional languages, so that a Russian history specialist must know Russian, French, and German. You might want to take a look at previous language exams to get an idea of how proficient you need to be before you choose a field. If you are one of those people about whom they say, "He doesn't have any trouble with his French, but the French do," you may want to rethink your field of concentration.

For information on software packages designed to make learning languages easier, see Appendix A.

▪ MISCELLANEOUS REQUIREMENTS ▪

Depending upon the department, there may be other, less common requirements, including the delivery of departmental seminars to demonstrate communication ability, practica, and preparation of research papers. Practica are common in education, psychology, physical therapy, and other fields where practical experience in treatment or teaching is important. If departments demand publishable research papers, they are to be commended for emphasizing publication and writing skills, since these are what will establish your academic reputation.

▪ THESIS PROPOSAL ▪

Before you begin work on your thesis, you must develop the proposal, which is a written, detailed plan of research. As you develop it, in close consultation with your adviser and committee, you will clarify your thinking, identify problems, and gain formal approval to undertake your research. As a final step in the proposal process, you may have to formally defend your proposal, in what amounts to an oral examination.

▪ THESIS ▪

Completing your thesis is the largest and most important task you will face, roughly the equivalent of writing a book. If you are a master's student, a successful thesis can provide entree into a related job or Ph.D. program. If you are a doctoral student, your thesis will establish your reputation as a competent researcher and also build the base for postdoctoral research.

▪ THESIS DEFENSE ▪

The thesis defense is almost invariably a public presentation of the thesis, followed by an "in chambers" oral examination by the dissertation committee. Although many students fear this examination, there is no reason to, because if you have maintained close contact with your professor and committee, it should merely be pro forma. They will have already decided that your thesis is acceptable.

12

MANAGING YOURSELF

"The horror of that moment," the King went on, "I shall never, *never* forget!"

"You will, though," the Queen said, "if you don't make a memorandum of it."

—LEWIS CARROLL, *Through the Looking-Glass*

DON HORAK'S FIRST DAY AS A GRADUATE STUDENT IN THE MOST PRESTIGIOUS physics department on the West Coast began with a lecture from a Nobel Prize winner. Don and his fellow students eagerly waited in the large lecture hall to be welcomed into the fraternity of physicists. The Nobelist, jauntily outfitted with a feathered Tyrolean hat, presumably to underscore his intellectual ties to the European origins of his discipline, ordered the students to look to the right.

With smug satisfaction he said, "Look carefully at the people sitting next to you. They won't be here a year from now, because half of you won't make the grade." He knew what he was talking about; his department set it up that way. The first year was a weeding process designed to exclude the undeserving. Most weren't thrown out, but life was made so miserable for them that they left on their own. They were befriended by no professor, put on no project, given no support, and, in Don's words, were "generally humiliated."

Hopefully, your departmental welcome will be more encouraging than Don's. However, you should take the same message to heart. The first year is critical, so you need to get off to a fast start.

▪ THINGS TO DO RIGHT AWAY ▪

You should do these eight things as soon as you get to graduate school:

1. Buy a good computer.
2. Set up a calendar system. One calendar should cover the entire period of your planned graduate school program and should display important deadlines, including self-set requirements like paper publication. Setting this up right away will help you start focusing on your long-term goals. You can use traditional paper calendars or make life simpler by using one of the personal-information-management computer programs I discuss below.
3. Set up a filing system. Keep track of thesis topics, bibliographies, personal contacts, and other information involved in the graduate process.
4. Begin keeping an hourly log of daily progress. At the end of every day, write down how every hour was spent. This will give you an accurate assessment of your progress.
5. Reapply for outside fellowships if you narrowly missed getting one the previous year. Some graduate fellowships, like those of the National Science Foundation, can be reapplied for in the first year of graduate school, although application deadlines are as early as November, right after you start school.
6. Set up regular meetings with your adviser.
7. Set up or join a graduate student support group.
8. Start searching for a thesis topic. Half of all students don't start actively looking for a topic until they have passed their qualifying examinations near the end of their second year. You can be ahead of half the pack if you start looking for a topic now.

FIND A QUIET PLACE WHERE YOU CAN WORK WITHOUT INTERRUPTION

SET UP YOUR OFFICE FOR ▪ ACTION ▪

The more you focus on your work and make it central to your life, the more progress you will make, the more your academic community will approve of you, and the happier you will be. An important first step is to set up an office command center that is devoted entirely to work and free of distractions. Make sure you have a large enough surface to work on easily and adequate file cabinets. Post calendars and schedules, and put a white board on your wall to list ideas and tasks. Put your pleasure books in storage and get rid of your television. Banish it to the attic or give it to an enemy. Keep your music only if it helps you write. Get an answering machine and turn off your phone when you're working. Below, I discuss some of the specific office material that can help you to be efficient.

Try a telephone headset

A lightweight telephone headset, like those worn by receptionists, can free up your hands so that you can talk on the phone and type or find papers in your file cabinet at the same time. If you are going to be on the phone for long periods doing research or other school-associated business, a headset will cut down on muscular and mental fatigue. Plus, if you need to take extensive notes on a phone conversation, with your hands free you can type the information directly into your word processor. You can purchase a headset from office supply or telephone supply companies for under $100.

▪ SET UP YOUR COMPUTER ▪

I'm lucky because in philosophy refusing to use a word processor is seen as an amusing eccentricity.

—Kathy Gardner

In the 1992 edition of this book, I assumed that many readers would not have personal computers and urged them to get one. Since then, computers have become so commonplace, cheap, and essential that every grad student should have one. You need a computer for researching on the Internet, sending and receiving e-mail, recording and analyzing data, organizing your bibliography, writing your thesis, and organizing your job search. In addition, many libraries have now made it possible for you to access their databases via modem and, in some cases, even browse through selections.

For more information on buying a computer, see Appendix A.

• MAKE DAILY PROGRESS •

The best advice I can give on not getting bogged down in graduate school is to maintain daily progress. Once you start working on your thesis, it's much better to work a couple of hours every day than the same number of hours in infrequent, concentrated sessions. Daily progress is the best antidote for procrastination. Also, if you keep focused on your research, your subconscious will work on it when you're sleeping or walking to school. In the same way that scenes from a movie will stay in your mind for several days after you've seen them, ideas for research or writing will magically appear at odd moments for a day or so after you have been working hard. But these insights won't come if you ignore the thesis during the week and only burst into feverish activity on the weekend. In your first year, when you are busy with classes, you may not have a great deal of time for the thesis, but at least schedule a few hours per week to read sample theses, research topics that interest you, or talk to professors.

SET UP A STRUCTURE:
• THE CALENDAR SYSTEM •

To keep motivated and working regularly, you need a schedule system to manage your time and make sure you respond to deadlines. There are many different time-management systems you can use effectively, including elaborate professional systems like Daytimer or Franklin Planner (named after Ben). I suggest you develop a system that has the following six parts:

1. A schedule of major events throughout your entire graduate career
2. A monthly calendar broken into days
3. A weekly schedule broken into hours
4. A portable weekly organizer also broken into hours
5. A daily log of hourly accomplishments
6. A list of tasks to be completed

In addition, you should write up short monthly progress reports. I know this seems like a lot to do, but you can buy an inexpensive computer program that will help you handle all this scheduling simply. These programs are called personal information managers (PIMs) and I review some of them below after describing why you need each of the six types of calendars and schedules.

GRADUATE CAREER SCHEDULE

National Science Foundation Fellowship applications were due in November of my first year in graduate school, and all the first-year graduate students, including myself, were so busy getting adjusted that we forgot the deadline. With this experience, you would think that the next year we would do better. Nope. We all forgot again.

One of the toughest things is to keep aware not only of what you've got to do today but also of what you've got to do in six months. It is easy to focus myopically on the paper due in three days, or the class you've got to teach tomorrow, and forget to think about your distant thesis proposal or defense. But if you want to make good progress, you have to keep focused on your long-term goals, always planning at least a year or two ahead. Once you are out in the working world, this is the time frame you will need for planning sabbaticals, job changes, setting up conferences, publishing books, and so on.

When you start graduate school, sit down with your department's guidelines and work out a schedule of your activities until graduation. Fill your schedule with all important deadlines, including bureaucratic deadlines for filing forms, self-set requirements for publishing papers, stages in thesis development, conference attendances, and any other important long-term deadlines or dates. You can do your schedule manually or you can use one of the PIMs, like Lotus Organizer or Baseline's Info Accelerator, to fill in all events for several years into the future. With a PIM, it's easy to alter the schedule as needed, and with most programs you can easily print out calendar pages for individual months with all events listed.

If you really want to get into the process, you can use a project management program that plots sophisticated time lines, helping you to figure out how long each step in your thesis will take and to juggle competing tasks. Most project management programs, which include Microsoft's Project Manager, Primavera's SureTrak, and Symantec's On Target, do much more sophisticated scheduling than PIMs, and are probably more than the average grad student needs. However, if you are doing a thesis involving complex projects, or if you are involved in projects with multiple researchers, these programs can be very helpful in thinking through who does what and how long each piece of the project will take. They will also print out project information in forms that include Gantt charts and monthly calendars with projects displayed as time lines. Although these upper-end programs are expensive, some of them offer substantial student discounts. If what you're interested in is primarily a way to display calendars with simple time lines for tasks, one of the low-end programs, like Symantec's On Target or Avantos's ManagePro are easy to learn and work well.

ManagePro has a nice on-line tutorial that can get you up and running in twenty minutes.

Once you've worked out your schedule, you can improve your chances of paying attention to it if you post it where you can't miss it. One option is to buy a 3' by 4' one-year calendar with a "mark and erase" surface at an office supply store. If you've got room for two on your walls, you can post two years' worth of deadlines. Or just write all your major deadlines on an erasable whiteboard.

MONTHLY CALENDAR

In addition to a multi-year schedule of your career events, you should use a monthly calendar to show in more detail what you plan to do on a daily basis. If you use your computer every day, you can use the monthly calendar in a PIM, but you might pay more attention to a traditional wall calendar posted where you can't miss it. To make sure you know what is happening more than one month ahead, pull out the staples from your calendar and pin the pages to the wall so that you show at least two months at a time. By looking at two months at once, you'll avoid missing the things you need to do in the beginning of the next month. Write all important deadlines, dates, and events on your calendar. Copy long-term deadlines from your multi-year schedule. Add classes and regular meetings with your adviser and other committee members. *Review this calendar every day to make sure nothing sneaks up on you. It only takes a minute in the morning.*

WEEKLY SCHEDULE

You may want to make a weekly schedule, like the one you used as an undergraduate, with each day divided into hours. Use this for planning courses and other regular meetings, particularly during your first year or more when you are heavily involved with classes. If you've got a PIM, the weekly calendar view will work well to schedule classes. All the PIMs I reviewed give you the option of marking a scheduled activity as a re-curring event, so that, for example, the PIM automatically enters your swimming class every Tuesday at 3 p.m.

WEEKLY ORGANIZER

Get compulsive about carrying a weekly organizer. This is one of those pocket calendar books carried by people with real jobs. Although called "weekly" organizers, each of their pages covers a separate day divided by hours so that you can see what you need to do at any time during the day. Because you carry it with you, you can set up appointments on the spot, and you don't have to depend on your memory when you're out of the house, wondering, "Was that meeting at three or three-thirty?" The information in this organizer should duplicate that on your month-scale calendar and weekly schedule.

Although PIMs also provide you with electronic weekly organizers, you can't haul your computer around with you to refer to. This is one place the old-fashioned three-ring Daytimers and other organizers win out. However, you can get the best of both worlds by using a PIM to maintain your schedule data at the office and then print it out to carry with you in a three-ring organizer. Most PIMs can print out your weekly schedule on three-hole paper in a variety of formats to fit Daytimers or other standard brands of weekly organizer notebooks. Franklin's Ascend, for example, will print your schedule onto pages to insert in a Franklin Organizer.

Daily log of activities

You can motivate yourself and keep track of your productivity by keeping a log of your daily activities. I use a large weekly organizer that I keep on my desk. At the end of each day, write in the space for each hour how you spent that hour. This will help you keep track of how you really spend your time. I'm sure you've had the experience of telling a friend, "I've really been working my ass off—nothing but studying for the last three days," when, if God were keeping score, He would know that you really worked six hours one day; ten the next, three the next, and spent the rest of the time playing. This is why support groups for dieters make members keep food journals—what they remember putting in their mouths is different from the reality. Likewise, you need to know how you're putting in your time, identify the big time wasters, and cut down on them.

The other benefit of the logbook is the Merit Badge Effect. People seem to have a chipmunk-like hoarding instinct, whereby once they start collecting something, whether it be Scout merit badges, bottle caps, or hours worked on a thesis, they want more and more. The secret is to turn your hours into a collection. It sounds silly, but it may work for you. After you've been collecting hours for a few days, you'll start thinking, "I earned ten hours yesterday. Wonder if I can get eleven today?"

"To-do" list

You will need a master list of things to do, so you don't have hundreds of scraps of paper with obscure notes to yourself scattered throughout the landscape. You can keep your lists on paper, or, again, most PIMs give you an electronic "to-do" list, including features like "rollovers," so that uncompleted tasks automatically show up on the next day's "to-do" list. Save all your old lists because you can use them to retrieve names, phone numbers, or other information that will be listed roughly in chronological order. If you're keeping your lists with a PIM, finding old information will be simple with a word-search function.

• MONTHLY THESIS PROGRESS REPORT •

The daily activity log will help you to assess your daily progress, but you also need regularly to assess how well you are doing at meeting your long-term goals. I suggest that once a month you write a one- or two-page report that (1) summarizes your accomplishments during the month, (2) relates them to your long-term schedule, and (3) describes the steps to be taken during the following month. Note not only successes but also problems you encounter, particularly places where you are stuck and need help. You should also give a copy of each month's report to your thesis adviser. This is much more impressive to your adviser than an occasional oral chat about how you are coming along, and it will focus his or her attention on your legitimate needs for help.

• MORE ON PIMS •

You can do all the above scheduling plus other things to get organized by using one of the personal information managers (PIM). Although programs differ in details and features, they all are combinations of appointment books, "to-do" lists, electronic address books, and calendars, all integrated so you can jump from one to another with a click of your mouse. Typically, the calendars allow you to check off items when finished, set alarms that will pop up on your computer screen to warn you before meetings, and set recurring events that automatically pop up on your calendar every week or month. An example of a recurring event is meeting with your adviser every Monday at 10 a.m. or paying the rent on the first of every month.

All the PIMs I looked at have provisions for printing out the different calendars. For example, Symantec's Act! does a great job of printing out a monthly calendar with all your scheduled events neatly fitted into each day. Lotus Organizer is unique in generating a time-line view to help you schedule multi-day tasks or events. For example, if you were going to be writing a thesis chapter from July 12 to July 20, Lotus Organizer could represent this in its planner by a red bar running through those nine days. However, to do this sort of time-line scheduling in detail, you really need a project manager program like Microsoft Project or Symantec's On Target.

All PIMs also have some type of electronic address book, which they generally call a "contact list" or "phone book." Information on each contact generally includes the person's name, address, phone numbers, and fax number, and some of the PIMs also contain e-mail addresses. With some PIMs, this information can be easily printed directly on Rolodex cards or address-book pages. Search functions let you look effortlessly for a contact, even if you can only remember part of the person's name or where he or she works. You can also associate key words with certain contacts so the PIM can pull up all the contact information for a certain group. For example, if you can't remember your aunt's name, you could pull up and scan the "elderly relatives" contact list.

If you have a modem, you can use the PIM's contact list to dial a phone number automatically or send a fax or e-mail message with a few mouse clicks. Many PIMs will also use the contact information to fill out word-processor templates for letters and memos, automatically inserting the salutation, names, and addresses of the recipients. A good PIM will seamlessly link to your word processor so you can click and insert the contact information directly into a letter or other document (they don't all do this equally well).

Some PIMs will also have a contact manager that can generate a contact history for you. For example, in Corel's Sidekick, if you ask for a history on John Smith, one of the colleagues in your contact list, you receive a list of all the letters, memos, phone calls, or e-mail you have ever sent the person, all arranged chronologically. If you use the PIM and your modem automatically to dial your phone calls, faxes, and e-mail, the relevant information on each activity will automatically be entered into the contact history. Some of the contact-oriented PIMs, such as Sharkware from CogniTech and Act!, link the contact history back to your word processor and other applications. For example, in Sharkware, if you see in your contact history that you used WordPerfect to write and send a letter to John Smith on June 14, 1995, you can click on the entry in the contact history and the original letter will be retrieved from your WordPerfect document directory for you to read or edit, assuming that you have not previously deleted it.

PIMs differ substantially in layout, ease of learning, ease of use, and capabilities. Some are modeled after the paper personal organizers we're all familiar with. Lotus Organizer, for example, mimics a paper organizer notebook, right down to the simulated three metal rings holding your simulated pages together. Others, such as Sharkware and Act!, use a desktop that looks more like a spreadsheet.

I checked out the following programs and found them all pretty good. Lotus Organizer, Corel's Sidekick, Baseline's Info Accelerator, Microsoft's Schedule, and Franklin's Ascend have layouts that mimic traditional paper organizers and calendars. Of them all, Lotus Organizer is easiest to learn and use, and the most fun, but they're all intuitive. Sharkware is easy to learn for a contact-based program, but I found Act! difficult, plus, the manual is complicated. These two are powerful at organizing contacts, so if part of your research involves calling and re-calling lots of people, or if you're job hunting, these could be useful.

Capabilities of these programs get updated quickly, so I won't compare them in detail, but I'll tell you some things to look for in a good PIM. Because it's almost impossible to tell much about a program from the box, be sure to buy your software from a store that allows exchange after you've opened it.

- For ease of learning, look for programs that have on-line tutorials, like the Answer Wizard in Microsoft's Schedule. Another great help are hypertext labels that pop up wherever you put your cursor to tell you what a command button does. Lotus Organizer, for example, has a feature called "bubble help." When you place the cursor on a button, a cartoon bubble appears that tells you exactly what the button is for.
- Make sure backup capability comes with the program—to back up your data with Baseline's Info Accelerator, you've got to shell out $30 more for a backup utility.
- Check for the quality of the calendar printouts—when you print out monthly views of your appointments with Info Accelerator, you lose some text that won't fit into each day's space, while with Act! everything fits in.
- This sounds picky, but programs are also easier to use if their appointment books and "to-do" lists are on facing pages, so you can see at a glance everything that's taking place on a given day. This is the case with Baseline's Info Accelerator, but not with Sharkware or Microsoft's Schedule.
- Programs differ in how easy it is to print your contacts' addresses and other information directly on Rolodex cards. Sharkware makes it simple by having a dedicated "print to Rolodex" command. The Rolodex cards come on a sheet, and you punch them out after the whole sheet has been printed, so you can insert them in your Rolodex.
- You also want a program that interfaces easily with your word processor, so you can insert PIM data into documents. Sharkware, for example,

automatically switches to WordPerfect or whichever word processor you are using when you want it automatically to create and address a letter using one of the entries in your contact list. Act!, on the other hand, uses its own built-in word processor, an approach I found annoying. Neither Lotus Organizer nor Corel's Sidekick has a simple way of getting information easily into a word-processing document (this is a big drawback and I expect they'll fix it in future releases).

- It's a big plus if the program automatically logs phone calls, faxes, and other activities in the contact history when you make them.

▪ **FILE SYSTEM** ▪

Early to bed, early to rise, work like hell and organize.

—ALBERT GORE, JR., 1988

The word "files" conjures up visions of hunched Dickensian clerks shuffling through endless stacks of dusty paper. Unfortunately, given the degree of organization demanded by graduate school, you've got to have organized files.

The first thing you need is a file cabinet or two, not the cardboard box under the bed you used as an undergrad. If you've been given an office at school, the university may also have blessed you with a file cabinet. If not, buy one. If you're doing a Ph.D., you will almost certainly end up needing at least one four-drawer cabinet, although a master's student might squeak by with a two-drawer. Get a good-quality cabinet with a sturdy roller mechanism. You will be opening and closing these drawers thousands of times, and if you buy a cheap cabinet whose drawers don't glide smoothly, you will regret it. New file cabinets are expensive, but second-hand ones are easy to find, if you aren't worried about aesthetics. Check ads and used-furniture stores, or ask office furniture stores if they have any shop-damaged but functional cabinets.

Place the file cabinet where you can open the drawers without getting up from your desk. This may sound silly, but keeping it within easy reach can make the difference between filing papers right away and putting it off until you are buried.

Next, buy lots of file folders, way more than you need, and don't run out. This is one of the places it is easy to be penny-wise and pound-foolish. If you try to scrimp on file folders, you will find yourself doubling up and filing papers where they don't really belong, rather than using a new folder for a new file. Then you will have trouble later on finding what you need.

Although you can use all sorts of filing systems, for the average graduate student it is usually adequate to divide the files into groups under basic headings, physically separating the groups with labeled dividers. You might, for example, have one group labeled "Life," which contains folders on insurance, vehicle registration, medical-insurance policies, and recreational activities. A second group might be "Job Applications," containing folders with your curriculum vitae, a summary of your research, job announcements, and individual folders containing correspondence for each job you apply for. Most important, of course, will be files dealing with your research. The following nonexhaustive list will give you ideas about some of the files you should keep:

- Applications to graduate school. Application is your first big job, so start your file system to handle it. You should have a folder with a timetable of important deadlines, a chart to keep track of which requirements you have completed for each school, and separate folders to hold application materials for each school.
- Thesis ideas. Start out with a single folder containing all ideas you glean from research, classes, etc. As you begin to develop some of the ideas through research, keep a separate folder on each main topic.
- Thesis proposal. As you begin writing your proposal, have folders for different drafts, adviser's comments, and bibliography.
- Thesis. You will end up with many files in the section devoted to your thesis, which may use most of your file cabinet. You should have a file for each chapter (perhaps one for each draft of each chapter), reviewers' comments, bibliography, figures and tables, and anything else relevant.
- Interview notes. Keep good notes on discussions with your adviser, committee members, and other contacts in the field, sorted into separate files. As described above, it will help to transcribe telephone conversations directly into your word processor and then file the printouts appropriately.
- Ideas for paper topics. As for thesis ideas, keep a file on ideas for future papers that you might write and publish. Ideas you decide to work on can be transferred to your "to-do" list, above. As you begin work on papers, each will generate a set of sub-files, as will your thesis proposal and thesis.
- Notes on graduate-student support-group meetings.
- Conference and seminar files. I keep a separate folder for each professional meeting I attend, each of which contains trip-expense receipts, a draft of my presentation text, the meeting agenda, and pertinent correspondence. These are filed chronologically because chronological filing allows easy cross-referencing to calendars. You can also include a cross-referenced

alphabetized listing of meetings at the beginning of the file section, in case you forget when an event occurred.
• Exam material. As you prepare for master's or doctoral qualifying exams, you will need to collect copies of past exams, study lists, and notes on discussions with teachers about exam material.
• Old "to-do" lists.
• Monthly progress reports.
• Financial aid information and applications.
• Job information.
• Professional credentials. You need files containing copies of material you regularly send out when applying for jobs or giving lectures, including curriculum vitae, summaries of research, and reprints of your published work.
• Photocopy files. You will be collecting many photocopies of publications relevant to your research, and you need ways of quickly finding the ones you need. Here's my method: for each project I work on, whether it be a paper or a thesis chapter, I collect all the photocopies relevant to that paper and file them together, arranged alphabetically by author, with a separate file folder for each author. Because publication of a paper or revision of a thesis is such a lengthy process, you will need to refer back to these copies when editing or responding to reviewers' comments for a year or more, and your life will be much easier if you keep the photocopies on a specific project grouped together. In cases where you use the same article for two projects, either you can file a duplicate with each project, if the paper is easily photocopied, or for the first project you can file in the appropriate author's folder a piece of paper that refers you to the complete paper in the second project's file.

One difficulty with managing a large collection of photocopies is that you may not remember where you filed an article. Let's say you are trying to find a file about wolves eating rabbits in Siberia. You may not remember whether you filed it under "wolves," "rabbits," "Siberia," or something else. But you can find your articles easily if you use a computerized index. For example, you can use a specialized bibliography system like Niles's EndNote, which lets you make a separate entry for each article, each of which has separate fields for author, title, key words, an abstract, and other key information. When you want to find a file, you can do a word search on the title, author, key word, or other field. Once the file is found in the database, just read the location where you filed it. Instead of a dedicated bibliography program like EndNote (which has lots of other nice bibliographic features, in addition to functioning as a file index; see page 235), you can make your bibliographic index using the database capability in WordPerfect (look under the merge command) or another word-processing program, or, if you have one, you can use a dedicated database program like Claris FileMaker Pro.

▪ DEVELOP GOOD STUDY HABITS ▪

The organizational tips given in this chapter will help you keep focused on your studies, but in addition, make sure you are using the techniques for good study set out in Chapter 8, including sitting in front of the class, reading assigned material before lectures, and regularly attending office hours.

▪ MAKE CONTRACTS ▪

One of the best ways to drive yourself forward is to make contracts with your adviser, other professors, or your graduate student support group. Promise them that you will complete a given task by a certain day. Don't wait for them to give you deadlines; set them yourself. If you then fail to deliver you will be embarrassed, and there is nothing like potential embarrassment for concentrating your mind on your work. As managers say: "What gets watched, gets done." For example, promising your adviser that you will complete a thesis chapter by Christmas Eve will give you a real deadline to work toward, one you won't want to miss. Obviously, you should try to choose these deadlines realistically, so you are not needlessly embarrassed. Make contracts with your adviser to (1) see him or her at regularly scheduled meetings, at least once a month when you are working on your thesis (every week or two might be better), (2) deliver a progress report once a month, and (3) complete any of the other tasks necessary to get your degree, including doing oral presentations and writing thesis chapter drafts.

Not only are these contracts an exceptional way of building in deadlines, but they involve the adviser in your progress and give him or her the (correct) impression that you are organized and forward-moving. If you see your adviser regularly, turn in progress reports, and meet most of your mutually set deadlines, your professor will think highly of you and become emotionally involved in your success, something that can help tremendously if problems arise with your thesis committee or thesis defense.

JOIN A GRADUATE STUDENT
▪ SUPPORT GROUP ▪

A Mexican graduate student studying in the United States was perplexed by how little the graduate students cooperated with one another. He said, "In the United States, graduate students won't work communally or even share notes. This was hard for me to get used to." Although most students in a typical American graduate school do experience high levels of competition and isolation, it doesn't have to be this way. You can make allies of your peers and band together to face the common threats of an indifferent faculty by joining or forming a graduate student support group.

A support group can build a psychologically healthy community of students. During different stages of your graduate career you can use the group to blow off steam, get and give psychological support, practice professional presentations, review for exams, critique research plans and manuscripts, and develop strategies for dealing with balky advisers. You can trade skills with each other: public speaking, photography, writing, and research. Junior students can benefit from the advice of more advanced ones. Finally, you can make contracts with the group members to fulfill goals.

Some hints on structuring a support group:

LOOK TO YOUR FELLOW GRAD
STUDENTS FOR HELP

• Don't make it too large or too small. You need enough people for good interaction, but not so many that meaningful criticism of manuscripts and oral presentations is awkward. Perhaps five to eight people would be good, depending on your goals, so that, given the natural tendency of people not to show up all the time, you have at least four or five present at any meeting.
• Pick your members carefully—you may be stuck with them for a long while.
• Make sure the people involved are committed. Ideally, you and your friends will be meeting together during the entire course of your graduate careers and be heavily invested in one another's success.

• Schedule meetings regularly to minimize scheduling conflicts and confusion over dates.
• Set a definite agenda ahead of time for each meeting. Be tough about keeping your meeting focused on business—you can socialize afterward.

In highly competitive programs you may run into resistance from students who don't want to join because they feel you are all fighting for the same Ph.D. slots or jobs. One beginning graduate student initially had a hard time starting a group in the highly competitive English department at the University of Virginia because the other students felt they were all in competition with one another. She finally convinced them that a small, self-helping group could improve the performance of all members *compared with the larger pool of nonmembers*. You and your companions can beat out the competition collectively if you work together as a team.

You may also be able to take advantage of formal thesis development seminars, offered by some departments, which fulfill some of the functions of a graduate support group. For example, Ohio State's psychology department requires each doctoral student to join a dissertation seminar, led by a teacher in the student's general area. Beginning students present thesis ideas for brainstorming, while advanced students present their latest results or use the seminar for a mock thesis defense. Although one doctoral student said that she often felt overwhelmed by the number of suggestions made for changes in her research, the seminar was invaluable in helping her stay motivated and focused, with the result that she finished all research and wrote her thesis in only one year.

▪ JOIN NAGPS ▪

You can get in touch with other grad students and help fight for graduate student rights by joining the National Association of Graduate and Professional Students (NAGPS). NAGPS is working to better graduate student working conditions and can provide you with information on conferences and jobs, and offers low-cost health insurance for grad students and family (phone: 708 256-1562; e-mail: NAGPS@NETCOM.COM, or http://nagps.varesearch.com/NAGPS/nagps-hp.html).

▪ MANAGE YOUR FINANCES ▪

Financially, you will have a hard time in graduate school, so it makes sense to budget carefully and keep track of expenditures. One software program that can help is Intuit's Quicken. Quicken lets you electronically record cash flow, checks written, and credit card purchases. It keeps a running balance of your accounts and makes it easy to balance them. Quicken has arrangements with some credit card companies so that your monthly bills can be electronically downloaded and automatically entered into your Quicken account. You can categorize all your purchases so that Quicken prints you reports displaying your expenditures by categories listed or graphed. For example, I can instantly generate a graph that shows what proportion of my income I spent on supplies for writing this book.

When it comes to tax time, a tax program like TurboTax can lead you step by step through your taxes, making all calculations automatically and printing out your tax forms. All you do is enter income and expenditures. TurboTax will even figure out the nasty stuff like depreciation on your house and alternative minimum tax. Best of all, it interfaces with Quicken, so you can import your Quicken financial data directly into TurboTax. Both Quicken and TurboTax cost under $50.

Even though you won't have much money, avoid being penny-wise and pound-foolish when making decisions critical to your professional success. Even though it costs more in the short term, it may be a better long-term strategy to hire a thesis typist if you are slow or incompetent, to hire a moving company instead of doing it yourself, or to buy a good computer with adequate software instead of limping along on a cast-off 286. Remember that once you finish school, you will be earning substantially more money and can pay back debts with relative ease, so don't be afraid to go into debt if it will get you out of school quickly. For example, if you have trouble meeting a deadline, rather than kill yourself staying up late, think creatively about paying other people to help you save time: you can pay a copy center to do heavy photocopying, hire a courier service to deliver a manuscript (this can be surprisingly inexpensive), or pay a typist. Other graduate students and undergrads are a good source of inexpensive help. Rather than spending days puzzling over complicated statistics, hire a statistics graduate student for a few hours. Likewise, a bright undergraduate might be glad to help you research a paper or part of your thesis in exchange for experience and modest payment.

If you work before starting school, you should try to save money for a "making things easy fund." It may even be sensible to spend additional time working before school to save money, if this money can be used to get you out more quickly.

13

PLAYING POLITICS:

BUILDING A

REPUTATION

START YOUR JOB SEARCH ON
· DAY ONE ·

It is natural to think only as far as your graduation (which, especially in the case of Ph.D.s, may seem impossibly far away). Nonetheless, you must think past graduation to getting a job—from the moment you begin school. Evaluate your performance in terms of whether it will improve your chances of getting a job when you get out. Are you developing good relationships with powerful professors? Are you publishing papers? Are you building a network of colleagues at other institutions? Make sure you read Chapter 24, "Bringing It All Together: The Job," now, while you are still in graduate school.

· PLAYING POLITICS ·

Whether you are headed for the academic or the professional world, recognize that careers are political. Contacts, friendships, and perceptions (valid or otherwise) of your professional worth will help determine your success. People with power help those in the following categories: those who may be able to do them a good turn, who know friends or colleagues, whose work they are acquainted with, whom they personally like, or whom they are afraid of. Since it's unlikely that you, as a recent graduate, will be fear-inspiring, you should focus on fitting into the other categories.

■ MAKE CONTACT ■

Because professors, like most people, help friends and rarely put themselves out for strangers, your goal is to be a friend. Start with your adviser and committee. To the degree they allow it, get to know them personally. At a minimum, start by making sure you meet with them regularly to discuss your work. In most cases, your adviser won't be someone to develop a beer-drinking relationship with, but invite her or him to dinner at your house, along with some other graduate students, postdocs, or lab technicians. Don't worry if you are a little nervous and the evening doesn't feel totally natural—to some extent this is a political and symbolic occasion that demonstrates the honor with which you regard your adviser. Look for opportunities to do your committee members favors: house-sit, do small research tasks, or give rides to school. At university functions, make a point of greeting and joining your teachers (don't be shy). For example, if there is a departmental seminar, sit with your adviser instead of another graduate student, even though you might be more comfortable with the graduate student. Go to as many departmental receptions as possible, and *force yourself to spend time talking with professors*, instead of huddling defensively with students.

Actively make opportunities to get to know other workers in your field. The more highly placed these are, the better, but don't spurn the lowly —you never know the heights to which they may rise. Begin professional correspondences. If you admire someone's work, see if you can invite him or her to visit your department to give a seminar (most departments will have funds to pay expenses for some visitors). If you are traveling to another town, find out who in your field is at the local university and meet them. If your research is advanced, you can also ask whether they might like you to present an informal seminar when visiting the department.

■ IMAGE BUILDING ■

When bringing yourself to the notice of your professors, make sure it's the right kind of notice. It is essential to cultivate a professional image so that the teachers and other researchers in your field—your judges—see you as a paragon of probity and dedication. Faculty will notice and gossip about graduate students to a degree you may not be aware of. Their perceptions will affect your career—everything from job recommendations to teaching assignments to whether you can get the money from the department to go to a seminar.

Therefore, be businesslike, punctual, respectful, *dress neatly*, get your work done on time, and appear serious about your work. Project goodwill, optimism, cheerfulness, maturity, sobriety, and modesty. Although Edgar Allan Poe could get away with saying, "My whole nature utterly revolts at the idea that there is any Being in the Universe superior to myself," you can't.

John, one of my fellow biology students at Stanford, made the fatal mistake of getting a reputation among faculty as someone who *wasn't serious about his work*—the greatest academic sin. Whenever he took a break from research, he practiced rock climbing on the sandstone walls of the biology building, shoeless, shirtless, and in cutoff shorts. When he ran into problems with his thesis, he could be viewed at all hours clinging precariously to the outside of the building. After he also began giving prolonged displays of shirtless juggling in the central courtyard, his future was decided. The departmental senate reviewed his academic progress, judged him inadequately serious, and he was exiled to a job in computer programming in which he made much more money than he ever could have as a biologist.

If you have an office or lab at school, apply the same standards here. Make sure you keep it neat and well organized. If you must decorate your office walls, make sure the pictures are associated with your field, as compared with posters of motorcycle babes, guys with great abdominals, or the Grateful Dead. If your adviser has regular working hours, make sure that yours overlap his, so that whenever he is there you are too and he gets the idea that you are always working. It's not a bad idea to leave your light on and your office looking occupied when you're not there, to give the impression that you have just disappeared down the hall for a moment.

If you practice acting like a professional, the role will become easier until it fits naturally. The actor Cary Grant was once asked how he rose from his humble beginning to become the screen's quintessential gentleman. He said, "I began by acting like the person I wanted to be, and eventually I became that person."

As final proof of the power of image, consider the case of a man named Thompson, who for some time lived the life of a successful academic on the basis of image alone. Thompson arrived at Stanford's business department, ostensibly with a Ph.D. from Harvard and recent teaching experience at major universities. Although no one had offered him a job, he represented himself as a visiting scholar and convinced the business school to provide him with an office. From this base he presented himself as a prestigious researcher and spent his time setting up appointments with anyone likely to hire him as a consultant, meanwhile tooling around campus trying to pick up women in his Lancia automobile with mink seat covers. His pièce de résistance was to organize a large conference at the Stanford business school, to which he invited the foremost experts in international development. When these worthy scholars arrived, they found that the only item on the agenda was Thompson himself, dressed in his rumpled blue blazer, who addressed them in a rambling monologue for three hours. His lecture made so little sense and so many people angry they began an investigation, which revealed him to be a complete fraud.

▪ KEEP A GOOD ATTITUDE ▪

Be careful not to develop a jaundiced attitude about graduate school and the professors. It won't help you to become angry because you perceive that "they don't care about students in this place." It's true that your adviser and other professors will likely be too busy to care much about you, but this isn't because they mean you ill. It is because the academic system demands that to get ahead they must spend as little time as possible with students. Therefore, as Shakespeare wrote in *Richard II*:

> . . . lay aside life-harming heaviness,
> And entertain a cheerful disposition.

This is easier said than done, particularly during some of the low points of writing your thesis, but do avoid some of the more self-destructive patterns, such as griping with other disenchanted graduate students, which can reinforce your negativity and earn you a reputation with the faculty as a loser with a bad attitude. Also, don't make philosophical statements by, for example, refusing to cut your hair or brush your teeth. One Harvard ecology student created such a distinctive air by smoking the strongest French cigarettes and refusing to bathe that the graduate secretary kept a can of air freshener in her office specifically to hose down his chair after every visit, no matter how brief. Needless to say, when he needed an administrative favor, she didn't rush to his aid.

Progress is the best antidote to getting sour. If you feel yourself getting stale or bored, arrange to go to a conference or travel to visit a colleague at another campus. Throw yourself into correspondence, start a new research project, or try to arrange some field research.

Although Ben Jonson said, "It's merry when gossips meet," don't be one. The professors will gossip about you, but you should never gossip negatively about professors. Word may get back to them, and an enemy on a key committee could scuttle your ship. It may be hard to restrain yourself, since there will be times when you need to blow off steam and other students will encourage you, but *make it a firm rule never to say bad things within the university community.* (Also, try to be friendly and uncompetitive with other graduate students, since they may be your best resources for information and support.)

• BE KIND TO SUPPORT STAFF •

One of the most common mistakes of both grad students and professors is to treat secretaries and support staff with condescension. Considerations

BE KIND TO SUPPORT STAFF

of human decency aside, this is really stupid because these people can either make life easy for you or not. If they choose to make your life hell, the chances are you won't even know it. It will seem an accident that your petition for a deadline extension was lost, or that the chairman's schedule is always too full to see you, or that the librarian never has change for the photocopier when you're going crazy trying to meet a deadline. One grad student says:

> I went out of my way to befriend the secretaries because, since I've been one, I know how much power they have. They've been

there for seventeen years, so they know everything. On secretary's day, a friend and I gave the secretaries champagne and flowers. I call the chairman's secretary, who's sixty years old, "Mrs. Green," which she likes, and all the other students call her "Joan." How would you like it if you were sixty and some twenty-year-old you hardly knew called you "Joan"? Because I've treated them nicely, the secretaries really help me out. For example, they tell me what's happening behind the scenes, during faculty meetings. Also, there was a choice job opening, with thirty graduate students applying, and somehow my application made it to the top of the pile while some of the others got temporarily misplaced.

▪ DON'T BE TIMID ▪

It is easy to shrink from pushing yourself forward, but you've got to do it. You simply must see your adviser regularly, hobnob with your colleagues, discreetly show off in classes, and confront problems head-on. If you have problems doing this, check with your school for counseling in assertiveness training or handling stress.

▪ CORRESPONDENCE ▪

Begin professional correspondences as soon as you can. Letter writing should be a regular task on your "to do" list. If you can find a reasonable excuse to write to someone, do so. In the professional world it is acceptable, for example, to send copies of your recently published papers to anyone working in the field who might be interested. Don't necessarily expect a response the first time—it is a realistic goal just to start by getting someone familiar with your work. You can also write letters responding to academic papers or opinion pieces published in journals like *Science*. If someone wrote something that fired you up, there's no harm in letting him know it. You can also write follow-up notes to people you meet at conferences or other professional venues, and you can include copies of your publications. You can be helpful by including copies of *other* people's publications that you think acquaintances might be interested in. Avoid asking people you don't know well for copies of *their* recent papers—although this was standard procedure before the age of photocopying, it is now considered an imposition. It is less annoying if you ask them what they have published recently so that you can track it down yourself.

▪ CONFERENCES ▪

You should attend a number of conferences where you can integrate yourself with your field. Look on the conferences as employment markets. You can meet researchers for whom you might someday be working and listen to them present their research. Use every opportunity to meet important people in your field, especially asking your adviser or other colleagues to introduce you (hopefully they will say kind words about you). Don't be shy—politic like mad and be charming. The more conferences you go to, the more people you will know and the more comfortable you will get.

When you run into someone for the second or third time he or she will seem like an old friend.

Begin delivering conference papers or giving seminars on your work as soon as possible. Find out which conferences give special awards for outstanding graduate papers. Good presentations will get you noticed and may generate new invitations to speak or even job offers. Again, consult your adviser to determine what parts of your own research lend themselves to good presentations. You can avoid duplication of writing effort if your conference presentations are essentially oral renditions of the same papers that you are submitting to journals, rather than covering entirely new subjects.

Most graduate students and indeed most professors are lousy public speakers and their presentations are boring. Make yours stand out. If a member of the search committee remembers an impressive presentation of yours when you are applying for a job, you'll have succeeded in distinguishing yourself from the rest of the applicant pool.

If money to get to conferences is a problem, check with your adviser or department. Your professor may be able to pay your way on a grant or the department often will have a small pot of money for just this purpose. Duke University, for example, maintains a Dean's Fund for travel by advanced graduate students who are asked to speak. Duke finds that "students have found this opportunity particularly helpful as a means to future employment contacts and overall professional development." Check into the possibility of travel aid early, since funds are usually limited. (Remember, one of the things to find out when you are looking at possible graduate schools is whether the school or the professor will have money for you to travel to meetings.) Many conferences also will waive application fees for students or reduce them to below the published student rate if you plead poverty. Also, check with the conference organizers to see if they have arranged special low airfares or hotel rates for attendees, although such "special" rates are often higher than some other discounted rates you may be able to find on your own.

Help organize conferences or seminars if you can. Many students have given a big boost to their careers by acting as conference coordinators. Often a professor nominally organizes a conference, but the student actually contacts the speakers and handles logistics. If there isn't a seminar series, you could organize one. By being involved with conference coordination you can rapidly get on a first-name basis with the big names in your field. One successful organizer told me, "As the conference organization progressed, I found I was treated differently by all the faculty. Instead of a student I was treated as a peer." Organizing a conference can be a mammoth job—expect to take a term doing it—but it can be well worth it in terms of political payoff. If the collected papers delivered at the conference are published as a book of proceedings, you may find yourself involved with editing, giving you further interaction with the contributors. Some graduate organizers of conferences even become full-fledged editors of proceedings volumes and receive royalties from the publishers.

■ COMMITTEES ■

You should push yourself to serve on academic committees. Again, ask your adviser about which committees students can serve on and how they are elected or appointed. Set a goal of getting on at least one committee per year. Eric Fajer, a biology student at Harvard, felt that serving on committees was one of the smartest things he did; it helped him to feel comfortable and collegial with the professors as well as to understand how academic procedures and politics worked. While the students on committees didn't have a vote, their opinions were often solicited and he felt that his presence made a difference in several decisions. When it comes time for your job search, committee service may count as administrative experience, marking you as the eager young assistant professor type.

■ PAPERS ■

Dear Contributor, Thank you for not sending us anything lately. It suits our needs.

—CHARLES M. SCHULZ, UNSOLICITED REJECTION LETTER TO
SNOOPY IN "PEANUTS"

If you are a doctoral student, set yourself the goal of publishing at least two or three papers in professional journals before you graduate, and at least one if you are a master's student. Because academic career advancement is closely tied to the number of publications, if you intend on an academic career you will need to publish vigorously throughout your professional life.

The benefits of publishing in graduate school are numerous. First, your adviser can teach you the ins and outs of what can be a complicated process. Next, publication in a peer-reviewed journal means that your research has been certified by the reviewers as a significant contribution; when you apply for jobs, the hiring committees have what amounts to a positive independent evaluation of your work. You have shown yourself capable of the professional skills involved in publication, including writing and revising. May Lim, a master's student in computer science, published a paper during school and when she was job hunting she found that prospective employers saw her accomplishment as a sign of initiative and advanced professional ability.

Early publication is also a good way to minimize problems with your thesis committee. It becomes very difficult for the thesis committee to find significant fault with your research if it has already been judged mature and useful. In some departments your thesis can virtually be a collection of previously published papers. Some students have used published papers to fulfill course requirements. One student co-authored a paper on utilization and conservation of tropical forests which was used as the basis of a report to Congress by the Office of Technology Assessment. The student successfully argued to his department that if he knew enough about tropical forest ecology to brief Congress, then he knew enough to skip an introductory course on the same subject.

Finally, the feelings of accomplishment you get when you publish your own work can be a very important step in developing your self-image as a professional researcher. Because grad students typically are insecure about whether their ideas are really worth anything, publication that affirms the value of work can be a wonderful tonic. You will find that your first publication awakens a powerful hunger to get in print again, providing impetus to continue with research.

How do you get published? You are lucky if your department makes a publishable paper one of the prerequisites for qualification, because the department then has a strong motivation for teaching you how to get a paper published. If it doesn't, you still aren't entirely on your own. Ask your adviser and other professors for guidance.

As your thesis plan develops in consultation with your adviser, ask his help in planning discrete units of research that can rapidly give publishable results. Then get his help in reviewing paper drafts and in deciding where to submit them (usually it is considered bad form to submit a paper to more than one journal at a time).

Start the publication process early; it usually takes a year or two from submission to publication. Because you can lose so much time waiting for what may turn out to be a rejection, it is important to be realistic about whether a paper is likely to be accepted by a particular journal. Ask your adviser to help you choose as prestigious a journal as possible *where there is a realistic chance of publication.* Regardless of the quality of the work, most journals have prejudices for and against certain types of work, so consultation with your adviser and others is key in targeting journals.

Because each journal has its preferred styles of writing, length, punctuation, and so on, you will need to craft the piece somewhat differently every time you submit it. A journal's guidelines are usually printed in each issue or you can write the journal and ask for them.

You can increase your publication rate by dividing your thesis or other publishable research into as many papers as possible. In academia, you are better off publishing three small papers than you are publishing one large paper containing the same information. So you should split up your thesis rather than try to publish it in toto. You also may be able to publish much of your work in toto as a book, but this will not preclude the same material from being published as articles. Also, you can often publish essentially the same or slightly different information in different places, provided it is rewritten somewhat to contain new data or interpretations. For example, I have republished essentially the same paper in three journals, five conference proceedings volumes, and a textbook (all dutifully acknowledging previous publication).

Don't be discouraged if the first journal you submit to doesn't accept your piece. If it is turned down, you have several options. If you feel the faults enumerated by the reviewers are valid and fixable, you can fix them and resubmit. (Even for pieces that are accepted, it is usual for substantial revisions to be requested by the editors.) You can also write and *politely* contest the reviewers' criticisms if you feel they are wrong; if your arguments are good, the editor may reconsider. If the first journal still won't publish your paper, try another. Most decent work is publishable somewhere; you just have to find the right place. So keep submitting your paper to different journals, with appropriate revisions, until you find a taker.

Don't be satisfied to have just one paper out being reviewed; as soon as one is sent out, start working on another so that you maintain a cycle: you should always have some papers out for review, others in the revision stage, and others being researched and written. And if it starts to look as though you will never get published, you can shoot for the rejection record—the popular book *Zen and the Art of Motorcycle Maintenance* was rejected 121 times before publication.

Even before you start your thesis, while still searching for a topic you may be able to do short bits of research in collaboration or consultation with your adviser that can yield publishable results. Reed Noss, an ecologist, had an amazing number of review papers published on a wide variety of topics before he graduated. Whenever he took a course that required a term paper, he planned each paper specifically with publication in mind. He consulted with the professor and did the quality library research and writing necessary for publication. He was getting A's, impressing his professors, and publishing papers.

If you are in a field where co-authored papers are common, it may be helpful to co-author your first paper or two with your adviser. You can expect to do the bulk of the research and writing in return for second or possibly first authorship, but you will receive guidance in producing a publishable paper. One advantage to co-authorship with an established researcher is that your name becomes linked with his or hers. Additionally, co-authorship can help you deal with the politics of getting published. If your co-author is a big name, the paper will be read more seriously and the reviewers are much less likely to trash the paper over small details or because they are in a bad mood. Some big names can get almost anything published because no one dares refute them—even though reviews are anonymous, identities can slip out. (Often there are so few people in a field that you can tell who the reviewer was by his writing style or choice of insults.)

If you do publish your first paper alone, ask if your adviser will help get it published by writing a cover letter praising the paper to the editor you are sending it to. If you pick a journal where the editor is a friend of your adviser, so much the better.

A final bit of advice: try not to get grandiose when writing your papers. They should be modest and sharply focused on results. Reviewers are particularly hard on uppity youngsters who try to revise an entire field or present moderately interesting results as a major breakthrough.

14

. . . .

MASTER'S COMPREHENSIVE
AND Ph.D. QUALIFYING
EXAMINATIONS

. . . .

> I was thrown out of college for cheating on a metaphysics exam: I looked within the soul of the boy sitting next to me.
>
> —WOODY ALLEN

MOST MASTER'S AND PH.D. STUDENTS MUST TAKE A COMPREHENSIVE EXAM that tests their knowledge of their field's subject matter. Master's students take their exams shortly before graduation, while Ph.D. students take their exams at the end of their course work, usually near the end of their second year in the program. Some students end up taking two sets of exams—if you are in a master's program and will continue as a doctoral student in the same program, you may first have to pass a master's exam to enter the Ph.D. program and then pass a Ph.D. exam within the following year or so to qualify you as a doctoral candidate. For the purposes of clarity, I will use the term "master's exam" to indicate an examination used only to determine a student's fitness to receive the master's degree, regardless of whether the degree is terminal or leads to the Ph.D. "Qualifying exam" denotes only the Ph.D. exam.

· MASTER'S EXAMS ·

Because the course of study in a master's program generally lasts only one to two years, the exam structure is usually simple—there is a single comprehensive exam near the end of the second year to test whether you deserve your degree. Master's exams may be either written or oral, and are typically given by a committee of three to four members, including your graduate adviser. They generally last from one to several hours, much less than the typical Ph.D. exam.

As in Ph.D. qualifying exams, examiners generally reserve the right to focus on material not specifically covered in class, maintaining that they are testing whether your general knowledge of the field is what it should be at the master's level. However, some departments graciously will provide you with lists of the material you are expected to master. In some cases you can choose the areas on which you will be tested so that they reflect your own concentration of interest.

The difficulty of these exams will in part be determined by the nature of the program. If you are in a terminal master's program, the department has little incentive to fail you, so the exam is likely to be relatively easy. If you are in a program leading to a Ph.D., your master's exam is likely to be particularly tough if it is used to cut people out of the doctoral program. Therefore, if you will be in fierce competition for a few Ph.D. program slots, take the exam seriously and study hard.

For nonterminal master's degrees leading to a Ph.D., departments often give different levels of passes, reflecting their judgment about your ability to do Ph.D. work. The University of Wisconsin's English department gives a Pass with Distinction, Pass 1, Pass 2, and Terminal Pass. Terminal Passes cannot go on for the Ph.D., and Pass 2s are discouraged from doing so.

▪ PH.D. QUALIFYING EXAMS ▪

Ph.D. qualifying examinations are large and terrifying. Their purpose is to certify that students who pass are qualified to be Ph.D. candidates. They are called different things by different departments, including: qualifying exams, comprehensives, general exams, certificate exams, doctoral exams, or preliminary exams. The reason these exams may be called "preliminaries" is that they come before the oral thesis defense. The oral thesis defense may also be called an "oral exam" in some departments, but don't confuse this with the qualifying oral exam.

Qualifying exams take many forms, but usually they have one part that focuses on breadth of knowledge in the field and another that focuses in depth on a specialty area (hopefully the one you've studied!). In addition, they often have both written and oral portions (hence "orals"). In some cases the portion of the exam on breadth of knowledge may be taken at a separate time from that on the specialty areas.

My brother's experience as a student in the English department at the University of Michigan was typical. There, each student chooses four specialty areas on which he will be tested. Then, in consultation with his adviser, he creates a list of the most important books in the four areas and spends a year or so preparing to be cross-examined on the contents. My brother chose the history of drama, fantasy and science fiction, Romantic and Victorian poetry, and the American Renaissance. The qualifying exam consisted of lengthy written exams in each of the four areas. Once he had passed these, there was a two-hour oral exam on the same areas in which the examination committee probed for weakness.

Examining committees are typically composed of four or five professors with specialties in the various areas to be covered. Usually, the examiners are chosen by the graduate school, and the adviser may influence their selection. It is common for one member of the examining committee to be from an outside department to act as a referee in preventing unnecessary roughness during oral examination. In one English department the outside person traditionally stands by with a stopwatch to prevent eager faculty members from exceeding eight minutes of inquisition apiece.

The actual written exam may take several days. Mario Ramos, a biology doctoral student, had to write fifteen pages in each of five areas, open book, over five days. He says:

> You felt that you could never stop writing or thinking about it. It was so much pressure that you couldn't think about original ideas to defend. You just worried about getting the right ideas down with adequate bibliographical references. The only good thing about the qualification exam was that for a month ahead the students got together in a support group and helped study in scheduled meetings to cover material.

In an attempt at standardization, it is common for the questions on written exams to be approved by the entire examining committee. However, the nature of the questions can be as off-the-wall as the professors who make them up, so it's difficult to describe a typical question.

Questions in biology have included:

• Compare the flight of vertebrates and invertebrates with respect to physiology, anatomy, and evolution.
• With respect to the amniotic egg, describe why its evolution was important, how it evolved, and how it functions physiologically.
• Trace, from a historical perspective, developments in understanding cell membrane function.

Questions in English have included:

- Choose four landscape poems, two from the Romantic period and two from the Victorian, and use them to show similarities and differences between the two nineteenth-century periods.
- Discuss how the incorporation of colloquial speech into English and American literature during the past two hundred years has had theoretical and practical consequences.
- Discuss the treatment of science and technology in the works of at least two of the following authors: Dickens, Butler, Hardy, Tennyson, Mill, Carlyle, Arnold, Ruskin.

Oral questioning typically lasts three or four hours. The field is wide open for questions, including some you couldn't possibly be expected to answer. One former professor, Peter Jutro, told me that he regularly asked his students an obscure or even self-contradictory question. What he wanted was an honest statement that the student didn't know the answer, followed by thoughtful analysis of the question and an explanation of how to do the research necessary to answer the question. He did this because "we're not only concerned with what people know but also with how they think." Look out for questions on recent literature in your field, even articles appearing right up to the exam, since professors often use the orals to try to figure out if you keep up with your journal reading.

Qualifying exams are for many the most purely terrifying part of graduate school. Although having to write a thesis may provoke overhanging feelings of doom, the exam stimulates more immediate terror. While it's natural to be nervous before the exams, you can do a lot to be prepared.

SCOPING OUT MASTER'S AND
· DOCTORAL EXAMS ·

Start early to find out what will be covered on the exam before you even begin studying. Be sure to review exams from previous years—this will give you the best sense of what will be asked. They will probably be on file with the department, which will often provide study lists of suggested books and articles as well. Ask older graduate students about their experiences. They may be able to give you tips on questions that particular professors are likely to ask. Draw on your adviser for support and guidance since he or she should have an interest in your success.

Find out who will be on the examining committee by asking your adviser or departmental secretary. Each examiner is likely to have special areas, corresponding to their professional interests and prejudices, in which they are prone to ask questions. Therefore, tune your studying and exam responses to fit the committee's character. If, for example, you know that Professor Curmudgeon believes that applying sociobiological theory to human beings is irresponsible, you will know not to champion sociobiology in your exam. Don't be so foolish as to omit reading the important research of your examining faculty, and when it comes time to take the exam, make sure you cite their work.

Ask professors, particularly those who will be on the examining committee, what they would advise you to concentrate on. Don't pay too much attention if they tell you the questions will be easy; they don't share a graduate student's perspective. For example, one neurophysiologist promised a zoology student that he would write very general exam questions and then asked about arcane minutiae, including "Describe exactly what happens biochemically to a cell membrane poisoned with the African arrow poison ouabain after five minutes, after half an hour, and after two hours."

Don't assume that the exam will be restricted to material covered in your courses—examiners for both doctoral and master's exams may go beyond the courses you have actually had and question you about material they feel you should have covered, even if you didn't. Princeton states explicitly that the "examination is not restricted to the content of graduate courses but is comprehensive in character." This comprehensive nature is why you must scope out the exam ahead of time so that you can fill in holes not covered by course work.

■ PREPARING FOR THE EXAM ■

Make sure you leave yourself enough time to study. Many students take a term in which they do nothing except study for the exam. Many students study for six to twelve months. The best defense against nervousness is to really know the material. Perversely, the adviser of a biology student at the University of Minnesota told him not to make a special effort to study, because "an open mind and a sense of humor" would see him through the exam. Fortunately, my friend didn't listen, temporarily stopped his research, and devoted himself to studying for six months. He reviewed all his past course work, as well as other areas suggested by previous exams and the examining professors. He did well on both written and oral exams, despite the fact that they turned out to be very difficult and several students failed.

Develop a list of possible exam questions from the sources mentioned above and research the answers. Have your adviser critique your list to see if you have forgotten important questions. The list will give him something concrete to respond to.

It will help if you work closely with other students facing the exam. If your exam is the type in which many of the graduate students will be asked the same questions, you can use the support group to help scope out the exam, pooling your knowledge about subjects you are likely to be tested on. As you review, you can use each other for encouragement. You can set up mock orals, in which each student takes turns being interrogated by the others. This can help you identify weaknesses and become familiar with answering questions under pressure. (Even if your qualifying exams will be on different subject areas from those of your fellow students, you can still help each other with mock orals.)

Stay focused on what you are likely to be asked. The most foolish orals taker I know was a plant ecologist who became unadaptively cosmic and decided that the best way to prepare for his qualifying exams was to study painting, listen to music, and contemplate nature. He believed this course of study would free his mind to see underlying patterns in biology, thereby astonishing his examiners. They were not too astonished to fail him.

▪ TAKING THE EXAM ▪

Several successful Ph.D.s counseled me that students should not put off the qualifying exam out of fear. Delaying the exam is one of the most common ways students increase their time in school. On the other hand, taking the exam too early can also be a mistake. By talking to graduate students who have already taken the exam you'll be able to find out how much studying is necessary.

If you have asked your examiners for guidance, studied thoroughly, and practiced answering questions with your fellow students, you should be well prepared. I won't bore you by telling you to bring No. 2 pencils, but do get everything ready that you need for the exam a day or two ahead of time, so that you are calm and prepared as the exam approaches. Don't do last-minute cramming—you will be tested on what you have learned over the preceding year or more, and the amount you can learn the last day or two isn't worth the fatigue. Do what you need to do to be your calmest, sharpest self. Regular exercise in the days leading up to the exam can help keep stress levels low so you are rested.

This may sound odd, but remind your committee to come to the exam. One student's professor forgot to show up for the orals. After waiting an hour, they located him at home mowing the lawn. By the time he got there the student was so exhausted from tension that she failed. Fortunately, she was allowed to retake her orals and passed.

Orals are particularly trying. You will feel more comfortable if you have practiced public speaking and if you have had frequent contact with the examining professors. During the exam, if you are asked something you don't know, don't freak out. The examiners are trying to push the limits of what you know, so expect that they will find gaps. It's not like a normal course exam where you are expected to know everything. If you don't know, say so instead of blathering nonsense and irritating the examiners. If an answer comes to you later, you can tell the examiners that you're ready to answer the question at that point. If you feel terrified during oral examination, don't worry, nearly everyone is, and the examiners expect it and will usually feel sympathetic.

▪ IF YOU FAIL ▪

Most schools give you a second chance to pass master's or doctoral qualifying exams. In some cases you may only need to make up the part that you failed. The second time around you may have a better idea of your weaknesses and can study more effectively. Even if you do fail absolutely, there can still be hope. At Cornell, one student failed his exam and left school, earning a master's at another university. His master's included an extensive thesis that was so good Cornell agreed to take him back as a Ph.D. candidate if he passed his orals and extended his master's thesis to Ph.D. length.

15

CHOOSING AND
MANAGING YOUR THESIS
COMMITTEE

Lots of folks confuse bad management with destiny.

—KIN HUBBARD

WHEN THE OTHER SIGNERS OF THE DECLARATION OF INDEPENDENCE BEGAN changing his draft around, Thomas Jefferson got upset at what he termed "mutilations," so Ben Franklin gave him some good advice. "I have made it a rule, whenever within my power, to avoid becoming the draftsman of papers to be reviewed by a public body." This is a great idea, but unfortunately your committee can mutilate your thesis if they want to. And they will. As H. G. Wells said, "No passion in the world is equal to the passion to alter someone else's draft." To keep the mayhem to a minimum, you need to keep firm but subtle control of your committee.

▪ WHAT DOES THE COMMITTEE DO? ▪

The thesis committee's formal obligations are to approve your thesis proposal and to judge the quality of your thesis and its defense. They also have a less clearly defined obligation to guide you in your research. Your thesis adviser (the committee chairperson) will be highly involved with the development of your thesis throughout the process, while the other members will vary in how involved they become. Some will be glad to let you go your own way, while others will want to exercise a high degree of control. Their involvement will depend both on their personal styles and on the degree to which their own research interests are related to your and how well these expectations are being met. Ask: Do you meet regularly enough? Does your adviser feel that she has adequate information on your progress? Does she need more frequent progress reports? Are you devoting enough time to research versus your other duties, such as teaching? Does she feel that you are maturing professionally? Are there ways the two of you can improve how you work together? Does she feel that you are responsive enough to her criticisms?

If your adviser gives you answers to these questions that are too general, follow up by asking for specifics. For example, if your adviser says that she is disappointed with how slowly your thesis is coming along, ask how she feels it can be speeded up. Has she noted where the problems lie?

These questions about your working relationship are often awkward to bring up, and both you and your adviser will have a tendency to avoid them. However, because it is so easy for misunderstandings to subtly poison a good relationship, you must make sure that these issues are raised *before there are problems*. If you find it awkward to bring them up casually during your normal progress meetings, it may be useful to tell your adviser that you want to schedule a special meeting to explore whether there are ways that you can be more responsive to her expectations.

Usually, your thesis committee will meet in its entirety only a time or two, often just for your thesis defense. However, additional meetings of the full committee may be helpful from time to time in order to get approval for your progress to date and to iron out disagreements involving multiple committee members. If you think such a meeting would be helpful, approach your adviser to see if he will agree to arrange one. A good way to structure the meeting is as an annual progress report from you, in which you present your completed work and plans for the future and ask for the committee's suggestions. This presentation can help you get accustomed to speaking in front of your committee. More important is that you and your adviser can use the meeting to make sure that everyone is in agreement on the direction you are taking and use peer pressure to herd troublemakers into line. If the committee members agree "on the record" that your research is on track, it will be more difficult for them later to change their minds as you near completion of the thesis. Many graduate students have had a committee member orally approve research in private consultation, only to later renege and demand substantial revision.

CIRCULATE MEMOS AND REPORTS

Whenever you meet with your adviser or another committee member, take notes and write a memo that reflects your understanding of the meeting. Say, "I plan to do X based on your recommendations." This will minimize misunderstandings. One student had typical problems with an adviser who couldn't remember what orders he had given from one meeting to the next:

> My adviser continually contradicted himself when he gave me instructions on my thesis drafts. First he would say, "Take out everything remotely editorial and leave only results." Then in the next meeting he would say, "This is so boring. It's only results. Why isn't there any commentary?" This back-and-forth craziness went on for months, and whenever I would tell him that he was contradicting what he'd said before, he would say something like "Oh, but that wasn't what I meant," so the whole problem was turned around to be my fault because I didn't listen closely. Finally, I started giving him notes of our conversations, so that he would recognize how contradictory he was. After that, things went smoother, and he even ended up apologizing. He wasn't a bad guy, just a poor communicator.

Whenever there is a full-scale committee meeting, make sure that the decisions taken are clearly spelled out and mutually agreed to. You can guide the committee toward clear decisions by asking, for example, "So what you want me to do is X. Correct?" Once decisions have been made, there should be a clear, written record of what was decided (often different committee members will come away from a meeting with very different ideas about what has been decided). Either write a memo yourself, summing up the major conclusions of the meeting, or ask your adviser to write one to circulate to all the members.

You should also make regular written progress reports, approximately one a month, to be circulated to your committee members. These reports act like newsletters, informing them of your existence and convincing them that you are moving ahead. They can also be used as the basis for discussion in regular meetings with your adviser and to help you plan and review your own performance.

PRESENT YOUR THESIS AS YOU GO ALONG

Avoid the temptation to show your committee how good you are by going off somewhere (I chose Texas) and writing your complete thesis, presenting it with a flourish and expecting applause. Suddenly presenting a complete thesis is a real bonehead move, both practically and politically. If you pull this, you will almost certainly be told to do serious revision. One master's student told me:

After my proposal was accepted, I charged off and wrote the whole thesis in three months without checking in with my adviser at all. When I presented it, my adviser was very angry because I hadn't asked her for advice, even though my thesis was good enough to pass and finally did. I think she thought up extra revisions for me to make just to teach me a lesson.

I made the same mistake myself. I wrote my entire thesis without getting any chapters reviewed as I went along. Between the time I started writing and the time I finished, my committee changed their minds about how my thesis should be structured, so I ended up rewriting all nine chapters. To avoid these sorts of problems, you should present chapters one by one as you finish polished drafts. This way you can involve the committee early and get each chapter certified as you go along. This is particularly important if your research direction changes substantially after your proposal has been approved.

You should make certain that the drafts you give your committee for review are *polished* drafts. First impressions will stick with your committee.

One of the most common reasons students are slowed down is that professors sit on manuscripts for long periods without reading them. In my own case, my first adviser took fourteen months to read my thesis proposal, losing three copies before I gave him a fourth and forced him to read it in my presence. To deal with this problem, when you give chapter drafts to your committee members, ask them to finish their reviews by a set date. Obviously you can't force your advisers to read your work, but you have more hope if you can get them to set firm deadlines with you, rather than accepting an "I'll read it during the next few weeks."

When your adviser or other committee members read your drafts, make sure you ask them for detailed written instructions on what should be changed. Not only will these give you a clear understanding of what changes to make, but also they will be documentary proof that a committee member actually told you to do what you did.

If one of your committee members is inadequately explicit in his written comments, tactfully suggest how much more helpful it would be if he were to annotate throughout, pointing out areas where clarity is poor or there are other faults. If his comments are too generalized or unclear, ask questions to focus the criticisms. If your reviewer says, "This section is weak," probe to discover exactly how it is weak. Is it lack of clarity in the writing or the logic of the point itself? Ask him how he would rewrite it so that you can understand exactly the type of changes he has in mind.

SOLVING PROBLEMS WITH
■ YOUR COMMITTEE ■

CONFLICTS BETWEEN COMMITTEE MEMBERS

If there are substantial conflicts between committee members, you will feel the pain. Animosity between the committee members will rarely be directly expressed, but they will attempt to win a personal or theoretical battle using your thesis for a tug-of-war. Peter, an economics doctoral student, told this story:

> I'm in my fifth year and hung up because I can't seem to take control of my committee. They just keep fighting. The chairman is a neoclassical economist and the second person, influential in the department, is a Marxist. Of course they have totally different interpretations of how my thesis should go. I can't see any end in sight because my adviser keeps asking me to write more and more chapters, saying, "Gee, now you understand this, how about a new intellectual problem?" Meanwhile, the Marxist demands that I rewrite everything from his perspective. When I do this, the chairman finds it unacceptable and refuses to sign off. The worst thing is that now they are both getting angry with me for doing what the other guy says.

Another student's committee got along fine until her adviser refused to publish a second member's article in a book he was editing. The unpublished professor transferred his anger to the student. Jane said:

> I felt like I was wearing a sandwich board with a target on it. He kept treating me badly in class, and we finally had a scene where he actually told me that he hadn't even wanted me in the department, that my adviser had pulled strings to get me in, but that I wasn't good enough to have been admitted.

If this type of feuding begins affecting your ability to finish, you need to act as soon as possible, because things rarely get better without intervention. Your first recourse is your adviser—ask him or her for help. If your adviser can't solve it informally, a meeting of the full committee may be in order to try to find an amicable way around any academic differences. If the problem stems from political or personality conflicts, rational discussion is less likely to work and your best option is probably to jettison one of the troublemakers.

CONFLICTS BETWEEN YOU AND YOUR COMMITTEE MEMBERS

If you have trouble with your adviser or another committee member, you've got to act quickly before negative impressions solidify. As a first approach, talk openly with the person to try to find out where the disagreement lies and how to resolve it. Most problems are simple misunderstandings. If you can't resolve the problem on your own, seek mediation. If your problem is with a secondary committee member, discuss it with your adviser. If the problem is with your adviser, or if he or she can't help, seek an outside mediator, perhaps the department chairperson or university ombudsman.

Your final resort is to replace an adviser or committee member you can't get along with. Booting off a secondary committee member is likely to have only minor repercussions, particularly if you do it early in the thesis process. Firing an *adviser* is another matter. If you have invested several years in building a relationship with the adviser, breaking up is like a divorce, replete with rancor. Added to whatever bad feelings made you decide to remove him or her, the professor will now feel rejected. In my own case, I changed advisers toward the end of my second year after a nightmarish experience with my first one. I foolishly thought I could placate him by keeping him on as a committee member, but he remained so hostile and obstructionist that I finally had to remove him from the committee. My advice to you is that if you do fire an adviser, don't leave him on your committee where he can sabotage you. Also, if you do remove a committee member, hide your ill feelings and help him save face. Don't tell him (or anyone else in your department) your negative reasons for the personnel change.

OTHER TIPS FOR SOLVING CONFLICTS

- *Nip problems in the bud.* Peter, who was caught between the Marxist and the neoclassical economist, waited much too long to deal with a destructive situation. He should have moved quickly to make the committee confront the problem, and if there was no resolution, should have replaced one combatant.
- *Be assertive.* The committee owes you professional behavior, including regular meetings, fast readings of chapter drafts, and rapid resolution of conflicts. Don't be afraid to ask for what you are paying for.
- *Be flexible.* Don't lose sight of the fact that your thesis isn't going to be perfect; nor will many people read it. Therefore, don't be stubborn about changes (unless they require a huge amount of reworking). Don't squabble about how many angels can sit on the head of a pin and other picayune

theoretical points. Don't take issue with larger-scale theoretical orientations of your adviser and committee members (if you must debunk them, you can do it *after* you have your degree).

• *Get perspective.* It is easy for the average graduate student facing committee problems to be temporarily insane from stress. Therefore, talk extensively with other people about the problems you are facing. The other grad students in your support group may help, as could the ombudsman, close faculty friends, or the counseling center. However, be discreet about whom you talk to—word can get back.

• DISAPPEARANCES •

LOSING AN ADVISER

If your adviser—the committee chairperson—retires, dies, or leaves for another department, you are in a career-threatening predicament. Here is what happened to Pauline, who lost *two* advisers while at one of the country's top biology departments:

> My first adviser left to teach in England during my second year when I had just started my thesis, so I had to start over with a new adviser and a new thesis topic. This put me a year behind. My second adviser, Greg, was wonderful at guiding us (there were four graduate students in his lab, all working on fish population genetics). But Greg didn't get tenure, so he left for a job where he couldn't have graduate students, leaving all four of us students orphaned. Because he took his grants with him, we didn't even have money to buy the chemicals we needed for our research. At this stage I was too far along to start over, even though there was no one else in the department doing my type of research. Fortunately, I did find a wonderful professor who was willing to be my adviser, but the only thing we had in common was that we both worked on fish. Our research areas were miles apart—he was a paleontologist and I was a population geneticist on totally different groups of fish—so he couldn't help much professionally. I finally finished, but my career was definitely set back, and I did not end up with the teaching job I wanted.

Given the importance of an adviser who actively supports your research, if your adviser leaves for another university your best option is usually to go with him. This is common practice, and many professors who take new jobs stipulate as part of the deal that their present students come along. It may seem that moving across the country to follow an adviser is a painful option—and it is—but in most cases it will give you more chance of success than staying behind with an unsuitable replacement.

If you are unable to follow your adviser, you have three options, depending on how far along you are in your research. First, if you are just starting on your thesis, you may need to follow Pauline's example and find both a new adviser and a new thesis topic. Remember that you need to find an adviser who has wholehearted enthusiasm for your topic, and it will not do to merely substitute a marginally interested committee member. Therefore, the person you choose may not turn out to be an existing member of your committee, and you may even need to change schools if you can't find someone appropriate in your present department.

Second, if you are nearly through with your thesis, you definitely don't want to choose an adviser who will change the direction of your research. Therefore, your best bet is probably just to push ahead with your present committee, naming one of the members as chairperson, although you essentially want him or her to play only a caretaker role. Your new chairperson is more likely to play this role without making your life difficult if you have kept your committee well involved in your thesis development all along.

Third, your department might let you retain your old adviser as committee chairperson even though he or she is at a new school. This would only be sensible if you are nearly finished with your thesis. The greatest drawback to this solution is that your adviser's relations with the other department members are likely to be soured, whether because she didn't get tenure or because she left for a better job. Also, a long-distance academic relationship takes extra work. You will have to be very strict about sending drafts on a regular basis, making regular phone calls, and visiting as necessary.

There is one final pitfall for students who have lost their advisers. Many refuse to let go of the old adviser's expectations and values. They fail to recognize that any new adviser, even one who was on their committee and therefore was involved in the development of their thesis, will have different standards and expectations than their old adviser. Mary, an economics doctoral student, ran into this problem when her adviser died suddenly. She had been well along in her thesis, with excellent relations with her adviser. She says:

> I made a big mistake in assuming that because I had Tom's approval for my thesis, the new adviser would also approve. After all, he was one of my old committee members, and he'd never voiced any substantial objections when Tom was alive, so I made the mistake of

taking him for granted. I assumed that if I continued in the path my old adviser had laid out, I was doing my part and everything would be okay. But there were real problems when it came time to get my thesis approved. It turned out that my new adviser had had reservations all along about the methodology. Now that it was his responsibility, he demanded substantial revisions. This caught me by surprise at the last minute, so I didn't graduate when I expected.

REPLACING SECONDARY COMMITTEE MEMBERS

When a secondary committee member leaves for another job, your options are to retain the person as an outside committee member or to replace him or her. The choice is not as crucial as it would be if you lost your adviser, but you should still manage things with an eye toward minimizing trouble. If you must find a replacement, think of the new person as a student enrolling late in class who needs extra exposure to the material. You need to involve her in the process as quickly as possible, sell her on your thesis, and identify and defuse any problems right away.

16

. . . .

THE THESIS TOPIC:

FINDING IT

. . . .

It is not worthwhile to go around the world to count the cats in Zanzibar.

—Henry David Thoreau

YOUR CHOICE OF THESIS TOPIC WILL PLAY A LARGE PART IN DETERMINING HOW quickly you finish, whether you can convert your thesis into publishable papers, and whether you are in a hot field when hiring time comes along. Particularly if you are getting a Ph.D., your thesis will continue to affect your life long after you have received your degree. If you are hired as an assistant professor, your research work for at least several years after graduation will likely be an extension of your thesis research, and your first book will be a distillation or extension of your thesis. Since the thesis is so important, it's not surprising that many students find choosing a topic the single most excruciating task in graduate school. Nonetheless, it can be quite easy to find a good topic if you set about it the right way.

My friend Mary started out looking for a topic the wrong way. Her primary technique was to worry a lot, mulling over one poorly researched possibility after another. This is a technique that I also used unsuccessfully for more than a year. Roy Martin has called this common search method "dreaming in a vacuum." He points out that those who search for topics by backpacking through the mountains or sitting on park benches in quiet contemplation of their topics are likely to learn a lot about mountains and parks but little else. Superficial thinking about a variety of possible topics won't get you anywhere.

Mary began to believe that her only hope was a sudden burst of magical insight. Her student friends couldn't help much; either they were also waiting for a topic to mystically appear or they belonged to that discouraging minority who seem to know exactly what they want to do from the moment they arrive at graduate school. Finally, she realized the secret of finding a topic: ideas are generated by intellectual cross-fertilization and the process of problem solving. To find a topic you must dive into research, discuss the ideas that interest you with as many people as possible, and write about the subjects as much as you can. This process of intellectual exploration is the core strategy of this chapter.

WRONG WAY TO FIND A THESIS TOPIC

WHEN SHOULD YOU START ■ LOOKING? ■

Start as soon as you begin school. You will waste valuable time if you wait until after your course work or qualifying exams. If you at least start the process of choosing a topic right away, you can get ideas from your classes, books and articles you read, and discussions with professors. You never know what stray bit of information—such as a teacher mentioning in class that "little is known about the subject"—may lead you to a topic. You must be actively thinking about the search to be receptive to the information. Once you have found your topic, then additional courses, seminars, and so on can be chosen to prepare you for actually doing the thesis.

One English grad student started looking for a thesis topic as soon as she started school, asking professors for suggestions and examining her course reading for possible topics. She says:

> I kept asking myself whenever I came across anything interesting, "Could this be a dissertation?" I was the only one to start looking so early. The other students kept asking me, "Why are you thinking about that now? We're not supposed to have a topic until the second semester of the third year." Now, even though I'm only a year and a half into the program, I'm already working on my thesis, I've written

two papers on my thesis topic, I'm taking my orals more than a year early, and most of the other people haven't even started looking for a thesis topic.

• WHAT IS A THESIS, ANYWAY? •

The words "thesis" and "dissertation" are often used interchangeably, although some universities use "thesis" for the product of a master's program and "dissertation" for that of the Ph.D. A thesis, particularly on the Ph.D. level, is expected to be an original contribution to knowledge. According to David Madsen, author of a book on thesis writing, "original" means "the potential to do at least one of the following: uncover new facts or principles, suggest relationships that were previously unrecognized, challenge existing truths or assumptions, afford new insights into little-understood phenomena, or suggest new interpretations of known facts that can alter man's perception of the world around him." However, as I discuss below, the degree of originality need not be earthshaking.

It can help if you think of the thesis as the answer to a research *question* rather than as just a written report on research. Rather than "thesis topic," think "thesis question," for you are essentially looking for a question that is intriguing enough that you are willing to take a year or more in answering it. Thinking of questions will help you to see the thesis as the outgrowth of an investigational process. You begin with a major question, develop subordinate questions that help you answer it, and plan *and refine along the way* research to answer these questions. Even if you aren't sure in the beginning where your research will take you, if you find a good question and answer it with well-planned research you will do well. Many researchers find that their experiments show the opposite of what they expected, but these results are just as valid and useful as the expected ones.

When it comes time to write your thesis proposal, it should include a statement of your basic and subsidiary questions, as well as laying out the research you intend to use to find the answers. An example of a research question is: What evolutionary selection pressures affect size in male pygmy swordtail fish? Subsidiary questions are: Do females choose their mates on the basis of size? Does male size convey advantage in fights over females? Is there size-dependent predation on males? Research questions in other fields include: How does the health of the American economy affect family stability? How did Jack London's socialist politics affect his writing? Does assigning grade school students to different groups according to academic ability enhance scholastic advancement?

WHY IT'S SCARY: THE MYTH OF
▪ THE PERFECT THESIS ▪

Many people become paralyzed because they are so afraid of choosing a topic that isn't perfect. This paralysis prevents them from beginning the most important step in finding a topic—actively exploring one or more possibilities. Choosing a thesis is a lot like choosing a mate—there are thousands upon thousands of thesis topics with which you can live happily ever after. After you have chosen and settled down with your thesis, the odds are that it will seem like the perfect one. Because there are so many good thesis possibilities for you, it is easy to find a topic if you search actively. Although there exist thesis topics that would fail because they are too large or otherwise unresearchable, if you thoughtfully choose a topic in consultation with your committee, the chances of failure due to the topic itself are small. There are some pitfalls to look out for, but I will warn you about them below.

If I can demystify the thesis process for you, finding a topic may not be so terrifying. One reason for the typical psychological block is that the student gives too much weight to the fact that a thesis is supposed to be an "original" or "significant" contribution to the field. You ask, "How can I, who have never done anything more ambitious than a term paper, make a significant contribution to the field?"

To start with, a "significant" or "original" contribution doesn't mean that you must come up with Nobel Prize–level research. My thesis described for the first time the sexual behavior of a particular species of swordtail fish of the genus *Xiphophorus*. Even though many papers had been written about the sexual behavior of other species in the genus, I used standard techniques and applied them to a new species. Similarly, one sociology student could study the effect of long-term unemployment on Chinese immigrant family structure, while another could do the same for a different ethnic group without fear of redundancy. Because your thesis can build upon similar (or *very* similar) work by other students or faculty researchers, it is relatively easy to come up with possible thesis topics by studying other theses and papers in areas that interest you.

There may even be drawbacks to being too original. As Machiavelli said, "There is nothing more difficult to take in hand, more perilous to conduct, or more uncertain in its success than to take the lead in the introduction of a new order of things." A student whose research is brilliant but off the beaten path may have difficulty in being recognized by the academic community compared with someone who pushes out the boundaries of knowledge slightly by elaborating on the theme of his mentor. Here is one example: Svante Arrhenius, the brilliant late-nineteenth-century chemist who postulated the greenhouse effect. His Ph.D. thesis elaborated the first correct theory of electrolytic conduction. However, he received the lowest possible passing grade on his thesis because his advisers, inured to a constant parade of incorrect theories by other workers, assumed that his also could not be correct. Nineteen years later his thesis won the Nobel Prize. All of this is not to say that you should not be brilliantly original in your research if you can pull it off, but that route also has pitfalls.

Even if you look for them, finding truly new paths can be difficult. Once, during the depths of my own topic search, I was occupied in the twin pursuits of brooding and cultivating my garden, when I turned over a rock, discovering a population of slugs. Each of the slugs was home to a gathering of small white mites that ran happily over the slug's mucus without getting stuck. Eureka! I would study the unique symbiotic relationship of my newly discovered slug mites, for I was certain that such an obscure and lowly topic could not have been studied in depth. I was wrong. Further investigation found that there exist several world experts on slug mites and my enthusiasm for the topic did not justify crowding in among them.

Therefore, instead of thinking of yourself as Einstein, think of yourself as an apprentice, learning techniques and ways of thinking from your adviser and other professors. At this stage, you aren't a great master who will find the secret of the universe, or even the secret of art history or biochemistry. You just have to find the secret of something as trivial as pygmy swordtail mating behavior and leave your magnum opus till later in life. Right now your goal is to learn how to do research from someone who is very good at it and then to demonstrate this knowledge with a good thesis. Your thesis is your final apprenticeship project, showing that you have evolved to the stage where you can do significant research on your own. If you choose a sound, safe thesis topic that yields good results under your adviser's tutelage, you should do well.

It is true that if you discover a new atomic element as a graduate student, your chance of getting a job goes up significantly, but don't feel that you must be flashy to succeed. In most fields, academic hiring committees are like those in any other business; they look for dependable specialists who have been well trained by reputable firms: they are likely to look for a young biochemist who knows how to do gene splicing just like her mentor, or an assistant professor of English literature who has received a firm grounding in deconstructionist criticism. They want the best students who received the training from the best mentors.

▪ TWO WAYS TO FIND A THESIS ▪

There are two ways to find a thesis. Either the topic can be provided or you choose by yourself (in consultation with your adviser). Many students despair of finding a topic on their own. As one student wailed, "I'm ready to do anything, if they'll only tell me what to do." Students may be too insecure to choose or they may not sufficiently immerse themselves in their chosen area, so in desperation they ask their adviser for a topic. In many fields, particularly the sciences, your adviser might suggest a piece of his own research for your thesis. This is common in physics or molecular biology, where you may need to join a research team because projects are too large for individuals, expensive equipment is necessary, and technical training is essential. A physicist says, "Let's face it. In particle physics there aren't too many major discoveries waiting around to be found by graduate students on their own." In the humanities, where research is usually an individual effort, many students still end up doing theses suggested by advisers. If you do accept a topic suggested by your adviser, life can be easier because (a) you have your adviser's immediate blessing and (b) you save time searching.

Even if you do allow your professor to choose or otherwise strongly influence your thesis topic, you must still make sure that it is suitable according to the criteria below. Because you will be committing yourself to from one to several years of research on a single topic, you had better, for example, make sure it really interests you. Also, be careful that in your adviser's enthusiasm to have you fill a chink in her research she doesn't start you on a project that is too limited in scope for you to use as the base for further research after you have graduated.

Whether or not you choose your topic yourself, it makes sense to closely ally your work with your adviser's research. Presumably you chose your adviser in the first place because you like his research, so working closely shouldn't be a problem for you. In the Stanford biology department students who nestled under their adviser's wing finished early, compared with independent students like the shark expert who took *twelve years* to do a monstrous and superb taxonomy of sharks (but he did have the added benefit of becoming a consultant on the movie *Jaws*).

If you are working on the same overall endeavor as your adviser, if your thesis and papers are seen as products of his research establishment (particularly if you co-author papers with him), he will have a powerful incentive to support and approve your research. Further, the closer your research is to your adviser's area, the more likely his advice is to be helpful. In experimental fields you can take advantage of existing equipment and methodologies. It can also help if there is a base of previous or ongoing work that can help you plan and interpret your own research. For example, if your thesis is on maternal care in elephant seals, it may be invaluable if previous workers have been marking seals and recording family relationships for the past fifteen years.

DON'T WORRY IF NOTHING ▪ INTERESTS YOU ▪

Don't worry if before you start actively searching for a topic nothing seems to interest you. If you are still standing back thinking about topics in a vacuum, I would be surprised if anything did, because interest develops from immersion and activity. Luckily, people have an amazing ability to become interested in almost anything once they are working on it.

GET PERSPECTIVE BY READING ▪ THESES AND ARTICLES ▪

Go to the departmental or graduate library and read the theses of recent successful graduates as soon as you start graduate school. Notice not only the topics but the structure of the theses: how do they handle the introduction and literature review, research methodology, results, and discussion? Notice who was on the advisory committees to get ideas about whom you might ask to be on yours. Look at the length—theses have recently been getting longer and longer and it will be in your interest to keep your thesis shorter. Note the scale of the writing—a thesis may be more detailed in treatment than a term paper. Note that some theses will be of better quality than others, and you can use the best as models. Look to see if the theses won professional or university awards or you can ask professors about which recent theses were outstanding. Obviously, you will pay special attention to the theses on topics that interest you. Their bibliographies may be invaluable for developing your own bibliography once you have decided on a topic. Above all, reading through theses will start giving you an intuitive feeling for the necessary conceptual structure—the interplay between fundamental theory, the specific problem you will tackle, and the technical aspects of the research and writing. Spending time with theses will demystify the process and help you believe in your own ability to do one.

In addition to the theses on file in your own library, you can access those at other universities. These will be useful when you begin closing in on your thesis topic and you wish to find similar recent research. You can locate relevant theses through computerized library databases, particularly Computer Dissertation Index. Check with your librarian about how to use this and the other computerized databases relevant to your area (such as ERIC, MAGIC, SOCIOFILE, and MLA), which will contain theses, books, and journal articles.

I suggest that you start familiarizing yourself with these databases as soon as you start school. Many of them should be free to students. With free databases, you can afford to start playing around: if you think you might be interested in Sumerian religion, just type in "Sumerian" and "religion" and you can get a detailed bibliography. Many of these databases will even give you abstracts of the articles. This is a quick and enjoyable way to get a rapid sense of the scope of a topic and an overview of previous research (it's the way I started research for this book). Usually you can get paper printouts of whatever bibliography you call up, which eliminates note-taking drudgery.

Of course, you can also search more arduously for dissertations using traditional hard-copy methods. One source that should be in your library is Dissertation Abstracts International, from whom you can order photocopies or microfilms of theses that interest you (University Microfilms International, 300 North Zeeb Road, Ann Arbor, MI 48109). The same source publishes dissertation catalogues on specific subjects that contain lists of theses published in the particular subject area. Other sources include American Doctoral Dissertations and the Comprehensive Dissertation Index. I won't go on to list all the possible bibliographical sources in the different fields because your librarian can easily tell you what you need to know.

Start reading through journals in your field for possible topics. If someone's research sparks your interest, you can contact the author to ask about related papers he may have written. The final paragraphs of many journal articles will point out necessary future research. The journals will tend to give you an even better feel than the dissertations for what is hot in your field.

▪ PHONE RESEARCH ▪

Once you have identified some topics you are interested in, you can research them rapidly by spending a few hours on the telephone calling up experts in the field and pumping them for information. Although it may cost you a few dollars in long-distance bills, it can save you *days* of arduous digging in the library. Another advantage is that this method decreases the chance, common with library research, that you will entirely overlook a whole body of research.

First, spend a few hours in the library stacks reviewing books and articles that can give you a broad understanding of the topic. You don't need detailed knowledge, just enough to talk intelligently about the issue. Next, after you have noted the names and university affiliations of the most important researchers, contact them by phone. You can get their numbers by calling directory assistance and asking for the university departments listed on their publications. If the professors themselves don't have time to help you, try their graduate students.

Once you are speaking with a researcher, politely tell him that you are a graduate student working with Professor So-and-so, and explain your interest in his area. Tell him you would like to know about his latest research (it won't hurt to flatter him) and ask for citations of his most recent publications. If he's feeling kindly, he may offer to send you copies (many people don't respond to written requests for articles but will to a personal request). Then ask him to recommend other people doing important work in the field. In a couple of hours on the phone you should be able to speak briefly to the top few people in the field, and they will point you to other experts and the latest literature. You can use the bibliographies of these recent papers to find earlier ones.

▪ START A RESEARCH PROJECT ▪

The best way to generate ideas is to be involved in an ongoing research project. I suggest attaching yourself to a professor (hopefully your adviser) whose research most interests you. Help him on his research or do an independent study on a topic in an area you are considering for your thesis topic. While you are researching and writing, ideas will come to you for exploration. A zoology student began working on a professor's bird-banding project, developed ideas for a thesis about how tropical forest migratory birds use their Mexican habitat, and went on to become one of the world's experts on tropical ornithology.

Once you are doing research, serendipity will play a big role—if you don't find the exact thing you are looking for, you will find another. Consider the example of Hugh Iltis, a renowned botanist, who traveled all the way to South America in search of a primitive strain of potato that could be useful for agriculture. The potato was nowhere to be found, but after hiking one morning up a steep Andean mountain, he sat down to eat lunch. He noticed at his feet a small wild tomato plant, which turned out to be the basis of genetic improvements in commercial tomatoes worth millions of dollars a year.

▪ USE YOUR PROFESSORS ▪

Ask for help from your advisers and other professors early on in the process. Tell them you want to get a head start on identifying a thesis area and ask them:

• What are the hot areas in the field?
• What were the best theses written during the past few years? Hunt these down in the library.
• Do they have projects associated with their research that could be good theses?

Drawing your professors into the process early will start them thinking about you as a self-starter ahead of the pack, even if you don't yet know what your thesis will be on.

▪ START A TOPIC FILE ▪

As you begin generating ideas about possible theses, place them in a thesis idea file. As you flesh out possibilities, have a separate file folder for each possible topic. Include your thoughts, notes taken on discussions with professors, and relevant journal articles. Spend a few minutes reviewing this file once a week so that your search stays in the forefront of your mind.

CRITERIA FOR EVALUATING POTENTIAL ▪ THESIS TOPICS ▪

Start identifying specific thesis questions by immersing yourself in your topic. Then, once you have identified three or four reasonable questions, start exploring them to see which one has the best potential for your needs. Use the following criteria:

Does sufficient background information exist? First, research what literature exists on each potential topic. Use a phone search, computer search, or other means to locate recent papers and theses on the topic and read them. Note whether there is sufficient research in the general area to help plan and interpret your own research. For example, I knew to look for stereotyped mating displays in pygmy swordtail fish because previous research had shown that closely related species used similar mating displays.

Is the topic narrow enough? One of the most common errors is to pick a topic that is too broad. Be as specific as you can, because it will be easier for you and your adviser to broaden a narrow topic than to focus a broad one.

Has it been done already? Check the literature, including theses, to make certain that the research you are planning hasn't already been done. Experts disagree about how big a problem duplication is; some assert that even if you are working on the same "problem" as someone else, you will each have a different approach. I think this assessment underestimates the degree to which two people are likely to duplicate each other's thoughts and experiments. After I had been running my own experiments for a year, another graduate student wrote to me about his planned research on the same species of fish. At first I thought it was a fake letter sent by one of my friends as a joke, because the other student's research proposal was amazingly similar to mine, right down to specific experiments. It read like a paraphrase of my own proposal. After talking with him, the reason for the similarities was clear; the unique behavioral and physical characteristics of the species were so obvious that any good scientist would set out to answer the same questions with essentially the same approach. In the sciences you can usually alter your experiments enough to get around the duplication problem even if someone is poaching on your turf, but in some fields, like English, it is more difficult to argue that your thesis on hunting metaphors in Shakespeare's poetry is substantially different from someone else's. The adviser of one English student suggested that for her thesis she should translate a German poet's book and write a critical introduction. She worked for three months before finding out that the book had already been translated and the introduction written, so she and her adviser agreed that she would have to find a new topic. How badly her career would have been affected by duplication is hard to say. Although she probably would have received her degree, publishing her research would have been difficult and she would not have been unique on the job market. I say better safe than sorry.

Is it tractable? Check your subject for tractability—will it work? If you are in sociology, make sure your subject group will stay available throughout the study period—migrant workers are likely to be a bad choice. If you are in biology, make sure your animals are easy to obtain and will stay alive. There is good reason why people use white rats and fruit flies: you can buy a lot of them, they are genetically standardized, we know

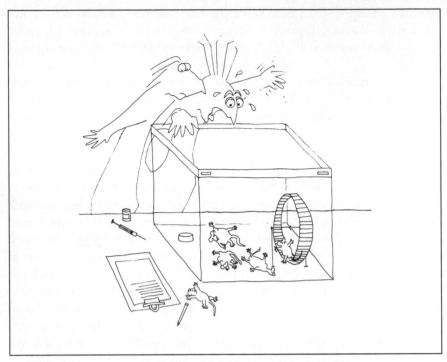

BE PREPARED FOR UNEXPECTED SETBACKS

how to feed them, and they breed well. It's like the old joke about chickens: A man buys a chicken farm and his friend says, "But, Joe, you don't know anything about breeding chickens." "That's all right," says Joe, "the chickens do." My swordtail fish didn't, at least in the lab. It took me two years to figure out how to breed enough of them for experiments. Unfortunately, you don't get extra points on your Ph.D. for figuring out that swordtails kill each other in close quarters.

Check out other aspects of the planned experimental design to make sure everything you want to do is possible. It would be terrible to find out halfway through that your thesis won't work. Here, people in the humanities have an advantage over scientists—it's rare for their theses to completely fail. As one scholar said, "The student in literature can always find something to say, whether this makes any contribution to scholarship or not." Pay particular attention to statistical planning if you will need to do statistical analysis of your data. If you aren't good at statistics yourself, it will be important to consult an expert *before you begin your research collection.* Bad research design can leave you with data that require complex statistical gymnastics or are ultimately useless. Again, ask your adviser about how to get statistical advice. You may be able to find a statistics graduate student willing to take on statistical analysis of your research as his own thesis project.

How long will it take to do your research? Take it for granted that shorter is better than longer, so it's probably not a good idea to study maturation rates in trees (at least by direct observation). Don't pick a topic where important literature is in a language you don't speak well. Don't pick a topic requiring extensive, expensive fieldwork or other travel unless you are wealthy or guaranteed funding. It would be a shame to spend one summer in the Caribbean setting up your experiments and be unable to return the following year for their maturation. *Do* rate highly a topic where there is a good chance of getting funding; it is worth repeating that this is more likely when you are nestling under a professor's wing.

Is it fundable? As you examine topics, think about which ones are fundable. If your research is closely linked to an adviser's, he may be able to provide funding for equipment, travel, and other related expenses from his grants. Your department may also have some funds available for graduate research—these are likely to be competitive, so apply early. More difficult, but possible, are outside funding sources like the National Science Foundation, which funds some graduate research. Unfortunately for those in the humanities, the National Endowment for the Arts specifically does not fund graduate education. Talk with your adviser, graduate department, and financial aid officer about ideas.

Because it is much easier to get additional funding for ongoing research than for new projects, beginning students are at a disadvantage. Their projects are new and they themselves don't have a proven track record of research. I ran into this problem when I proposed to study the ecology of pygmy swordtail fish in Mexico. I naively figured that because nothing was known about their ecology and because pygmy swordtails belonged to an otherwise much-studied group of fish, the reviewers would approve of my plans to fill this gap in the ecological literature. I was wrong. The reviewers of the proposal harshly criticized me for daring to suggest doing research without preliminary research. Because I didn't already know what I would find, I was accused of "going on a fishing expedition," which was indeed exactly what I wanted the money for.

Two things can help with this problem. First, as with getting papers published, submit grants jointly with your adviser so his contacts and reputation help. Second, do some preliminary work, which makes the need and ultimate success of your research more plausible. In my own case, my grant for extensive fieldwork in Mexico might have had a better chance if I had taken a brief (and relatively inexpensive) trip to Mexico on my own to do a quick survey of the study site.

Don't be discouraged from doing an ambitious thesis just because expenses at first glance are beyond your means—you or your committee members may come up with the funding sources. Just make sure you have a backup plan if your thesis does depend upon the uncertainties of getting a grant. One of my friends made the mistake of moving with his wife to Africa and starting research in anticipation of support that never materialized. After three months he had to return and find another topic. If you have ties to the working world, perhaps working part-time, be creative about ways to get funding from work for your thesis. For example, if your work regularly takes you on travel to a foreign country, you may be able to do work there that otherwise would be prohibitive.

Is it hot? If you can do your thesis in an area that is in vogue, you may have more success being hired upon completion. It is difficult to predict for certain what will be in fashion a few years ahead when you graduate, particularly if you take a long time, but by reading the journals and talking to professors you should be able to see the general direction of your field. Luck plays a part too: one English student chose a thesis in deconstructionist criticism, in part because she knew it was a hot topic, and her timing was just right—she rode the wave of interest into a good job just before the fad for deconstruction subsided.

Avoid fields full of theoretical or political controversy, even though it may be good to focus on a new, rapidly expanding area. As a newcomer you will have a hard enough time getting your work published and accepted without stumbling into the midst of internecine warfare. If the big boys are thrashing around biting each other like dinosaurs in a grade C prehistoric world movie, you could get squashed in the undergrowth. Theses that are controversial for nonacademic reasons can also be problematic. A Stanford graduate student went to China to study and did his research on a topic unauthorized by the Chinese authorities—involuntary abortions. Because the Chinese raised a storm of protest, he was dismissed from the university after a number of hearings and lawsuits. (The upside of this tale is that he became a darling of the U.S. conservative establishment and ended up with a fellowship at the Heritage Foundation.)

The preceding suggestions primarily focused on topic characteristics that affect your ability to finish the thesis. One successful professor of English warns that you should also think about how the thesis will affect your chances of getting a job by showcasing your abilities. She feels it should do three things:

- Allow you to show off your background knowledge of the field. For example, if you are a literature student who is writing a critical study of the minor seventeenth-century author "Williams," use your thesis to demonstrate that you are conversant with the entire field of seventeenth-century literature.

- Focus on a narrow enough topic so that you can become *the* expert—you become *the* "Williams" scholar. If you do a broad thesis that tries to cover all the major seventeenth-century writers, you become an expert in none.
- Provide a springboard for future research. In any academic job interview you will be asked what brilliant research you will be doing in the next couple of years to make their department look good if they hire you. You could, in this case, have in mind an extension of your work to other seventeenth-century writers, or you could continue some important themes by applying them to another century for comparison.

■ START WRITING IMMEDIATELY ■

As you start evaluating your three or four thesis topics, start writing about them. Writing is the best way to initiate, organize, and extend ideas. You can start by writing a detailed evaluation of each possible topic using the criteria listed below. If you don't know enough about a topic to evaluate it, you'd better find out more before you commit to do your thesis on it. Rate each topic according to: (1) financial support, (2) interest to you, (3) extendability after completion, (4) controversy, (5) time to complete, (6) "hotness," (7) adviser's enthusiasm for topic, (8) closeness of topic to adviser's research, (9) depth of existing research, (10) duplication or uniqueness, (11) narrow focus, and (12) tractability, including availability of research subjects or materials, existence of preplanned experimental methods, degree of methodological difficulty, and simplicity of statistical design.

For each topic under serious consideration you should also outline a thesis proposal in which you ask the major research questions and outline the experimental or research steps you plan to take. Don't fall into the trap of waiting until the proposal is nearly due to start writing it as though it were a class assignment. You should use proposal outlines as tools for sharpening your topic search as soon as you begin to identify possibilities. Outlining a proposal will force you to explicitly ask the research questions and plan the research itself; it will also help you get a feel for how much the topic interests you, and—very important—it will give you a concrete document to discuss with your professors. One of the mutually frustrating dances of graduate school is when the student comes to the professor unable to find a topic and the professor can't help because the student's ideas are so vague. The key is specificity. If you can give your advisers a written outline, then they can make useful comments about the project's doability, scope, and experimental and statistical design.

As you begin to focus on a particular topic and are planning the research, get as much feedback as you can. Live and breathe your topic to the point of being annoying: Talk to your adviser, outside experts you have identified from your preliminary research, other graduate students, your mother, and your cat. Get immersed in planning. Draw in researchers outside your own university by writing, calling, or visiting them to ask advice about the research you propose. They may be willing to do you the favor of looking over your proposal outline for suggestions. Remember, by contacting them now you can start the career-long process of cultivating colleagues and friends with whom you may later collaborate.

Make sure that your final topic has the approval and enthusiasm of your adviser. You are now ready to write your thesis proposal.

17

THE THESIS

PROPOSAL

▪ WHAT IS A THESIS PROPOSAL? ▪

Most departments require that Ph.D. students write a thesis proposal that describes in detail on what, why, how, and on what time schedule they plan to do their thesis research. Master's students also may have to submit some type of proposal or prospectus before beginning a thesis. Depending on your department and the whims of your adviser, your proposal may follow a traditional structure or be relatively informal. Whether required or not, I believe you should write a proposal for your own good. Most of the proposal can be easily integrated into your thesis itself, so even doing an unrequired proposal won't be a waste of time. On the contrary, it will be a head start on your thesis.

Like making an outline for a term paper, but on a larger scale, writing the proposal will force you to think clearly through all aspects of what you plan to do, illuminating weaknesses and unknowns and sharpening your arguments. The proposal will be reviewed by your advisory committee so that they can help you discover problems and correct them before you blunder off track while working on your thesis. If you are a Ph.D. student, the department is also likely to require that you make an oral presentation of your proposal, coupled with a "defense," in which you answer questions from your committee.

As you write your proposal, bear in mind that both the process of writing the proposal and the finished product have several complementary purposes. The proposal is at once a research plan, an evaluation, a trial run at writing your thesis, a contract with your department, and a sales pitch. Because of the scope and importance of the proposal, you should devote considerably more time to it than you would a course paper of similar length. The process of writing the proposal will be a complex one, requiring extensive research and thought, in which, ideally, you resolve all the major issues of your thesis problem. I say "ideally," because in reality it may be impossible to know exactly where your thesis will go before you do substantial research on it.

▪ A CAUTIONARY TALE ▪

Before going into detail about the attributes of a proposal, let me tell you about one student who had problems with his, but who ultimately managed to get a good thesis under way. In Paul's own words:

> My first thesis topic was monstrous. I planned to trace the development of two whole traditions of literary theory, and then to discuss the theory in terms of the tradition of philosophy, linking all the way back to Descartes. I would include important examples like the Searle-Derrida debate, capping off with Ludwig Wittgenstein. I banged out eight to ten pages on what I wanted to do, rather fuzzy, and gave it to my committee. They thought the project was way too big, but they more or less said, "We think you're about to charge into a swamp, but it's your funeral."
>
> The next step was to outline what I was actually going to do. I had to come up with a much more detailed prospectus than the ten pages of mush I'd already produced, and this is where it started to get ugly. I wasted a lot of time reading everything that was remotely relevant before I realized that I desperately needed to narrow these hundreds or thousands of books down to a dozen that could be dealt with in detail. I spent almost a year trying to do this detailed prospectus and finally recognized I didn't have anything new to say, only hundreds of pages of crabbed, arcane notes that went nowhere. Finally, I had to face the fact that I had thrown a year of my life away. During this whole year I isolated myself, became depressed, withdrew from the social circuit, and became a crazed hermit. I lost touch with my professors—a very bad thing. If I saw one coming toward me, I would dash into the bathroom and sit in a stall until I figured he was gone. This was silly, because they certainly weren't going to throw me up against the wall and demand to read my latest efforts. They're not that eager to read a hundred pages of crap.
>
> What saved me? I went to my adviser, who was becoming disgusted with my incoherent babbling; he told me, "Why don't you drop this?

Forget about your thesis for the moment and just get something written. Write a paper on something you know about, like Sir Walter Scott." He'd given this advice before and I'd rejected it, but now I was desperate enough to listen. So I took some old papers on Sir Walter Scott that I'd written for classes and cobbled them together. When I finished I had fifty concrete pages that formed a coherent paper, so I wasn't embarrassed about having people read them. I presented this to my committee as a possible first chapter of my thesis—even though I had no idea what the whole thesis would look like. I just asked them whether this *could* be the first chapter of a thesis and let them make suggestions for where the rest of the thesis should go. They liked my first chapter, gave me suggestions for additional chapters, and I was on my way. In my case I'm sort of going at things backwards, developing the plan as I go along, but it seems to be working well. (The only problem is that I keep inserting Wittgenstein into Sir Walter Scott, like a nervous twitch.) So tell your readers that even after a bad start they can still pull it together if they get focused.

Paul's first thesis topic was much too broad, a common mistake. He was more concerned with doing a grand thesis than with finding a concise, doable topic. He didn't stay in touch with his professors and didn't really listen to their advice. Finally, his story points out the hazards of writing without a detailed outline; in his wasted year of writing, Paul meandered all over the place. He should have realized earlier that the reason he couldn't create a clear proposal was that there were basic flaws with the conception of his thesis. He forgot that the proposal writing process is a time of assessment, when you have to decide as soon as possible if the thesis is viable or whether to cut your losses. On the positive side, he finally climbed out of his depression by taking action. He talked with his adviser, listened to advice, got a more focused topic, and started writing.

▪ USES OF A THESIS PROPOSAL ▪

RESEARCH PLAN

To use a house-building analogy, the proposal is a blueprint for your research. Therefore, your proposal should describe in as much detail as possible the theoretical framework within which your research will take place, what textual sources you will use, which statistical methodologies will apply, and, in the case of an experimental thesis, which specific experiments you propose. Other questions to be explicitly answered in your proposal include: How will your research contribute to the existing body of knowledge? What literature has bearing on the topic? What are the major hypotheses to be tested? What results do you expect, based upon prior studies by others? What is your timetable leading to completion?

EVALUATION

At the proposal step both you and your committee do a final assessment of whether the topic you have chosen is a good one. Therefore, as you write your proposal, answering the above questions, continue to evaluate your proposed research carefully. If serious defects turn up, now is the time to cut your losses and modify your original plans. Ask yourself if what you are proposing is realistic. Can the research be done in the time allotted? Are the necessary research materials available? Can you do the promised modeling or statistical analysis? Will the topic hold your interest?

HEAD START ON YOUR THESIS

Because the proposal usually mimics the final thesis structure, with some changes, much of the writing you do for the proposal can form the foundation of the thesis. Notably, the introduction and literature review (in which you discuss relevant literature and justify your problem in terms of the theoretical and research history of your field) may become the first chapters of your thesis. The more complete you make them now, the less work you will have to do later. The methodology section may also make it to your thesis relatively intact.

CONTRACT

The proposal is a contract with your committee and by extension with your department. You propose to complete the research detailed in the proposal. By approving the proposal, your committee agrees to reciprocate with a degree. The proposal protects you against later arbitrary changes in the committee's expectations. At the same time, if you want to change your research later, you will have to renegotiate the contract—that is, get your committee's agreement. In some departments, you may have to formally amend the proposal. You should not have a problem if you later need to change your research for good reason; most committees realize that proposals are provisional. As one professor said, "In my field, proposals are largely fiction because you have to start your research to know where it will take you." Nonetheless, regardless of how easygoing your committee seems, you would be foolish to make any major changes in research plans without prior approval.

One of Judge Wapner's favorite statements on the television show *The People's Court* is that for a contract to exist there must be "a meeting of the minds." This means that both parties must understand and agree to the specific provisions of the contract, which may be impossible if the wording is ambiguous. Likewise, because your thesis proposal binds you and your committee to specific provisions, it is vital that the final proposal be clear, as detailed as possible, and agreed upon by all committee members.

Because of the contractual nature of the proposal, it is important not to get carried away when you write it, selling research you do not really intend to do. This can get you in trouble down the road if you find you can't deliver. If you have poor language skills, do not wishfully put in your proposal that you intend to search through libraries in Spain for original documents to substantiate your thesis that Christopher Columbus left Spain to get away from his mother.

SALES PITCH

Write a clearly written, forceful proposal that makes a strong case for the importance of the research and for the specific methodology you intend to use. Your written proposal and oral defense of it give you the chance to determine the way in which your committee will view your research from now on. You will get better support and less trouble if you convince your committee members that your research is exciting and well planned.

A strong proposal and defense will decrease the chance that the committee will nitpick and tack on unnecessary work additions. However, no matter how perfect you believe your research plan is, the committee will suggest changes. This is to be expected, and let's face it, they have much more knowledge than you about what makes a good thesis. But if you can convince them you know what you are doing, they are more likely to keep the tinkering minimal and constructive. You don't want the experience of one English student, preparing to do his thesis on how science-fiction authors use musical images, whose committee decided on the spur of the moment that, in addition to two languages, he should also become "substantially grounded" in music theory.

▪ TYPICAL PROPOSAL STRUCTURE ▪

Because proposal structure will differ among disciplines and departments, I will give here a generalized recipe. Feel free to skip this section if you already understand how proposals are constructed. You can familiarize yourself with the detailed requirements of your department by (1) getting official departmental guidelines (do this *early*), (2) getting advice and samples from other students who have recently defended their own, and (3) talking with your adviser and other committee members. In addition, two good books that go into more detail, complete with examples of Ph.D. proposals, are *Completing Dissertations in the Behavioral Sciences and Education*, by Thomas Long, John Convey, and Adele Chwalek, and *Successful Dissertations and Theses*, by David Madsen.

LENGTH OF THE PROPOSAL

The length required can differ considerably from department to department, anything from a few pages to thirty or more. My advice is not to worry too much about the length per se, but instead do as much as is necessary to get the maximum benefits of planning and evaluation, bearing in mind that much of your proposal can be adapted for use in your thesis itself. You should ask yourself, "Is it possible to tell from this proposal precisely what I plan to do?"

Even if your committee will let you get away with a vague proposal, don't do it. One student, who got formal approval for a ten-page proposal, later said, "I think it would have been better if I had done a more complete proposal. Even though at the time I wasn't sure what form my research was going to take, I still should have spent more time planning. Then I would have had a greater feeling of confidence that I knew where I was going."

Although I have suggested you write a proposal that is detailed, I also want to caution you about becoming compulsively perfectionistic. Remember that a proposal is just that, a proposal; it is a working document that is likely to be changed, and if you are too wedded to it, it may be difficult to accept the committee's valid suggestions for improvements. One history student, for example, became so compulsive about her proposal that she spent an entire year working and reworking it before she felt it was good enough to show her committee, during which time other students actually completed their entire theses. Another student spent three months researching a single section of his proposal, believing that in order to write this piece he had to master all relevant literature. His committee ultimately decided that this piece of his thesis was too ambitious, and they therefore struck it from the proposal, so he had pretty much wasted three months. Work closely with your adviser and committee members as you develop the proposal, put in enough work to explore the topic thoroughly and get a good head start on your thesis, but don't overdo it.

Proposal outline

As I said above, you should determine early exactly what type of structure your department requires, since different departments and disciplines demand different structures and terminology. Here is a generalized outline similar to what you might end up writing. After the outline, I discuss in detail some of the common elements of a typical proposal. In both the outline and subsequent discussion, I have called the various sections "chapters" to keep them congruent with the corresponding thesis chapters that will be adapted from them. In some cases the proposal sections will indeed be of chapter length. In others, notably humanities proposals, the methodology chapter in particular may be quite short. Use your department's guidelines and common sense to glean from the following outline and discussion what is applicable to you.

- cover page
- abstract (one page)
- table of contents
- Chapter I. Introduction to the proposal. This may include:

  A an introduction to the "research problem," describing the area of your field where research is needed.
  B a brief overview of the research you propose to do in order to investigate the research problem. This is commonly called a "statement of purpose."
  C a list of the specific research questions you propose to answer and/or hypotheses you intend to test.
  D a list of the limitations and assumptions of your research.
  E a definition of your terminology.

- Chapter II. The literature review
- Chapter III. Methodology (includes the method of data analysis)
- appendixes
    schedule of completion dates
    budget
    provisional table of contents for your thesis
    bibliography

DETAILED DISCUSSION OF
■ PROPOSAL OUTLINE ■

THE INTRODUCTION

Chapter 1, the introduction, sets the stage for your research, explaining to your committee what you propose to do and why. The introduction's structure typically moves from the general to the specific, beginning with an overview of the general problem and ending up with the specific research questions you will answer.

Often, the introduction is broken into closely related subsections, A through E in the outline above, although your particular proposal may not contain all the subsections described. An English proposal, for example, will probably not have formal research hypotheses (described below), while a psychology proposal will.

- *A: Introduction to the research problem.* This is a short review of relevant theory and research, only a couple of pages long, which provides a context for the work you want to do. It describes the general research problem, tells why it is important, and points out that the world will end unless someone solves the problem with brilliant research. The research problem may be a controversy, an information gap, or even a taxonomy in need of revision.

Here is an example: Imagine that you are a sociologist who wants to investigate people who believe in UFOs and parapsychology. You begin by asserting that it is important to understand how subcultures are able to persist for long periods of time within dominant cultures. Next comes a brief review of relevant theories and research describing what is now known about the persistence of subcultures. This discussion should be slanted so that it leads up to the research problem—i.e., something that is both unknown and important. In this case, you state that little is known about how individual members of a subculture seek reinforcement for their belief structure. And you, of course, are ready to do the important research that will solve this problem. At this point in the discussion, just like evolutionists who draw family trees with human beings perched triumphantly on the top, you have presented the entire development of your field as leading right to your research.

- *B: Statement of purpose.* Here you should briefly describe the particular research you will do to help solve the research problem you've just presented. Also explicitly state the significance of your study—how will it contribute to theory or practical knowledge? Your statement may be as short as a paragraph or two, but make sure you have thought it through very carefully, because this is the heart of your thesis. Keeping with our UFO example, an abbreviated sample statement of purpose is:

In order to refine present theory on how members of subcultures maintain their belief structures, I propose to study the degree to which members of UFO Hunters, an organization dedicated to researching UFO sightings, reinforce their beliefs by selectively reading materials that substantiate their own positions and avoiding materials that are contradictory.

• C: *Explicit research questions and/or hypotheses.* Following the description of your general research plan, it is usual to present a list of finely focused research questions or hypotheses you intend to answer or to test while carrying out your research. Refer to your adviser or department for the exact style required. Such a research question might be "Is there a relationship between the frequency with which people report UFO sightings and the frequency with which they read supermarket tabloids?" To turn this research question into a research hypothesis, the question is rephrased as a statement that can be tested to see whether or not it's true. In this instance we could state, "There is a positive correlation between the frequency with which people report UFO sightings and the frequency with which they read supermarket tabloids."

If you have a traditionalist for an adviser, you may have to state your hypotheses as *null hypotheses*; a null hypothesis is just a turned-around version of the hypothesis, where instead of stating that there *is* a correlation, you state that there *is not* a correlation. Then you test this negative statement to see whether it is true. The null hypothesis of the above would be "There is *no correlation* between the frequency with which people report UFO sightings and the frequency with which they read supermarket tabloids."

• D: *Limitations and assumptions.* In some fields you may need to list limitations and assumptions of your research plan. For example, the UFO study may be limited to interviews with *volunteer* subjects (which may be unrepresentative of the wider community). Therefore, the use of volunteers is a *limitation* of the study. In your interviews you might assume that the subjects will answer the interviewer truthfully. That they will tell the truth is therefore an *assumption* of the study. You need to explicitly state these limitations and assumptions, discussing ways in which they may affect the research conclusions of your thesis.

- *E: Terms to be used in your thesis.* The introduction may also contain a section in which you define terms whose precise meaning will be essential for further discussion in your thesis. For example, "supermarket tabloid" might be defined to distinguish it from related materials that are not considered in the thesis research. An English professor cautioned me that in her field it would be seen as somewhat insulting to the committee to define accepted terminology, since the committee would be expected to know it, but in many fields definitions are an expected part of the proposal, in part to show that the student has mastery of the required terms and concepts.

THE LITERATURE REVIEW

The primary goal of this chapter is to convince your committee that the topic you have chosen is important and that your research will yield important results. A secondary goal is to demonstrate mastery of the major concepts and research in your field. You fulfill both these goals with a careful, synthetic review of the literature that provides a context for your work. Among other things, you should describe the empirical studies relevant to your problem, the specific methodologies that have been employed by other workers, major theories that your research will test or that will influence your interpretations, and specific research needs identified by yourself or others. Trace important historical developments and controversies; it is especially nice if you can make the case that your research will help to resolve a theoretical or practical controversy. You may be fortunate enough to find and quote statements by other researchers saying that your proposed research is needed. Marshal evidence that shows there is good reason to believe that the relationships between your variables are real and that the hypotheses you intend to test are likely to be true (or, in the case of null hypotheses, false). For instance, in the example we have been using, your review would describe related studies that lead you to expect that there is a correlation between belief in UFOs and regular tabloid consumption.

Since this review develops the ideas presented in your introduction, it might be helpful to write it first.

Here are a few additional tips to help you structure this chapter:

- If you haven't written critical reviews before, familiarize yourself by reading review chapters in theses related to your work. Also read review articles published in journals in your field until you have a good instinctive feel for structure and language.

- Make sure you develop a detailed outline first, to be reviewed by your adviser.
- Use headings within the chapter, conforming to your outline, which allow you to break the review into discrete sections that are more easily handled.
- Write more about studies that are closely related to your research and less about those that are not. For example, imagine three studies, one of which is more closely related to your research than the other two. In the most closely related study, Johnson in 1991 showed that Iowa farmers who report witnessing UFOs also read supermarket tabloids. The less closely related studies were: (a) one by Plotkin which showed that farmers who read tabloids also reported mysterious circles of crushed wheat in their fields, (b) one by Madrigal which showed that supermarket clerks who regularly read tabloids during smoking breaks were more likely to watch the Geraldo show. These three studies might therefore be reported, to emphasize their relative importance: "A study by Johnson in 1991 found a high correlation between UFO reports and tabloid readership in a population of Iowa farmers, and similar studies by Plotkin and Madrigal showed correlations between tabloid readership and belief in unsubstantiated phenomena."

THE METHODOLOGY

In the methodology chapter you describe in as much detail as possible exactly how you will conduct your research. (In some cases, notably for humanities proposals, the methodology description may be so short it is better included in one of the previous chapters.) The chapter is essentially a list of tasks to be done, descriptions of how you will do those tasks, and a time line of when the tasks will be accomplished. For a psychology thesis this could include descriptions of the subject groups, the questionnaires (instruments) you plan to use, and planned statistical analysis. For a history thesis it could include a listing of specific source materials and the particular theoretical approach you plan to use. Because methodology differs so much between disciplines, I won't go further into structure of the chapter, but I will briefly discuss some general points.

The methodology chapter of your proposal is the road map you will follow. Therefore, make it as specific as possible, both as a guide for yourself and as a contract of work to be done for your committee. Think carefully about each task you propose to do: Will you have adequate access to research material? How much will this task cost? How long will it take?

Are there ethical concerns involving human or animal subjects? What computer programs will be necessary? Do you have the requisite technical skills? For example, if you will need advanced statistics, and you need to learn them, figure this into your time line.

If you do not know the answers to these questions, actively research them. You will have to find the answers eventually, so you might as well find them during the proposal process when you have plenty of time to make changes. For example, if you need access to rare manuscripts in restricted library collections, find out now about library rules for access. If you need original theses or obscure papers photocopied and sent to you, find out approximate charges. If you will be feeding experimental animals for three years, find out what they eat and how much it costs. If you need to travel, call a travel agent now for estimates of expenses. Some of the answers may cause you to revise your thesis plans. When I set out to study my fish, I neglected to investigate carefully how long it would take to breed an adequate number for my experiments (they couldn't be bought). It ended up taking two years just to raise enough animals to begin experiments.

I want to stress again that now, when you write your proposal, is the time to set up your statistical analysis—*before* you begin any experiments or data collection. Proper experimental design will make statistical analysis easy, and improper design can create a nightmare, including invalidation of your entire study. If you feel insecure doing statistical design, this is the time to hire a statistician. You can even create dummy results, in line with what you expect, and run a preliminary statistical analysis in order to identify potential problems. This can also give you a good gut feeling for the data as you collect it, helping you better understand what's going on.

A time line (schedule) of all thesis activities is essential. Not only should it be included in your proposal but a large copy should eventually find its way to the wall of your dissertation office. List each task in order and estimate the number of days each will take. Estimate how many days will be necessary for each experiment, for library research, instrument design, writing of papers for publication, data analysis, writing the thesis, revisions by your committee, thesis defense, and *vacation*. Check your estimates against the experience of more advanced graduate students.

Make sure that your committee doesn't just gloss over your time line. They should review it carefully for feasibility, helping you add or subtract time in line with what seems realistic. This goes doubly for your adviser. In future discussions over your progress, the time line will be an agreed point of reference. If your adviser feels you are behind schedule, you can discuss exactly where and why things took longer than expected. Obviously, the time line is just an estimate and some things will take considerably more time than you imagined, some less. Nonetheless, it can help you keep on track and remind you of the relative importance of the tasks you have ahead. If you have allotted only thirty days to library research and were last seen six months ago disappearing into the stacks with a duffel bag of high-caffeine soft drinks and candy bars, your time line may alert your committee that something is wrong.

Even though a budget is not a traditional part of thesis proposals, I strongly suggest you make one and include it as an appendix to the proposal. Estimate photocopying, long-distance phone, postage, equipment, and travel costs (if you are a scientist, some of these may be picked up by your lab). If you're not sure how to do a budget, check out some of your adviser's grant proposals.

When you write the methodology chapter, refer to the budget to make sure it is not overlooked when your committee is reading the proposal. By making your committee consider your expenses at this time, you can begin drawing them into the process of helping you get funds. Do they have grants that could cover some of these expenses if your research is closely associated with theirs? Can they help you identify and apply for your own grants or scholarships? Are there departmental funds available? Will your committee help you get them?

APPENDIXES

Other miscellaneous parts of the proposal may be best handled as appendixes, although other structures are also possible. These include the budget (above), a provisional table of contents for the thesis, and a bibliography.

A draft table of contents will help you and your committee understand the structure of the finished thesis. One student said, "I never really worked out a table of contents till halfway through writing my thesis. My advisers and I kept going back and forth with a million changes to my thesis structure, until I was going crazy. I finally realized that none of them had a firm grasp of how the entire thesis fit together, so I wrote out a detailed table of contents. Once we had that to work with, I finally got them all to agree."

The bibliography should include the literature cited in the literature review chapter, as well as other literature that has important bearing on your thesis. Various authors have different opinions about how long the proposal bibliography should be, ranging from "brief" to "massive." I tend toward the "massive" end of the spectrum. Clearly a very complete bibliography can't hurt, and creating it isn't wasted time, since your *thesis* bibliography will have to be massive anyway. Moreover, now is the time to do an in-depth literature review so that you can bring the most ideas to bear on planning your work. Also, a strong bibliography can impress your committee with your diligence, and putting it together can help prepare you for your proposal and eventual thesis defense. By way of warning, writing even a brief bibliography is time-consuming because the bibliography form must be correct and consistent and the typing must be impeccable. If you're up against a deadline, be sure to leave *plenty of time* for the bibliography, especially if it's going to be a long one. Don't think you can get it done the last day—several full days or even weeks is none too much time for a good job.

■ TACKLING THE PROPOSAL PROCESS ■

Before writing your proposal, also read Chapter 18, "The Thesis," for suggestions on how to write a large document. It will also help you understand how the proposal and thesis are related.

LEAVE PLENTY OF TIME

The proposal writing process has several stages and involves substantial interaction with your adviser and possibly other committee members, so make sure you start early, at least several months before the proposal is due.

THE PREPROPOSAL

Before writing the actual proposal write a shorter preproposal, a few pages in length. You may already have such a short treatment on hand from your earlier topic evaluation process. The preproposal can resemble a detailed outline, although you should flesh out key sections such as the statement of purpose. Ask your adviser to look it over and make suggestions. If he suggests substantial changes, do the necessary research and incorporate these changes into a second draft of the preproposal. Once this meets his approval, you are ready to draft the proposal itself.

THE PROPOSAL

The finished proposal should be your best work, since this is the document that convinces your committee that you are ready to do major research. Therefore, the writing should be clear and straightforward. Make sure the final copy is clean and typo-free. Consider getting it spiral-bound to give it some substance.

Don't try to read everything on the subject first. Identify the key sources you need to include and then cut yourself off from the library and start writing. It's much more important at this point to develop your ideas, methodologies, etc., than it is to touch base with every relevant reference. Besides, if you miss important sources, your various reviewers will be delighted to point them out to you.

As you finish drafts, even fairly preliminary ones, get them reviewed. A good place to start is other graduate students and *junior* faculty. Let's face it, no one will want to read fifty pages of arcane mumbo jumbo, so you basically have to bribe people to read your proposal (and later your thesis). With graduate students it's quid pro quo. Your average grad student working on his proposal will be stumbling around in a haze, certain that the only thing that should matter to the world is the effects of fourteenth-century mercantilism on the Catholic Church, and peevishly perplexed that no one is interested. If you volunteer to read his thesis, he will be pathetically grateful, in which case you can ask him to read yours, and he will have no choice. In the case of junior faculty, they will be new in town, socially isolated, low in the pecking order, and delighted if you ask them over for dinner or drinks, to the point that they also may be willing to review your thesis. One recent grad said that "the comments of junior faculty are likely to be more valuable than those of the tenure class because their own theses will be fresh in their minds, and they are apt to spend more time and care helping you."

AN ADVISER MOTIVATING STUDENTS TO
IMPROVE THEIR THESIS PROPOSALS

Draw your adviser into the review process early. At the latest, have your adviser review the proposal before it goes to the other committee members. There shouldn't be any unpleasant surprises here if you have been involving him since the preproposal stage, and he can help with some final smoothing. As with your later thesis defense, it is in his interest to have you look good to the other committee members.

THE PROPOSAL DEFENSE

Although some departments merely require you to have your committee and possibly department chairman sign off on your proposal, others will demand a formal defense in front of your entire committee.

A typical defense consists of a fifteen-minute opening presentation by you, followed by an hour or so of questioning and discussion. Make sure that you schedule this well ahead of time, since it may be tricky to reserve a room at the same time that all your committee can get together. In preparing, you can use many of the same techniques as for your comprehensive exam or thesis defense. Prepare your talk well ahead of time and practice until you can give it in your sleep. Do a trial run in front of other grad students and have them ask difficult questions. For a proposal defense, slides would seem like overkill, but many students find it helpful to illustrate their presentation with transparencies on an overhead projector. These are easy to make on a photocopier just by inserting blank transparencies in the paper tray and copying whatever figures or text you have prepared (don't forget your proposed thesis table of contents).

Pump students who have made their defenses recently for typical questions asked by the committee. You can expect everything from open-ended questions in the manner of "What will your thesis contribute to the field?" to specific questions on statistical analysis. They might ask, "Why are you using the particular statistical procedures that you propose? Has similar work been done that gives you confidence in a significant outcome?"

Don't be worried if you do have to give an oral defense. It won't be as stressful as your comprehensive exam and will be good practice for your later thesis defense. One professor says: "The defense should be less like an exam than like a group of colleagues gathering to discuss an interesting research project. At the defense you can establish yourself as a colleague. Realize that even though the committee members are senior and know more about theses in general, you may already be more expert than they are in the particular area you have chosen to study. Therefore, take their criticisms seriously but be prepared to defend your proposal if you don't agree with their objections."

In this light, don't be upset if your committee gives you a conditional acceptance subject to changes. Remember that the process of developing and defending the proposal is not a test; it is a process whereby you and your committee work together to develop the best possible thesis project.

If revisions are requested, there are a couple of ways to handle the process. You may not have an option, but in case you do, here are some pros and cons of two slightly different methods. One version is for the committee members to give you notes or a formal memorandum requesting changes. In consultation with your adviser, you then either make these changes or begin discussions with the committee as to why they should not be made. You finally circulate the new draft for approval. This method makes sure that the committee's requests are communicated to you clearly, but it has the drawback that the committee members crystallize their objections on paper and therefore are more difficult for you to ignore if you want to. Another method is for *you* to take notes during the meeting which form the basis of revisions. This gives you more leeway about which objections to take seriously. In either case, wait a couple of weeks before presenting your major changes so that spur-of-the-moment or ill-considered suggestions will have faded from their memories.

Finally, an additional benefit of an oral defense is that it gives you a good look at the dynamics of your committee. As one professor said, "If some guy is a crotchety, nitpicking roadblock, now's the time to know so you can throw him out before you get heavily into your thesis."

18

. . . .

THE THESIS:

WRITING IT

. . . .

Your manuscript is both good and original; but the part that is good
is not original, and the part that is original is not good.

—SAMUEL JOHNSON

SAMUEL JOHNSON ALSO SAID, "SIR, NO MAN BUT A BLOCKHEAD EVER WROTE
except for money." He's probably right, but you may not have a choice,
so let's make it as painless as possible.

If you are like most students, facing up to a major writing task fills you
with a level of anticipation somewhere between greeting a blind date and
undergoing dental work. H. L. Mencken said of writing, "It is lonesome,
unsanitary, and maddening. Many authors go crazy." These relatively
accurate attributes make writing up research in thesis form the single most
daunting task of graduate school. However, by using good organizational
skills and understanding basic truths about the writing process, you will
have an easier time and may even enjoy the job. To help make writing
your thesis easier, the bulk of this chapter is devoted to suggestions about
how to fight fear and procrastination. First let's look briefly at how theses
are structured and then move on to how to get yours written.

· STRUCTURE ·

To research this chapter, I first read all the books I could find that talked
about thesis structure. The authors confused me because they contradicted
each other about structural details. One author maintained that theses

should have five chapters, while another gave an example with nine. One discussed research hypotheses in minute detail, while another did not even mention them. In part, the authors' differences reflected the biases of their fields. Like the five blind men describing an elephant, each depicted an ideal thesis based on his own experiences. Scientists, for example, tend toward a standard five-chapter thesis structure, while humanities professors like theses that are more free-form, as befits their outlook on life. But the authors' prescriptions differed even within a single field. After a fruitless week of trying to reconcile how and why one author's method differed from another's, I took the step I should have taken in the first place—I went to the library and reviewed several hundred theses so I could draw my own conclusions.

Theses differ substantially from each other depending on the field, the guidelines of the department and committee, and most important, the intrinsic logic of the thesis itself. If you are writing a history thesis, and you need nine chapters to fully develop your ideas, then nine chapters is right for you. If your committee expects you to state explicit research questions, then you should. Likewise length can differ dramatically dependent upon need, ranging from the twenty or thirty pages found in some theoretical theses in physics or mathematics to many hundreds of pages. Ph.D. theses in English, for example, typically run from two hundred to three hundred pages. Within a field, Ph.D. theses are expected to be more complex, in greater depth, and usually longer than master's theses, but many master's theses approach the length of Ph.D.s.

This variability in form means that you should not try to structure your thesis according to a book written by an author who knows nothing about your particular thesis topic (including me). Instead, you should use guidelines set down by your department and committee to plan a structure that meets the needs of your individual thesis project. If you haven't already done so, spend at least a few hours in your school library reading over theses to get a sense of scope and style in your field. Also, make sure you check early on with your adviser, department, and graduate school for guidelines so that you don't waste time doing things wrong. Generally your graduate school will set format requirements, including form of the title page and reference style, while your adviser and committee will be responsible for approving the actual structural composition, content, and writing style of the thesis.

Flexibility of thesis form being noted, it is also true that most theses are similar in gross structure. They have three main sections: the front and back matter, which are straightforward and similar in all theses, and the body, which is where everything gets complicated (the thesis structure has also been described as having a beginning, a muddle, and an end).

FRONT MATTER

Front matter typically includes the following trivia, without which you will not graduate: a title page, a copyright page, signed certifications by your committee and other important functionaries testifying that your thesis is "partial satisfaction of the degree," acknowledgments, a table of contents, and a list each of tables and figures. These are all straightforward and will be covered by your departmental or school guidelines, so I only have a couple of suggestions here. First, when you pick a *title* for your thesis, work in as many descriptive, precise key words as possible without making it absurdly long. If you have chosen the key words in your title well, it will be relatively easy for future researchers to find (and cite!) when they are doing computer searches or otherwise rooting about for the latest contributions to the field. My own thesis was called "A Dimorphism in Male Mating Behavior Associated with Size Class in the Pygmy Swordtail Fish *Xiphophorus pygmaeus Nigrensis* (Poeciliidae, Pisces): A Study in Competing Male Strategies." "Dimorphism" and "mating behavior" are key words that a researcher would typically use in looking for works on sexual selection. On the other hand, "competing male strategies" is somewhat obscure, so it would have been better to use "sexual competition," a more common phrase.

Second, in your *acknowledgments* don't forget to mention all politically important people who helped you, especially members of your committee and other luminaries. Check out the correct professional tone by reading the acknowledgments in papers published by other authors—avoid gushing. You don't need to mention everyone, just those who materially helped. As a guideline, you can leave out people you won't remember in ten years. My own acknowledgments were full of people presently unknown: Pete Seymour? Don Horak? John Tolan? Who *are* these people?

BACK MATTER

This includes the bibliography and whatever appendixes are necessary. *Bibliographies* take different forms depending on the field and the demands of the thesis. In the sciences, it is usual to list only literature actually cited in the text, in which case the bibliography is titled "list of references" or "literature cited." In other fields the bibliography may include additional sources not actually cited but which were consulted by the author or would be useful to the reader. Subdivisions within such expanded bibliographies vary: a history thesis divided its references into "primary" and "secondary" sources, in accordance with how heavily they were used in preparing the thesis. An art history thesis included separate sections for sales catalogues, manuscripts, books, and articles. In any case, your references must be impeccable in form, punctuation, and completeness.

Appendixes include any material that would be out of place in the main body of the text. This may include tables of original data, facsimiles of supporting documents, or questionnaires used for collecting data. Do include genuinely useful material, but avoid filling up the thesis with dross, if only because excessive length will decrease the chances that other researchers will order copies of your thesis (they usually will have to pay by the page to have it copied). Ask yourself if what you want to include genuinely adds to the credibility or interest of your thesis. Remember that your committee isn't likely to judge your work by the pound.

THE BODY

The body of the thesis contains two groups of chapters. The introductory chapters set the scene and tell how you did your research. The "presentation" chapters make up the meat of your thesis.

Introductory chapters: introduction, literature review, and methodology. Most theses will have some recognizable version of the introduction, literature review, and description of methodology. Often they appear as distinct chapters, particularly in the sciences (see exemplary outlines below). In other cases, these three chapters may be collapsed into one or two introductory chapters. Such condensed introductions are common in humanities theses, where a "methodology" section may consist of little more than a brief list of sources to be researched or a statement of which theoretical approach was used. More rarely, the complexity of the introductory material demands additional chapters to present it clearly.

These introductory chapters are essentially updated versions of the first three chapters of the thesis proposal. Therefore, if you did a sound job on your proposal, you should be able to adapt it easily to create these introductory chapters. If you did not do a comprehensive proposal, you can refer back to Chapter 17 for a description of how to structure these chapters.

Even if you did write complete versions of these chapters for the proposal, you will need to revise them to reflect the additional knowledge and changes in direction gained during research completed since the proposal was finished. For example, the introduction may be changed to reflect new theoretical insights or research questions that you developed during the thesis process. Your original literature review chapter, even if excellently done and comprehensive, will have to account for more recent publications. Finally, the methodology chapter must reflect the work you actually did, which will almost certainly be somewhat different from what you originally proposed. Particularly in experimental theses, the early data you collect is almost certain to point in unplanned but rewarding directions.

Presentation chapters: results, discussion, theme chapters, and conclusions. In the presentation chapters, thesis structures diverge substantially from each other, depending upon field and content. Although theses can be categorized in many ways, for our purposes I will divide them loosely into two main types, "data" theses (including most in the hard and social sciences) and "thematic" theses (including most in the humanities).

In data theses, the usual practice is to write two final chapters, called "results" and "discussion," which follow the three introductory chapters just described, for a total of five thesis chapters. In the results chapter, describe your findings without interpretation. As Sergeant Joe Friday said, "Just the facts." In the discussion chapter, interpret the significance of your results in relation to other theory and research in the field.

In a data thesis your final conclusions and suggestions for further research are usually incorporated into the discussion chapter. A typical thesis outline of the data type would look like this:

Data thesis outline Type 1

• Front Matter
• Chapter I. Introduction
• Chapter II. Literature Review
• Chapter III. Methodology
• Chapter IV. Results
• Chapter V. Discussion (including conclusions)
• Back Matter

Even this relatively standardized form may be adapted to individual needs. For example, a complicated experimental thesis in biology might be best handled if each major experiment were given its own chapter, each of which would have its own methodology, results, and discussion sections. My own thesis was of this form:

Data thesis outline Type 2

• Front Matter
• Chapter I. Introduction
• Chapter II. Literature Review
• Chapter III. Experiment 1 (Methodology, Results, Discussion)
• Chapter IV. Experiment 2 (Methodology, Results, Discussion)
• Chapter V. Experiment 3 (Methodology, Results, Discussion)

- Chapter VI. General Conclusions
- Back Matter

In thematic theses, there are no results or discussion sections because there are no experimental results to discuss, although you may be working with historical facts or other types of evidence. Instead, a typical thematic thesis develops intellectual arguments, substantiated with reference to other works. A history thesis, for example, might make the central argument that the Mayan civilization was susceptible to rapid collapse during the Spanish conquest because of its extremely hierarchical nature. The narrative chapters of this thesis could chronicle key historical events, analyze evidence about Mayan social structure, and draw comparisons with the social structures and cultural resilience of other groups. In this type of thesis the number of chapters used is more variable than in the sciences because thesis structure reflects the intrinsic logical organization of the arguments developed by the author. Theme chapters in a thesis on the American China trade in 1784–1844 included "American Merchants and the China Trade" and "The Middle-Class Consumer of Chinese Goods." Here is a typical outline for a thematic thesis:

Thematic thesis

- Front Matter
- Chapter I. Introduction (including literature review and methodology, if condensed)
- Chapter II. Theme 1
- Chapter III. Theme 2
- Chapter IV. Theme 3
- Chapter V. Theme 4
- Chapter VI. Conclusions
- Back Matter

Theme chapters can be structured in many ways. One common structure is a chronological organization, in which the chapters cover successive time periods. For example, the Ph.D. thesis of an English major traced the literary development of one major author during his lifetime, with separate chapters for the 1920s, 1930s, and 1940s. Another common method is comparative; a Spanish literature student contrasted the works of three twentieth-century authors, with each author given a separate chapter. A third structure is causal, in which different contributory factors are treated in separate chapters. A political science student examined the predominant social and political factors leading to forced collectivization of Ukrainian farmers during the 1930s, with a different chapter for each major contributing factor. A good structure will become clear to you as you begin research, exploratory writing, and talking over your ideas with professors and other colleagues.

Whether you use a thematic or data thesis structure, the body of your thesis will end with your major conclusions. In thematic theses this summing-up is usually presented in a final chapter aptly called "Conclusions." In a data thesis, the conclusions are often placed in the end of the discussion chapter, which also contains detailed discussion of the significance of your results. As in the Type 2 data thesis outline above, data theses may also have a conclusions chapter if the author feels it necessary to pull together the threads of a complicated thesis. In either case, the conclusions section is your opportunity to state the importance of what you have done, answering the following questions: What are your most important results and why? How is your work unique? How do your results answer the research questions laid out in your initial chapter? If your results were unexpected or contradicted your initial hypotheses, why was this so? Do your results or conclusions substantiate or contradict similar studies by other researchers? If so, why? How do your results reconcile with existing theory? Finally, what future research needs do your results demonstrate? (This is a chance to think about future grants you might apply for.)

Given how different the final chapters are between fields, I will not go into further detail about how to structure them. Again, I point you toward other theses and published papers in your field to get a sense of structure and writing style. Of the self-help books available, I particularly recommend Chapter 6 in Madsen's *Successful Dissertations and Theses*, and Appendix B in Long, Convey, and Chwalek's *Completing Dissertations in the Behavioral Sciences and Education*, which describes different types of research.

OVERVIEW OF THE THESIS
▪ WRITING PROCESS ▪

HOW LONG DOES IT TAKE?

Writing up your thesis is a monstrous task, so you should expect to take somewhere between six months and a year, provided you don't seriously procrastinate. In general, students in science and technology take a shorter time than those in humanities because their theses are more formulaic. Writing a results chapter, for example, may be tedious, but is conceptually straightforward. Humanities theses tend to be longer, structurally more complicated, and in some fields, notably literature, the author must pay more attention to writing style.

One productive scholar says that a reasonable writing rate is three pages per day, including time for research. With steady writing at this rate, and weekends off for good behavior, you could produce about seventy pages per month. So it would take about three months to write the first draft of a two-hundred-page thesis. To this estimate you should add time to take into account writing blocks, unavailable resource materials, domestic crises, and errant committee members. This scholar's estimate jibes well with my own writing experience. Often I will spend several days doing research only, and then write fifteen pages in a day, but an average of three pages per day is a good ballpark number for figuring out how long a first draft of your thesis will take you.

Expect to go through several complete drafts. Even after you feel satisfied with what you have written, your committee will usually demand substantial revision. Incidentally, don't make substantial revisions based on input from only a single committee member, since their instructions will often be contradictory and you should resolve contradictions *before* extensive rewriting.

In planning how much time you need, do not expect your final drafts to be much quicker than your early drafts, because the picky details at the end can take a huge amount of time to get right. In the last stages you will incorporate your committee's final suggestions, proofread for punctuation and other errors, and check every bibliographic reference for accuracy. If you were sloppy with your bibliography at earlier stages, you will pay for it now. A single missing reference, the exact location of which you have forgotten (let's see, was it in *Science?*), may take hours to find.

WHEN TO START

Some people write up bit by bit as they research, while others wait until all research is finished and then write everything up in a lump. Your particular type of research may make one method more practical than another. For example, the entire research of a Ph.D. student in education was one massive survey, and she had to wait until the survey was complete to write up any results or discussion. On the other hand, it is common for the research in a scientific thesis to consist of a series of separate but related experiments, each of which can be written up as it is completed.

Regardless of the type of research you do, I strongly suggest that you write as much as possible as early as possible. If you did a thorough job with your thesis proposal, you should have the beginning chapters in good shape, suitable for further revision. If you haven't done these already, you should start writing them as soon as you can. There are good reasons for an early start. The most obvious is that you start whittling down the amount of outstanding writing and reduce your anxiety about the size of the job. Equally important is that an early start at writing will give early warning of problems. One student in English wrote a brief thesis proposal which was accepted by her committee. She then wrote her thesis introduction right away and gave the draft to her committee for approval. To her surprise, they rejected it completely and asked her to find another research topic. The reason was that substantial theoretical and practical problems with her topic appeared in the full introduction that were not obvious in the abbreviated proposal. She was fortunate that she chose to write and submit her introduction before spending a year or two researching her complete thesis.

In the experimental sciences, at a minimum you should thoroughly analyze data and write research reports on each experiment as it is completed. This will allow you to spot and correct problems before they weaken your entire foundation, and to identify promising new directions for research. On several of my own thesis experiments, I deferred statistical analysis until it was too late to correct for sample sizes that were too small to give significant results, invalidating some of the potentially most interesting findings of my work.

Don't put off writing under the misapprehension that you need to read everything ever written about your topic before you start. If you're not careful you can waste months or even years before daring to scribble anything on paper. Realistically, your head can only hold a limited number of facts and ideas for more than a few days. This means that a month into a reading orgy you will retain only a general sense of what the first book you read was about. Of course, you can always reread it, but it's pretty easy to see that this will put you in a perpetual loop of reading and rereading. Fortunately, in most cases only a few days of library research should be enough to get you started on an outline or rough draft. When you come to knowledge gaps, stop writing temporarily while you research the answers. Or you can leave a gap and fill it later. The important thing is to start writing so you can develop ideas, identify areas where you need to think or read more, become comfortable with the writing process, and complete a preliminary product to discuss with your committee.

HOW TO GET A HEAD START ON YOUR THESIS

One excellent way to trick yourself into starting your thesis is to make course papers do double duty as thesis research. Whenever possible, choose paper topics that cover material you need to know for your thesis. One master's student did much of her thesis research on women's roles in U.S. government by choosing to write about women's issues when she took government classes and vice versa. Writing papers on your thesis topic is also a good way to tell ahead of time whether the topic you have chosen for your thesis will sustain your interest over the long haul (if you are bored after a term paper, imagine how you will feel halfway through the thesis process). As Nietzsche wrote, "Is not life a hundred times too short for us to bore ourselves?"

Another productive way to get the thesis written in stages is to write it in units that can be separately published as you go along. Early publication will help maintain your enthusiasm and increase your marketability after graduation. Further, publishing parts of your thesis will make them "bulletproof." It is hard for a committee to fail a thesis that has been largely validated by peer review and publication, and, frankly, peer review is sometimes more generous than your committee. One lucky chemistry student's adviser instructed him how to write his thesis: "Just bind up your papers. You've already done your thesis."

When deciding whether to use the paper publication strategy, be aware that you may have to put in more total work than if you do not publish. The amount in part will depend on the type of thesis you are expected to produce. You may have relatively little duplication of effort if your committee will accept a thesis which is essentially separate papers cobbled together with transitions. In this case you can publish the papers as you go along, with little left to do at the end to finish the thesis except write the transitions and general conclusions. This is often acceptable in scientific fields where you are reporting the results of experiments, rather than weaving a book-long argument. If, on the other hand, your committee believes that the thesis should be an organic whole of well-integrated parts, more similar to a book than to a collection of papers, you may find that published papers would have to be substantially rewritten and total time expenditure proportionally increased.

▪ GETTING THE DARN THING WRITTEN ▪

Don't put off till tomorrow what can be enjoyed today.

—JOSH BILLINGS

By far the biggest problem most writers face is remaining motivated. Harry Bauld, the author of a book on application essays, wrote, "The hardest thing to do is budge an object from a dead start, particularly if that object is your brain." You can consult other books about the mechanics of writing, including the excessively recommended *Elements of Style*, by William Strunk, Jr., and E. B. White, or the *MLA Style Manual* for those of you in humanities. My purpose is to provide perspective and techniques that can help you write your thesis as rapidly as possible with a minimum of pain. I'm going to assume that if you're in graduate school you can write a complete sentence and are able to string ideas together in a coherent manner. If you really do have trouble with basic English composition, if you are a foreign student perhaps, then you will need a course or a tutor in composition rather than a how-to book. Another possibility if you're in real trouble is to hire an English graduate student or professional editor to work with you to carve your thesis into good form. This is common practice, but you should check with your adviser if it's okay to do this, because some departments might not like it. (For an amusing overview of the moral and practical dilemmas of hiring help, see "A Visit to the Prose Pros," in the October 1991 issue of *Lingua Franca*.)

Most thesis writers are in danger of procrastinating, which Thomas De Quincey found heinous. He said, "If once a man indulge himself in murder, very soon he comes to think little of robbing; and from robbing he next comes to drinking and Sabbath-breaking, and from that to incivility and *procrastination*" (my italics). To illustrate the danger, consider my friend Joanne, who did what I hope you will never do: she accepted a job when she was almost finished writing her thesis. Even though when she started work her thesis was only days from completion, four *years* later she was still lugging it around in a battered cardboard box. She says, "I put it on my desk and didn't work on it. I put it on my table and didn't work on it. Finally, I put it under my bed and tried not to think about it." At last, because she'd been hired with the understanding that she would finish her degree, her employer gave her eighteen days' paid leave to finish it "or else." Given the threat, she easily finished on time. She now says, "I can't believe I subjected myself to four years of guilt just to avoid two weeks of work."

Students who have become mired in this state of permanent, epic procrastination, often lasting years, are called ABD—all but dissertation. It's a horrible state in which, as Bernard Berelson wrote, the "uncompleted dissertation hangs over the candidate like a black cloud, interfacing with his career, his domestic life, even his peace of mind."

One reason students don't get their theses written is that they have poor writing skills. I'm not talking about bad punctuation. What I mean is that most amateur writers, including novice academics, fail to understand that large writing projects require consistent, well-organized effort and a system of self-imposed incentives to overcome procrastination and writing blocks, to organize your work clearly, and to sustain progress. Moreover, they seriously misunderstand the nature of writing.

People also procrastinate because they're afraid. You are afraid that what you write won't measure up or that you simply won't be able to manage something as complex as a thesis. As you try to write, you hear the phantom voices of your thesis committee saying things like "You call that brilliant? I knew it was a mistake to let you into the program." Added to this wretched insecurity is that good writing is just plain hard work and anyone normal would rather be going to a movie or having a few beers.

All this aversion causes what animal behaviorists call displacement activity. A displacement activity is what an animal—i.e., you—does to burn off emotional energy when he's frustrated. A young male elk chased away from eager females by an older bull is angry and afraid, so he beats up a bush or pretends to eat. In the case of graduate students, you want your thesis to be finished and it isn't, and you want to go to a movie instead but you shouldn't, so you end up buying a candy bar and then talking on the phone to a friend about how much trouble you're having getting started on your thesis.

Here's a story about the writer Robert Benchley, told by his son, that illustrates the perils of displacement:

> Once, he had been trying to start a piece but couldn't get it under way, so he went down the corridor to where a poker game was in progress, just to jolt his mind into starting up. Some time later, he returned to his room, sat down to the clean sheet of paper in the typewriter, and pecked out the word "The." This, he reasoned, was as safe a start as any, and might possibly break the block. But nothing else came, so he went downstairs and ran into a group of [friends], with whom he passed a cheerful hour or so. Then, protesting that he

had to work, he went back upstairs, where the small, bleak "The" was looking at him out of the expanse of yellow paper. He sat down and stared at it for several minutes, then a sudden idea came to him, and he finished the sentence, making it read "The hell with it," and got up and went happily out for the evening. [From *The Oxford Book of American Literary Anecdotes*, edited by Donald Hall]

Ending the cycle of fear and procrastination is simple. If you make consistent progress, writing every day, even if only for a short period, the job gets easier and easier. Partly this is because writing takes practice. Not only do you get better over time, gaining more fluency, but the converse is true. If you stop for even a few days, you start getting rusty. People rarely think of writing this way, as something needing regular practice, like piano playing, tennis, or running, but it does.

At this point you're probably saying, "Big deal. If I could write easily every day, I wouldn't be reading this book for advice." Therefore, let's move on to some concrete suggestions.

How to get started

A recent study by the National Academy of Sciences concluded, alas, that subliminal-suggestion tapes won't help you lose weight, quit smoking, or earn more money selling real estate. However, the scientists also concluded that one thing does work to improve performance—plain old relaxation. A relaxed person will outperform a stressed person on everything from math problems to tennis. Even bouncing a tennis ball once or twice before serving can drop your heart rate and blood pressure enough to improve your next serve. For writing, this means that in order to get started, you should first get comfortable.

Each person will have his own ritual of comfort. One eccentric writer, Charles K. Ogden, spent every night scribbling away until dawn, surrounded by two dozen blaring radios and ticking clocks. Truman Capote said, "I am a completely horizontal author. I can't think unless I'm lying down, either in bed or stretched on a couch and with a cigarette and coffee handy. . . . As the afternoon wears on, I shift from coffee to mint tea to sherry to martinis." The system of Clavius Frederick Earbrass, Edward Gorey's mythical writer, is the opposite of Capote's. Earbrass is a "straying, rather than sedentary, type of author. He is never to be found at his desk unless actually writing down a sentence. Before this happens he broods over it indefinitely while picking up and putting down again small, loose objects; walking diagonally across rooms; staring out windows; and so forth. He frequently hums. . . ."

Despite their different methods, writers have one thing in common, the need for a place reserved for writing where they will not be disturbed. For example, Katherine Anne Porter described how she wrote *Ship of Fools*: "No telephone, no visitors—oh, I really lived like a hermit, everything but being fed through a grate!" My friend Mark Plotkin, while writing a book about his adventures in the Amazon jungle, had a small cell-like room constructed in his basement. He purposely made it without windows so that he would not be tempted to look out. Follow these writers' example and set up a tranquil place for your own writing, remove anything that distracts you, and during your writing time unplug the phone.

One of the best ways to get started is to talk about your ideas to anyone who will listen so that your ideas crystallize. Howard Becker, an excellent academic writer, says, "Although I have written a fair amount, I have spent relatively little time at the typewriter. I would begin what eventually became a paper by talking to anyone who would listen about the topic I was going to write about. . . . I learned what points I could get to follow one another logically, which ways of making a point people understood, and which ways caused confusion, what arguments were dead ends that were better not entered at all."

I always talk to people about my own writing ideas. I will explain the structure I'm using in a particular chapter, or the terminology I've had to invent. Not only does talking it through help me organize, but there is an additional, almost magical benefit. Talking is the first step in the immersion process I describe below—your head will become so full of ideas that there is a pressure to write. Before talking the ideas through, I am often afraid to write, perhaps because I'm not sure what I want to say, or how to say it; after talking, I am comfortable with the ideas and eager to get them down on paper.

Of course, some people are really good at talking about their subjects but can't seem to make the transition to paper. The secret here is, once you've built up a conversational head of steam, park your butt on a chair in front of a word pro-

IF YOU STAY FOCUSED ON YOUR WRITING, INSPIRATION MAY STRIKE AT ANY MOMENT

cessor, even if you think you've got nothing to write about. Don't make excuses that you haven't done enough research, or haven't thought through everything you want to say, or that your writing will be wasted because you won't actually use it in your thesis. Just start. Set yourself a schedule, which may be as little as an hour per day at first. When your schedule tells you to work, sit in front of your word processor for the allotted time, even if nothing happens. Even if *you're* not working, your subconscious will be. Eventually you will be so bored staring at the paper that you will create something. You may not produce during the first hour, or the first day, but eventually you will begin to write, unless, like Benchley, you've gone down the hall for a game of poker.

If you don't have the discipline to keep to the schedule, ask your significant other, mother, or friend to tie you to the chair. Beth, a thirty-six-year-old nutrition student, was in the sixth year of her doctoral program, out of money, with no end in sight, so she called her mother for financial help. Mom said, "No money. But you can stay at my house, and I'll feed you while you work. You'd better get used to the idea of writing every day." Writing hours in Mom's gulag were nine to five, seven days a week, with a half hour off for lunch. It wasn't fun, but Beth finished her thesis in six months and now says, "I resented her for making me work so hard, and I kept trying to sneak away, but now I realize that without her I never would have finished." Tom, a master's student in history, couldn't get started either, so he volunteered as a guinea pig in a pharmaceutical study which required him to stay in the hospital for monitoring every day for two months. When they let him out, he had $1,500 in pay plus most of his thesis done. He said, "It's amazing how much you can write when you're bored out of your mind."

At this point, I'm assuming that you have found the discipline to at least sit down to work. Maybe you've even started writing a few paragraphs, but there's a problem. You still feel unable to write and would really be much happier watching television. *Don't* get out of that chair. Realize that your brain needs to warm up. I need at least an hour to warm up, and I do my best writing after I've been at it for at least two hours. In part, I simply get too tired to criticize each word and sentence as I write, so the flow is smoother. If you give up during the warm-up period, you lose all the time invested. Also, recognize that the more days you've been without writing, and the more anxious you are about getting started, the longer your warm-up period may be.

One of the biggest obstacles faced by novice writers is when they approach writing the way they would diamond cutting, where one wrong cut can destroy a stone worth a fortune. It's not surprising that diamond cutters spend months preparing the first cut on a big stone, but you shouldn't move that slowly when you're writing. Instead, realize that writing isn't at all like diamond cutting; what it's really like is sculpting clay. First you take handfuls of clay and slap them together into a big lump that looks vaguely like what you are trying to make. Then you smooth a little here, cut a little there, add a little to the nose, and with enough refinement your sculpture ends up looking pretty good. If you realize at the beginning of writing that you don't need perfection, that you are just doing the equivalent of making a pile of clay for future use, it will go much easier.

In writing, slapping the clay together is called exploratory writing. There are various tricks to use, but the basic idea is to turn off your critical sense and simply write, without worrying about whether what you are producing is good. Don't worry about spelling, about whether the word you chose is right, or, above all, whether you are saying something "the best way." Write not to create a finished product, or even a good first draft. Instead write to (a) work through your ideas and (b) create fragments of writing that you may later use in putting together a first draft. By removing the pressure of perfection and writing drafts meant to be thrown away, you can relax, turn off your critical appraisal, and create. Some of the fragments you write will be balderdash, others redundant, some useful, and a few will be gems. If you hit a hot streak, you may suddenly be able to dash off a whole section that is worth saving. Whatever happens, the key is to suspend judgment, write freely, and, above all, keep at it. Once you have enough useful fragments, you can quilt them together, adding new sections, discarding some old ones, and rewriting as necessary to come up with a decent draft.

Despite this freewheeling, clay-slapping approach, you still should construct an outline to guide you. This outline should be adaptable, not permanent, and it should evolve constantly to reflect the new ideas and changes in structure that develop throughout the whole writing process. Even though your outline is evolving, it remains a relatively structured map for figuring out how the parts of your manuscript relate to each other, where you are now, and what you need to write next.

Eventually, as you fill in your outline, the piece you are writing will coalesce to the point where you can accurately call it a first draft. Continue rewriting until you get a draft good enough to show to your committee. Edward Gorey describes Mr. Earbrass's dislike of rewriting: "This is worse than merely writing, because not only does he have to think up new things just the same, but at the same time try not to remember the old ones." Revision involves "first, transposing passages, or reversing the order of their paragraphs, or crumpling them up furiously and throwing them in the waste-basket.''

Do not underestimate the amount of work to be done once you have a half-decent first draft. At this point you are less than halfway finished. For this reason, one excellent book on writing calls itself *Rewriting Writing* in order to stress how much work you have to put in to get from any first draft to a quality finished product. It says:

> The writing process is also a *recursive* one. Its nature is circular and self-feeding. Professional writers seldom compose unblemished text at one sitting. More commonly they compose in increments, often pausing to read what they have just written to get ideas about what to say next. When they get stuck, as all writers occasionally do, they go back and look over what they have already written for further ideas.
>
> Implicit in this recursive process is the notion of rewriting, restating, a continual patching of this sentence or that, this phrase, this expression. You jump from this paragraph to the start of the essay and, while lingering briefly there, find a better word, a better image, a less crooked sentence.

Accordingly, you should expect to go through at least three or four drafts for each section of your thesis, rewriting for clarity and style, just to develop to the point where you can show it to your adviser.

Once you have gotten to the stage where you are working on complete drafts, don't be afraid to throw stuff out and start over. Be ruthless. If what you have written doesn't seem absolutely clear, and you can't fix it with minor editing, throw out the original and rewrite it. Your second attempt is almost certain to be better. I typically throw out three complete paragraphs for every one I keep, despite the fact that many individual paragraphs may have taken an hour to write. For example, when I originally wrote the section above on procrastination, it was entirely different from the present version. The original structure was split into two sections, one on procrastination and one on techniques for generating ideas. However, as I wrote, I realized that the distinction between procrastination and lack of ideas was not clear-cut, certainly not enough to justify basing the entire structure of the section on it. So I threw out everything I had written—two days' work—except for a couple of paragraphs which survive, mutated, in the present version. Those two days of work were not wasted, because they forced me to develop my ideas until I could come up with a sound structure.

My own writing technique begins with brainstorming. For the section you are now reading, "Getting the Darn Thing Written," I took half an hour to make a list of everything I could think of about how to start writing. Because I was short of ideas, I skimmed my collection of research materials and added to my list whatever ideas I could borrow from them. Then, with my list of ideas typed into the word processor, I deleted those that were duplicates or pea-brained, and organized the survivors into groups of related ideas, such as "techniques for getting started." Next I invented a heading for each group, such as "Getting Started" for the subsection you are reading right now. At this point what I had created was an outline. Next, working within the outline, I began my exploratory writing, gradually developing my ideas and learning how they connected with each other. As my ideas evolved, I moved them around within the outline as necessary, and altered the outline itself—all easy to do on a word processor. I kept the good writing, threw out the bad, and kept reworking until I arrived at a final draft. If I got bored with one part, I skipped to another that interested me, coming back to the first later on. Whenever I got really stuck, I either talked it through with friends or read my research sources for further ideas. Often I would find a good anecdote or quotation to start me off in a new direction.

If you would like to read more about writing techniques, try *On Writing the College Application Essay*, by Harry Bauld. Don't be misled by the title. This is an entertaining book on basic writing that can help you if you're having problems with course papers, proposals, or your thesis. Also, read Howard Becker's *Writing for Social Scientists*, which is the most useful, amusing, and personal book that I have seen on how to do good academic writing. Again, don't be put off by the title—it will help you regardless of your field. Another excellent book, focusing more on structure and editing, is the aforementioned *Rewriting Writing*, by Jo Ray McCuen and Anthony Winkler.

KEEP GOING

Writing something as big as a thesis is like running a marathon—a modest, steady pace is much better than sprinting. Instead of infrequent bursts of intense writing, which leave you exhausted and conditioned to dislike writing, keep to a regular schedule of moderate but constant progress.

The purpose of writing according to a schedule is to ensure that you write at least the minimum necessary to keep your engine tuned. Over time, as you get more comfortable with writing, you may find yourself in periods where you work hours at a stretch, for days at a time. That's great. Just make sure that when you finish a stretch, you don't stop writing completely. Instead, fall back to your minimal schedule for forward progress.

One of the reasons to keep writing every day is that your writing will be better and easier if you are immersed in the process. If you are immersed, you will be thinking about what you are writing all the time, while walking to school, taking a shower, or eating. You will see ideas everywhere—in a newspaper article, in something someone says, or in a movie.

There are certain times when it is particularly critical to keep your writing in mind. One is late at night; if you read over what you wrote during the day just before you go to sleep, your sleeping mind will work on it, and you will usually have new ideas in the morning. Critical times for me are the last minute before I go to sleep, in the shower, first thing in the morning, and walking. These are the times that new ideas, structural rearrangements, and even language will surface from your subconscious.

Katherine Anne Porter, when asked why it was important to avoid breaks or distractions while writing, said, "To keep at a boiling point. So that I can get up in the morning with my mind still working where it was yesterday." When you take breaks during a writing period, don't watch TV, read, talk to people, or anything else that will reprogram your mind. Instead, do the things I just mentioned that let your subconscious work: go for a walk, take a shower, or wander into the kitchen and make tea. I would be surprised if you could get through an entire shower without a couple of good ideas for where you need to go next with what you are writing.

If you follow the above regimen of daily exploratory writing and revision, it is unlikely that you will suffer the most dreaded of maladies, writer's block. Writer's block is usually just a bad case of procrastination, where you are less willing to work than usual, possibly because you are angry at your adviser, or because the thesis looks so big you're afraid you can't do it, or just because you're feeling lazy. If writer's block does strike, you can usually climb out of the slump if you force yourself to sit at the typewriter until you break down and write something. It scarcely matters what you write; just get your brain moving. Try not to judge your work. Don't try to be brilliant, just hack the stuff out; you can add brilliance when you edit. One trick I use when I'm stuck is to take a pad of paper to a restaurant, order coffee, and write whatever comes to mind. Usually the walk to the restaurant, plus the lack of pressure, frees me up. Another trick is to start writing about why you are stuck: if you can't figure out how to handle two ideas because they blur into each other, start by writing, "The reason I am having trouble with these two ideas is . . . The first idea is . . . The second is . . ."

You can also talk out loud to yourself. Ask yourself, "What am I really trying to say here?" Answer the question out loud, and then get your answer down on paper. For example, if you can't get started on a section, ask yourself out loud, "What is the first thing I would tell someone about this issue?" If you're in a section that is getting too muddled up, ask yourself, "What am I really trying to say here? In the simplest words possible, what is the basic idea?" If you're really stuck, call someone up and try explaining the idea to them.

You may also be blocked because you really *don't* have anything to say, perhaps because you haven't done enough research. Try brainstorming, as described above, writing down all your ideas on a list. If you don't have enough ideas, develop some by reading more articles and talking with people.

ADVICE ON WRITING CLEARLY

In 1992, I edited a book containing scientific articles by twenty-five biologists. If you have spent much time reading the academic literature in your own field, it will be no surprise to you that three-quarters of these articles were incomprehensible. I tried sending them back to the authors with detailed requests for corrections, but the authors seemed incapable of making them. What they mailed back to me was often more feeble than the first attempts, so I finally had to rewrite most of the articles myself. If you had listened outside my study window late at night, you would have heard me screaming, "What the hell is this miserable knucklehead trying to say?" In many cases I remained unable to decipher an author's meaning, even after lengthy study, so I eventually had to phone most of the authors with long lists of questions before I could even attempt to rewrite their papers. It was appalling that all the authors were senior in their field and responsible for teaching graduate students to write, but that's another and more horrifying matter entirely. One of my friends, an English professor, also edited a book of papers, in this case contributed by *English* professors. She gave them simple instructions on how to write their citations. She told me, "The directions were the same ones I give to college freshmen, and every single author screwed up. I want to know how can these guys manage to get in their cars and drive to work in the morning."

While racking my brain over the chapters my authors had sent me, I began to have a sense of déjà vu, in that many of the same faults were repeated over and over, almost as though some diabolical mastermind, dedicated to the destruction of the English language, had sabotaged academic writing throughout the United States. I realized that if academic writers could be trained to avoid even a few of these problems, the lives of academic readers would be much easier. Therefore, I will give you a few rules for clear writing.

First, however, here is a description of an extraordinary experiment which explains one reason why most academics write so poorly. Because he did such a good job of summarizing the experiment by Naftulin et al. (1973), I will quote from a paper by Scott Armstrong, from the Wharton School, University of Pennsylvania:

> Dr. Fox was an actor who looked distinguished and sounded author-itative. He was provided with a fictitious but impressive biography and was sent to lecture about a subject on which he knew nothing. The talk, "Mathematical Game Theory as Applied to Physician Ed-ucation," was delivered on three occasions to a total of 55 people. One hour was allowed for the talk and 30 minutes for discussion. The audiences consisted of highly educated social workers, psychologists, psychiatrists, educators, and administrators. The lecture was com-prised of double talk, meaningless words, false logic, contradictory statements, irrelevant humor, and meaningless references to unrelated topics. Judging from a questionnaire administered after the talk, the audience found Dr. Fox's lecture to be clear and stimulating. None of the subjects realized that the lecture was *pure nonsense* [my italics].

To be academically rigorous, I must tell you that subsequent researchers have criticized this study for poor methodology and that further research has shown that audiences may not always be so gullible. Nonetheless, the Dr. Fox Effect appears real enough to have stimulated additional serious research. One study of particular relevance to thesis writers, called "Un-intelligible Management Research and Academic Prestige," was published in 1980 by the same Scott Armstrong. Armstrong created difficult versions and easy-to-read versions of serious articles that had been published in management journals, and he sent them out to academic reviewers. Even though both easy and difficult versions had identical intellectual content, reviewers rated the difficult-to-read versions as significantly higher in "research competence." Armstrong concluded, "Overall, the evidence is consistent with a common suspicion. Clear communication of one's re-search is not appreciated. Faculty are impressed by less readable articles."

I told you about Dr. Fox partly because this twist of human nature is funny in a depressing sort of way, and also because I feel that I owe you complete disclosure before blithely telling you to simplify and clarify your academic writing. However, if you are now cheerfully concluding that you don't have to write your thesis clearly, I must disillusion you. I believe the Dr. Fox Effect doesn't apply to your thesis, because you aren't writing for Armstrong's academic reviewers, you are writing for your thesis committee. What's the difference? First, understand that reviewers generally aren't paid, and they're very busy, which means that they won't spend much time deciphering a difficult article. So if the article is very difficult to read, the reviewer often takes it on faith, basing his judgment on the reputation of the researcher, perhaps reading only the summary and a few figures and skimming over the tough parts. Your thesis committee is different—they're supposed to read all of your thesis carefully, and you want them to. A muddled, dull, verbose, and pretentious thesis will not impress them; it will irritate them and may keep them from reading closely enough to give you good advice. It would be like going to the doctor and hiding your symptoms—you're not likely to get cured.

Given that you now have a burning desire for clarity, I will give you a few pointers. For my sake, please pay attention in case I someday wind up editing one of your papers.

• *Say it in English.* As Einstein said, "Make it as simple as possible, but not more so." Avoid writing like an academic, especially in the critical first draft. This will be hard to do, because you will have read so many turgid, poorly written papers in your field. And in many ways it is easier to write badly, using jargon and stilted language, than to write clearly in simple English, partly because to write clearly you have to truly understand what you want to say. Nonetheless, if you can learn to write simply, it will be easier to see where you have redundancies, where your ideas contradict each other, or where you just plain don't make sense.

Here's an example of obscurity taken verbatim from a book by the Conservation Foundation on environmental policy. The book went through an extensive editing process designed to clarify it for a *lay audience*— that's you. Nonetheless, even after editing, this sentence remains a good example of the jargon-filled abstruseness typical of academic papers and technical reports:

[The Environmental Protection Agency] has developed an industry-specific cross-media pollution-abatement model that also estimates the reduction in human health risks attributable to adopting various sets of abatement measures. The model has been applied to the iron and steel industry.

Didn't you breathe a sigh of relief when you got to the words "iron and steel"? You may not know anything else about the model, but at least you're sure it has something to do with the iron and steel industry. Here's a rewrite:

> In order to understand how to reduce pollution in some specific industries, the Environmental Protection Agency (EPA) has developed a computer model which examines how pollutants in air, water, and other environmental media interact. In addition, the model can estimate how selected measures to reduce pollution would also reduce human health risks. As a trial run, the EPA has used this model to examine pollution reduction in the iron and steel industry.

My version is what I call "explanatory" writing. It may not sound as impressive as the first, but it *explains* the ideas to the reader. I tried to make clear what was affecting what, I explained all the jargon, and I threw out the vague, passive phrases "attributable to" and "has been applied to." Assuming that the writer's original goal had been to communicate, the second version would have been a better choice.

Academics may argue that they use jargon words because they are essential technical terms. Not so. They use them because they want to sound impressive (and because they don't know any better), as explained by one of Howard Becker's students in an essay she wrote on why certain pedantic constructions are attractive:

> Instead of choosing to write "he lives at" I prefer "he resides at." Instead of saying "Couples spend their extra money" (or "additional money" or even "disposable income") I'd choose "surplus income." It sounds more grown-up. Here's a favorite of mine: "predicated upon the availability of" is classier than saying "exists because of." Maybe it sounds more awesome. Here's another one. I could say "domestic help," but what I choose to do is say "third party labor." The first time I use it I put a "that is" after the phrase and explain it. Then I am at liberty to use "third party labor" throughout, and it sounds fancier. I think the point here is that I am looking for a writing style that makes me sound smart.

Becker describes the type of image this writing is meant to convey: "a classy person . . . wears a tweed jacket with leather patches at the elbow, smokes a pipe (the men, anyway), and sits around the senior common room swilling port and discussing the latest issue of *The Times Literary Supplement* or *The New York Review of Books* with a bunch of similar people." Nice life if you can get it.

- *Keep it brief*. One of the most annoying writing traits is poorly focused verbosity, which is guaranteed to irritate your reader. So keep your writing tight. Shakespeare said, "Since brevity is the soul of wit, I will be brief." Dorothy Parker said it better: "Brevity is the soul of lingerie." In any case, condense—ask yourself if each paragraph, each word is necessary.

- *Break it up*. Avoid seamless, multipage sections. These tend to be harder to write well than short sections, and harder for the reader to follow. Instead, write in short sections with headings.

- *Don't be self-important*. Many novice academics overemphasize the earthshaking importance of their research. Avoid sentences like "This clearly proves that a major revision of existing critical thought is necessary." Overstatement will make you sound professionally immature and will irritate committee members and journal reviewers.

- *Start your paragraphs with topic sentences*. It's amazing how many academics, particularly in the sciences, think that the correct way to start is to string together a bunch of facts, which, if the reader is lucky, the author interprets at the end. For example, a typical paragraph in a biology paper might begin: "Carter (1982) found that *Xiphophorus pygmaeus*, when subjected to strobe lights, swam in circles. Jones (1983) found that the same species responded to disco music by increasing basal metabolic rate, while a six-month regimen of big-band music induced premature maturation." It would be better to start this paragraph with a statement that guides the reader in understanding what follows. One possibility is: "Two studies have shown that *Xiphophorus pygmaeus* responds to stimuli commonly found in discos by changes in physiology or behavior. Carter (1982) found that . . ."

- *Don't write a detective novel*. The same type of thinking that creates paragraphs without topic sentences also creates whole sections where the conclusion is postponed till the end, whereupon the writer announces it with a tone of misplaced triumph. After the reader has trudged through paragraphs or pages of buildup, the writer finally says something like "Thus we see clearly that Napoleon was short." Don't do this to your reader. Start out your discussion with a statement of what you will prove or conclude. Say, "Much evidence exists to support my contention that Napoleon was short. Let's turn first to pictorial evidence. . . ."

- *Don't try to handle too many ideas at once*. Everyone knows that you shouldn't put three strings of Christmas-tree lights together in the same box because next year you will have to spend a couple of hours untangling them. Likewise, unless you are skilled at handling complex writing with clarity, don't put too many ideas into a paragraph. It's cruel to tie your reader's mind into knots trying to follow you. One trick I use, if my paragraph is muddled, is to underline each separate thought with a pencil. I then often find that the first version of the paragraph has a structure something like AABCAB, where like letters stand for related thoughts. This might be all right as an obscure poetry rhyme scheme, but it's not great for a coherent paragraph. The best solution is usually to put all the A's in one paragraph and the B's in another. Or, if the ideas flow into each other, to switch them around until you end up with AAABBC. The same rule goes for sentences—if your sentence has too many ideas, cut it up.

- *Use key words.* Key words are the friendly guides that lead your reader through the thicket of text—so don't disguise them. If, for example, you begin a section discussing "free will," in the next paragraph don't start suddenly talking about "latitude of choice" or "volition" unless you want your reader to think that there is a difference between free will and latitude of choice. Despite what some English composition teacher once told you about the importance of not using the same word twice in your essay, this does not apply to key words in expositional writing, so stop hunting for synonyms in your thesaurus. Use your key words as often as necessary to keep your meaning clear. Don't replace key words with words or phrases that look like nouns but are so vague that they are really pronouns, such as "these issues," "these effects," or "various options." Likewise, do not replace key words with true pronouns unless their antecedents are crystal clear.

- *Signpost with transitional phrases.* Use "however," "nevertheless," "for example," "moreover," "admittedly," "specifically," and other sign-posting words as needed. It's better to overuse these than to underuse them. Likewise, if you are introducing more than one point in a discussion, signpost them with appropriate numbers, as in "first," "second," and "third."

- *Repeatedly summarize.* Whenever you have presented some complicated material, summarize it for the reader. One of the least intrusive ways is to write a summarizing, transitional phrase between paragraphs, or a summarizing, transitional paragraph between sections. For example, following the above discussion of how *Xiphophorus pygmaeus* responds to disco music, you might write this transitional sentence, summarizing the evidence, which leads into a paragraph on contradictory evidence (the italicized segment is the summary): *"This physiological and behavioral response of Xiphophorus pygmaeus to disco music,* however, has not been found in closely related species. For example . . ."

- *Avoid passive constructions.* Whenever you find a construction like "attributable to," "it is important to," "it should be stated that," or "it was assumed that," chop it out.

- *Avoid adverbs.* Search and destroy the words "very," "extremely," "seriously," and so on. The phrase "extremely redundant" is redundant.
- *Delete double negatives.* You will sound not unlike a windbag if you write things like "it is not inconceivable that," "it is not impossible that," or "his work is not entirely without promise."
- *Chop off your first paragraph.* Usually, the introductory paragraph you first write will be vague, generally just a warm-up to get you thinking. Unfortunately, most novice writers let this paragraph survive. You can rewrite it to make it sharper, but try this instead: after you have finished your section, remove the first paragraph and see how the section reads without it. The chances are that the second paragraph—now the lead paragraph—will be sharper and stronger than your first. You can often do even better by searching through your piece for a colorful, sharp paragraph, often an anecdote or a summarizing paragraph, and use this as a lead.
- *Read it out loud.* As you progress toward your final draft, read your text out loud to help you hear stylistic or logical faults.
- *Read it again cold.* Make sure you leave yourself enough time to read over your material at least a week after you have written it so that you can review it with the eye of a stranger. If you can't understand it two weeks later, no one else will either.
- *Move back and forth between word processor and paper.* Because what you have written will appear much different on paper than on the word processor, make sure you are reviewing in both modes.

KEEP IT SHORT SO YOU CAN FINISH THE DARN THING

As you work, particularly as you near completion, struggle to keep your thesis as short as will do justice to the subject. Remember that your goal is to finish a thesis good enough to convert into published papers or a book *in as little time as possible.* The key words here are "good enough," not "perfect." Resist the urge to put in just one more major idea. As one Ph.D. in electrical engineering said, "Remember, few people other than your advisers will read your thesis (if even they do), and it will soon be consigned to the mustier back shelves of the library stacks." You may publish pieces of it, but most people never publish their thesis in its entirety, and hence its completeness doesn't matter. Also, if you are applying for a job, realize that the search committee isn't going to read your six-hundred-page thesis—published papers are the accepted currency of brilliance among academic search committees, and that's what they will read, if anything. Therefore, once you've achieved a level of adequacy acceptable to your committee, you're better off putting the extra energy into turning one of your chapters into a published paper or looking for a job. Moreover, if you leave yourself a few well-thought-out but unanswered questions, you can use them to justify future grant support once you're an assistant professor.

When judging how much work to put in, think about opportunity costs. If you spend an extra year on your thesis, that is one less year in which you can earn a salary. Will an extra year of work really make your thesis so much more impressive that you will land a job which pays enough more to make up the missing year?

You can significantly shorten your thesis while improving its readability by good editing. As a rule of thumb, you should always be able to cut your first draft by a third or even by half without sacrificing any of the ideas. I once cut from 120 pages to 40. Tough but possible.

BACK UP EVERYTHING TWICE—THE MOST ■ IMPORTANT ADVICE IN THIS BOOK ■

For months this forlorn ad ran in Stanford's student paper:

$1,000 REWARD for contents of blue canvas backpack taken from Stanford Coffee House on November 13. NO QUESTIONS ASKED. This backpack contained three years of original data for my Ph.D. thesis which cannot be replaced. I am desperate. Please call John.

BACK UP YOUR MANUSCRIPT

Don't let this be you. Make sure you have photocopies of all original data in a separate location from the original. Make sure you back up and double back up computer disks. Keep copies of old drafts, so that if you lose your most recent one, you have a fairly up-to-date version to resurrect. Keep both paper and disk copies in case an electromagnetic catastrophe wipes out your disks. Keep backups in a separate building from your originals in case of fire or other disaster. When I was writing this book, I didn't follow my own advice on backing up. When the air conditioner in my office building failed, the main hard drive on our network crashed, and I lost two complete chapters. Rewriting them was no fun.

▪ COMPUTER HELP ▪

I cannot recommend too strongly a Windows program by Niles called EndNote. This program can manage your thesis bibliography and footnotes or endnotes, saving you days of effort. As you undertake your thesis research and find references you may wish to cite in your thesis, enter them in EndNote's database. EndNote accepts information on titles, authors, dates, type of publication, and much more. Once you are writing your thesis and come to a place where you wish to put an endnote or other type of citation, simply change windows to enter the EndNote database, click on the correct reference, and EndNote instantly places the correct citation in the text and puts the full reference in the document's bibliography. You don't have to worry about making errors with spelling of names or dates because they will be electronically entered into the text from the database. As you add additional footnotes to the manuscript, EndNote will automatically renumber all footnotes and update the bibliography. Over the years, you can build up a complete bibliography of references that were cited in your thesis and other publications, ready to use in new publications. Niles also makes a companion product called EndLink that allows you to download references from library databases and enter them directly into EndNote.

19

. . . .

THE THESIS DEFENSE

. . . .

They endured.

—WILLIAM FAULKNER
The Sound and the Fury

THE AFRICAN EXPLORER DAVID LIVINGSTONE, IN DESCRIBING HOW IT FELT TO be badly mauled by a lion, wrote:

> It causes a kind of dreaminess, in which there was no sense of pain nor feeling of terror . . . a merciful provision by our benevolent creator for lessening the pain. . . .

Unlike Livingstone, most students remember both the pain and the terror of a thesis defense. One doctoral student, now a successful academic, told me:

> For several days before the defense I felt like I was sleepwalking through a nightmare. I was so afraid that I couldn't focus on preparing. I couldn't conceive of what the ordeal would be like, I couldn't imagine the questions that would be asked, and worst of all, I couldn't visualize myself answering them. Things didn't get much better during the defense. I was sweating, blanked out from time to time, and talked nonstop at others. Part of the problem was that I didn't know ahead of time whether a couple people on the committee approved of my thesis, so I kept thinking paranoid thoughts, like they were thinking I was stupid and that my even getting into grad school had been a huge fiasco. I ended up passing with some minor revisions, but it was an awful experience.

On the contrary, other students I spoke with were so well prepared for their thesis defense that they felt it was an enjoyable experience. An English student told me:

I was on very good terms with my committee, I knew they thought my thesis was great, and I'd really prepared my presentation well. So I gave my talk, they asked interesting questions, and then we all had a spirited discussion for about an hour. All in all, it was more like giving a seminar than taking an exam.

As these two examples point out, the secret to having an easy defense is preparation—you need to select your committee wisely, manage them well, and prepare thoroughly for the defense itself.

▪ WHAT IS THE THESIS DEFENSE? ▪

Most departments require Ph.D. students to defend their theses, although a few have abolished the defense, figuring that if you wrote a satisfactory thesis, a verbal examination is superfluous. The majority of master's students do not have to orally defend their theses.

When students in Europe first began defending their theses several hundred years ago, it was a metaphorically bloody affair. The defendant, outnumbered and alone, armed only with his wits and his bulky manuscript, was expected to defend his thesis in open debate against a hall full of antagonistic academics trying to prove that he was an incompetent dolt. If he held his ground, besting his attackers with skill in the art of what was then called "disputation," he was awarded his doctorate.

In today's thesis defense you will still be outnumbered by your examiners five to one if you are a doctoral student, three to one if a master's student. Mercifully, however, the average defense is now more civilized, and many departments consider them to be largely ceremonial presentations of work which has already been judged sufficient to warrant the degree. Nonetheless, there are still departments inhabited by crusty "old school" academics who believe, like tough drill sergeants, that the best way to determine whether you are both brilliant and academically rigorous is an ordeal by fire. Further, in an era of extensive subcontracting, your committee may cross-examine you to make sure you actually wrote your own thesis.

Most likely you will begin your defense by presenting a brief overview of your thesis work, which can last anywhere from a few minutes to an hour. When your presentation is completed, the committee cross-examines you for another hour or two, asking about either specific aspects of your research or more general questions about the broader implications of your research, or even asking detailed questions about your field which are not covered by your thesis. The defense is a final opportunity for your committee to probe for flaws in your work, and it is also a test of whether you can present your work in a professional manner and of how skillfully you can think on your feet to defend it under pressure. It is excellent training for holding your own in faculty meetings and in squelching students who ask difficult questions. You can expect challenging questions that demand, for example, that you justify the specific methodology you chose, prescribe which research steps should be taken next, explain why you did not place more emphasis on a particular theoretical approach, or cite related work which supports or contradicts your conclusions.

Depending on the tradition of your department, in addition to your committee there may also be a wider audience present, including other faculty and students. If so, you may want to invite some of your fellow students for moral support. My own defense was divided into two stages; the first was my presentation, which was open to all members of the department, and the second was the oral exam, for which the committee and I retired to a private room.

Before the questioning begins, the candidate is usually asked to leave the room for a few minutes while the committee chairperson explains to the rest of the committee the procedure for asking questions and other ground rules of the examination. Once you are brought back into the room, the committee chairperson traditionally asks the first question. This first question, if skillfully asked, can put you at ease and draw you out so that you show to best advantage. For this very reason, some advisers will give up the right to ask the first question so that they do not appear biased toward you. Next, the other faculty members each ask you a question (or questions) in turn. After everyone has had a chance in the first round of questions, the chairperson opens the floor to additional questions from any of the committee members.

Once your committee has satisfied its appetite for questions, the chairperson asks you to leave the room while they vote on whether your years of struggle have produced work of sufficient value. In some departments the vote must be unanimously favorable for you to pass. In others you only need three-fourths or two-thirds (making it easier to deal with troublemakers on the committee). Assuming you have passed, and almost all candidates do, it is de rigueur for your new colleagues to pour you champagne in welcome to the panicked ranks of academic job seekers.

▪ CAN YOU FAIL? ▪

Almost no one fails outright if they have worked closely with their committee during the development of their thesis. To do so not only would reflect badly on you but also would show dereliction of duty by the committee. They are morally obligated to judge that your thesis is acceptable before they let you schedule your thesis defense. However, if you have *not* worked closely with your committee, you may go into the defense blind, with no indication of whether the committee likes your work. If you have irritated them by being aloof, they may let you fail your thesis defense to teach you a lesson. This nearly happened to one insect taxonomist. He says:

> I really blew it. By the time I started getting somewhere with my research, I wasn't talking much to my committee. They didn't like some things about my research, but I knew it was going in the right direction, so I pretty much went off by myself and finished it. By this time I hadn't talked with my adviser in over a year, and I was determined to write an excellent thesis that would show my committee how good my work was after all. So I wrote really hard for six months, polishing and polishing. Finally, it was good, well written, so I circulated it to my committee and scheduled my thesis defense. I practiced a lot for my defense, and then at the last minute the committee canceled it. My adviser said that they had found my thesis unsuitable in its present state, and that I would need major revisions. I don't think most of their demands were well taken, but I didn't have much choice. For a while I was too angry to work on it, but I finally revised it and did my defense.

Even though total failure is rare, it is common for defendants to receive provisional passes, with eventual acceptance of the thesis dependent upon either major or minor revisions. You shouldn't consider it your fault even if they demand major revisions at this stage, provided that you have had them review the thesis in progress. It merely means either (a) that your committee has belatedly realized the need for further research, writing, or other revision that they themselves had previously overlooked or (b) that a late addition to the committee wants to give you a hard time.

The worst a provisional pass means is that you must put in additional work before your thesis is finally accepted. Normally you will not have to undergo a second defense. For minor revisions it may be enough to have your committee chairperson sign off on your changes, while for major revisions you may need to have each committee member sign off.

Try to minimize the number of revisions necessary to achieve acceptance by using your best negotiating techniques on the committee. Try to distinguish between tasks they see as essential and those they (a) can be talked out of or (b) will forget about. If a late addition to the committee requests major changes which your adviser and other core members of the committee don't consider essential, lobby them to intervene. You can also try to finesse some of the changes by circulating a memo to the committee, written either by yourself or by your adviser, which lays out the changes you propose. In writing the memo, you can do a certain amount of subtle picking and choosing of tasks so that you minimize the work. If you can then get them to agree to restrict revisions to those laid out in the memo, it could save you weeks or months of revising.

There is one more possible outcome of your defense. If you have written a good thesis but are unprepared or otherwise do poorly on your defense, the committee may accept your written thesis but fail your oral defense. You could fail the defense because you get an attack of nerves that is so bad you can't think clearly, because your presentation was poorly prepared, because you failed to anticipate complicated questions and were unable to articulate clear answers on the spot, or because the committee asked questions about recent literature or theoretical aspects of your field that you hadn't studied up on. All these problems are best dealt with prophylactically by preparing well so that you don't fail in the first place. However, if you do fail the oral portion, it shouldn't be a matter of great concern —if your thesis was acceptable and your committee likes you, you will just have to prepare more carefully and pass a second oral exam.

Often a committee will find a way to take pity on someone who is truly incapable of standing the stress of the examination by questioning him or her informally, using the justification that the formal requirement of the committee is to satisfy themselves that the student wrote and understands the entire thesis, and can intelligently discuss it in the context of the relevant literature. One philosophy student told me this story:

> There was a student named Helmut in our department who was so terrified of his oral exam that he canceled it five or six times. His committee thought Helmut's thesis was brilliant, but they simply couldn't force him to go through with an exam. Because they liked him, they put together a conspiracy. A fellow graduate student invited Helmut out for a drink, whereupon, by strange coincidence, they ran into one of his professors. The three of them sat down for a few beers, began to discuss philosophy, and the professor naturally asked

a few questions about Helmut's research. Being well lubricated by alcohol, Helmut answered them brilliantly. When, by further coincidence, a second committee member wandered into the bar, he was jovially hailed, joined the conversation, and in turn asked his own questions. Before long, the entire thesis committee was there, all without Helmut suspecting a thing until they cheerfully congratulated him on passing his defense.

The fact that you aren't likely to fail doesn't mean that some committee member won't cause you grief. He may do this because the defense is a last chance to beat up someone who can't fight back, because he doesn't understand the subject well enough to ask intelligent questions, or because he sincerely believes your approach is wrong and that this is his last chance to veto ideas he doesn't like. Outside committee members may be particularly nasty because they know they aren't going to be able to fail you in the long run, so they don't need to pull their punches. One student who had problems with an outside committee member but was rescued by his adviser says:

> I was trained by my adviser as a cultural historian, and my thesis was a somewhat subjective one focusing on how politics is portrayed in literature. My outside committee member was a visiting Italian senator who was only on campus once a week, a big shot in structuralism, very famous, who trashed my defense because he kept saying my thesis wasn't quantitative enough. My committee couldn't get him to pass me, so I had to go through a second defense, but this time they scheduled it when the Italian guy was out of the country, so I passed with flying colors.

▪ PREPARING FOR THE EVENT ▪

Before discussing the specific things you need to do to prepare well, I want you to hear the story of my friend Frank who put together a successful strategy. His thesis was on how South American medicine men use jungle herbs to treat illness.

> I decided to follow a friend's advice and hit them with a first-rate oral presentation. My friend says, "Make 'em laugh, make 'em cry, leave 'em feeling religious." So I carefully chose the best slides of plants and Indians that I've got and wove them together into a powerful slide show. I mentioned all the important points I wanted the com-

mittee to focus on, even if they weren't specifically in my thesis.

I was very close to my adviser, and we met before the defense to talk strategy. He gave me pointers about what to expect and what to say. I also met with my other committee members—except for the outside person who was added late—and made sure they would be supportive. After my presentation, my adviser launched into a spirited defense of my thesis, talking about how valuable my work was. Equally important, he stressed how diligent I had been about keeping in touch with the whole committee, and how I had responded to all their comments when revising my thesis. This made it tough for them to give me a hard time. Then he gave me a couple of nice, fat, slowball questions right over the plate.

I did have trouble with my outside guy. He wasn't really trying to sink me, but he did believe that the student should be grilled. But he was slowed down considerably by the other members. Whenever he'd start getting hostile, asking too many harsh questions, another committee member—not my adviser—would break in with answers to the questions, mostly long, involved anecdotes about his own adventures in the Amazon. Pretty soon, they were all telling stories, which took up the rest of the time. So my advice to your readers is to try and make sure that you've got someone on your committee who is ready to blindside the person who is trying to blindside you.

PREPARE YOUR COMMITTEE

- *Make allies.* As Frank's story shows, you've got to make allies of your adviser and the other core committee members as you involve them in your thesis process. They should all have accepted your thesis in advance, either formally or in their own minds, and be ready to help you out if you get stuck during the oral examination or if a hostile committee member attempts to scuttle your defense.
- *Schedule your defense far in advance.* Otherwise, it can be very difficult to get all your committee members together at one time. If you have to hold your defense with little advance warning, you may be forced to accept a substitute who can give you problems.
- *Distribute your thesis early.* Give your completed thesis to all committee members well before the defense so that they have time to read it thoroughly. It is common for committee members to go into the defense without having read the thesis, which greatly increases the chances that they will make objections because they don't fully understand either the specific sections or how these sections fit in with the body of your work. One way to avoid this is to meet with each committee member after

they have had time to read the thesis and before the defense, in order
to discuss any last-minute revisions. This will ensure (a) that they actually read the document and (b) that they go into the thesis defense
already having accepted your thesis.

- *Prepare an abstract.* Prepare an abstract of your work to accompany your
  thesis. Despite your best efforts, some committee members may fail to
  read your thesis thoroughly. A good abstract can go a long way to
  convincing them that your thesis is competent and coherent. An abstract
  can also guide them in their reading of the thesis, helping them understand how the parts fit to make a logical pattern and making sure that
  they do not miss or misunderstand important points. Once your thesis
  is accepted, the same abstract can be submitted to University Microfilms
  International, which publishes most theses for wide distribution, so you
  won't waste time by writing it (they require that the thesis abstract be
  no more than 350 words).
- *Make your thesis look sharp.* A ragged-looking thesis can make a bad
  impression on your committee, so the typing should be crisp, the paper
  of good quality, and the binding professional.

Prepare yourself

Much of your preparation will be similar to what you did for the comprehensive exam or your proposal defense, so read those sections for other
ideas to add to these:

- *Talk to other students.* Seek out other students who have passed their
  defense and ask them what to expect.
- *Observe the defenses of other students.* Watching the performances of
  other students can warn you of pitfalls, as well as accustom you to the
  process so you aren't afraid when it is your turn. Just like giving an oral
  report in junior high school, it's easier if someone else goes first.
- *Ask your committee members for tips.* Are there any particular areas
  they would like you to cover? To help you start off your defense
  smoothly, your adviser may be willing to tip you off ahead of time to a
  couple of the first questions he will ask.
- *Play devil's advocate with your own thesis.* Probe for every weakness.
  Plan responses that not only defend these weaknesses but turn them into
  strengths. For example, if you are criticized for not answering a particular
  research question, you can acknowledge its importance with a well-
  thought-out analysis of future research you have planned to answer it.
- *Read up on the latest literature.* If a committee member tries to depth-
  bomb you by quoting from a two-month-old journal article that pur-

portedly refutes your entire thesis, you want to have read it too so you can defend yourself. Also, know intimately the latest papers that have been published by your inquisitors.

• *Make a list of possible questions.* List every question that you and your friends can imagine, including those that seem absurd or obvious. The night before my own defense I jokingly told friends that my committee would probably ask me the silliest question I could think of: "Tell us how your thesis fits into the entire field of biology." Because I didn't believe they would actually ask this question, I didn't bother to formulate an answer, and of course it was the first question they asked. In another case of poor preparation, a student in an Environmental and Public Policy Program defended a thesis in which he had correlated the severity of a river's noxious plankton blooms with episodes of high pollution. When his committee asked how his thesis could affect public policy, which was a reasonable question given the nature of his program, he didn't have an answer because he had focused so restrictively on the biological aspects of his work. Nor, when asked, was he able to define "public policy." So make sure you're at least able to define the field you're in. Once you've got a complete list of questions, practice answering them over and over until your responses are fluent.

• *Prepare your formal presentation carefully.* Use good-quality slides, even if you have to pay to have them made up, and make your presentation sharp and professional in every other way you can. One temptation will be for you to overdo the detail, but don't. Avoid using too many slides crammed with data that will cause brain overload and committee irritability.

• *Practice your formal presentation repeatedly.* Your delivery should be smooth as silk. With enough preparation, even if fear causes you to blank out, you will deliver your presentation on autopilot. If your department doesn't require a formal opening presentation, you should still prepare and practice a brief overview of your research, because the chances are that one of the first things you will be asked for in your defense will be a summary of your research. You can use your abstract as an outline of what to say.

• *Do a mock defense.* Ask your fellow students to critique your presentation and to role-play inquisitorial professors by asking you the toughest questions they can during the mock exam.

• *Familiarize yourself with the exam room.* You will be less nervous during the actual defense if you are familiar with the room where it will be held. Ideally, you should use the actual room both to practice in and to hold your mock thesis defense.

• *Read your dissertation.* You would be surprised how many students forget to leave themselves enough time to read over their dissertation, probably because they're so sick of it. As you read yours, memorize some of the key conclusions and data, just as if you were studying for an exam on any other topic.

▪ SURVIVING THE EVENT ▪

KEEP YOUR PERSPECTIVE

Remember that not only is the defense an open-book examination but you wrote the book! Hold tight to the knowledge that your chances of failing are zero if you have kept contact with your committee and they feel your thesis deserves a pass. If they have read your thesis and let you schedule your defense, they believe your thesis is good enough. Even if an outside committee member tries to scuttle you, the worst that will happen is that you'll have to make revisions.

IF YOU GET IN TROUBLE

If someone starts contradicting you or questioning your interpretations, although you shouldn't come across as arrogant, don't be cowed. Instead, respectfully refute his arguments. Remember that you know more about your thesis subject than anyone else, including any of your committee members.

If someone asks you a question you can't answer, don't be afraid to say you don't know. If the answer comes to you later in the exam, you can answer it then. Remember that this defense isn't really about what you know and don't know; it is about whether you can conduct yourself as a professional. So demonstrating confidence and skillfully taking charge can earn back the points you lose by not knowing an answer.

One tactic to use when you don't know an answer is to admit that you don't know, or give a partial answer, and then ask the questioner or one of the other committee members for his thoughts on the issue. This can often get a discussion started that (a) gets you off the immediate hook and (b) gives you enough ideas so that you can then add intelligent comments to the discussion.

Don't babble on out of nervousness or to cover up what you don't know. If you have been regularly speaking in public, you should know by now that it is all right to pause for ten or fifteen seconds to think, so don't be afraid of a little silence. One doctoral student in comparative literature said:

I had a severe attack of nerves and went completely blank during part of my defense. One of my committee members asked me a question about Octavio Paz, which I should have been able to answer easily. Instead of answering it, I walked to the blackboard, picked up a piece of chalk, and began a fifteen-minute lecture on Sartre, complete with diagrams and connecting arrows. I felt like a sleepwalker, talking on and on, faster and faster, drawing huge circles on the board to illustrate the relationship between Sartre and something or other, while my committee members exchanged perplexed glances. I kept hoping that if I talked long enough, something would eventually connect up with Octavio Paz.

If someone asks a question that doesn't appear to make sense, don't panic. It is much more likely that the question *doesn't* make sense, or at least reflects ignorance of the issues involved, than that you have suddenly become stupid or that the person is asking a question that is too brilliant for you to grasp. Remember that the questioner may not have read your thesis thoroughly. During my own exam, it was clear from the questions that at least two committee members hadn't read my thesis at all. My adviser admitted to skimming it the night before the defense, and she asked at least one question that was foolish enough to throw me off balance. She asked, "Why couldn't you have done as good a job of writing your thesis as you did on that wonderful paper for the journal *Evolution*?" She hadn't read my thesis well enough even to recognize that the first chapter of my "poorly written" thesis was the *Evolution* paper word for word.

AN OVERCAFFEINATED STUDENT
PRESENTS HIS THESIS DEFENSE

Deal with questions you don't understand by calmly asking for a restatement or clarification. You can paraphrase the questions before answering. This gives you time to think, and keeps you from looking like a fool as you blithely rattle off a treatise on Sartre. If the question reflects the committee member's ignorance, note that the question is interesting, correct gently, restate the question or formulate a related question that does make sense, and discuss this point.

If you do get seriously rattled, you can seek refuge in the ultimate source of authority, your thesis. David Sternberg writes in *How to Complete and Survive a Doctoral Dissertation*:

> [Your thesis] is *prima facie* evidence and expert witness to your qualifications for the doctorate. If the going gets rough or the defense seems to be going against you, try to get your committee and your rattled self back to basics: open up your 300-page tome and remind them—if necessary by reading chapter and footnote—what the defense is at bottom all about: the written document of your researched dissertation.

Finally, if you get totally stampeded or emotionally exhausted, you can ask for a brief intermission to get a drink of water or go to the bathroom. This will usually give you enough of a break to let you get your composure back. Once when I was panicked in the middle of a lecture, I walked off the stage in front of five hundred people, splashed some cold water on my face, and returned to finish the lecture. The audience actually applauded my fortitude when I came back. A break also can give your adviser and other protectors a chance to take control and redirect the proceedings if a hostile committee member has been hammering at you.

Afterward

If your committee asks for revisions, make them as soon as possible. Then finish off the bureaucratic requirements, get your degree, and send your thesis off to University Microfilms International. Likewise, you should publish as soon as possible, while your thesis is fresh in your mind. Work with your adviser to make whatever changes are necessary for submitting chapters to journals, and get them out the door within a couple of months. Because most graduate students put off reworking their thesis, they never publish, even though this hurts their career. Once you have left school and are working, the demands on your time and energy are so great that it will be very hard to go back and resurrect your thesis.

20

■ ■ ■ ■ ■ ■ ■ ■ ■ ■ ■ ■

ORAL PRESENTATIONS:

THE KEY TO

BEING A STAR

■ ■ ■ ■ ■ ■ ■ ■ ■ ■ ■ ■

It usually takes more than three weeks to prepare a good impromptu speech.

—MARK TWAIN

SPEAKING WELL UNDER PRESSURE
▪ IS ESSENTIAL TO YOUR CAREER ▪

Because most of your fellow graduate students—the competition—are poor public speakers, you can develop a tremendous advantage if you learn how to give impressive presentations. If your thesis defense presentation is polished and powerful, your committee is more likely to pass your thesis, and if your job seminar is strong, you are more likely to win an academic job. Likewise, verbal skills that you hone by perfecting your formal speaking ability will improve your success even in less structured speaking situations, such as job interviews or panel discussions.

The strongest argument to convince you that speaking skills are important is to remind you how annoyed and bored you have been when forced to sit through some badly organized and poorly presented lecture, or how painful it was to watch some wretchedly nervous student give a presentation. Conversely, strong presentations make us respect the speaker and even ascribe to him (and his work) a brilliance which he may not possess. This phenomenon may explain how a moderately talented actor was twice elected President of the United States.

With good presentation skills you can persuade your audience to believe or do things which they otherwise wouldn't. Because an audience doesn't have the same amount of time to mull over your words as they would with a written document, they are more easily swayed by good visual aids, tricks of rhetoric, emotion, and the force of your personality. A skilled presentation can make mediocre research results seem good, or good ones brilliant, or can fire up your committee about your thesis so that the members become more active in finding you a job.

Becoming a good speaker will strengthen your professional reputation, ensuring that you are taken seriously and helping you become someone with what the Romans called *gravitas*, weight and worth. In my own field, junior scientists with outstanding speaking skills are regularly invited to speak at conferences where most of the other speakers are of higher rank. There is a reinforcing effect: the more conferences at which you are invited to speak, the more people will know about your work, the higher your reputation will rise, and the more invitations you will get. Look at it from the point of view of the conference or workshop organizer. As one who has organized conferences, I can tell you that there is huge pressure to organize an impressive meeting, one that everyone will agree was informative and interesting. One of the first things the organizer asks when prospecting for potential speakers is "Is he a good speaker?" If the answer is yes, that person is more likely to be invited to speak in the more prestigious plenary sessions or even to give a keynote address. Conversely, I know of good researchers who are rarely invited to speak at major conferences because everyone knows that their talks will be poorly presented, uninteresting, and therefore uninformative.

When it comes to getting hired, studies have shown that oral communication skills outweigh written skills, letters of reference, and even technical knowledge. One survey of nearly two hundred businesses, the Endicott Report, found that poor communication skills was the most commonly given reason for rejecting a job applicant. Employers hire people who come across in presentations or interviews as bright and personable —let's face it, *no one* is going to hire you on the basis of your résumé alone. As one manager says, "A one-page résumé doesn't tell you about poise, communication skills, effective answers to hard questions, or even technical expertise." One professor on a hiring committee explained how they make their choices:

When we're hiring, we look for whether potential faculty are personable and good communicators. Partly this is because we're looking for good teachers, partly it's because we want to hire someone we can get along with and who won't embarrass the department when he's speaking at a conference. We scrutinize people carefully when they give their seminar. If they can't project competence and ease, if they can't interest us in their topic, we don't want them no matter how good their thesis was.

Don't underestimate the importance of communication skills even if you're headed for a technical job. A middle manager who runs a large computer department which provides word-processing and computer support to the rest of his organization says:

> I hire a lot of people at the master's level. Even though our department is highly technical, I won't hire people without good communication skills. Because we're a support unit, there's a lot of interaction with other staff, and it's important that my people listen well and clearly communicate our goals and capabilities. It's also important for my own career survival that other departments have confidence in our ability to get the job done, and their perception of our quality is strongly influenced by the image we project when we communicate. Our organization as a whole thinks communication skills are so important that they regularly hold workshops on presentation skills, one-on-one communication skills, and effective listening.
>
> When it comes to comparing the relative importance of communication and technical skills, you obviously need both, but I would much rather have someone who lacks some technical skills but is smart, articulate, and trainable than someone who is highly skilled but noncommunicative and therefore ineffective. Therefore I don't hire people who make bad eye contact, mumble, whose sentences run on and on or trail off weakly, or who can't stick to the subject.

A final reason to put effort into developing your speaking skills is the emotional reward of turning a potentially nightmarish experience into something you can enjoy. An expert on the preservation of historic buildings actually fainted during her first talk before a large, prestigious audience. She says:

> I hadn't practiced my speech enough to realize how long it would run, and once onstage I talked too slowly and made too many digressions. When I realized that I wouldn't be able to finish on time, and that I didn't know what to do about it, I panicked and hyperventilated until I passed out right onstage. It was very dramatic. Since then, I prepare more carefully, and with practice I've come to love speaking, particularly the part where total strangers come up afterward to tell you how wonderful you were.

• TRAIN YOURSELF IN PUBLIC SPEAKING •

The first step in developing good speaking skills is to understand that they don't come as a gift but must be earned. Just as with writing, tennis, and other skills, you need training and practice. Take my own case. When I gave my first graduate seminar paper at Stanford, I was terrified of the audience, and, with good reason, afraid that I would make a fool of myself. When I started my lecture, I was so frightened that I couldn't even read my notes, and after fifteen minutes I was too exhausted to continue. Although my subsequent presentations did improve, public speaking continued to be an unpleasant ordeal throughout graduate school. This all changed a few years ago when my friend Mark Plotkin, who is one of the best speakers I have seen, offered to teach me how to do it. He showed me that good public speaking is a matter of mastering some relatively simple skills, coupled with lots of preparation and practice.

TAKE A LONG-TERM APPROACH

You can't expect to give a top-notch thesis defense or an outstanding job seminar unless you have put in the time and practice to learn the necessary speaking skills, any more than you would expect to pass a driving test by trying to learn how to drive the day before. Therefore, you should start a long-term, consistent effort to improve your skills as soon as you start graduate school. Don't use fear of public speaking as a reason to avoid learning how, and don't make the mistake of thinking, "This is a gift I don't have." Public speaking ability is not a gift; it is a learned skill that you can master if you work at it, and practice will dissipate your fear.

Just because I'm advocating long-term training doesn't mean that you can't improve rapidly. You *can* greatly improve your performance in a short time with intensive practice. Even a single session with a good coach can help substantially, particularly if you can be videotaped to help you see your faults.

One place to look for training is university career-counseling centers, many of which have workshops in public speaking or videotaping facilities so that you can tape yourself doing mock presentations. Also, university or college courses in public speaking can both teach you new techniques and provide a support group you can use for motivation, to habituate yourself to audiences, and to get feedback on your performances. Nancy Chapman, a lobbyist and speechwriter, found that a class greatly improved her skills:

I started writing speeches for a member of Congress when I was on his staff, and my speeches weren't very good, too labored and heavy with data; I was obfuscating the important details in a mass of content. So I enrolled in a course at Georgetown University which ran for three consecutive Saturdays. The first benefit of the course was that the time it took me to write a speech dropped from four or five days to four or five *hours*. My new speeches were not only clearer and more interesting, they were also shorter and easier to write.

Before you sign up for a speech class, be sure to examine the curriculum. Find a class that will maximize actual practice and minimize, as one student experienced, tedious dissection of Plato's discourses on the difference between speech and rhetoric.

If you are well heeled, there are also private courses, like Dale Carnegie's High Impact Presentations course, but at nearly $1,000 a pop, these courses are real wallet busters. You can contact Carnegie at 800 231-5800. Toastmasters clubs (or other public speaking self-help groups) are low-cost alternatives, with annual dues of approximately $35 per year, although training is much less intensive. Toastmasters meetings are typically held twice a month, and, as a member, you would have an opportunity to give a short speech every few meetings, as well as more frequent short talks lasting only a couple of minutes. The president of one club says that you should count on attending for at least six months to see significant improvement in speaking skills.

You should augment formal instruction by searching out as many opportunities to speak as possible. Deliver papers at conferences, give departmental seminars, or teach classes. One biology student organized a weekly seminar where both graduate students and faculty were invited to present talks. He says:

> Although I didn't set it up for this reason, the weekly seminar taught me how to be a good speaker. I gave at least one forty-minute lecture a quarter in which I could practice my techniques, and I also had a chance to observe many other presentations, learning what worked and what didn't. For example, I learned the importance of keeping it short and sweet, using good slides, keeping abstruse data slides to a minimum, and putting in a little humor.

Like this student, whenever you watch a presentation pay attention to the speaker's skills and learn from both the good and the bad. Note how the speaker talks and uses his body. Are the visual aids effective? When watching, I write down particularly effective anecdotes, turns of phrase, or anything else that I feel might be useful. Here's how one speaker adapted a borrowed phrase:

> I once attended a seminar where the speaker's slide—a map of North America—was upside down. The speaker quickly said, "This is what North America looks like from the Southern Hemisphere," which got a good laugh. A year or so later, I was speaking and my map of Brazil was backwards, so I said, "Here's what Brazil looks like when seen from the center of the earth." It took them a minute to get it, but they laughed at this one too. Even though I'm very careful to get my slides in right, sometimes you screw up, and if you're prepared with one of these stock jokes, you can always get the audience on your side.

▪ WRITING A PRESENTATION ▪

Here are some pointers on writing a good speech. For further tips on writing and delivering speeches, try the books *Make the Most of Your Best*, by Dorothy Sarnoff, and *Sweaty Palms*, by Anthony Medley.

• *Know your audience.* You should have a firm picture in your mind of who the audience is so you can aim the presentation directly at them. Obviously, if you're speaking to a *general* audience of academics from several fields within your discipline you need to be more explanatory and less technical than if you are presenting your research results to your thesis committee or to experts in your own subfield. If you're not sure what the audience will be like, do your homework. Nancy Chapman says:

> Before every speech I do detective work to find out the composition and biases of the audience. Often I will take a member of the audience out to lunch ahead of time and pick their brains. I want to know what their general level of knowledge is about the issue, what sorts of information they would like to learn, and whether or not they will be antagonistic.

When you are writing your presentation, it can help if you imagine your audience and speak directly to them, creating a dialogue that focuses your ideas and brings them to life. An experienced speaker told me:

The worst speech I've given in recent years was when I was torn between the main audience, who needed a relatively simple and untechnical talk, and one particular member of the audience—a potential employer—whom I wanted to impress with my brilliance and technical competence. To please the employer I tried to show that I knew a whole bunch of technical stuff, and I put in too many concepts, too much detail, and too much jargon. Also, because I couldn't decide on which audience I was trying to reach, the presentation wasn't even a good technical talk—it wandered all over the place and I could never figure out quite what I wanted to say. I would have been much better off doing a competent speech targeted at the main audience. Then at least the employer would have been impressed that I knew how to reach an audience.

- *Take extra care with your beginnings and endings.* These should be strong and clear, for studies show that the beginning and ending of a presentation are where the audience pays the most attention. Even if they've slept through the rest of your talk, they'll start waking up during the last few minutes in anticipation of escape, so here is where you should give them your most important take-home messages. Likewise, they tend to be more alert at the beginning, before you've put them to sleep, and here is where you should give them a clear, point-by-point statement of exactly what you will cover in the presentation so that they will be able to follow your erudite twists and turns.
- *Use humor.* With this instruction comes a caveat: there is nothing worse than an inappropriate joke inserted forcibly into a speech, so make sure you try out your presentation—jokes and all—on a trial audience first. Slides of appropriate cartoons often work well.
- *Be specific and avoid generalities.* Even more than in writing, you must paint pictures that are easily graspable by the audience. So use examples and analogies wherever possible.
- *Don't clutter your speech.* One of the most common and unforgivable sins of poor speakers is that they cram their talks with so much information that the listeners miss the main points. So don't try to impress your audience by squeezing in everything you know, and don't labor under the delusion that your role in lecturing is to force-feed mountains of data to the audience. Remember that even in a well-presented talk, the audience will only absorb a few main points, and within a month they will have forgotten 80 percent of the information you presented. Therefore, pare your talk down to the most important points and to interesting examples that will reinforce these points. By focusing this way, you increase the chance that your audience may remember your

major conclusions, and even more important, that they will remember you as a strong, clear speaker. If the audience feels more detail is necessary, they will ask during the question period.

- *Speak plainly*. Your words should be simple and your sentences short. As Emerson said, "Speech is the power to translate a truth into a language perfectly intelligible to the person to whom you speak." Edit and edit again until you have found the clearest, simplest way to state each idea.

- *Write out the text fully*. There are several ways to prepare your text, but I would advise novice speakers to have the complete speech printed word for word, in clear type, on regular-size paper. This way, if you freeze up in terror while speaking, you can keep going by reading directly from your text until you recover your poise. Nonetheless, reading your text should be a last resort.

- *Make your text a performance script, complete with stage directions*. During your speech it will be easier to refer to your text if, by using a word processor with variable font capabilities, you print the text in an oversized font or in "speech type" (which is all capital letters). For ease in keeping your place when moving your eyes from the text to the audience and back again, the text should have many more paragraph breaks than regular writing. They should come wherever there is a natural break in your speech—for example, at every new point, example, or slide. Here is sample text from one of my own lectures, in which I present two slides, one showing a thermometer reading three degrees and the second a photograph of an ice-blue glacier:

(THERMOMETER): **Climatologists project** that within the next fifty years the average temperature of the earth will rise by THREE DEGREES CENTIGRADE.

This may not seem like much, but from an **ecological point of view it is unprecedented.** ➤ (PAUSE)

—**if the earth warms by three degrees** (HOLD UP THREE FINGERS), it will make the planet warmer-than-at-any-time-during-the-past-100,000-years.

—and **if the earth warms by four degrees** (HOLD UP FOUR FINGERS), it will make the planet warmer than at any time since the EOCENE, 40 MILLION YEARS AGO . . . long before humans even evolved.

(GLACIER): **For purposes of comparison**, during the depth of the last ice age, when much of Europe and North America were covered by ice, it was only FIVE-degrees-colder-than-today.

Notice that I separate my sentences as though they were paragraphs, indent related points or examples so that my eye groups them together, and capitalize words needing emphasis. I use hyphens within phrases where my delivery needs to be slowed down and each word needs to be separated slightly for emphasis. I use a down arrow to remind me to drop the pitch of my voice at the end of lines, particularly where the last word needs to be stressed, or anywhere else where stress is needed. Most inexperienced speakers have the bad habit of raising their pitch at the end of lines, a trait that makes them sound querulous and weak. Try saying "but from an ecological point of view it is unprecedented" both ways, with the final pitch both up and down. Getting this right takes some work, but it is one of the most effective things you can do to lend authority to your talks.

My text also includes stage directions, which I often handwrite in the margins, such as "hold up five fingers," "smile," and "make eye contact." Finally, I often boldface words or phrases that start new sentences to help me keep my place in the text, and I also boldface phrases that I want to speak word for word, exactly as written. This way, if I'm looking at the audience when I come to that phrase, it is relatively easy for me to flick my eyes back to exactly the right spot and read the line without hesitation.

- *Write your own introduction.* The moderator will ask you ahead of time for biographical information so he can introduce you to the audience. Instead of raw information, write your own introduction and give it to him. The moderator will be glad you've saved him time, and you can control exactly what is said.

SOFTWARE TO HELP ▪ YOUR PRESENTATION ▪

Designing slides has become ridiculously easy. Computer programs that can help you include Lotus's Freelance Graphics, Microsoft's PowerPoint, and Harvard Graphics. Corel gives you a choice of two programs—Presents, which comes packaged with CorelDraw!, and Presentations, which comes with WordPerfect Suite. Although they differ in frills and interface, all these programs are built around the capability to let you quickly design a series of slides. Once you've designed them, you can take the saved file to a commercial firm to have them made into transparencies for your Kodak projector or print them as handouts to accompany a lecture. Another option is to program your computer to display them in sequence as a slide show. In this case you can even add sound and other special effects to the show. Some university conference halls now have the capability of displaying your computerized slide show on a big auditorium screen.

To design a slide, you choose among many templates that automatically set the style of the slide, including background color, location of bullets for text slides, and font size for the slide's title and text. Unless you override it, all slides in the series you are making will have the same style based on the template. And you can change the slide's style with a mouse click or two. This system is so fast that it takes only a few seconds to make a text-only slide—the time it takes you to type in the text—and you can quickly add clip-art figures, geometric shapes for flowcharts, and simple bar charts and graphs, and you can import photographs that you've scanned or even downloaded from the Internet. One word of caution is not to get carried away making bullet slides—I've seen too many presenters who fell in love with slide technology and now barrage the audience with dozens of bullet slides outlining even the most trivial information. Then, instead of speaking conversationally to the audience, the speaker just reads from the endless procession of bullet slides.

All the programs provide a "slide sorter" that allows you to see miniature versions of all the slides in your presentation at once and to change their order simply by clicking on an individual slide and dragging it to a new position. Once you've got the slides in the order you want, you can test whether you like the presentation by running it on-screen, displaying the slides one by one on your monitor. If you don't like the order or the backgrounds, you can change with a few mouse clicks. You can even add sound to your slide presentation. Another nice feature is that, if you are showing your computerized slide show to someone else, you can draw on the monitor with your mouse, overlaying the slides with comments and diagrams à la Joe Madden.

All programs also provide an outliner that can help you plan your presentation by letting you type in slide titles and text as though you were outlining the talk on paper. The advantage is that the outliner is linked to the slide editor, so that whatever you type into the outliner is instantly transferred to the appropriate slide. It also works in reverse—for example, when you change a title in the slide editor, the change automatically shows up in your outline. In most cases, your outline can be exported to a word processor in case you need to base a memo or other document on your talk outline.

Another useful feature is the ability to associate speaker notes with each slide. You can type the speaking script that goes with a particular slide and then print both the slide and the script on the same piece of paper. Once you've made pages for all the slides, you have a complete speaking script with pictures of slides to help orient you.

You'll probably be making slides of photos and charts and graphs that you've created with other programs, such as Microsoft Word, Corel Photo-Paint, or QuatroPro. All the presentation programs allow you to import a variety of these data files, but all programs won't accept all file types. For example, although Lotus Freelance Graphics will import some types of image files, it won't import JPEG files, commonly downloaded from the Internet. Microsoft's PowerPoint will. So think about import compatibility before you buy a program—if you've got questions, you can phone the company and ask about capability. You can often get around this problem by converting the files using another program. For example, if you own Corel Photo-Paint or a similar image-editing program, you can convert JPEG files to Windows Bitmap files or another format that your presentation software will accept.

All the programs I named will do the job for you, but I found some easier to learn and use than others. Harvard Graphics has always been the standard for presentations, and in some ways I like it the best. It has a good interactive on-line tutorial to get you started, something some of the other programs don't have, plus it puts a side help panel on your screen that gives you tips as you go along that are keyed to the task you're working on. Corel Presents has a good manual, but it doesn't have an on-line tutorial and the interface is tough to figure out intuitively. This program frustrated me because I often had a hard time finding what I needed using the on-line help. Corel's Presentations doesn't come with a manual, at least when bought with the WordPerfect Suite, and although there's an interactive tutor for a few of the common tasks, it's tough to figure out all the tools from the on-line help. Lotus's Freelance Graphics, like the other elements of the Lotus SmartSuite, has an intuitive interface that's easy to use, as well as pretty good on-line help to guide you in completing specific tasks. PowerPoint has the best help system of all the programs, which can really speed learning—when you ask it how to do a specific task, it often moves the cursor to the appropriate buttons. This is great because I hate reading a help file that says, "Click the feenblodget button," and then I spend fifteen minutes just trying to find the feenblodget button. Another feature that's important in usability is the ability quickly to see and choose from the offered style templates. Of the programs I looked at, Harvard Graphics and PowerPoint make it easiest for you to see quickly what your finished slides will look like.

Flowcharts. If you need to make slides or other figures that contain flowcharts, you can create some modest effects with the presentation programs, but there are a number of programs that specialize in flowcharts. For professional engineers and other hard-core process modelers, there's RFFlow from RFF Electronics, which lets you select from 65,000 shapes.

But most people can have all the capacity they need from products like Micrografx's FlowCharter and Corel's Flow. Corel's Flow comes packaged with WordPerfect Suite, so it's ready to use with Corel's Presentations. The basic idea in using these programs is to choose a shape, like a square or triangle, from a sample box, and click to place it on the page. With more mouse clicks, you can choose lines to connect the shapes and text to describe their relationships. Once you've finished, you import the page into PowerPoint or another presentation application.

▪ PREPARING TO GIVE THE SPEECH ▪

- *Edit while you practice*. The first thing to realize about practicing your presentation is that writing it and practicing it are intertwined. Each time you practice your talk, you will find ways of saying things that are more fluid, simpler, more colorful, or that sound more like spoken language and less like you are reading a dry academic treatise. Make these changes to the text, practice your talk again, and then make more changes, so that you improve both the text and your delivery with each repetition.
- *Practice a lot*. I practice a new talk at least six or seven times, ideally over several days. *You* may not need that many trial runs, but make sure you overpractice. By this I mean, once you think you can do the talk perfectly, practice it once or twice more for good measure. *Never* underestimate how easy it is to forget what you want to say when you are onstage. Practice the beginning of your talk the most, since this is the part where you are most likely to be rattled.
- *Time yourself*. When you are onstage, you will have no sense of time —it will either fly or move at a glacial pace. Therefore, you've got to time yourself while practicing so you can alter the length of your text to match the amount of time allotted. You would be wise to make your final version a couple minutes shorter than the amount of time you have because it is very common for stage fright or interruptions to cut into your speaking time.
- *Record yourself*. Use a tape recorder or, better yet, a video recorder for your trial runs to check for annoying mannerisms, lack of speech clarity, or other problems.
- *Talk extemporaneously*. To be a good speaker, you should neither read your text verbatim nor try to memorize your speech word for word. Reading is excruciatingly boring to listen to and memorization is dangerous, because (a) it is tremendously difficult to do, (b) most people can't recite well enough to sound natural, and (c) it is too easy to get amnesia. Instead, you should speak extemporaneously, which means

"prepared but not memorized," using your text as notes to jog your memory and keep you on track. You will have your complete text with you in case you do get lost or panic, but instead of reading from it, you should only refer as needed to the boldface words and other cues to keep you on track. You may want to read some phrases verbatim, perhaps because you repeatedly stumble over them or because they contain precise data, in which case you can highlight these for easy finding. (I often have trouble with transition phrases leading from one major point to another and therefore highlight these.) However, the more times you practice your talk, the less often you will need to refer to your text.

After you have practiced your talk several times, as described above, revising the text so that it adapts to your speech patterns, the written and spoken versions will become very similar. Nonetheless, note that even though you may eventually be speaking a very close approximation to the written text, the process is quite different from memorization. In memorization you write out a text and then memorize it, forcing your mind to conform to the text, whereas in the extemporaneous method, the text itself is gradually adapted to match your natural speaking patterns. This type of speaking not only takes much less effort than memorization; it is also more interesting to the audience because it seems spontaneous, as though you were making it up as you went along. In reality, this apparent effortlessness will be the result of the numerous practice run-throughs and text smoothings.

- *Do a mock presentation.* Once you are happy with the way you give your talk, do a mock presentation for your graduate student support group or other friends. Include a question session at the end and ask your audience ahead of time to pose not only friendly questions but hostile ones as well, so that you can have practice handling them. At the end, ask them to critique you honestly. Some things for them to watch for are: Is your diction clear? Are you projecting well? Do you say "uhm" or use other place-holding grunts? Were any other speech or body mannerisms annoying? Were hand gestures used effectively? Was your talk too long or too short? Are any parts unclear? Did you speak too rapidly or slowly? Were any slides or other visual aids hard to see, confusing, excessive in number, or otherwise inadequate?
- *Make sure you have everything you will need.* I can imagine few things more upsetting than arriving in a foreign city to discover that the airline has lost the only copies of my speech and slides. To avoid this, I always take two copies of my speech, packed in separate bags. I would like to always have two sets of my slide show too, but this is often impossible

when traveling. However, I always leave a complete duplicate set at home so that it can be sent to me by rush delivery if necessary. If you will be using slides, you should also take a slide projector bulb and a long extension cord for the remote control, two things that your hosts often overlook. If you will be using an overhead projector, take extra blank transparencies and marking pens. Make sure that you have the home and office phone numbers of your hosts so that you can reach them for last-minute emergencies, and if you are traveling, double-check your destination. Being an absentminded-professor type, I once ended up in Lafayette, Indiana, when I was supposed to be speaking in Fort Wayne.

Once you've arrived, try to get access to the lecture room ahead of time so that you can familiarize yourself with the podium, microphone, lights, pointer, position of the slide screen, availability of drinking water, and anything else that would affect your talk. Ideally, you should use this room for a final practice run-through of your talk.

If you are using slides it is especially important to do a last-minute practice run, because so many things can go wrong. Therefore, call your hosts beforehand to make sure that you will have access to a room with a slide projector. Most professionally run conferences will have such a special room set up for practice, although it is not uncommon for inexperienced conference coordinators to neglect this, so ask ahead of time. Even if you don't have time to run through your entire talk, at a minimum you should project each slide in turn to make sure that they are all oriented in the projector correctly. Note that if they will be shown on a rear-screen projector, each slide will have to be reversed. Also check to make sure that your hosts will have a pointer available for slides—a light pointer is best.

▪ DURING THE PERFORMANCE ▪

First of all, don't worry about being nervous—most experienced speakers are. If you are well prepared, this nervousness will feel like exhilaration instead of terror, powering your talk with energy that you can transmit to the audience. People who are too calm usually end up giving lackluster presentations. It's like taking an exam—you do better if you are keyed up because the adrenaline sharpens your wits.

Remember that, with very rare exceptions, the audience wishes you well, and that they are just poor mortals like yourself, in need of love and approval. Because you are onstage, you become in their eyes an authority figure, so it is up to you to make *them* feel good. Try to feel affection for them, projecting as much warmth as you can. If you can forget about yourself and be genuinely concerned about the audience and their need for information and stimulation, you will not have time to be afraid. Try to be the type of teacher Carl Jung admired:

> One looks back with appreciation to the brilliant teachers, but with gratitude to those who touched our human feelings. The curriculum is so much necessary raw material, but warmth is the vital element for the growing plant and for the soul of the child.

One other thing to realize is that it is usual for an attentive audience to stare at you with what can seem somber faces, with little expression, and without smiling or laughing. Inexperienced speakers often get frightened by this because they think the expressionless faces are showing disapproval. This isn't so. You really only need to worry if a large proportion of the audience is actually sleeping or throwing vegetables.

• *Study how the audience reacts to other speakers.* If you are one of several speakers, use your waiting time to study both the other speakers' styles and how the audience reacts, and amend your own talk accordingly. If the previous speakers were long-winded and the audience is obviously tired, tell them that you will shorten your talk—they will love you for it. George Bernard Shaw, once the final speaker on the program, got the audience to roar with approval by rising to say only, "Ladies and gentlemen, the subject is not exhausted, but we are."

If you notice that the speaker before you is very dry and the audience is falling asleep, wake them up when it is your turn. Double the energy of your voice, stand closer to the audience, walk around the stage, use more jokes, and use every other trick you know to get their attention. If you observe that the audience responds well to jokes, you might want to slip in an extra one to start off your speech (I always have several ready, just in case).

Often you can begin your own talk by using humor that plays off the past speaker. Once the speaker before me was an agricultural specialist whose main point—with which I disagree—was that people don't have to worry about the greenhouse effect. He said that modern agriculture can cope with even the harshest environmental conditions, and to prove it he showed a picture of tomato plants growing in a field that had been so overirrigated that white salt was lying on the surface like snow. "Isn't this wonderful?" he asked. "The ground is so salty that even the weeds can't grow, only these new super-tomatoes." I wanted to rebut this technocentric viewpoint, and his tomato slide gave me an idea of how to do it. By chance, I had brought with me some extra slides, one of which was a photograph of typical supermarket tomatoes basking under fluorescent lights. They were rock hard, whitish green, and coated with wax. When I slipped this into the beginning of my slide show, commenting how much I indeed appreciated the succulent firmness of modern tomatoes, the audience roared, and that one slide did more to refute his talk than an hour of heated debate.

- *Pauses are okay*. When you first walk to the lectern, pause for a few seconds before starting, while you look at the audience. This will get their attention, calm you down, and give you a feeling of control. Pauses are all right anytime during your speech, whether you want to collect your thoughts, search through your notes for something you might have forgotten, or recapture the attention of a wandering audience.
- *Make eye contact*. This doesn't mean that you should stare at individual members of the audience. Instead, think of the audience as one huge organism to whom you are speaking, and sweep your eyes from one side of the hall to another, stopping for just a second here or there. You can, however, look directly at an individual for a few moments if you want to get his attention. For example, if someone is talking to a neighbor, a friendly but direct look will usually make him behave. *Don't* look down at your notes for more than a few seconds, and try to read as little as possible.
- *Stay close to the audience*. The nearer you can be to the audience, the better you can relate to each other. If the lectern is too far away, move it before your talk. I often come out from behind the lectern, right to the front of the stage, if there is one, speaking as directly to the audience as possible. In informal settings, or during the question period, I will often sit on the edge of a chair or on the edge of the stage to make the audience feel more at ease.
- *Move around*. You can keep the audience's attention by moving from one position to another, by walking to the front of the stage and back to the lectern, or by approaching the projection screen to point out detail on a slide. Likewise, change your facial expressions as much as you can. Express happiness, concern, or whatever else seems appropriate to your text.
- *Speak loudly*. It is better to speak too loudly than not be heard. If the lecture hall is large, I often begin by asking for anyone in the back who cannot hear me clearly to raise his hand.
- *Avoid nervous habits*. Don't lean on the podium (unless you are intentionally trying to be informal), put your hands in your pockets, touch

your face or hair, or say "uhm." These bad habits will disappear if you concentrate on them during practice.

- *Never call attention to your nervousness.* Don't say, "I'm not much good at public speaking," or "I've never done this kind of thing before, so I'm a little nervous." This sort of apology is painfully amateurish, draws the audience's attention off the subject matter and onto you in an unflattering way, and will set them to thinking, "Well, if he's so inadequate, why didn't he just stay home?"
- *Use visual aids.* Good slides or other props can increase the audience's interest dramatically, and they can also help you if you are nervous by focusing the audience's attention away from you. They also give you an excuse to work off nervous energy by walking back and forth and pointing. However, make certain that your visual aids are very good, because bad ones are worse than none. There are few things as deadly as a succession of fuzzy black-and-white slides of obscure graphs with microscopic captions.
- *Don't overrun your time limit.* In public speaking, shorter is better than longer, and the one unforgivable sin of public speaking is to go over your time limit.
- *Handle the question session skillfully.* Although many speakers treat question sessions as an afterthought, they are actually the time of maximum interaction between you and your audience. Often, people are hesitant to ask the first question, causing an embarrassing pause between the end of your talk and when the first brave soul raises his hand. You can fill this gap by having a confederate in the audience ask a question that you chose for him or you can say, "Here is one question I am often asked . . ." and then answer it yourself.

Try to figure out ahead of time, perhaps during your preliminary detective work on the nature of the audience, which questions you will be asked. You should practice good answers, just as you practice your formal presentation. Be ready also to politely cut off hostile questioners, or those who ask too many questions. If you let someone drone on and on, it will annoy the rest of the audience and make it seem as though you aren't in control. There are many ways to skillfully put the skids under a monopolizer. One is to break in and say, "It seems as though you are asking several questions. Let me answer the first one." Or you can break in and paraphrase by saying something like "It seems to me you are asking why Napoleon was short. That's a very good question and here is the answer." If someone still continues hogging the floor, you can nicely say, "Because time is short, let's move on to the next questioner to give everyone a chance." Don't be afraid to take control—it's your presentation.

• *Use humor to get out of jams.* During my speaking career I have put in slides upside down, had slides melt in the projector, split my pants all the way up the back, tumbled off the stage, and knocked an entire pitcher of water off the lectern. When accidents happen, if I laugh, the audience laughs. I once saw Joan Baez, wearing a beautiful white dress, onstage before thousands of people at the UCLA auditorium. After she had sung a few minutes, a stagehand ran up and whispered to her. She turned back to the audience and said, "I have just been informed that you can see through my dress. Since I only brought one dress with me, I hope you enjoy it." The audience roared and she continued singing. The lesson of these stories is that it hardly matters what you say, because as long as you laugh at yourself and appear indomitable, the audience will love you.

I'll close with a story about Chauncey Depew, a nineteenth-century humorist, who had to follow Mark Twain onstage. Unfortunately for Depew, Mark Twain gave a speech that was so similar to the one he was planning that Depew's would have been an anticlimax. He saved himself, to great applause, by saying:

Mark Twain and I agreed to trade speeches tonight. He has delivered mine very well, and I am grateful. Unfortunately, I have lost his and I can't remember a word of it.

21

DEALING WITH STRESS

AND DEPRESSION

If the day and the night are such that you greet them with joy, and life emits a fragrance like flowers and sweet-scented herbs . . . that is your success.

—HENRY DAVID THOREAU

Start every day off with a smile, and get it over with.

—W. C. FIELDS

BY THE TIME YOU'VE READ THIS FAR IT SHOULD BE CLEAR THAT GRADUATE school—particularly on the Ph.D. level—has a variety of special stresses that make it more difficult than both undergraduate school and most jobs, notably the confluence of poverty, low status, long hours, total length of the ordeal, social isolation, and difficult interactions with your adviser or thesis committee. In this chapter I make suggestions for how to deal with these stresses, but I can't pretend to have brilliant cure-alls, partly because the problems are inextricably part of graduate school. One of my Ph.D. psychologist friends says, "No matter how much advice you give your readers, they'll still go through pain—it's part of the process." Nevertheless, even in the cases where you're stuck with a problem, knowing what causes it can help you bear up.

A critical first step toward keeping healthy, happy, and sane is to recognize that thesis-demanding programs cause psychological or physical problems for almost everyone. David Sternberg, a professional counselor of Ph.D. students undergoing the dissertation ordeal, says:

I believe that the vast majority of emotional disturbances exhibited during dissertation days date their origins within the thesis period and from the unusual stresses of the course . . . one can discuss the "temporary insanity" of the ABD, with the assumption that he will be his old, nonsymptomatic self when the dissertation is done.

If you appreciate how difficult the process is *for everyone*, you are less likely to blame yourself when problems arise and less likely to experience feelings of depression and worthlessness. Likewise, if you can communicate the magnitude of the challenge to the other people involved in your life, they may be more supportive and understanding. If they won't take your word for how difficult it is, make them read this book.

• COPING WITH STRESS •

By 1979 a frustrated Stanford graduate student in mathematics named Theodore Streliski had spent eighteen years in futile pursuit of a Ph.D. When the last in a string of advisers requested further thesis revision, the student killed him with a hammer. Although the historian Cecil Gray has remarked that there are times when "a few judicious blows with a bludgeon impart a variety, expressiveness, and rich charm," I hope that you find a less artistic way to express your stress than Theodore did.

A certain amount of stress can be good for you. Like the nervousness before a speech or the pressure of a deadline, it can keep you on your toes and demand your best performance. Stress causes your adrenal glands to flood your bloodstream with three hormones, epinephrine, norepinephrine, and cortisol, which make you alert and speed up your reactions—evolution's answer to saber-toothed tigers and other threats to prehistoric longevity. This alertness can even help you learn—studies show that students learn more when they are under *moderate* stress than when stress levels are low. On the other hand, high levels of stress impede learning.

You can be debilitated by long-term, chronic stress, whether it is caused by ongoing hostility from your adviser, chronic fear of failure, or a single traumatic event with long-term emotional repercussions, such as failing your orals or suffering a divorce. Such chronic stress can exceed the mind's and the body's ability to adapt, causing both psychological and physical problems. As Friedrich Nietzsche wrote in *Ecce Homo*, "Simply by being compelled to keep constantly on his guard, a man may grow so weak as to be unable any longer to defend himself."

Physically, chronic stress has been related to back pain, sleep disturbances, ulcers, depressed immune response and increased susceptibility to colds and other illnesses, and even hair loss. When stress hormones prepare your body to fight or flee, blood is shunted away from nonessential areas, including the liver, which then does a poor job of removing harmful cholesterol from the blood. This can result in, among other problems, arteriosclerosis and heart attacks. You should also be on the lookout for irritable bowel syndrome (IBS), an aptly named chronic inflammation of the lower intestinal tract which is common in graduate students.

Psychologically, stress can make you depressed, irritable, emotionally exhausted, unable to cope easily with what should be minor problems, and downright not fun to be around. It will also exacerbate existing psychological problems, including eating disorders and abuse of alcohol or other drugs. In terms of career survival, high stress levels will sap your energy, affecting your ability to perform well. Without even realizing it, you may withdraw from the source of stress by avoiding your department, further alienating yourself, and thereby creating a cycle of stress, withdrawal, poor performance, and more stress.

High levels of stress during graduate school may burn you out to such an extent that when you finish you are unable to gear up properly for the next stage in your career. For example, if you are headed for a teaching job, you may be too exhausted to do the necessary revamping of your thesis for publication, or be unable to set up a research program strong enough to get you tenure. Complete recovery after lengthy periods of high stress can take months or years, and some of the physical effects, such as heart disease, may be largely irreversible.

Stress is insidious. More often than not, we fail to take action to reduce it before we and the people close to us are exhausted. Lynda Powell, an expert in stress management at Yale University, says, "Many of our patients are stockbrokers and lawyers who are so habituated to stressful lives that they aren't even aware of the intolerable stress they are in until they have a heart attack." I counsel you to take periodic assessments of how much stress you are under, what is causing it, and how you can reduce it.

Unfortunately, it is common for people to cope with stress in ways that are maladaptive. One example is to minimize your fear of an exam by fooling yourself into thinking it isn't important, with the negative result that you don't study enough. Another is to avoid thinking about a stressful event by engaging in other activities—i.e., procrastinating. Instead, let's look at some *productive* ways of dealing with stress:

• *Take control.* Studies show people perceive threatening situations as less stressful if they feel in control—most people feel happier in a car under bad driving situations if they are behind the wheel. Therefore, the sooner you try figuring out how to deal with a stressful problem and come up with some plans for implementation, the better you will feel.

Recognize that even if you cannot remove the source of the stress, you still have great power to determine how you respond to it. For example, you can learn to be less afraid of your adviser or more comfortable with public speaking. You can learn, through relaxation techniques or changes in thinking, to remain calm when faced with stressful events. Lynda Powell says:

> The average person encounters thirty potentially stressful events every day—"hooks"—including everything from getting rude service in a restaurant to being stuck in a long line at the bank. We try to teach people that they aren't mere pawns at the mercy of their environment, but that they can choose how to respond to these hooks, whether to become hyperreactive or remain calm.

Here is how one graduate student learned to cope with a moody adviser:

> I would meet with my adviser one day to talk about my work, and he would love it, be very supportive. The next time I saw him, he hated it. I would crawl away crushed. Finally I noticed that his response on a given day had nothing to do with my output, it just had to do with his mood. So I learned how to handle him. I would never tell him about my work until I had spent ten minutes chatting about inconsequentials to test his mood. If his mood was good, then I gave him a report about my work. If it wasn't, I'd say, "It was nice chatting. See you later."

GROUP THERAPY CAN HELP YOU REALIZE
THAT YOUR PROBLEMS AREN'T UNIQUE

• *Order your universe.* Stress will decrease if you organize your time efficiently and develop an effective system for completing tasks.

- *Remove the cause.* If your adviser chronically belittles you, your best option may be to get rid of him. If your housemates are inconsiderate boors who play Wagner or Wayne Newton at full volume when you are trying to sleep the night before a big exam, move.
- *Negotiate to reduce the cause.* Even if you can't get rid of the cause entirely, you may be able to negotiate a decrease in the stress source. If you're having problems with your adviser, talk with him directly, or call in a mediator. If your housemates are a problem, likewise try negotiating with them. The key to making negotiations work is to do them early, before everyone involved is too estranged and angry to be rational.
- *Look for help.* Many university counseling centers have stress management workshops. Kate Harris, the stress management coordinator at American University, says:

> Our course has five sessions, during which many students dramatically improve how they respond to stress. Some students report improvement after even a single session where they learn a relaxation technique. We provide a variety of relaxation techniques and cognitive therapy because different things work for different people.

Ironically, the people who most need stress counseling may be the last to get it. Kate Harris says:

> Although master's students come in, we rarely get Ph.D. students in our stress program. My own theory is that they feel under so much stress that they don't make time to get the counseling they need. It's also interesting that women are smarter about coming in early—the men we see are usually suffering more by the time they get to us.

You should deal with stress *before* it becomes a great problem. School may be the last time in your life you can get free counseling, so take advantage of it.

- *Investigate the source.* Psychological studies show that providing students with foreknowledge about stressful events, what has been called "stress inoculation," can reduce their stress levels. Forewarned is forearmed. One commonly identified source of graduate student stress is lack of feedback about how the student is doing in the program. You can help alleviate this in your own case by regular contact with your professors. Likewise, you can find out early what is expected of you in the way of your thesis proposal or comprehensive exams.
- *Increase your competency.* If stress is related to fears of inadequate

performance, you can decrease your anxiety by simply becoming more competent. If you are stressed by public speaking, then practice and become better. If you are stressed because you have been procrastinating on your thesis writing, take a systematic approach to getting it done.

- *Improve your interpersonal skills.* Your basic personality was molded well before you entered graduate school, so if you are presently a boorish, antisocial chump, to some extent you're stuck with yourself. But don't give up hope. You can still learn effective techniques to minimize bad communication and to improve the chances that you will get what you want out of personal interactions. Check with your university counseling or wellness center for workshops to train you in assertiveness or other types of interpersonal skills. In addition, many formal university courses in communication teach not only public speaking but also active listening, conflict resolution, and other communication skills. Finally, you can volunteer as a peer counselor, a role in which you help others while receiving training yourself in how to clarify problems.

TAKE A BREAK FROM STRESS

If the interpersonal problems you are having are long-term or severe, whether they be with advisers, roommates, parents, or significant others, and you're not getting the help you need from family and friends, get psychological counseling. Even if you feel your problems are manageable, a counselor or therapist can give you perspective on what's going on and help you think through your options. Group counseling may be useful, particularly if you are feeling isolated or need the honest perspectives of several people—two, four, or six heads may be better than one.

• *Don't avoid, habituate*. You can reduce your reaction to some types of stress by habituating yourself to the stimulus. Repeated airline trips will desensitize flight phobics, repeated public speaking experiences will banish stage fright, and repeated contacts with a scary professor will often diminish your fear.

• *Have fun*. Graduate students forget to have fun. Invite some friends over to play cards (a lost art in the age of television), throw a Frisbee, or organize a roller-skating expedition.

Get away to the outdoors and experience nature. According to anthropologist Lionel Tiger, our whole appreciation of air, light, texture, and sound evolved on the savanna of Africa, which is why "greenery has a reassuring effect." Even a one-hour walk through the woods or feeding ducks at a pond can do wonders for your state of mind.

• *Exercise*. Exercise can make both your mind and your body feel better. Exercise burns up the adrenaline and other hormones released by stress. The more intense the exercise you do, the greater the effect on stress reduction. At the same time, exercise releases endorphins, opiate-like substances which are your body's natural tranquilizers, responsible for "runner's high."

Exercise is easier if you do it in a group. Your companions will motivate you and provide an element of fun and camaraderie missing from, for example, the more solitary sport of running (apologies to those who run in mirthful packs). If you don't have the willpower to exercise on your own several times a week, exercise with a friend or join a class or club.

You are most likely to put off exercise when you are writing under deadline pressure or otherwise under high stress. Yet these are the very times you most need to exercise, to shake off the effects of long hours hunched over a keyboard so you can remain maximally productive. So make the time you need.

When you do exercise, do it, as the doctors say, "in moderation." One university counselor says that she often sees students who become unhealthily dependent on working out, some exercising five or more hours a day. The gym where I work out is filled with grim-faced individuals reading law books while pedaling their exercise bikes, hour after hour. This is the wrong idea—pick exercise that is fun and interactive. It's not only better for you psychologically and physically; you're more likely to keep at it over the long term. Also, recognize that as you reach your mid-twenties, your body is beginning to slow down a little—you are reaching the age where you will become less flexible, often more out of shape, and therefore more prone to injury. You will need extra time to stretch and warm up.

Along with exercise, it's important to eat right. Avoid the basic graduate student food groups of sugar, grease, caffeine, and chocolate. Instead, concentrate on fruits and vegetables, lean meats, bread and other grain products, and milk products.

• *Relaxation techniques.* Many relaxation techniques can successfully reduce stress. They include meditation, positive imagery, and anxiety management training in which you imagine stressful situations while maintaining a relaxed state. Many of these techniques are available on audiotapes. You can track down tapes through your counseling center, "new age" bookstores, massage centers, or physical therapists. Feldenkrais muscle relaxation techniques, which are helpful for removing generalized stress as well as healing muscle pain in specific parts of the body, such as the back and shoulders, can be ordered on tapes from Feldenkrais Resources, PO Box 2067, Berkeley, CA 94702, phone: 800 765-1907. A good book on meditation, which boils down transcendental meditation (TM) and other meditation techniques into one simple method, is Herbert Benson's *Relaxation Response.*

Massage can be very useful in relieving stress and associated physical pain. There are several common types, including Swedish, shiatsu, sports massage, and the various types of deep-tissue massage, including neuromuscular massage, myofascial release, and Rolfing. All will help you relax, but for muscle spasms and related pain, I recommend searching out a deep-tissue specialist. Often you can locate such body workers by looking at "new age" holistic newspapers distributed at health-food stores, by using the Yellow Pages to find massage schools, or by calling physical fitness spas and asking whom they recommend (spas will often have massage therapists on the premises). Avoid "massage parlors," unless you are looking for relaxation of a more personal nature.

Some people who have not had serious professional massages feel embarrassed at the idea of letting a total stranger pound their naked body. Don't be. It is no different from going to the doctor; the massage therapist is a dedicated professional whose sole aim is to make your mind and body feel better. He or she will avoid culturally sensitive areas, and will usually keep most of your body covered with a sheet, only exposing the part he or she needs to work on.

If you have a significant other, you can help each other deal with stress by learning how to give each other professional-quality massages. You can either buy massage guides, such as *The New Massage*, by Gordon Inkeles, or enroll in massage classes.

A final relaxation technique that reduces stress is sex. Because stress depresses sex drive, this is a remedy that is best used preventively.

- *Cognitive therapy*. There are also a variety of cognitive techniques, in which the goal is to exchange your negative, irrational, and stressful thoughts for ones that are positive and relaxed. These techniques are best taught to you by counseling professionals—many stress management workshops will teach them—because most people need external motivation plus group feedback. Nonetheless, you can try some self-therapy by being on the lookout for irrational, stress-producing thoughts. Many of these thoughts derive from an unhealthy perfectionism: "If I don't do this perfectly, I'm a failure." As such thoughts come to you day by day, try to notice, refute, and replace them with more positive, rational thoughts. For example, if you must give a presentation in class, don't think, "I have to do a perfect presentation so that the teacher will think well of me." Instead, think, "The professor will judge me on my overall work, not just on this presentation, so even though it is important that I do a competent job, it doesn't have to be perfect." One book that can help is *The Relaxation and Stress Reduction Workbook*, by Martha Davis, Elisabeth Robbins Eschelman, and Matthew McKay (New Harbinger Publications, Oakland, CA).
- *Get enough sleep*. Your need for sleep will increase when you are under stress, possibly because neurotransmitters used up by your body's reaction to stress need time to be replenished. If you don't get enough sleep, bad things happen. Studies of sleep deprivation have shown that effects include a significant increase in errors on tasks, difficulty in thinking, sensitivity to criticism, inappropriate affect (i.e., behaving like you're crazy), deficits in recent memory, and most alarming of all, the development of *black humor*. Sounds dangerous.
- *Do not self-medicate*. It will only make things worse in the long run if you try to hide from stress with alcohol or other drugs. Likewise, avoid caffeine. According to a study by Kirby Gilliland, a psychologist at the University of Oklahoma, "coffee drinkers also felt considerably more anxious, frustrated and depressed. And the more they drank, the worse they felt. . . . These 'background' levels of anxiety and depression build up slowly over a period of time, so many people never connect their anxiety with their coffee intake."

Nicotine is seductive to people under stress because it releases endorphins that give you the feeling of relaxation. Unfortunately, there are serious side effects. To start with, nicotine potentiates some of the worst physical effects of stress. For example, smoking, when combined with stress, raises blood pressure and heart rates more than either alone. Other reasons to avoid smoking are emphysema, cancer, and—most terrifying of all—premature wrinkling of your face.

• *Keep your perspective.* Although your schoolwork should be your prime focus, remember that it's not everything. Here is a cautionary tale which I have borrowed from Clifton Fadiman:

> The brilliant Greek scientist and mathematician Archimedes invented Archimedes' screw (a primitive water pump), mathematical theorems, and various war machines useful to his home town of Syracuse when it was attacked by the Romans. Unfortunately, despite the possibly apocryphal use of giant mirrors to enflame the Roman fleet, the town fell and Archimedes was taken prisoner. In honor of his wisdom, Marcellus the army commander left instructions that the scientist was not to be harmed, but alas, this was not to be. When commanded to move by a Roman soldier, Archimedes ignored the order because he was too absorbed in drawing mathematical symbols in the sand. Engrossed in his work, Archimedes gestured impatiently, indicating that the soldier must wait until he had solved his problem, and murmured, "Don't disturb my circles." The soldier, enraged, drew his sword and killed him, a common response of nonacademics to the philosophically minded.

COPING WITH DISCOURAGEMENT
• AND DEPRESSION •

Many graduate students experience periods of discouragement about their work and life in graduate school. Given the amount of stress you experience, this is to be expected. A former education doctoral student says:

> I was very depressed in graduate school, largely because I hated it. It was hard, boring work, and it didn't look like I'd get a job anyway because in 1979–80 there weren't any. My last year in school before I dropped out was particularly bad. I was discouraged about the bad job situation, I couldn't find a good thesis topic, and then my back went out. I'd always had a bad back, but before graduate school I was always doing athletic stuff to keep in shape. But in graduate school I got no exercise, sat in a chair for ten hours a day, plus got uptight

from stress, so I ended up on my back and pretty helpless for six months. Then my wife says to herself, "I'm stressed out getting my own Ph.D. I don't have time to take care of this guy." So she left me. At this point I asked myself why I was killing myself for a degree that wouldn't even get me a job. So I left school and got a job. It's amazing how much better you can feel once you're earning a decent salary.

You may become discouraged (1) because you are making poor progress in school, (2) because your lowly graduate student status is giving you low feelings of self-worth, or (3) because you are burned out after a long period of stress. Lynda Powell says, "One hypothesis about the development of reactive depression is that you are struggling against time or other people over a long period, and then you're suddenly in a depletion phase, worn out." It is common for students to feel depressed after having accomplished some major task, and many people experience something akin to a postpartum depression after finishing the thesis.

If periodic blues turn into chronic or deep depression, you should seek professional help through the school's medical or psychological counseling center. Serious depression, which can be caused by either biochemical imbalances or devastating loss or disappointment, can entirely prevent you from working or even be life-threatening. Warning signs are a persistent low mood or irritability, loss of concentration, feelings of hopelessness, worthlessness, weakness, inadequacy, or guilt, a loss of interest in activities that you normally enjoy, including sex and eating, and either insomnia or excessive sleeping.

Even mild depression is usually harder to treat with simple coping techniques than stress-produced anxiety. Kate Harris says:

Some people under stress seem to show symptoms of anxiety, and others are more likely to feel depressed. The depressed people are harder to treat with short-term group techniques because the benefits of treatment aren't as immediately apparent and because the depressed students may be slowed down and don't interact as well. If their depression persists, they generally need individual counseling.

Nonetheless, there are things you can do to help lift yourself out of mild depression. To start, it can help to realize that depression is circular. Once a person becomes depressed, he becomes withdrawn and passive. He minimizes human interaction and recreational activities and becomes ineffective at work. The more he withdraws, the fewer pleasurable interactions he has to lift his spirits and the more depressed he becomes. A student who is too depressed to get his thesis chapters done on time will certainly not win praise from his committee and is then likely to become even more depressed.

The obvious way to break this cycle is to do things that reward you with good feelings, so that you begin a cycle of action, positive results, and power for new action. You can use some of the same activities that help with stress in general, including regular exercise—which has been shown to help many people with depression—avoidance of alcohol and other drugs, and doing things that are fun and different from your usual rut: it's hard to be depressed when you are skiing down a mountain. Other tactics include:

- *Increase human contact.* Depression thrives on isolation, so force yourself to search out opportunities for interaction. Get together with classmates to study, walk to school with friends or join a car pool, or replace your individual exercise with group activities. If you're living alone, it may help to move back to the dorms or into a house with roommates.
- *Act undepressed.* If you act negative and lifeless, even your best friends will get fed up and flee, so try your best to act cheerful. Furthermore, if you act happy, your feelings will often fall in line. One psychologist who counsels depressed patients told me, "If you want to conquer an undesirable emotional tendency, act as if you feel the way you want to feel, and the feelings often will follow."
- *Avoid negative thoughts.* Note whenever you start sentences with absolute words like "all," "every," "ever," and "never," as in "I can't ever get what I want" or "All the other students are ahead of me." Such sentences are almost never true and show that you are letting unrealistic negative thoughts take over.
- *Get moving on your work.* Much of graduate student depression comes from procrastination and isolation from your professors.
- *Identify and escape from traps.* People commonly feel depressed when they see themselves as trapped in hopeless situations, powerless to escape. For example, if you have two people on your committee giving you contradictory commands on how to structure your thesis, you can become paralyzed if you are afraid of both of them and don't know how to resolve the conflict. The obvious solution is to take prompt action to break out of the trap. If you don't know how, or are afraid to take action, seek the advice and support of friends, sympathetic faculty, or professional counselors, but get moving.

Recognize that fear, often unrealized but nonetheless lurking in the back of your mind, is a key element behind why people are unable to take what are often obvious escape routes. It can help to confront the fear directly. Think carefully about what you are afraid of, assess the probability that these fears will come true, and ask yourself, "What is the worst thing that can happen to me in this situation?" In most cases, even the worst outcome isn't as bad as you think. You might be afraid that if you confront the contradictory committee members, one of them will shout at you. You might be afraid that one will bear you a tremendous grudge and try to destroy your career or say bad things about you to the other faculty. Ask yourself whether each of these possibilities is likely. Will Professor Williams actually shout at you? If so, can you stand it? Will he try to destroy your career? If so, will he be able to? Often, as you examine these questions, you will see that many of your fears are unfounded, or that even if there is a real possibility that the professor will react in the worst way possible, the repercussions for you and your career are not nearly as destructive as you might at first imagine. In nearly all cases, the worst outcomes aren't as bad as the paralysis of not doing anything, and it is better to find out the worst sooner rather than later, after the worry and stress has had time to grind you down psychologically. If a faculty member is going to scream at you and be unreasonable, the sooner you find out and get rid of him, the better.

• *Consider leaving school.* A final solution to stress and depression caused by graduate school, if you are truly miserable, is to leave school. My friend Michael found he was much happier leaving school than finishing his thesis, and he has had a good career in the computer industry without his Ph.D. For too many people, graduate school is like holding a wolf by the ears—you don't like it, but you can't let go either. Many people stay despite the fact that they don't enjoy school and may not even have great love or aptitude for the field they're in. They stay because of internalized parental expectations, because of an overdeveloped sense of persistence, or because they're afraid of the real world. But realize that there is no disgrace in deciding that graduate school isn't for you.

22

. . . .

THE SOCIAL

MILIEU

. . . .

The mutual and universal dependence of individuals who remain indifferent to one another constitutes the social network that binds them together.

—KARL MARX

· RELATING TO YOUR FELLOW STUDENTS ·

Your greatest source of support should be your fellow students, but as with professors, there will be some departments where the students are friendly, interactive, and supportive and others where they're not. A psychology doctoral student was fortunate:

> I'm lucky to be in clinical psychology. There are only seven people in my class, and our work throws us so much together, being involved in process groups, and so on, that we are all very close. We socialize together and work together. People say that's not the case with the experimental groups, although a few labs have good camaraderie.

A study by Nathalie Friedman, called *Mentors and Supervisors*, found large differences among six departments in how supportive the graduate students were of each other. She found that students get a double whammy—in departments where the advisers are unhelpful to their students, the students in turn don't help each other as much as in departments where the faculty are supportive. One explanation for this is found in psychological studies that show that students under stress reduce their level of sharing and helping activities, and aggression among them increases. This makes for a vicious cycle in which high stress leads to more isolation and negative social behavior and in turn more stress.

DOCTORAL PROGRAMS CAN BE ISOLATING

As I've said before, doctoral programs are particularly isolating. Although your first year or so may be spent in classes with fellow students, after that you all get out of sync, passing your hurdles at different times, huddled alone in carrels or traveling into the field for research. This has led one educator, Bernard Berelson, to observe that "the medical or law student seeks to be graduated 'with his class'; the doctoral student has no class to be graduated with." Students in M.D.–Ph.D. programs have both experiences. One said:

> I've finished my medical degree and I'm now working on the Ph.D. Compared with med school, the doctoral program is the pits. All the students in my program are unhappy. In med school we did everything together; there was a sense of community. In the Ph.D. I'm isolated. No one cares about me; no one tells me what to do.

Although master's students spend a larger percentage of their time together in classes, many of them also suffer from isolation, in part because so many master's students are part-time and therefore aren't much involved in student life outside of class (according to the National University Continuing Education Association, two-thirds of master's students were part-time in 1993). A master's student in education described her experience:

> The other students were nice, and I got to know them in class, but we didn't spend a great deal of time working or socializing together. Many of us were working, some were married, and most of my classes were in the evening—I worked during the day—so I was too tired to socialize after class.

Don't forget undergrads as a source of friends. Many graduate students, perhaps from a false sense of their elevated status or because of shyness, don't socialize with undergrads, even though there may only be a year or two difference in age. Nonetheless, I believe that you may be happier interacting with undergrads as well as your fellow graduate students— they will provide you with a reminder that life is meant to be enjoyed. Also, realize that they may be shy of you because you are older, so you may have to reach out to them. For example, if you are a teaching assistant, invite some of your students over for dinner and let them know that you would enjoy being included in some of their other activities.

One factor contributing to isolation is that graduate students are often largely excluded from living on campus. For example, a student who did his sociology doctorate at Princeton tells me that most of the graduate student dorms are twenty minutes from campus. Many of the grad students live in aged living quarters built during World War II for servicemen. Under the terms of the original owner, the land reverts to a polo field when the buildings come down, so the university is permanently stuck with the antiquated structures. Who lives in them? The grad students of course.

If you are a single graduate student, it may be hard for you to meet the opposite sex. As Seymour Halleck, the author of a report entitled "Emotional Problems of the Graduate Student," wrote:

> To achieve intimacy with others, one must first have the opportunity to meet others in a climate that allows intimacy to develop. . . . Graduate students who work with only a few people and who are likely to see the same individuals day in and day out can find themselves easily rutted into an extremely isolated, lonely life.

If you are a doctoral student, you may turn into such an overworked, stressed-out, unhygienic troglodyte that you won't be attractive even if you do manage to meet someone. One student, recognizing his own plight, in desperation published a personal ad reading, "Anal retentive seeks perfect love."

Because male grad students outnumber women on most campuses, their search can be arduous. The Princeton sociology student said:

> I was lucky to live in a little enclave, the Woodrow Wilson center, where the sex ratio was relatively balanced, but basically, on campus there were way more men than women and the social scene was awful.

You might expect that your lofty position as a graduate student would make you irresistible to undergrads of the opposite sex, but the reverse is often the case, because undergrads may believe, often with good reason, that graduate students are hopeless nerds. At Harvard, one male student who ran into this phenomenon dedicated his thesis to the girls at Adams House, an undergraduate dorm, who made early completion of his thesis possible by completely rejecting his advances.

In summary, be aware ahead of time that isolation will be a threat. Before you make your final decision about which school to attend, talk with some of the grad students about their experiences and factor this into your final choice. Once you're in school, you will have to work much harder at creating a social life than you did as an undergrad. Finally, I recommend that you live on campus if possible—think about living in a mixed grad-undergrad dorm, if your campus has them.

BUILDING RELATIONSHIPS
▪ WITH FACULTY ▪

In many departments the hierarchy between professors and lowly grad students is pronounced, professors prefer to keep their distance from students, and the two groups rarely socialize outside of departmental functions, where the graduate students huddle in little clumps saying brilliant things to each other in the hope of being overheard by faculty. Nevertheless, some students are able to become genuine friends with the faculty in their departments. Nathalie Friedman quotes an economics doctoral student who says of her adviser:

> Our relationship goes far beyond the dissertation . . . we're friends. I can go in and talk with her whenever I want and she's interested in knowing what's going on in all aspects of my life. On the one hand, she's maternal and makes you feel that she's solidly behind you. On the other hand, we're friends—we socialize, we play racquetball, just talk.

Every student would like to have a relationship like this with his or her adviser. This may or may not be possible, but there are things that you can do to foster relationships with the faculty in your department, to move them along the continuum from strangers to colleagues to friends. I talked in earlier chapters about the importance of maintaining close contact with your adviser and other faculty. This is vital for the first step of building a good mentor-student relationship. In addition to regular professional meetings, you should take every opportunity to talk with faculty at professional and quasi-professional occasions, such as postseminar sherry hours.

As you spend more professional time with your professors, teaching or doing research with them, collegial relationships will develop naturally. Depending on your natural affinity, some of these professional relationships may develop into deeper friendships. You may then feel comfortable inviting your adviser over to a dinner party or out to join you and other students for beer, or you may indeed end up playing racquetball.

Although the student above enthusiastically described her close personal relationship with her adviser, there can be risks involved with such relationships. First, when personal relationships go bad, they are harder to salvage than more professional ones. Second, it will be natural for your adviser to be wary of developing a close relationship with you, for fear that it may affect his ability to judge your work objectively. To prevent him from feeling taken advantage of, *never* ask for special consideration based on your friendship (it's okay if the professor offers it occasionally, but don't ask).

A related and very touchy area is that of romantic relationships between students and faculty. One cynical view of dating between female graduate students and male faculty is expressed by Pierre van den Berghe in his book *Academic Gamesmanship*:

Female students have an obvious advantage in competing [for their professor's attention, favor, and esteem], and they should make the most of it because this is the last occasion where being a woman in academia is an advantage. . . . Male professors love female graduate students who pay them homage, but dislike female colleagues, especially if they are brighter than themselves.

Contrary to this utilitarian viewpoint, I believe that dating professors is a dangerous proposition. Like dating housemates or people at work, once the romance burns out, the embers lie around waiting to burn your feet. Because of the inequality in power between students and professors, it is difficult to defend yourself against retaliation for rejected love or lust. Retaliation and other forms of sexual harassment occur frequently enough even without encouragement. This potential for trouble has led a few universities, such as the University of Iowa, to specifically prohibit romantic fraternization between professors and graduate students. The Iowa regulation, in speaking about relationships between faculty and the students they supervise, says, "Voluntary consent by the student in such a relationship is suspect, given the fundamentally asymmetric nature of the relationship." Most universities don't go as far as having such an explicit prohibition, but their concern suggests you should think twice or thrice before getting involved.

▪ RELATIONSHIP STRESSES ▪

Studies show that students with supportive spouses, ready to give encouragement and logistical support, have a better chance of finishing school than single students (however, see Chapter 23, which describes the plight of married *women*). Moreover, a study by Lester Bodian has found that you are more likely to finish a Ph.D. if you are married to another graduate student rather than to someone not a student, because you both empathize and help each other. Despite this advantage while in school, the later stresses of trying to find good jobs in the same place for both members of a couple can be daunting (see the February–March 1992 issue of *Lingua Franca*). For this reason, one professor warns that "an academic is best off with someone movable, someone with skills easily transferred from place to place."

Marriages and other long-term relationships often founder as the graduate student becomes increasingly devoted to his work, or depressed and stressed. There are things you can do to increase the chance that when you finally get your degree, you've got someone to share it with:

- *Choose a nondisruptive thesis topic.* Try to be realistic about strains on your relationship when you choose the topic. Most relationships cannot stand long or repeated separations (either physical or mental), so avoid planning lengthy research in the Serengeti without your spouse.
- *Make sure your significant others give informed consent.* To play fair with your spouse, children, or other significant people in your life, before you commit to going back to school, make sure that they fully understand the magnitude of what you are proposing to do, and that they fully agree ahead of time that it is worth the strain. Don't cavalierly announce to your husband or wife that you have decided to return to school, thereby guaranteeing to make their life hell for the next five years. Otherwise you may have the experience of one of my friends, whose husband told her he wanted a divorce the day after she passed her thesis defense. Likewise, if you have older children, you should make them feel included in the initial decision, so that later on when graduate school deprives them of your company, they will be less resentful.
- *Involve your family in your endeavor.* Valerie Epps, director of the Multicultural Student Services Center at George Washington University, who recently received her Ph.D. in higher education administration, says:

It's important to encourage children to be part of the school process. My two sons helped me collate papers, stuff envelopes, and anything else they could do. My youngest, Kareem, who is twelve, moved his computer downstairs next to mine, so that we could work next to each other for company. Children can be a real source of inspiration and help you to keep from giving up because you want to set them a good example by finishing.

- *Give them equal time*. Don't assume that your relationships will always be there—unless you work on them. This means taking time regularly to set aside your work and enjoy each other. Don't fall into the trap of thinking that there will be plenty of time to have fun after school is finished, because relationships can't survive long periods of starvation.

23

. . . .

SWIMMING WITH THE MAINSTREAM: RETURNING STUDENTS, WOMEN, MINORITIES, AND FOREIGN STUDENTS

. . . .

I have been a stranger in a strange land.

—Exodus, 18:3

"Who's 'im, Bill? A stranger! 'Eave 'arf a brick at 'im."

—*Punch*, 1854

TRADITIONALLY, UNIVERSITY CULTURE HAS BEEN DOMINATED BY WHITE MALE academics. The preferred student was like the preferred army recruit—male, white, young, aggressive, well disciplined, and respectful of authority. Although times are changing, white male faculty, and to a lesser extent white male students, continue to predominate in most departments, and the institutional culture reflects that fact. The result is that "nonmainstream" students—older students, women, racial minorities, and foreign students—often suffer from culture shock. Minority students coming from heavily minority colleges may feel lost without their accustomed support group. Women students entering predominantly male departments may be acutely aware that in most disciplines the percentage of women in graduate school is smaller than on the undergraduate level. A foreign student not only may feel out of place in his department but will also have left behind his family and the entire culture of his native country.

Double or triple minorities, such as older Hispanic women, may be multiply challenged.

Although overt or intentional discrimination is relatively uncommon in graduate school—indeed, many programs actively recruit women and minorities, and foreign students make up majorities in many departments— studies show that subtle, often unconscious, types of prejudice frequently remain, including subtle (or sometimes not so subtle) differences in how students are judged and encouraged in class. Even where little prejudice exists, students may be handicapped by their own insecurities and fears of the foreign culture, by language difficulties or differences in modes of social communication, and by loss of their social support groups.

Before talking about specific types of students, I'd like to make a few generalizations. First, if you are a nonmainstream student, expect to work harder than mainstream students to be taken seriously, at least until you establish yourself with your professors. Studies show that teachers often expect less of nonmainstream students. Coupled with this is the "affirmative action" stigma. Some people may believe that you made it into the program only because you're a minority (or a woman or whatever). Set these doubters straight right away by excelling in your work and by taking an active role in class.

Second, you may need to work harder to fit in socially. If you are a woman student in a largely male setting or a Nigerian student in a predominantly Anglo-American department, the faculty or other students may overlook you because they're not sure how to treat you socially. Nonetheless, as I've said repeatedly, active participation in your department is critical for success, so reach out to other people as much as you can. As Samuel Johnson said, "If a man does not make new acquaintance as he advances through life, he will soon find himself alone." Carrell Horton, professor and chairman of psychology at Fisk University, says:

> As a minority student you are likely to feel out of your own culture
> to the extent that your previous contacts have been predominantly
> with people of your own ethnic group. You do, however, need a
> cohort, so make yourself part of the departmental group. You don't
> have to love everybody, but don't exclude yourself.

A related thing to remember is that your failure or success in graduate school, as in most other essentially social endeavors, is a self-reinforcing spiral. If you make an extra effort to be outgoing, competent, and professional, most likely you will get positive feedback from your professors and fellow students, enabling you to continue doing well.

Several of the minority counselors whom I spoke with made a third recommendation: avoid the trap of seeing prejudice where it isn't. Realize that most people will mean you well and that what you might at first perceive as prejudice may actually be only the isolation and lack of care-taking most students experience in graduate school. Indeed, many of the women, foreign, and minority students and faculty I spoke with said they experienced little or no discrimination during their graduate years. Raymond Winbush, a psychology professor and assistant provost at Vanderbilt University, says:

> Don't confuse the everyday difficulties of graduate school with discrimination. You may feel ignored, but remember that most graduate students feel ignored. It comes with the territory. One of my fellow classmates at the University of Chicago was very unhappy with the program when he first arrived. He thought the atmosphere was unwelcoming to minorities and decided to transfer. But when he talked to graduate students at other schools, he found out that grad school was tough everywhere for everyone, so he decided to stay and did fine.

When you do run into discrimination, it is often unconscious discrimination by someone who would be willing to change if you ask him. Carrell Horton says:

> Absolutely talk to the person if you feel they are treating you differently. Many people are unaware of the message they're sending, and if they realize it, they'll change.

You are more likely to be successful in changing minor discriminatory behavior if you take a nonaccusatory, objective approach. Focus on asking for the changes you want, whether they be for more guidance, attention, fairer grading, or balanced course content, rather than demanding apologies or immediate conversion of the professor to your way of thinking. For example, if you courteously but firmly tell the professor that you would like to be called on more in class, or would like the class to cover theories out of the cultural mainstream, then you are more likely to get what you want than if you call the professor a racist, chauvinist, or imperialist.

If you are unfortunate enough to run into discriminatory behavior that is frequent or flagrant, such as continued incidents of sexual harassment, and the person does not respond to firm but polite requests to change, you may need to take more forceful steps. These can include the registered letter described below in the section on sexual harassment or formal charges lodged with the appropriate university office. Recognize, however, that there may be costs associated with such escalated responses, including being labeled a troublemaker, academic retaliation, or even the filing of legal complaints for libel (these have little chance of succeeding). Realize also that once you have begun open warfare with a committee member or another powerful faculty member, you may need to end up changing committee members or even schools for a fresh start.

Several minority graduate counselors and students said to me that they thought the best approach once you're in school is to not worry too much about discrimination and just get ahead with the job (obviously this isn't the case when there is harassment severe enough to cause you substantial pain). Worrying just takes energy you need to get your work done and produces stress you don't need. A counselor said:

> I seldom give the grad students a shoulder to cry on. I just help them figure out what to do. They need to solve the problems, focus on their work, and put everything else aside. I tell them, "If you're being ignored in the classroom, don't get mad, just be more aggressive about contributing."

Raymond Winbush said:

> Graduate school is like going out your front door when it's raining cats and dogs. When someone throws a bucket of water on you too, don't spend too much time figuring out which water is rain and which got thrown on you for discriminatory reasons, just get to where you're going so you can dry out.

A Hispanic student said of discrimination:

> You learn to manage it. Live life. You just have to believe that you can handle what comes your way. You'll always face ignorance, but you just have to take care of it. I'm busy and don't have time to worry about people who are ignorant and bigoted. I've got too many goals to meet.

Finally, the most important thing, which I have been hammering at you throughout this book, is to do your detective work ahead of time. Find out before you apply to schools which ones have good reputations for treating students like you well. Are there good institutional programs for helping nonmainstream students? For example, if you're a parent, are there day-care facilities? Will there be a community of similar students, or will you be one of a handful of tokens? Find out before choosing an adviser whether a particular professor has a reputation for making sexual advances to students or being culturally insensitive.

I suggest that you read each of the following sections on specific types of nonmainstream students, even if a particular section doesn't immediately apply to you. For example, if you are a male member of a racial minority, you should still read the section on women's issues, not only to give you perspective about the problems women face but also because the section describes tactics that can be adapted to your particular case.

▪ RETURNING STUDENTS ▪

At seventy-seven it is time to be earnest.

—SAMUEL JOHNSON

Many professional programs prefer older candidates with work experience because they are more mature and better motivated. Even in academic programs, many professors believe more mature students do better in graduate school than those coming straight from college. At the same time, other professors prefer to admit younger students, who are seen as more committed to the field, with a longer career of academic contribution ahead. In either case, although your study skills may be rusty, you can use your greater maturity to sustain you in overcoming obstacles, give you more self-discipline in ordering your life, and help substantially in your interpersonal relations with professors.

Getting reacquainted with school can be tough. A George Washington University stress counselor says:

> Reentry is very stressful, and returning students may initially be at a disadvantage compared with those that come in straight from undergrad. The first quarter is the worst—they're not used to taking tests, and they have problems with their sudden loss of status, what the students call "infantilization." They are very self-questioning and need a quarter or two to build confidence.

Older students may also face "ageism." One graduate school dean said, "Many departments feel that admitting older students is a waste of the university's resources because these students don't have as much time ahead of them to contribute." Faculty may also believe that older students, particularly women, aren't serious about their work ("They just want to get out of the house for a while"). They may be uncomfortable teaching students who are as old as or older than they are, so they ignore these students in class or otherwise treat them differently. Such problems can partly be overcome by your attitude. If you are confident and friendly, participating fully in what goes on in the classroom, you will be taken seriously. One of my older friends at Stanford who succeeded on a combination of charm and talent is Harriet Doerr. She returned to Stanford to finish her undergraduate degree in English in her seventies—she had dropped out of Stanford more than fifty years earlier—and went on to become a Stegner Fellow in Stanford's graduate writing program, and published an award-winning book of stories based on her life in Mexico —*Stones for Ibarra*. She says:

At first I told myself I was a fool even to attempt going back to school. I was scared to death I wouldn't be good enough for Stanford. But once I'd started, I liked it very much, and the professors were very encouraging. I concluded that age doesn't matter if you are exercising your talents; it doesn't matter if you are twenty or ninety. Just be your natural self, and friendships will naturally grow with the professors and other students, even if they're not your age. Funny things do happen—I could tell the other students were often wondering if I was the teacher's mother, and once someone asked me if I was the chairman's secretary. I thought it was terribly funny.

Be aware also, before you decide to invest the time and money in graduate school, that you may also face discrimination once you have graduated. For academic jobs, hiring committees often put a premium on youth. Conversely, if you have been in the working world and are going back to school for a master's to improve your credentials, age may not be a handicap.

Before you actually start school, you can act to decrease your reentry trauma by doing homework to catch up. Read recent journal articles in your field. You can cover a lot of material rapidly by reading appropriate textbooks and general review articles in journals like *Scientific American* and *Bioscience*.

You should also be competent at using a computer to do word processing. If you're not, take a course in Wordperfect or a similar common word-processing program, or learn by using a computerized tutorial. Many public libraries have videos that instruct in the use of computers and specific word-processing programs. These can be more useful than manuals for computer novices, as they actually *show* you what you are supposed to be doing. If your typing needs work, typing tutor programs for personal computers can brush you up.

Once in school, if you have other demands on your time—a family or a job—you have to realize that you can't study in the same way you did when you were an undergraduate. If you are married or have children, you will have to balance your priorities—you may not be able to stay up until 3 a.m. every night during finals. Unfortunately, most schools are not yet very good about providing child care. One way around this time dilemma is to pace yourself—remember that the amount of work you have to do in most programs is not overwhelming, often less than in undergraduate school, provided that you work every day, just as you would with a job. Second, be smarter about what really counts and where to expend your energy. A good example of a place to put in minimal work is a class where the professor is outside your field, so you will never need him for a reference. Do the minimum you need in his course for an adequate grade, but conversely, do your best in a course taught by one of your committee members. Don't be perfectionistic where it doesn't pay off. One English student said:

> In one class we had to read thirteen novels. I figured that because there are eighty people in the class, the professor would never know whether I'd read them or not. So I focused on reading the novels I was going to base my paper on, did some extra reading to back up the paper, and the professor ended up complimenting me on how well prepared I was. Another way I saved time in preparing for my orals was to pretend to my committee that I hadn't read some books I knew backwards and forwards. So they assigned me these to read for the orals.

One final optimistic thought is that many universities offer reduced tuition to senior students.

▪ SPECIAL PROBLEMS FACED BY WOMEN ▪

Most hierarchies were established by men who now monopolize the upper levels, thus depriving women of their rightful share of the opportunities to achieve incompetence.

—LAWRENCE J. PETER

FACING A MALE-DOMINATED ENVIRONMENT

First the good news. The number of women attending school has been rising in most fields, even those traditionally reserved for men. According to the National Research Council, in 1960 only 11 percent of Ph.D.s were earned by women, while in 1994 women earned 39 percent. In some areas, notably the social sciences, psychology, and the humanities, nearly half of the doctoral degrees are awarded to women. In chemistry, 28 percent of the Ph.D.s awarded in 1994 went to women, up from only 12 percent fourteen years earlier. Overall, this means that women have more role models and that the institutional climate is becoming more accepting.

Moreover, in many departments women experience little overt or intentional discrimination, to the point that one zoologist who received her degree in 1991 could say:

> I had problems in graduate school, but discrimination wasn't one of them, neither because I'm a woman nor because I belong to a minority group. However, I did have friction with my professor, a woman in her sixties who suffered early in her career from being one of the few women in the field. She kept trying to get me to join a group for women in science and was very irritated with me that I didn't see the point in joining.

Nonetheless, women are poorly represented in many fields, including engineering (11 percent), mathematics (21 percent), the physical sciences (24 percent), and, to a lesser extent, the life sciences (42 percent). In the critically important field of computer science, only 15 percent are women. In science something mysterious happens to women along the career trail. Take physics, for example. According to an article in *Science* by Faye Flam, although 35 percent of students in high school physics classes are female, more women drop out at every stage along the way. Statistics compiled by the American Institute of Physics in 1991 show that women constitute only 16 percent of physics BAs, only 10 percent of Ph.D.s, 7 percent of assistant professors, and 3 percent of tenured faculty. Likewise in mathematics; although women made up 22 percent of Ph.D.s in 1991, only 4 of 303 tenured positions were held by women at the ten best mathematics departments in the United States.

Why is this happening? There may be several intermingled reasons. One is that in many departments role models are hard to find, so women may lack encouragement to continue. A second reason is that subtle discrimination may remain as the residue of an earlier policy of exclusion. Women weren't admitted at all to physics or astronomy programs at Harvard, MIT, or Caltech until the 1960s, and older faculty in many departments may still consider the presence of women inappropriate.

Furthermore, even if intentional discrimination isn't present, a number of factors operate to make graduate school tougher for women than for men. They include:

• The male-dominated social structure creates an institutional "climate" that encourages men at the expense of women. You can read about the causes and effects of this climate in an excellent study by Roberta Hall and Bernice Sandler, *The Classroom Climate: A Chilly One for Women?*—available from the Association of American Colleges and Universities (1818 R St. NW, Washington, DC 20009, phone: 202 387-3760). It describes how people rate work by women as of lower quality than identical work by men, and negatively judge women who show behaviors that are interpreted as "masculine" rather than "feminine," even though these behaviors may be essential to excel in graduate school. Males who act dispassionately may be viewed as "objective," but females are "cold." Men may be "forceful," while women are "hostile." Moreover, subtle differences in the way faculty treat male and female students, such as giving less eye contact to women and interrupting their comments more, may leave students of both sexes with the belief that women make less valuable intellectual contributions.

• Women themselves enter graduate school with a set of learned behaviors and values that put them at a competitive disadvantage. These include feelings of academic insecurity. A study reported by Hall and Sandler has shown that women undergraduates feel less prepared for graduate school than men from the same institution. Some women also hold beliefs, previously reinforced by society and school experiences, that women should stick to feminine fields, speak deferentially, and otherwise act in a feminine manner. These factors may actually convince women not only that it is difficult for them to succeed but that they *shouldn't* succeed if they are to successfully fulfill their role as "feminine" women.

The Classroom Climate notes that researchers on sex differences in language have shown that women, along with other low-status individuals and groups, use particular speech patterns that signal lack of status to the listener. These patterns include hesitation and false starts ("I think . . . I was wondering"), high pitch, "tag" questions ("This is important, don't you think?"), and excessive use of qualifiers ("Don't you think that maybe sometimes . . . ?").

- Family structures often dump more of the household duties and child rearing on women, even if both parents work or are in school. This makes for an interesting situation in which single women get through graduate school more easily than married ones but married men—with the support of their wives and the motivation of ultimately being the breadwinner —are more likely to finish and to finish earlier than single men.
- There may also be stressful sexual tension between female students and predominantly male faculty. This often makes it difficult for women to develop the same degree of comfortable "buddy" camaraderie with their male advisers that men are able to develop, which gives the men an advantage when it comes to the bestowal of teaching assistantships, job recommendations, and the other benefits of a close relationship with your adviser. A graduate student in American studies found:

> This was one of my greatest frustrations in grad school, that it was impossible to develop the same level of camaraderie with male professors as the male students could. The feeling between the professors and me was more formal. The men could go drinking beer with their advisers, or play tennis, which didn't feel appropriate to me. I think informality helped the male students in feeling that they could more easily approach their professors for help. I *do* think that buddy-type relationships develop between female professors and students, one reason I recommend that female students search out women for advisers.

Additional bad news is that whatever discrimination exists in graduate school, it is much more severe on the professional job front. For example, in a survey of astronomers, almost 40 percent of women reported that they had experienced discrimination of some sort. The result is that many women persevere through graduate school only to find they have trouble getting jobs or advancement at later stages, as indicated by the statistics above for mathematics and physics.

EVENING OUT THE ODDS

Here some things that you can do to try to even out the odds in graduate school:

- *Check out schools ahead of time.* When you are scoping out schools and professors, as described in Chapters 5 and 6, pay extra attention to whether the departments you are interested in provide a welcoming environment for women. Are there women at the top levels of the university? If the president, vice presidents, and all the deans are men, there's likely to be a problem. Is there a university-wide or departmental association of women graduate students? Are there courses that deal with women? If you're in history, art, psychology, or music, and there is nothing about women, this should be a tip-off that the department isn't particularly interested. If you are headed for a nontraditional field, are there special programs designed to welcome and smooth the way for women? For example, some engineering departments go out of their way to recruit women, implement a buddy system whereby new women students are teamed with more experienced ones, and otherwise try to smooth the way.

- *Choose your adviser extra carefully.* Female advisers are obviously likely to be sympathetic with your aspirations and understanding of the special effort you will have to make. When evaluating male professors, look for ones who have already produced female graduate students, particularly ones whose students have been successful in finding jobs. One way to get this information is to search through the literature for publications by women whose work interests you. Note their home institutions and call them for advice and ask them about their own experiences. If they aren't recent graduates themselves, do they know any who might be willing to talk to you?
- *Look for support from other women.* Join women's professional groups or support groups. If none exist on your campus, you can form one of your own, at least an informal one. One way to locate groups is to contact your local branch of the American Association of University Women (AAUW)—some, but not all, of their branches have groups for graduate students. The AAUW can also be a source of information if you run into trouble. If your local branch can't help, try their national office (1111 16th St. NW, Washington, DC 20036; phone: 202 785-7700).
- *Think hard about whether you have a pioneer temperament.* It takes a strong personality to overcome the bias you will confront if you are one of the few women in a field still dominated by men. Therefore, try to assess how hard it will be by talking to women grad students or recent graduates in your field. Try to realistically assess whether you have the drive it takes. In some cases it might make sense to switch to a related field that is more accepting of women.

These days there are also advantages to being a pioneer. If you can excel in an untraditional field, and if hiring in the field is subject to the effects of affirmative action, you actually have an advantage at hiring time, compared with a field, like English literature, where more than half the students are women. Moreover, unfortunately, the fields with many women are also the fields that are overcrowded, with poor job prospects overall.

• *Be aware of the risks of academic "ghettoization" and soft subjects.* It is tempting for women who are conscious of their struggle for equality to devote themselves to research focused on women's issues. These studies are important, but there is a danger. Women's studies are often seen by the academic establishment as substandard compared with more traditional fields, a perception that can hurt your career. The way around this problem is to make sure that your research is well grounded in traditional research, in a traditional department, even if your main focus is women. This is particularly important early in your career. Your job chances in English literature are better if you are a specialist in nineteenth-century novelists, with a few papers written about women novelists, rather than a specialist in women novelists per se. It is much easier to get a job in a women's studies program because you have a strong grounding in your primary discipline rather than vice versa.

A related problem is that, even within fields, women are often tracked into "softer," qualitative areas of concentration, which have less prestige. Instead of becoming economic anthropologists, women head for descriptive anthropology. Instead of molecular biology, women become field-ecologist types. You can increase your prestige and employability by entering more rigorous, quantitative specialties. Before going to graduate school, pay extra attention to figuring out which field holds out the best chance of success.

• *Think carefully about teaching versus research tracks.* Careerwise, academic women tend to choose or be tracked into teaching positions rather than the more prestigious and financially rewarding research positions. This happens early in graduate school, in terms of both what type of thesis is chosen and whether women get teaching assistantships rather than research assistantships. A women's graduate school counselor says:

I recommend that women think carefully about whether to try for TAs versus RAs. TAs offer the advantage of letting you get to know more professors, assuming that you teach a variety of classes, but an RA carries much more professional weight. In some cases a research assistantship may even pay you to carry out some of your own research.

- *Strive for scholastic visibility.* A researcher on women's issues says, "Women are often in the idealistic mode. They think, 'If I do good scholarship, I will be rewarded.' They *don't* think about how to get their scholarship seen." This "wait to be noticed" strategy won't work, in part because women's work is often devalued. Instead, you must actively strive to build your reputation.
- *Watch out for your personal safety.* Women on campus are prime candidates for assaults because the friendly atmosphere lures them into dropping their guard, and graduate students are particularly vulnerable because they're often on campus late at night or during breaks when the campus is empty. Consider taking a self-defense class, take care not to put yourself in dangerous situations, and use campus escort services when you must travel across campus late at night.

HANDLING HARASSMENT

Sexual harassment happens to both women and men, but the large majority of cases occur when male professors or students harass female students. Bernice Sandler, senior scholar at the National Association for Women in Education, estimates that more than 90 percent of harassment is by men directed toward women, and that over 30 percent of women graduate students report some form of sexual harassment (including relatively minor incidents such as sexually explicit comments). However, the following discussion can be applied to male students harassed by either men or women. *No one* should stand for harassment.

Graduate students are easy marks for sexual pressure from professors because they are relatively powerless and dependent upon faculty for the help that will lead to a job, and because they are older than undergraduates and therefore lack the protection of being "underage." Further, it can be difficult for a student to prove harassment, particularly in its subtler forms, and a student may risk her career by formally complaining. These fears mean that 90 percent of sexual harassment experienced by graduate women goes unreported. However, in February 1992, the Supreme Court ruled that the federal law barring sex discrimination in schools and colleges permits students to sue for damages for sexual harassment and other forms of sex discrimination. This ruling may put pressure on schools to prevent harassment.

One reason this area of sexual harassment is a messy one is that when professors and students date, it can be difficult for outsiders, in the absence of objective evidence, to judge whether the relationship is exploitative or not. Nonetheless, many cases of harassment are clear-cut, as the following story shows. In the words of a departmental chairman at a highly regarded school:

> A few years ago a female student came to me, closed my office door, and confided that she was being sexually harassed by her adviser. The guy was married, but he told her to be his mistress, saying, "I want to be free to visit you at any time." She initially gave in, but was now at the point of bringing charges to free herself. I took the matter to the provost, who handled it quietly. A senior colleague spoke to the adviser, and persuaded him to leave her alone. She was convinced not to file charges because the adviser was up for tenure and it would have hurt his career. The woman eventually left the department and now has a good career in business.

The weakness of this departmental response, which seems common, suggests that you should not place great reliance on formal university procedures, particularly given the difficulty of proving harassment and the possible repercussions to yourself. Although you may eventually need to resort to formal complaints, you are better off dealing with the issue informally if you can.

In this case, what should you do? Ignoring continuous harassment generally doesn't help—the harasser often takes this as tacit consent. Therefore, your first line of defense is to make it absolutely clear to the offender that his behavior is unacceptable. Say, "No," clearly and firmly. If this doesn't work, the Center for Women Policy Studies suggests:

- *Keep records*. Keep a journal of events and preserve any letters or notes you receive from the person harassing you. Record the dates, places, times, witnesses, and the nature of the harassment. This evidence can be used as substantiation for any later case you need to make.
- *Tell someone*. Talk with other students to find out whether others have been similarly harassed. What kind of action did they take? Were these actions successful? Often you will find that the same person has also harassed others. This evidence can be used to substantiate a formal complaint or at least to help you feel less alone with the problem.
- *Identify an advocate*. Find a counselor, ombudsman, or other sympathetic faculty member who can give you advice, discuss the formal and informal options available to you, and perhaps intervene on your behalf.
- *Write a registered letter*. Sending a particular type of private, but registered letter to the offender has proven to be very successful at stopping harassment. Such a letter should have three parts. In the first part, you state the objectionable behaviors. ("On November 17, in your office, you

put your hand on my knee during a discussion of my thesis draft.") In the second part, you tell how these behaviors make you feel. ("This made me feel afraid and angry.") In the third part you ask for specific changes. ("I want you to refrain from touching me and to leave the door of your office open when we are meeting.") Dr. Sandler says that this type of letter has a high success rate, stopping 90 percent of harassment, and carries more weight than an oral communication. It works because it gives the harasser a chance to see his behavior from your point of view, and it also warns him—the registered letter lends gravity—that he cannot continue without formal repercussions. This technique was developed by Mary P. Rowe, a labor economist, who is special assistant to the president of the Massachusetts Institute of Technology. Rowe says that this letter is "the *only* method that usually works and at little 'cost.'" To read more about this and other methods of dealing with harassment, order articles on harassment from the Center for Women Policy Studies (2000 P St. NW, Suite 508, Washington, DC 20036, phone: 202 872-1770; there is a small charge for the articles). Your counseling center or women's support group may have someone familiar with this type of letter to help guide you through the process.

Finally, despite the fact that there are remedies available to you to deal with sexual harassment, remember the overwhelming importance of maintaining good relations with your adviser and committee. In most cases, it isn't enough to stop the behavior. You must stop the behavior while maintaining or reinstilling goodwill. If you can't do this, if you continue to have doubts about whether your adviser will do his best for you given your interpersonal history, you may be best off changing advisers.

▪ MINORITY STUDENTS ▪

In this section, I will talk about challenges that minorities have in common, while trying to note situations specific to different ethnic groups. I will confine my analysis to the four official minority groups recognized by the federal government for purposes of affirmative action—namely, African-Americans, Hispanics, Asian-Americans, and Native Americans. However, many of the observations and recommendations will also apply to other students of unique cultural background.

If you are a minority student, it will be hard for you to find many role models of your own race among faculty. The National Center for Education Statistics reports that as of 1993, across all institutions of higher education,

African-Americans held only 5 percent of regular full-time positions, although they make up 12 percent of the total U.S. population; Hispanics held only 2 percent of positions, although they comprise 9 percent of the total population; and Native Americans made up 0.5 percent of tenured faculty and 0.8 percent of the U.S. population. Asian-Americans were slightly overrepresented; although they make up only 3 percent of the U.S. population (as of 1990), they held 5 percent of full-time faculty positions. Whites dominate, with 88 percent of full-time faculty positions. Minorities, including Asian-Americans, are concentrated at the lower levels of academic employment and are more likely to be nontenure track.

These patterns in faculty concentration roughly reflect the percentages of minority students in graduate programs. In 1992, African-Americans earned 3.7 percent of all doctoral degrees, Hispanics earned 3.0 percent, Asian-Americans 2.5, Native Americans 0.06, and whites 88 percent, according to Deborah Carter and Reginald Wilson in a report published by the American Council on Education. The following statistics are also from their report.

Between 1983 and 1993, the number of African-Americans earning doctorates held steady, and African-American master's degrees rose by 6 percent between 1981 and 1992. Asian-Americans, Hispanics, and Native Americans increased the number of both Ph.D.s and master's degrees they earned during this period (the number of Asian-American master's degrees rose by 101 percent!).

In some fields you will find more of your peers than in others. For example, in 1993, 28 percent of all African-American doctorates were earned in the single field of education, while only 15 percent were earned in the physical and life sciences combined, and only 3.7 percent in engineering. On the other hand, Asian-American students are increasingly concentrated in engineering, this field alone holding 24 percent of them, and their share of all engineering doctorates increased from 3.7 percent in 1975 to 9.7 percent in 1993, more than three times their representation in the general U.S. population.

Minorities show shifts in fields in recent years, in part due to an increased emphasis on earning potential. For example, there has been a large shift by African-Americans away from education degrees on the master's level—down 25.5 percent from 1981 to 1992—while at the same time the number of African-Americans MBAs increased nearly 70 percent. Hispanic education degrees remained steady during this period, while MBAs increased 124 percent, and Native American MBAs increased 42 percent.

The lack of minority graduate students in certain fields has been a continuing frustration for departments that go out of their way to recruit both minority graduate students and minority faculty. The dean of graduate admissions at a top school that does have relatively high African-American attendance said:

> Good African-American graduate students applying in some departments are so rare that, for example, I can still remember the name and file information on a magna cum laude student who applied to our government department four years ago. We admitted him, as did Berkeley, Harvard, Yale, Princeton, Stanford, and everywhere else. After being accepted with full support, he decided not to go to graduate school at all, so no one got him. Highly qualified black applicants can make so much more money outside of academia, for fewer years of preparation, that it's difficult to keep them in doctoral programs.

This continuing shortage of minority graduate students in many fields will make substantial increases in minority faculty difficult to achieve because there will be no large pool of qualified applicants to fill faculty vacancies. Reginald Wilson, senior scholar at the American Council on Education, has warned:

> We have the potential for achieving parity for minority faculty, but if we don't have the faculty there to hire, then the chance will be lost. Unless there is a substantial change in the production of black and Hispanic Ph.D.s, that parity won't be achieved.

Michelle W. Zak, director of faculty development for the University of California, asks:

> What's this country going to look like in the next couple of decades if we have a population that's 55 or 60 percent nonwhite, and all the educated people, all the leaders, are white?

If you are a prospective minority graduate student, this very shortage of minorities can be good news for you because universities are hungry for qualified minority grad students. This doesn't apply as much to Asian-Americans because they are already overrepresented in many fields, but if you are African-American, Hispanic, or Native American, your minority status can help you with admission and later with getting a job. A dean of graduate admissions says:

> Many of the blacks and Hispanics who notify us of their status on the application get their application fees waived. In addition, for

professional degrees, like the two-year MBA or the foreign service master's, the department tries to shape the class to be culturally diverse and therefore minorities have a definite edge on admission. For academic master's or Ph.D. programs, the minority advantage isn't so clear-cut. You still have to make the first cut as an acceptable candidate by the department—unlike in undergraduate admissions, there is no adjustment of GREs or other criteria for minority admission. We're very strict on having students meet the academic criteria because we only want students who can succeed. Unlike with undergraduate programs, there is no support system to help underqualified students through. However, once you've made this cut, minorities get very, very, very special reading of their files. Qualified minority candidates are so rare in most fields that we jump at them.

PROBLEMS

Many of the problems minorities face are analogous to those faced by women in a male environment.

- *Lack of role models.* Because only one of every 344 full-time faculty is a Native American, one out of 51 is Hispanic, one out of 22 is African-American, and one of 21 is Asian-American, you may very well end up in a department with no faculty of your race.
- *Loss of cultural support.* The demographics of graduate school mean that there will be fewer minority students to provide you with a community than there were when you were an undergraduate. African-American students, for example, in 1994 made up 10 percent of the total undergrad enrollment in higher education institutions, but comprised only 4 percent of graduating doctoral students. Hispanics made up 7 percent of the undergraduate population, but only 2 percent of graduating Ph.D.s.
- *Social differences and preconceptions.* You may suffer from the paradox of "too little" and "too much" attention, in which minorities receive less attention from professors during normal scholastic activities, but are called upon to speak for their race during discussions of culture or ethnicity. ("Maria, can you give us the Hispanic perspective on this issue?")

Cultural and language differences that exist between whites and minorities will cause miscommunication and misjudgments, even though all parties have the best intentions. For example, Sarah Nieves-Squires, author of the report "Hispanic Women: Making Their Presence on Campus Less Tenuous," says:

The closer personal space that is comfortable for some Hispanics may make Anglos uncomfortable or may be perceived as inviting intimacy. . . . Overt hand and arm gestures, coupled with a Spanish accent, may be perceived as a lack of verbal ability.

• *Academic "ghettoization."* Just as for women who focus on women's issues, there is a tendency for the academic mainstream to reject or devalue work by minorities on minorities. A related issue is that minority philosophies and attitudes toward mainstream academic interpretation may not be welcomed. A minority professor says:

We find that minority students seem to feel less intellectually isolated, less alienated, in mathematics, engineering, and the sciences, because here the measure of their work is objective—opinions don't matter as much. Students in the humanities and social sciences have a harder time because determining the "right" approach is more subjective, and often the opinions of minorities are out of sync with the mainstream. One example is the recent controversy over how to treat the "discovery" of America by Columbus.

• *Fewer research and teaching assistantships.* Although there are special aid programs for minorities, minorities overall receive fewer of the research and teaching assistantships vital for career progress and financial survival. For example, a 1994 report by the National Research Council shows that while 78 percent of Ph.D. students in the physical sciences received university support (primarily teaching and research assistantships and fellowships), such support was received by only 59 percent of African-Americans and 64 percent of Hispanics. As a result, cumulative debt at graduation due to school loans is greater for these minorities than for the general student body—63 percent of African-Americans and 65 percent of Hispanics graduate in debt, compared with 47 percent overall. These differences may be caused less by discrimination than by resources available at schools differentially attended by minorities.

• *Overwhelmed advisers.* Like female advisers, minority advisers tend to be overwhelmed. One adviser said, "Because of the paucity of black professors at my university, I am placed in the dilemma of being all things to all black students."

• *Double whammies for minority women.* Minority women not only have the difficulties of being minority, but suffer the inequities, described in the section above, of being female as well. According to Yolanda T. Moses, author of a report called "Black Women in Academe" for the Association of American Colleges' Project on the Status and Education of Women,

"A double bias exists in which black women are judged on the basis of preconceived notions about women *and* blacks."
• *Competition between and within ethnic groups.* One graduate adviser said, "Although our minority affairs office technically takes care of all minorities, in reality it focuses primarily on black students, who are the dominant minority on our campus." Even within an ethnic group, such as Hispanics, there can be friction. One Hispanic master's student told me:

At our campus there was a Latino group, which was composed mostly of upper-class students, primarily with parents from Central or South America, and a Hispanic group, primarily lower- or lower-middle-class students from the United States. There was almost no interaction between them, because the Latinos perceived the Hispanics as low-class, and the Hispanics thought the Latinos were snobs.

EVENING OUT THE ODDS

The steps you can take to succeed are similar to the common-sense things for women to do:

• *Investigate the school ahead of time.* Contact the minority affairs office on campus to find out what's available in terms of financial aid and general campus tone. Find a school where your particular minority group is treated well. Note, as I just mentioned, that just because there is a minority affairs office doesn't mean that it will look out for the interest of your group.
• *Choose a school with a critical mass.* Raymond Winbush advises:

Try to choose a school with a critical mass of minority grad students and faculty, so that there are a reasonable number of people like yourself for support. When I went to grad school, I was fortunate that there were three other black students in my program, so we could bounce ideas off each other. If there aren't enough students of your race, you can make common cause with other minorities.

If you do want to choose a school with a concentration of minority students, there is a publication that can help you called *Minority Enrollments: A Guide to Institutions with the Highest Percent of Asian, Black, Hispanic, and Native American Students* (Garrett Park Press, PO Box 190B, Garrett Park, MD 20896, phone: 301 946-2553).

- *Make it known to the admissions committee that you're a minority.* This will help you get admitted and considered for special financial aid.
- *Look for special financial aid.* Check with any schools you are attending for special programs for minorities.
- *Network.* Network with other minority students and faculty. Reach outside your department for advice and support—alumni are an often overlooked resource, but they can be particularly helpful, since they've already been through the course.
- *Get counseling if you need it.* Even if you have had past negative experiences with counselors, give it a try if you're under stress or experiencing other problems.
- *Participate fully in classes.* Be assertive about speaking up. An African-American master's student says:

> Classes are for communication, so I say what I want to say. Being loquacious, the professors sometimes cut me off, but it's better to talk too much than too little.

An Asian-American said:

> Because people assume, as an Asian woman, that I'll be soft, passive, and submissive, I compensate by being ultra-aggressive in class. Once you act like that, people will take you seriously. You just have to establish yourself.

- *Be aggressive about competing for RAs and TAs.* As I've said before, teaching assistantships and, even more so, research assistantships are important for your career. Be aggressive about searching them out. Go directly to professors to ask if they have TA or RA funds.
- *Be extra careful about choosing an adviser.* Look for one who has a proven record for treating minority students well. It would be ideal to get an excellent, politically well-connected adviser of your own ethnic group, but recognize that this may be impossible. However, as long as the adviser you choose has your best interests at heart, then good guidance skills, academic excellence, and political connections are more important to you at this stage than ethnicity. An African-American student says:

> Don't discount people who aren't black. Most of the people who have got me where I am have been white, so you *can* connect with white people. White professors took an interest in me as a person and helped me.

• *Be aware of the dangers of academic "ghettoization."* My advice here is the same as that I gave for women. Don't insist on doing ideologically pure research at this stage if you have reason to think this may hurt your career. Focus on the mainstream. As an African-American student said:

The name of the game is getting through with solid training. Once you're a professor or other full-fledged professional, then you have the power to effect change. Once you're a prof, you can make an African-American language class or a Hispanic culture class part of the standard curriculum. But first you have to get through the standard way; that's the key, whether we like it or not.

• *Have self-confidence.* The trait that stood out most clearly to me when I was interviewing successful minority grad students, faculty, and administrators was their strong sense of self and self-confidence. A student in international relations said:

I'm the only person in my family's history to go to college, but my father was telling me I would go to Harvard from the time I was seven years old. He said, "There's nothing you can't do; race isn't going to be a barrier." Now that my program is nearly over, I'm interviewing for jobs in international banking. I'm competing with primarily white men, and I do feel different, but not disadvantaged.

Carrell Horton, who got her Ph.D. twenty years ago, says:

Students are always asking me how I kept my identity in a predominantly white school. I tell them, "How could I lose it? I had it when I arrived, and I had it when I left."

▪ FOREIGN STUDENTS ▪

Modern man . . . is educated to understand foreign languages and misunderstand foreigners.

—G. K. CHESTERTON

> I've always had a weakness for foreign affairs.
>
> —MAE WEST

If you are a foreign student planning on attending a U.S. program, you won't be alone. Peter Syverson, director of information services at the Council of Graduate Schools, writes that the numbers of foreign students in U.S. graduate schools are increasing rapidly, at about 5 percent a year. In 1992–93 there were over 200,000 foreign graduate students enrolled. They composed 11 percent of all U.S. master's students and 26 percent of U.S. doctoral students, for a total of 14 percent of all graduate students. Foreign students are heavily concentrated in engineering and the sciences—they earned 61 percent of all U.S. engineering doctorates in 1994 and 43 percent of doctorates in the physical sciences.

Although coming to a foreign country can be exciting, it can also be difficult to find yourself for a long period away from your friends and family, getting used to a new language and new customs. Nevertheless, take confidence in the fact that most foreign students do well; actually, foreign students are more likely to finish their Ph.D. programs than are U.S. citizens.

APPLYING TO GRADUATE SCHOOL

Foreign students have the following special concerns when choosing and applying to graduate programs. You should:

• *Judge your capabilities carefully.* Be aware that increased competition for graduate students among U.S. universities has made what the Council of Graduate Schools calls a "buyer's market." This means that schools are actively recruiting foreign students, and in some cases you may be recruited to attend a school even if your academic or English-language capabilities are too weak for you to ultimately succeed. Therefore, be realistic in evaluating your potential. The dean of one school said:

A lot of universities in the United States are hurting financially, so they are taking students whose English isn't ready for them to do well. To make sure all *our* students are qualified, we have a strict policy that graduate students must have a TOEFL score of 550 or above, and 650 or above if they are going to teach. Even so, we have had a few students whose spoken English wasn't good enough for them to continue in the program.

If your contact with U.S. schools is through private, profit-seeking organizations, scrutinize them carefully to ensure that they are reputable. The Council of Graduate Schools says:

> Many such agencies are legitimate and provide useful services; others are not. When an institution works with any external recruiting agency, there is always the possibility that the student's main objectives in pursuing graduate study may be neglected.

If you do consider using a recruiting service, ask students who have previously used the service about their experiences. You can also get information about specific recruiting organizations by writing to Sarah Herr at NAFSA Association of International Educators, which maintains records on third-party recruitment agencies (1875 Connecticut Ave. NW, Suite 1000, Washington, DC 20009, phone: 202 462-4811).

- *Attain English proficiency*. The better your English is before you start school, the easier your life will be. Schools will generally require that nonnative speakers of English score at acceptable levels on any of several English proficiency examinations, the most common of which is the Test of English as a Foreign Language (TOEFL). Other tests you may be asked to take include the Test of Written English (TWE), the Test of Spoken English (TSE), and less frequently the American Language Institute of Georgetown University (ALIGU) or the Michigan Proficiency Test (MPT). The TSE is often required of students who want to be considered for teaching assistantships. For information on the TOEFL, TSE, or TWE tests, write to TOEFL, TSE, or TWE, PO Box 6151, Princeton, NJ 08541-6151, USA.

If your English is below the acceptable standard but close to it, some schools will admit you provided that after admission you take English classes and pass the appropriate English exam. If you are given this opportunity, make sure that you plan carefully for the extra time and money you will need to attain acceptable proficiency.

- *Take standardized tests early*. In addition to English-language proficiency tests, you will have to take standardized admissions tests, such as the Graduate Record Examination. Given that your educational background and language may put you at a disadvantage in taking these tests designed for U.S. students, you should practice carefully and take them early. Because foreign students are at an obvious disadvantage when taking the GRE verbal test, many departments accept lower verbal scores from foreign students than from U.S. citizens. In deciding when to take the tests, remember that it will take at least six weeks to report scores to the institutions you are applying to.

• *Choose your school carefully.* Because you probably won't be in the United States when choosing a school, it may seem difficult for you to do the research necessary for identifying good schools and advisers. Nonetheless, you should still try as hard as possible to approximate the methods laid out in Chapters 5, 6, and 7 for choosing an adviser and a school, particularly if you are going into a Ph.D. program. You can write directly to professors whose work you know about. A Venezuelan student said:

I found my adviser by meeting one of her graduate students who was doing fieldwork in Venezuela. I was very interested in the work the student was doing, and he contacted his adviser on my behalf. Then his adviser and I corresponded, and my husband and I both ended up coming to the United States to study under her. This really worked well, because the graduate student ultimately got a position with the New York Zoological Society and was able to fund much of my thesis research.

You can write directly to schools, addressing your letter to the office of foreign students, to inquire about how many foreign students are enrolled and what special counseling or other programs are available to make your life easier.

Given that the happiness of graduate students differs dramatically from school to school and department to department, speak to current students or recent graduates of the programs you are interested in. Ask the department or the office of foreign students for the names of students whom you can write or phone.

A further source of free information and counseling about graduate school programs are the offices of organizations in your country that specialize in educational exchange. They include the Fulbright commissions and the offices of the United States Information Service, the Institute of International Education, and America-Mideast Education and Training Services, Inc.

• *Start the application process at least one year before application deadlines.* You need to start early to deal with the slowness of international mail, the need for special forms, and U.S. immigration requirements for a passport and visa. Some schools will also require that foreign students file a preliminary application, which is reviewed first to see if you meet minimum requirements. Once the preliminary application is approved, then you can formally apply.

Some students report considerable difficulties with their own nations' bureaucracies, which may be unfamiliar with U.S. procedures. So leave time for this. A student from Gabon said:

> One of the greatest troubles was getting a transcript. No one in my country knew what a transcript was. Getting one that was acceptable to the American school was very hard.

- *Take special care with your application.* Type your application if possible. Make sure that your name is written the same way on all forms. Transcripts of your previous academic record must be official, bearing the signature and academic seal of the registrar—photocopies are not acceptable. Do not send documents that cannot be replaced. All documents must be in English. If your previous school cannot issue documents in English, include the original non-English documents accompanied by notarized translations, which must be complete and exact translations of the originals.
- *Letters of recommendation and essays are especially important.* Because application committees may have a hard time evaluating an undergraduate record from a foreign institution, your letters of recommendation and application essays, which can show the clarity of your thought and your reasons for wishing to attend graduate school, will carry special weight.
- *Financial aid for foreign students.* Much of the foreign aid available to U.S. students will not be available to you. According to the Council of Graduate Schools, as of 1994, 45 percent of foreign grad students depend upon private sources of funding. Nevertheless, about one-third of foreign students receive either research or teaching assistantships from the institutions they attend, so make sure you fill out the appropriate school applications. Policies differ significantly from institution to institution; some routinely offer support, particularly to doctoral students, while others will not admit foreign students who are not entirely self-supporting. Therefore, although the U.S. school may provide some help, you also need to look for aid elsewhere. Try your own government, fellowship foundations in your country, your employer, and the U.S. embassy or Fulbright commission in your country, which may have a

limited number of fellowships. You can also read *Funding for U.S. Study: A Guide for Foreign Nationals* (Institute of International Education, 809 United Nations Plaza, New York, NY 10017-3580, USA, phone: 212 883-8200).

Note that before you can receive your student visa you must be able to demonstrate that you have enough financial resources to support yourself during your studies, from either private funds or financial aid.

Don't count on supporting yourself by working part-time while you are a student; the Immigration and Naturalization Service (INS) places many restrictions on international students and their spouses. For example, if you are on an F-1 visa you may be restricted to on-campus employment during your first year at school. Students caught doing unauthorized work may lose their student visa and be sent home. *Because INS regulations are complex and presently being changed, for up-to-date information you should contact the international student adviser at the school you wish to attend.*

If you are restricted to on-campus work, you will find out that jobs are hard to get and are poorly paid. Kathy, a student from England, tells this story:

Last summer I was desperately short of cash, but because I have an F-1 visa, I can only work for the university. I tried to get a job waitressing for conference services, but apparently my personality wasn't winsome enough. So I was put on a dorm-painting crew at $5.50 an hour. Because I'm from England, the locals who ran the crews couldn't understand me. They thought I couldn't speak English, so they put me on a crew where everyone else was Chinese. My crew painted 300 rooms, which was incredibly tedious. The only good thing about the job is that it was so excruciatingly boring that we developed a jaunty camaraderie.

• *Budget carefully.* Living expenses in the United States may be greater than you are used to. For example, many U.S. communities are designed so that a car is nearly essential if you want to live a fulfilling life. You may need a car to get to the supermarket, see a movie, or simply visit friends. So find out before you arrive at school whether you will need to budget for this major expense. Yves Djoko, a student from Cameroon, said:

I went to school in Mobile, Alabama, where the public transportation system isn't very developed. If you don't have a car, you stay home. I stayed home.

Housing can likewise be expensive—it varies greatly from school to school. Don't assume that the school will find you a place to live. Graduate students are usually forced to find their own living arrangements off campus, and rents can easily be more than $300 per month for a room in a house shared with other students.

Health insurance is something that most foreign students don't think about. Unlike some countries, the United States has no national health insurance, and a relatively minor accident, such as breaking an ankle, can cost you $5,000 or more in medical care. Many schools will provide health insurance for students, and sometimes for their dependents. If the school does not provide insurance, it can be *very* expensive to buy on your own. If there is no insurance provided, you can contact the National Association of International Educators, Washington, DC, for referral to recommended programs designed for international students.

Don't forget to budget for expenses during the summer. Anticipate, even if you originally planned to go home over the summer, that unexpected research, extra English instruction, or other demands may keep you in the United States.

• *Additional information.* You can order two publications that may be helpful from the Council of Graduate Schools (CGS), 1 Dupont Circle NW, Suite 430, Washington, DC 20036, USA. They are *Graduate Study in the United States: A Guide for Prospective International Graduate Students* and *International Graduate Students: A Guide for Graduate Deans, Faculty and Administrators.* The second guide, although not specifically for students, is more helpful because it is more detailed and provides samples of "Certification of Finances" and other forms. Because these guides were published in 1991, check with the international-student adviser where you will be attending school to make sure any vital information is still current.

There is an excellent report, which I drew on for some of this section, by Nathalie Friedman for the Institute of International Education. The report, called *Mentors and Supervisors*, compares experiences of U.S. and foreign graduate students at six universities. It is filled with interviews and will help you understand the challenges faced by foreign students. You can order it from ERIC Document Reproduction Service/DynCorp

I & ET, 7420 Fullerton Road, Suite 110, Springfield, VA 22153, phone: 800 443-3742 or 703 440-1400 (ask for document ED 295-541).

PROBLEMS FOR FOREIGN STUDENTS IN GRADUATE SCHOOL

The genius of you Americans is that you never make clear-cut stupid moves, only complicated stupid moves, which makes us wonder at the possibility that there may be something to them we are missing.

—GAMAL ABDUL NASSER

Culture shock. If the culture of your native country is very different from that of the United States, even the food here can be hard to get used to. Even more important, the social atmosphere of American departments may seem strange. For example, students from Asian countries often have trouble with the relatively informal manners of U.S. classrooms. A professor said:

> We have a real problem with the Asian students. Their cultural upbringing makes it difficult for them to be aggressive enough about seeking out help from the faculty. In the case of my students, I practically have to order them to come in to talk with me. This makes it difficult to establish a friendly rapport.

At the other extreme, Latin American students often experience U.S. academic culture as cold and impersonal. Here is what a zoology doctoral student from Venezuela had to say about her department:

> In Venezuela I was used to different human relationships, more friendship and socializing with faculty and students. Even the U.S. grad students make a hierarchy. In my master's program in Venezuela, students and professors invited each other for meals, or we would all go dancing together. There wasn't a need to always maintain a professional front. In the United States, my husband and I invited the professors and students to dinner a couple times, but it was a disaster. Everyone was too stiff. I said to my husband, "The last time I was at a party like this I was twelve years old." So we gave up and got nonacademic friends.

According to Nathalie Friedman's study, foreign students, who have left behind their family, friends, and entire culture, suffer much more in an emotionally cold atmosphere than U.S. students. They need friendly and supportive faculty, and when they don't get it, not surprisingly they are unhappy. She quotes a Chilean's cry of grief:

> This is a terrible university! Grotesque, I would call it. I did learn a lot in my field, but you're left too much on your own here. Everything is very individual—no relations with anyone. I did some graduate work back home before coming here and it was very different. I was treated very well there. Faculty there related to you and worried about you. Here, it's a different system—faculty are too busy publishing to pay attention to you.

• *Poor advising*. Foreign students don't get worse advising from the faculty than American students, but, as a group, they suffer more, particularly during the dissertation process. Again, I quote Friedman describing the difference between how American and foreign students respond to poor advising:

> American students are angry, annoyed and resentful but, at the same time, not devastated by the absence of attention, assistance and input from the advisor. They tend simply to get on with the task of finishing the dissertation, sometimes turning to peers, sometimes to another professor, for support and feedback. They were generally quite acute in diagnosing the cause for the situation: an advisor who was overloaded with administrative responsibilities or industrial consulting, or a general departmental or university-wide ambiance of indifference to students.
>
> Foreign students, in contrast, were devastated and in several cases seemed almost paralyzed, powerless to move ahead, to get on with the task at hand. They spoke bitterly about advisors who did not read their material, who were unavailable for meetings, and who were not willing to provide concrete direction and assistance. But even more, they spoke of advisors who were unconcerned with their needs, uninterested in students, unprepared to offer encouragement and support during the difficult dissertation years. In other words, while the American students interviewed complained about the lack of instrumental help from nominal advisors, foreign students missed both the instrumental and the expressive support that they felt should be forthcoming from a dissertation sponsor. . . . Apparently, foreign students— particularly those from the Middle East and Latin America where faculty-student relationships are on a warmer, more informal footing—acutely resent the lack of such relationships during both the early and the later graduate years. . . . Asian students, who tended

to form their own peer networks, seemed less distressed than other foreign students. . . .

- *U.S. education is aimed toward problem solving.* Some foreign students were raised in more "memorization"-oriented systems and have trouble adapting to the American system, which emphasizes creative thought and problem solving over knowledge gathering and analysis.
- *Language difficulties.* Passing the TOEFL is no guarantee that you won't have language problems. Expect to have some frustration when you start. Yves Djoko found:

> I passed the TOEFL without being able to speak English. It's easy to pass. When I got here for school, English was a big problem. I learned to speak it by sitting in my apartment for the summer and watching television ten hours every day, only with a break to play soccer. In school, my first class was in marketing, and I didn't know anything about U.S. culture. The teacher was talking about General Foods, and I wondered who that was. In one quiz, I was supposed to write about the packaging decisions I would make as a marketing director for Campbell Soup, but I didn't even know what Campbell Soup was.

Even if you speak English fluently before you get here, you may still run into hidden difficulties because your natural speaking patterns and conversational signals may be different from those of native U.S. English speakers. For example, a case study by John Gumperz and Deborah Tannen presents a graduate student from India having a discussion with several U.S. graduate students. The Indian student interrupts the other students frequently, although she doesn't intend to; moreover, they interrupt her. The result is that everyone is frustrated, and the American students perceive the Indian as irritating. The reason is that U.S. and Indian speakers of English use different language cues to signal when they are finished speaking, so that each erroneously believes the other is finished when in fact she has more to say. This cultural difference in the language patterns is analogous to the differences between minority and mainstream white language patterns within the United States, but on a larger scale.

Another problem observed by a grad school dean is that the language capabilities of some foreign students actually decrease after they arrive here:

> We have had problems with foreign students who only hang around with their compatriots. They don't spend enough time with American students, and therefore their English skills go down. Some eventually

had to leave school because their skills deteriorated to the point that they couldn't function in the lab.

• *Separation from family.* A stress counselor says:

Many of our students are foreign, and the master's students often leave their spouse and children in their home country for the two-year program. You can imagine that this causes a lot of stress.

EVENING OUT THE ODDS

• *Learn all the English you can.* English is the key to getting teaching assistantships, being noticed in class, relating well to professors, and otherwise excelling. If your English is poor enough so that you are having problems keeping up with your work, consider asking your department for permission to defer courses to lighten your load while you focus on English.
• *Be assertive about getting to know professors.* If, because of cultural differences, you're not sure about the cultural rules for how to act with professors, ask American students or counselors at the office of foreign students for advice.
• *Be assertive about teaching assistantships and research assistantships.* Look into the options for additional financial aid once you have established yourself in the department. If you are seen as a good student and you have made good political connections, new sources of departmental support may open up. You may have to do an especially good job selling yourself to get teaching assistantships because some professors don't like to give these to foreign students; they are worried about language difficulties or believe that foreign students don't know how to handle U.S. undergrads.
• *Understand your undergraduate students.* Many foreign students who do teach feel they don't understand their American undergraduate students. Accept the fact that American undergrads will be informal and rambunctious, and may not treat you with the respect you expect. However, if you overlook this and treat them warmly, your teaching career will be more rewarding.

Also, don't worry about appearing perfect to the students—just be human. If you don't know something your students ask, don't try to bluff them. Just say you don't know but you'll find out the answer. Or ask if anyone else in the class knows the answer. The best attitude to take is that your job as a teacher isn't to have all the answers; it is to help the students learn by themselves.

- *Contact the office of foreign students and other foreign student organizations.* Although many students only approach the office of foreign students for necessary bureaucratic reasons, the personnel are also there to help you adjust, they can counsel you if you run into problems, and they often provide social activities. The office also may be able to act as a mediator if you have culturally induced misunderstandings with your adviser or other professors. Ask whether there is peer counseling available for foreign students.
- *Reach out to your fellow American students.* The more interaction you have with American students, the better your English will become, the faster you can adjust to American culture, and the richer your stay here will be.

24

BRINGING IT ALL

TOGETHER:

THE JOB

Work is of two kinds: first, altering the position of matter at or near the earth's surface; second, telling other people to do so. . . . The second kind is pleasant and highly paid.

—BERTRAND RUSSELL

There's no point in living if you have to work.

—ANDRÉ BRETON

MOST OF THE FOLLOWING ADVICE APPLIES WHETHER YOU ARE HEADED TOWARD an academic or a nonacademic job. Although the two are usually talked about as different career paths, and there are real differences, basic strategies still apply to seeking both types: academic and nonacademic careers will flourish if you get an early start on planning, ideally while you are in graduate school. Both depend on personal contacts in order to find jobs and to get them. And both depend strongly on well-developed interpersonal and presentation skills—if you bomb the interview, you're out of luck.

YOU NEED A CLEAR VISION OF
· YOUR FUTURE CAREER ·

Regardless of what type of job you are headed for, you need an overall career strategy to follow from the time you begin graduate school. If you have a clear vision of the job you want, you can take the right classes, choose the right thesis, do relevant internships, and make the connections to obtain political and personal influence. For example, if you are getting a master's in physical therapy and want to specialize in rehabilitating people with sports injuries, then you should take classes focused on orthopedics and do a practicum in a sports medicine clinic.

Marva Gumbs, a career consultant and director of career services at George Washington University, describes this planning process as "career management." She says:

> We try to show students that they need to take on responsibility for planning and managing their careers. They need to make sure that the curriculum they're following leads to what they really want to do. You can confirm if you're going in the right direction by talking to people in your field who are actually practicing their profession.

Unfortunately, many graduate students enter school without clear career goals. Although you may have labored for days over your grad school applications, it is likely that you didn't even spend a few hours to investigate the full range of career possibilities in your chosen field. One career counselor says:

> I see many floundering graduate students who just figured that a graduate degree would be a good thing to have without nailing down why. School is a way for them to put off deciding which career they want—they may have chosen a general field, but that's different from deciding specifically what they want to do. In school, these students take standard courses without focusing on specific career goals, so when it comes time to graduate, they're lost. Often they find that the face value of their degree won't qualify them for the jobs they want. For example, an MBA who wants to do international work is probably out of luck unless he played a smart game in school. Without good planning, he's headed toward being a desk jockey doing standard financial analysis.

Don Brezinski, director of placement services at American University, says:

> I just gave a talk to a class full of college juniors—all of them were going to grad school, and none knew why. I told them that they'll have trouble getting a job when they finish school unless they start planning now. We try to make students aware that they shouldn't go to grad school unless they have a purpose. A master's degree is called that for a reason—you're supposed to master something. In

the ideal scenario, we try to get students to have a focused purpose with every paper they write and every class they take.

If you are reading this while already well along in graduate school, perhaps even nearing graduation, don't lose heart. You just need to start putting your job strategy together right away. Don Brezinski says:

> Grad students who just come into the counseling center at the end of school, wondering how to get a job, have to scramble to catch up. Fortunately, there's a lot that can be done in a relatively short time, meaning a few months, if they're willing to work hard on putting together a good job-search strategy. They should recognize, though, that a successful job search typically can take up to six months or more.

Even if you are fortunate enough to have your career goals clearly defined, you may still be wise to begin a careful, broader assessment of job options. Just because you know what you want to do doesn't mean that the job market will cooperate. This is particularly true if you are in a Ph.D. program, headed for an academic job, in a field where your chances of getting a decent academic position aren't certain. Traditionally, 90 percent of humanities Ph.D.s entered the teaching profession. Today, however, the tight job market ensures that many would-be teachers won't be, so you need to have an alternative strategy. Roger Wyman and Nancy Risser, in *Humanities Ph.D.'s and Nonacademic Careers*, a report for the Committee on Institutional Cooperation, write:

> Humanities graduate students whose primary career objectives remain academic positions will best be served by a two-pronged strategy that can prepare them for employment in both the academic and nonacademic worlds. "Plan A" concentrates initially and primarily upon an academic job search. "Plan B," pursued concomitantly, provides the tools needed to launch a nonacademic job search if an initial academic appointment does not materialize, or if that appointment is terminated and prospects for further academic employment are dim.

A happy note for displaced academics is that studies show that Ph.D.s who have gone into administration, government, or business actually have higher job satisfaction than those who are college teachers. Teaching college can often be a thankless task. Remember St. Cassian of Imola, the patron saint of stenographers and teachers. He was condemned to death by the Romans for refusing to sacrifice to their gods, and two hundred of his students cheerfully carried out the sentence by beating him over the head with writing slates and stabbing him with iron pens.

HOW TO DEVELOP A CLEAR VISION
▪ OF YOUR FUTURE CAREER ▪

When I realized I had turned out to be a lousy, two-bit pool hustler and drunk, I wasn't depressed at all. I was glad to have a profession.

—DANNY McGOORTY

As they go through life, people naturally assess what they like and don't like. Most of the time you've done this intuitively, deciding, for example, that you like to play volleyball and don't like shuffleboard, or vice versa. What you need for a good job search is a structured version of this intuitive process.

Regardless of the field you are in, there are four steps that you can use to identify a good career path:

- Assess realistically your own abilities, likes and dislikes.
- Research what kinds of jobs possess the characteristics you want and investigate the career paths necessary to reach them.
- Talk with as many people as possible in the field to find out in detail what their jobs are like and how you might fit in.
- Gain as much on-the-job experience as you can by taking appropriate summer jobs, interning, and, if you are headed for an academic career, teaching.

For most people this process of exploration and focus will be a gradual one, in which you refine your goals as you gain more information and experience. You may well change paths several times during your graduate career—from one specialty to another or from one thesis topic to another. The point of early preparation, however, is to plan as carefully as possible from the beginning. You don't want to get a master's in electrical engineering only to go back several years later for a degree in English.

Your goal, by clearly identifying your unique skills and affinities, is to find the job that matches. The better you can evaluate yourself, and the better you identify the jobs that fit, the more employable you will be and the more you will ultimately enjoy your work. Robert Wilson, director of the Community Vocational Counseling Center at George Washington University, says:

EVALUATE YOUR UNIQUE
CHARACTERISTICS

Each person should identify the fundamental components of their training and personality that are unique to them and not to the herd of graduate students. Once you've figured this out, decide how to present this unique package in a way that makes you attractive. Suppose you've got a Ph.D. in English, but one of the things you love and know about is folk music. Start looking at organizations that include an element of folk heritage in their work. You could be a staff writer on a journal or a researcher for a professional organization.

To motivate you to undertake the following career exploration process, you should know that students who prepare this way do better on the job market than those who don't. For example, a study of business students at New York University by Stephen Stumpf, Elizabeth Austin, and Karen Hartman found that those students who had engaged in career exploration activities, including self-assessment of aptitudes and informational interviewing, were rated by potential employers as giving better interviews. They were also offered more jobs.

STEP 1:
• EVALUATE YOUR SKILLS AND AFFINITIES •

Robert Wilson says:

> If you're not sure what you want to do, you've got to start looking at your whole life, asking what experiences really energized you. You can't make career decisions without getting a good fundamental sense of self. Don't let the market make you a computer programmer if you don't like programming computers.

> You need to ask yourself which jobs you particularly enjoyed in the past. What aspects of those jobs? Do you want to live in a particular geographical area? Are you self-motivated or do you do best on a team? How much money do you need to be happy? Ask yourself these and other questions in a systematic way. Just as a thesis topic won't come to you

by virtue of occasional, disjointed musings, neither will a clear realization of what you want to do with your life. Appendix A in *What Color Is Your Parachute?* by Richard Nelson Bolles will do an excellent job of leading you through a structured assessment. I strongly suggest you read it and *actually do the exercises it contains*. If a book isn't enough to get you motivated, find a counselor at your school's career counseling center to push you through an assessment.

STEP 2:
▪ RESEARCH YOUR CAREER POSSIBILITIES ▪

The human race has a cruel choice: work or daytime television.

—ANONYMOUS

Once you have an idea about what your needs are and what specific job qualities would suit you—whether you need a structured working environment, a large salary, or warm co-workers—then you should research what types of jobs exist that both fit your abilities and offer the qualities that will make you happy. Most people who feel that there aren't any jobs they would like to do simply haven't done enough research. Bob Orndorff, a career placement consultant at the Georgetown University career center, says:

> Most of the time people don't know what they want to do because they don't know what opportunities are out there. The best thing is to simply explore options and be exposed to opportunities. This means *start gathering information*.

Obviously there are limits on what you can be, and you must be realistic, but there are many more options available than you might imagine. Robert Wilson says:

> Once you've figured out who you are, then look at the universe of possible jobs, tempered with reality. The computer scientist who wants to be a musician may not be able to jump into being a classical pianist, but he can find out how his computer skills fit into the world of music, maybe working in a sound mixing studio, using computers for musical education, or writing programs for composing on home computers.

There are a number of sources to help you identify which jobs are out there for someone with your background:

- *Career counselors.* Career counselors are trained to think creatively about jobs. For example, Don Brezinski says:

  I help people think about the less obvious jobs, which are often the most rewarding. If you're interested in international affairs, don't just send your application off to the State Department, which has a thousand applications for three openings. I can tell you that the Department of Agriculture is also internationally oriented and that there may be far fewer applications for each international position than at the State Department. Likewise, I was just counseling a lawyer who wanted an entry-level position to do international law on sovereignty rights. Again, he was thinking State Department. When I told him to check the Interior Department, he thought I was crazy. I said, "They work on Indian Affairs—human rights, sovereignty, treaties."
  So the answer is to outsmart the market. Everyone goes to the obvious places, and your best bet is to find the little niches they miss.

- *Alumni.* Your department is likely to have statistics on where previous students have ended up. If ten out of forty graduates in your field are working in a certain area, that's a likely bet. But also track down the single individuals in unusual jobs. One of these jobs might be right for you.
- *Other people working in the field.* Talking with people in your field is the best way to find out about what kinds of jobs are available and what these jobs are like.
- *Personnel departments.* Call the personnel departments of organizations that work in your field. Ask someone to spend time talking with you about whom they hire and where they would place someone with your background.
- *Want ads.* You may not find a job you want through the classified ads—most people applying for graduate-level jobs don't. But ads can give you an idea of the breadth of jobs available. One job counselor says, "I never fail to find a job I've never heard of in the Sunday want ads."
- *General business magazines and newspapers.* Even if your artistic soul rebels, get used to reading publications that write about business. Try *Business Week, The Wall Street Journal,* and the business section of your local newspaper. Especially good is the *National Business Employment Weekly,* published by *The Wall Street Journal,* which you can buy

at a newsstand. It contains both job ads and articles on networking and other aspects of the job search.

- *Trade magazines.* Find them listed by subject in the National Research Bureau's *Magazine and Editorial Directory*, Volume 2 of *Working Press of the Nation*. Another reason to spend time reading your field's press is to learn the jargon. You look good to employers if you speak their language.
- *Books on your field.* There are books on specific fields, exemplified by the Career Associates' series, including *Career Choices for Students of Mathematics*, *Career Choices for Students of Art*, and "career choices" for students of history and at least nine other fields.
- *Directories.* There are directories for a huge number of fields which offer what is essentially biographical information about organizations. You can find out where a firm is located, how many people it employs, who the top officers are, and whether it publishes newsletters, magazines, or books that might contain additional information. If you might like a career working with books, you can get ideas by looking through the *American Book Trade Directory*, which lists 24,000 bookstores, wholesalers, auctioneers of literary property, importer/exporters, book appraisers, book trade associations, and foreign-language dealers. If you think we're still in the 1980s and you want to make a few million dollars through leveraged buyouts, there's the *Merger Directory*, which lists three hundred firms providing acquisition services. To be really thorough you can go through either *Directories in Print* (formerly *Directory of Directories*), by the Gale Research Corporation, or *Guide to American Directories*, by Bernard Klein. Each lists hundreds of directories, which in turn list thousands of organizations.
- *Associations.*

> People of the same trade seldom meet together even for merriment and diversion but their conversation ends in a conspiracy against the public, in some contrivance to raise prices.
>
> —ADAM SMITH

You can read about associations in the *Encyclopedia of Associations*, by the Gale Research Corporation, and *National Trade and Professional Associations*, by Columbia Books. In their subject indexes you will find associations for almost everything from numismatics (American Numismatic Society) to nuts (Northern Nut Growers Association). Associations distribute information about their activities, so they're a good place to get information and contacts.

Check with your career counseling center for other ideas.

Try to be as honest with yourself as possible about what will make you happy in the long run. The world is filled with unhappy lawyers who went to law school because they were seduced by dreams of large salaries or because the route to follow was clear-cut. Going into a field that you aren't really enthusiastic about can be poison—not only will you be unhappy, but the chances are you won't excel. One of the reasons it took me eight years to finish my Ph.D. was that animal behavior bored me. Once I changed fields to something I loved, conservation, I was motivated to do the equivalent of a second Ph.D. in less than four years, pioneering a new field (how global warming would affect biological diversity) and establishing a national reputation. Richard Nelson Bolles said this a lot more succinctly: "If a thing turns you on, you'll be good at it; if it doesn't, you won't."

STEP 3:
• TALK WITH PEOPLE IN THE FIELD •

It is hardly ever any use to go and interview people. If they are at all nice, they will not want to meet you.

—EVELYN WAUGH

Once you've got an idea of what sorts of jobs are available, talk with people in the field to find out what these jobs are like and whether your skills match the employers' needs. This is the notorious process of "informational interviewing." Most career counselors and many books can describe the process in detail. Again, I recommend either *What Color Is Your Parachute?* or *Jobs for English Majors and Other Smart People*, by John Munschauer.

Informational interviewing is simple in concept: people enjoy talking about what they do for a living, so if you ask them nicely, they're apt to give you half an hour of their time to answer questions about their work. You'd be surprised how willing people are to talk. At the same time you are absorbing information, the person you are talking with gets a chance to know you and to evaluate you as someone who might be worth taking a second look at later if a job opens up.

The best thing about informational interviewing is that it's fun. Because you are in quest of information, not begging for a job, you don't have the same performance pressure. Also, the people you're interviewing can feel free to give you honest advice about their organizations without having to deal with your job expectations. One middle manager says:

> I'm very leery about interviewing people if they say they're interested in specific jobs. There are too many ways I can get in trouble, partly because in a formal interview a whole new set of rules kicks in having to do with equal opportunity and the personnel office. On the other hand, if someone comes to me *just for information*, then I'm perfectly happy to spend time with them.

In practice, most people put off informational interviews until they are actually looking for a job, so both you and the person you're interviewing know that a job is really what you're after. However, by maintaining the fiction that it's just an informational interview, you keep the pressure off, because (a) formal guidelines don't come into play and (b) even though you're looking for a job, you may not expect to get one from the specific person you're interviewing.

Informational interviewing does several things for you:

- It provides you with information about the types of jobs available.
- It puts you in contact with people who can hire you or recommend you for jobs.
- It gives you practice in interviewing that can help when you are doing real job interviews.

Often people looking only for information are offered jobs out of the blue. My friend Nancy told me:

> When I first moved to Washington, I started informational interviewing with congressional committees. I talked with all the leads I had, asked those people for more leads, and tried to find out everything I could about what sorts of jobs were available in the nutrition field. One of the people I spoke with was administering a committee which dealt with nutrition issues. We hit it off and a week after our meeting she called to say she liked me so much that she'd fired her current assistant and wanted to offer me his job. I hadn't been expecting a job when I went to see her, but it sure turned out great.

Whom do you talk to?

If you feel hesitant about calling up total strangers, start by interviewing people you already know or who are connected to people you know. Ask your professors, fellow students, friends, and family for the names of people working in your field.

You may also feel more comfortable approaching people who are on record as wanting to help pitiful waifs such as yourself. Your career counseling center is likely to have a list of alumni who have volunteered to be contacts for fellow alumni trying to break into careers. There are also networking organizations dedicated to helping their members help each other. For example, the Women's Information Network in Washington, D.C., regularly hosts breakfast lectures and happy hours specifically so that people can explore mutual career interests.

Once you get braver, you can contact the organizations you're interested in directly. Call the receptionist or public relations department and ask them who can help you with information about your field. For example, if you're interested in finding out about an organization's research on economic patterns in the Sahel region of Africa, ask who is working in that area. Then call that person. A typical opening gambit would be:

Mr. Seymour? My name is Maria Tolan. Don Horak suggested I call you. I'm a grad student at Johns Hopkins and I was wondering if you might have a half hour or so next week to talk with me about the research you're doing on peanut farming in the Sahel.

This raises the question of whether you should phone the person cold or precede the call with a letter saying that you will call. I always call cold, and I get good responses. The Georgetown University career center did a survey of alumni and found that half preferred the letter first, while half were happy with the phone call alone. My advice is to do what you feel comfortable with. If you're good on the phone, dial away. If you choose to send a letter first, include your résumé and say in your letter that you will be calling within the next week. This way your targets will keep your letter and résumé on their desks and in their minds.

When you begin interviewing, practice on the most nonthreatening and least critical people. You can begin by interviewing at organizations where you're pretty sure you never want to work. Or you can even interview people in fields other than your own. Start by interviewing lower-level people—they're likely to have more free time and feel more flattered that you want some of it. Bob Orndorff says:

It's natural for students to be hesitant about walking in cold to talk with strangers. That's why we tell them to start with personal contacts and alumni. To get them over their fear of talking with strangers, I ask them to do a visualization. Imagine that an undergrad from your

college calls you to ask for advice about graduate school. Do you want
to help? No doubt you do. This exercise helps students realize that
it can actually be a pleasant experience for the person who is in a
position to help.

If you're targeting a large organization, rather than head for the president of the company, your best bet is to approach people appropriate to
your level. Talk to the people who actually do the work you're interested
in. If you're an entry-level person with a new graduate degree, and you
want to do policy research in Washington, talk to policy researchers, not
to the upper management. Even if it takes someone in upper management
to hire you, you'll have better luck if you approach them with the recommendations of their staff.

Don't take it personally if some people act as though your request to
talk is an imposition. As long as you're not unduly pushy, informational
interviewing is a perfectly acceptable thing to do. People who are asked
for an interview may groan a little inside, but they realize that it's part
of their job to keep an eye out for new talent; moreover, most people like
helping people. Mary found that often all it takes to open someone up is
the right password:

> I went to interview a woman at the National Marine Fisheries Service
> who warned me ahead of time that she was very busy. When I got
> there, she was downright unfriendly. After a little stilted conversa-
> tion, she asked me where I went to school and I told her, "Harvard."
> It turned out that she had too, and from then on it was old home
> week.

The moral is to take informational interviewing as a percentage game.
Some people will be useless, others unfriendly, but some of them will be
gold mines. Robert Wilson says:

> What you are looking for in interviews is collegiality, a meeting of
> minds. If you are truly well focused on what you want to do, you
> will find kindred spirits. The chances are you will eventually have a
> happy, friendly, energized conversation with someone working in that
> field.

Often, such conversations will lead to warm relationships in which someone will go out of his or her way to help you. Several times over the past
few years someone interviewing me sparked my special interest because
of a combination of superb credentials and great interpersonal skills (i.e.,

I liked them) and I therefore went out of my way to introduce them to colleagues and track down job possibilities.

How do you prepare?

• *Research background information.* Paradoxically, even though you are going on an interview in search of information, you should still do research ahead of time. If you are hoping that the interview might turn into a job offer, you should be even more prepared. It's a basic rule of informational interviewing that you shouldn't ask someone something that you could have found out by reading the company's annual report. If you go for an interview at AT&T, and you don't know what AT&T stands for, you'll feel like an idiot. Likewise, if you will be interviewing someone who has published, make sure you're familiar with his or her work. If you walk into the office of a Nobel Prize winner and say, "So I understand you're a writer," you won't get far.

There are two ways to get information: from published sources and from people. Jeffrey Allen, author of *How to Turn an Interview into a Job*, refers to the coward's way (namely, rooting about in the library) and the hero's way (namely, phoning people). The most fruitful written source is the organization's annual report. This should also be the easiest source to get. Just call the receptionist and request it. Failing to get this, you can visit the library and read company profiles in *Standard and Poor's Register of Corporations, Directors and Executives*, the *Business Periodicals Index*, or other similar tomes pointed out to you by the reference librarian.

These printed sources have limitations. Although they may tell you net profits and who's on the board of directors, they're not likely to tell you much about company morale, about which departments within the company have the best future, and the fact that the person you're going to interview graduated from Harvard. Also, small companies aren't likely to be listed in the published profiles. To get this information, you'll have to resort to the phone and do mini-informational interviews to get the background necessary for your full-scale informational interview. Don't waste your prime informational interview candidates for this; instead target peripheral people who can give you general background on the company and on the person you are going to interview. Try people outside but connected with the department you want to work for.

If you have no contacts in the organization, you can make your own by calling cold. Call the publicity department (also called "communications" in many organizations), or the sales department, or even accounting or the receptionist. When you reach someone, tell him or her you're curious about the organization and want to ask a couple of questions. Your goal is not just to get statistics—you can get that from the annual report—but to draw the person into a conversation with you in which they will give you the inside scoop. I've found one good way to get someone to open up is to ask them, tactfully, whether they like their job.

QUESTIONS TO ASK IN THE INFORMATIONAL INTERVIEW

Remember that everyone likes to talk about themselves. You can ask:

- How did you get your job?
- When did you first decide you wanted to pursue this specific career?
- Did you have a mentor who helped you? Any other role models?
- What satisfactions do you get from your position?

Ask about the work:

- What sort of backgrounds do the people have who work for you?
- What's the primary project your group is working on now? What's the next one planned?
- How long does a typical project take?

Ask about the organization:

- Did the organizational culture turn out to be what you expected when you first started here?

Ask about job hunting:

- How were the most recently employed people in your group hired?
- How would you suggest that someone with my background go about searching for a job?

Finally, make sure you *don't leave the interview without the names of other people to contact.* As with any good pyramid scheme, if each person you talk to gives you the name of at least two more, after your twentieth round of interviewing you should be able to speak with 1,048,576. If the person you're speaking with suggests you call someone else, ask if it's okay to use his or her name when making the call.

INTERVIEW ETIQUETTE

As with grad school interviews and formal job interviews, observe normal decorum, dress appropriately, and thank the person you spoke with in a personal letter.

STEP 4:
■ EARNING KNOWLEDGE AND EXPERIENCE ■

> Experience teaches you to recognize a mistake when you've made it again.
> —ANONYMOUS

Your graduate years should be a time when you put together an attractive package of skills and experience through a combination of course work, thesis, internships, and summer jobs.

Not only will well-planned experience make you more employable; it will help you assess whether you like the direction you are headed. A lecture course in wildlife ecology may not tell you much about what it would be like to be a Fish and Wildlife Service ecologist, but if you spend a summer as a research assistant collecting moose droppings and you find it less than enchanting, this may be a clue that you need to reorient.

The more practical experience you can gain, the more attractive you will be to employers. Marva Gumbs says:

> Fine. You've got a degree, but without practical experience you're still an untried entity and will need training from scratch. There are lots of master's and Ph.D.s on the market—it's not unique anymore—and you'll be a lot more competitive with some experience.

Bob Orndorff got his own job as a career counselor because of a perfect match between what the Georgetown counseling center needed and his master's project. For his master's work Bob had created a small workshop where students critiqued videotapes of themselves being interviewed. Meanwhile, the Georgetown counseling center had been told by employers that the Georgetown students needed to brush up their interview skills. So when Bob applied, Georgetown hired him to set up an interview clinic.

You can choose a thesis or internship that puts you into the work environment where you can meet the people who can get you a job. Don Brezinski himself, for example, is about to enter a Ph.D. program in history so that he can advance further in his career. His focus will be on labor economics and technology transfer. He plans a thesis that describes how the state of Maryland can adapt to the rapid changes occurring in high-technology industries. It's easy to see how his thesis will put him into regular contact with potential employers at state agencies and that the expertise he develops will make him an attractive job candidate.

You can be more attractive if you develop complementary skills. For example, if your field is computer science, you might want to learn enough about composition to write good documentation. Marva Gumbs says:

> Ask yourself whether you are developing all the skills to make yourself maximally competitive. Many people are too specialized—in biology they take all the biology courses but don't get on the computer enough. In the humanities, the more multi-talented you are, the better, because increasingly the most employable liberal arts students are what we call "portfolio" people. They have developed a number of different skills and can go from job to job adapting to market changes.

ON THE HUNT:
▪ GETTING SERIOUS ABOUT GETTING A JOB ▪

When more and more people are thrown out of work, unemployment results.
—CALVIN COOLIDGE

For the job search itself you will intensify and focus your previous efforts to identify alternate career paths and make professional contacts. The best strategy is a diverse one. In the story below, for example, Lisa got a job by applying to an advertisement she found in the newspaper, but this strategy proved successful only because she had previously made professional contacts who were able to influence her future employer's hiring decision. Your tactics will include a systematic search for job openings, more informational interviews (this time focused on getting a job), regular consultation with your career counselor, solicitation of recommendations and other types of personal influence, carefully crafted résumés or other types of personal qualification briefs, and a well-prepared job seminar if you're looking for academic or other research jobs.

How long does it take?

The amount of time necessary to get a job varies from field to field and degree to degree, but count on it taking longer than you expect. At one extreme, if you will be applying for academic teaching positions, you will have to start the process of submitting applications at least a year in advance. In English, for example, doctoral students apply for positions beginning around October of the year before they would start their appointments. For nonacademic jobs you might expect to be actively looking for several months or more. Because several months to a year is a lot of time to support yourself on savings or handouts from home, you would be wise to start the job search process well before you graduate.

How do you find out about jobs?

Some jobs are advertised. Notices appear in the employment section of newspapers, in trade journals, in academic journals, and on the bulletin boards of career centers. Check out the book *Where the Jobs Are: A Comprehensive Directory of 1200 Journals Listing Career Opportunities*, by J. Norman Feingold and Glenda Ann Hansard-Winkler, which contains what its name suggests. Some jobs are listed with headhunters or the other variants of employment agencies described below.

Academic jobs and government jobs are relatively easy to locate because they are usually advertised for reasons of equal opportunity. Academic positions in English, for example, show up in the *Modern Language Association Journal*, while science positions often are advertised in *Science*. Others may only be locally advertised or circulated by flyer to other departments, so check your department and career center for listings. You can find out about jobs with the federal government by calling federal agencies directly—many have recorded job listings.

Don't be discouraged if advertisements suggest there aren't any jobs in your field. Approximately 75 percent of all jobs are never posted; they go to someone inside the organization, a friend of the boss, or the friend of a friend. Aside from academic jobs, at the graduate level most of the better jobs won't be posted; they're part of the hidden job market and will be snapped up before advertisements are even drafted.

Two true stories

Before discussing the nuts and bolts of the job search, I want to tell you about the job-hunting strategies of two recent master's graduates. Jane's tale is a "how not to," while Lisa's has a happy ending.

After graduating with a master's from a top department in public admin-istration, Jane began looking for jobs in women's health. Although she had some near-misses, she was unable to find a job in three months of looking and began to work as a temporary secretary, sent by her agency to fill short-term vacancies, each lasting a week or two. She soon found that to avoid penury she had to work full-time as a temp, making job hunting so difficult that her efforts dwindled to nonexistence. After a year of this dead-end work, she was further away from getting a permanent job in her field than when she started because she now had an unproductive year of drifting to explain.

Lisa was more fortunate. She had nearly completed her master's in education when she realized that the last thing she wanted was to spend her life inserting French grammar into unwilling high school students. Therefore, master's degree in hand, she set out to become an administrator in international education, a different but related field.

Like Jane, Lisa also began her job search by answering ads and calling personnel departments of likely organizations, primarily nonprofit insti-tutions. She did little networking. Although she had an excellent academic record, her job search was initially discouraging. After six months she had no job, not even any close calls. In order to support herself, she began working as a waitress, a job that exhausted her and left little time or energy for job hunting.

There were several reasons for Lisa's initial lack of success. First, her background in teaching did not strike employers as adequate preparation for a field which depends primarily on good administrative and commu-nications skills, areas in which she was not formally trained. Second, because she was changing fields, Lisa had few contacts to open doors for her, and she was shy about actively networking to make new contacts. Third, because she waited until after graduation to hunt for a job, she suffered from the negative perceptions that employers usually have of the unemployed, no matter how excellent their reasons for being out of work. Fourth, her waitressing job ate up her time.

How did she turn the situation around? First, she recognized that it would be cost-effective to borrow money so that she didn't have to drain her energy by working full-time while trying to look for a job. Second, she recognized that, because she lacked formal training in her new field, she needed experience that would prove to employers that she had the skills they needed. Third, she knew she had to work harder at making personal contacts who would be willing to provide her with introductions, recommendations, and advice.

Lisa's new campaign was very different from her first approach. She borrowed enough money from her father to live for six months—he had the foresight to realize that this was a good investment in her future. Assured of support, she quit her waitressing job and began calling likely organizations to see if they would accept her as an unpaid intern. Within two weeks she found an internship at a nonprofit institution which organizes international exchanges of high school students. She says:

> I worked full-time just like it was a real job. I even took work home with me. Within six weeks, my boss recommended me for a full-time position which suddenly became available. Unfortunately, one of *her* boss's protégés got the job, but at least this showed me I was on the right track—contacts are everything. A month later I saw an ad in the newspaper for an even better position at a different organization. Instead of a typical entry-level administrative assistant job, this one was to be the coordinator of a program to give educational funding to students from Eastern Europe. When I told my boss I wanted to apply, she did everything she could to help me. She not only praised me to the person doing the hiring; she also called a couple other people there whom she knew. My first interview went well, and I was offered the job without even a second interview. I know it was because of the recommendations from my internship.

Although Lisa did find out about her job through a newspaper advertisement, it was because her first boss was willing to use influence on her behalf that she was able to slip into the job, despite a lack of administrative experience.

It's who you know

The most important lesson of Lisa's search is that "it's who you know" that gets you a job. Indeed, U.S. Department of Labor statistics show that four out of five jobs are filled through personal contacts—either you know the employer directly or you know someone who can refer you. "Who you know" also counts in academia, even though the system at first appears to pick people on the basis of their merits as displayed by their curricula vitae. Actually, the power of your recommenders and their connections to the hiring committee have a lot to do with who gets the job.

The connection factor is why it's always easier to get a second job than a first, because once you're in the first job you can easily make the contacts to get a second. But don't despair; there are ways to get to know employers, many of which you will be familiar with from preceding pages of this book.

The secret to knowing a lot of people who can help you get a job, is to meet them. The more people you meet, the greater the possibility that you can convince one to give you a job. This is why I have been repeating throughout this book that you need to do everything possible to make professional contacts. The list by now should be familiar: go to conferences, make conversation with professors wherever possible, create professional correspondences, and, most important, hold more informational interviews. Deepen these relationships whenever you can by working with the people through internships and part-time or short-term jobs. Even the most unexpected meeting can pay off. Tom Hall, a recent master's student in international relations, tells this story:

> I got my present job by keeping my eyes open. The government agency I worked for was closing down for lack of funding, so I was looking for a job. The last month I worked there, representatives from other agencies came trooping through because they wanted to rent the office space. I just started talking with one of these guys and his outfit sounded interesting, so I sent him my résumé. A week later he called about an interview, my boss called his boss to recommend me, and I got the job. There were a million people more qualified than me, but they didn't know the people doing the hiring.

Make sure that you have business cards with you to hand out whenever you meet people—it's the accepted form of grown-up greeting. Put on it your name, university affiliation, address, and phone number, and give yourself a title. Use "Research Assistant" or something else that sounds professional. Don't use "Student."

▪ INFORMATIONAL INTERVIEWS REVISITED ▪

One of the best ways to meet a lot of potential employers in a hurry is to pick up the pace of your informational interviews. Set them up just as I described above, but this time around you have a new goal. Under the guise of informational interviewing, you try to find out about job possibilities and internship possibilities and raise your visibility so that as many people as possible know that you are available.

When asked, "What is the best single method of job hunting?" Bob Orndorff says:

> I believe in a combination of techniques for job hunting, but if you held a gun to my head and said, "Choose just one," I'd say, "Infor-

mational interviewing coupled with a powerful cover letter for your résumé.''

How do you go about turning an informational interview into a job offer? When I was first looking for jobs, I was irritated by *What Color Is Your Parachute?*, *Who's Hiring Who*, and similar job-hunting books which said that the key to finding a good job was informational interviewing. I was irritated because I couldn't figure out how to make the jump from talking to people in a general way about my interest in the field to a real job offer. It seemed downright silly that I could wander into someone's office after reading a little about their organization and they would be so taken with me that they'd offer a job. Understanding how and why this works requires putting yourself in the mind of the employer.

The first thing to remember is that the average person whom you approach for a job is a mere mortal. He may already have decided he has a position to fill, or he may merely be aware that he is overworked and could use some help. In either case, hiring someone is a hassle fraught with difficulty. He'll have to read hundreds of résumés and interview tens of people, and there's a good chance that he'll screw up and hire someone terrible, someone who leaves right away, making him look like a fool, or even worse, someone incompetent or nasty who stays forever, making his life miserable. These days it's often hard to fire someone because of the lawsuit potential, so a manager will have to live with his mistake for a very long time. It's no wonder the hiring process is a dreaded event for a manager whose job depends on his ability to hire good staff.

Even though you may never have hired someone, think about the times you were involved in some other large, potentially disastrous transaction, such as buying a car or renting out your house. Focus on the worry you felt. Now imagine that a friend suddenly popped up before you even advertised that your house was for rent and said, "Hey, I want to rent your house. And you know me, I'll take good care of it." If you're like me, you would rent it to your friend in a second, even if she offers a little less money than you were hoping for. You've saved yourself both the trouble of interviewing and the worry that you might screw up and rent to someone who would use your hardwood floors as an indoor roller-skating rink.

The same goes for a job. Your goal, by getting to know a potential employer, is to become someone they know, someone whom they'd feel comfortable working with. If you have shown yourself to be bright, personable, and competent, knowledgeable about their organization and needs, then if a job opens up the chances are that they would like to hire you, their new friend. In fact, the chances are that they would *much* rather hire you, a known quantity, than go through the hassle of interviewing many more strangers, *even if some of them might have better qualifications than you.* By getting in early like this, you can cut the competition down.

There isn't any surefire prescription for how to entice a job offer from a likely prospect. You just have to use your intuition and judgment. If the interaction between the two of you feels good, there's nothing wrong in saying, "From what I've seen of the organization, I would be very interested in working here."

If you've impressed someone, he or she can express interest in several ways. If there's no job open, he may just tell you to keep in touch—*in which case you should.* He may also send your résumé with a recommendation to someone else in the organization who does have an opening. Such an internal reference can carry substantial weight. If there *is* a job, but the person isn't sure about you, he may ask you to come back for another informal chat, or even for a formal interview with himself or others. It's partly a matter of the corporate culture—even if he wants to hire you on the spot, he might be obligated to bring you back for formal interviews with other staff.

As you go through the process of interviewing and waiting, don't be impatient. Remember that your goal is not to get *any* job, but a job that is right for you, which takes time. A rapid hire is rare and it is much more likely that the best you can expect from any particular interview is to establish yourself as someone they would like to hire when an opening occurs, or as someone they would be willing to recommend to others.

After an interview, always follow up with a positive, well-crafted letter, enclosing your résumé or curriculum vitae, even if you've given it to them before. Be warm and genuine in your letter, avoiding the fine line between fawning and toadying, and make it clear that you appreciate the time they gave you. Be specific about why you liked the organization and what you learned in the interview. Try something like:

> I enjoyed talking with you very much and felt we had a lot in common. From the way you described your program, especially your plans for new projects in sustainable agriculture, I would be very interested in exploring the possibilities of working with you if an opening comes up. My experience in proposal writing could help you bring in funding, and I would be very enthusiastic about getting the chance to work in Madagascar.

Let's say you've had a good informational interview with someone, established good rapport, sent a nice follow-up letter indicating your interest in the organization, and nothing happens. What do you do to let the person know you're still alive, to keep your visibility high?

Don't ask for another interview unless you have a very good reason— you've already presumed on the person's time. However, it's fine to write or phone to express your continued interest in the organization. Again, rather than trying to sell yourself, I prefer something honest like:

> Hi, Bill. This is Donna Celler. You were kind enough to talk with me a month or so ago about jobs in the fashion industry. I just wanted to say thanks again and to let you know I am still job hunting, so if you come across any possibilities for me, please keep me in mind.

Another good gambit is to put the person in the role of *consigliere* and ally. Everyone likes to give advice, so ask for some. Make it advice that you really need. In other words, don't ask something obviously fabricated about your burning need for their thoughts on the future of U.S.-Japanese trade. Try something like:

> Hi, Bill. This is Donna Celler. You were so helpful when we spoke a few weeks ago that I wondered if you'd mind giving me a little more advice on something that's come up. I've been talking with some people over at Designs Unlimited—Carole Mills primarily—and it looks like there are possibilities for me there. I was wondering if you could tell me anything about their organization. I heard a rumor that they may reorganize, and I'm worried about what that would mean for the sales department. Do you know anything about what's going on over there?

You can also write to send them articles you've written, relevant articles from journals or newspapers that you think might interest them, or an updated copy of your résumé to reflect changes since you last spoke.

Even if an interview doesn't scare up a job for *you*, keep your fellow job hunters in mind. If you have a friend who would be perfect for the employer you're talking to, tell him. You make a guaranteed friend for life if you find someone a job.

Here's a final caution on informational or other job interviews. A number of the self-help books on job finding advise you to figure out why an organization needs you and then convince them they've *got to have you*. You're supposed to get an interview with the person who has the authority to hire you and then say something hyperbolic along the lines of:

My analysis of your production figures indicates that widget output has fallen substantially over the past five years. My extensive background as a crackerjack time-management consultant leads me to believe that I can solve this problem for you. Applying new ideas to bring up productivity is the kind of work that turns me on. Frankly, if you hire me to deal with this problem, you won't regret it.

My own background as a crackerjack skeptic led me to believe that this approach would cause your listener to guffaw, so I asked a few career counselors what they thought. Bob Orndorff can speak for all of them:

Don't do corny stuff. We definitely don't recommend marching in and saying, "Here's what I can do for you." What you're trying to do in an informational interview is build a relationship, which is a gradual process. You're not trying to close a quick deal on underwater real estate.

■ THE FORMAL JOB INTERVIEW ■

One way or another, you'll make it to some formal job interviews. How are these different from the informational interviews you've been doing?

My friend Andy says that "the main difference is that you're scared silly because you could lose the job." He's right. Both you *and the employer* have more on the line. In the informational interview, like the preliminary stages in a courtship, you were both having a good time and probably avoided areas of potential disagreement. Now you're thinking about tying the knot, and you both want to know whether the other has disgusting personal habits. This means the questioning will be more pointed. You can expect questions like:

- Why did you leave your last job?
- Can you describe how you handled a situation in your last job where there was interpersonal conflict?
- Have you had much trouble with absenteeism?
- What's the greatest challenge you ever faced?
- Can you tell me why you should have this job?

And the perennial favorite, "What's your greatest weakness?" (To which you're supposed to answer some variant of "Gee, my greatest weakness is that I pay too much attention to detail and meeting deadlines.")

If you are interviewed by several people, make sure your answers jibe, because they'll compare notes. One applicant wasn't hired because she told one person that she "really wanted to focus on the technical side of her work," while she told another that she was "really interested in moving out of the technical field into management." In each case she was responding to what she thought the interviewer wanted.

What your questioners will want to know is: How do you respond under pressure? Are you truly enthusiastic about working with the organization? Do you get along well with colleagues? Do you follow directions? Are you self-motivated? How do you respond if you're given an order you don't like? How good are your technical skills? The bottom line is that they will be trying to figure out, however they can, whether you will fit the organization emotionally, socially, and technically, *whether you'll be personally loyal to the person who hires you*, and whether they'll be glad they hired you a year from now. Do your best to put the poor souls at ease.

Show that you're eager to learn and ready for new responsibility. One manager said:

> The best person I ever interviewed, now a senior engineer, was very enthusiastic, smart, asked great questions, and was aggressive about wanting to learn new areas that were related to but a stretch from what she had learned before. For example, we were talking about the overall computing environment. I said, "We do x, y, and we also do a little Unix." She said, "Oh, I've always wanted to do Unix."

You also want to demonstrate concern and thoughtfulness by asking questions about what your role would be, what they would expect of you, and how management functions. Don't ask things that reflect a petty interest in your own well-being, such as whether you would get an office with a view, or what will happen to you if you're regularly fifteen minutes late for work. Ask things that reflect your mature consideration of the job that needs doing and your enthusiasm for learning. Try:

- Mary, it seems as though the project we'd be working on will require regular interaction with the technical support group. Can we get good cooperation from them?
- How strong is our secretarial support?
- What new technical skills will I be able to learn?

Although most interviews last only an hour or so, be prepared to spend more time unexpectedly if the first interviewers like you and pass you up the chain of command. Academic interviews are particularly lengthy and grueling. The applicant is invited to the campus to present a job seminar and to "meet with faculty and students." An English professor describes a typical experience:

> I flew for four hours and as soon as I got to the school the ordeal began with a cocktail party, followed by a formal dinner and too much wine with the faculty until midnight. The next day I taught a sample class, followed by meetings with the departmental chairman and the dean, then my ninety-minute job seminar, then open hours to be grilled by faculty and a committee of students. I sat in a chair and was cross-examined by sixty people who were trying to make points for political reasons. It started to get surreal after a couple of hours when new people kept coming in and asking the same questions over and over. My warning to job applicants is that you need great bladder control and the ability to eat while being asked nonstop questions. Also, when you set up the trip, try to schedule at least an hour of free time *alone* to recuperate before your seminar—you'll need it.

Prepare for formal interviews in the same way as you would for informal interviews, your thesis defense, or any public speaking—practice under conditions of maximum similitude. Prepare the answers to questions you expect, have your support group grill you in a mock interview, and, if you're doing an employment seminar, overpractice it. Be especially prepared to explain any weaknesses or irregularities in your employment history in a positive way. You should have little to worry about if you have been getting regular practice by doing informational interviews.

Finally, *don't talk too much.* Richard Nelson Bolles points out that studies show that the employer will like you best if (a) you don't talk more than 50 percent of the time and (b) you don't speak more than two minutes at a time.

INTERNSHIPS AND PART-TIME JOBS

I want to reemphasize the potential of part-time work. In my interviewing, I found that *the most common way that recent graduate students got their first jobs was through internships or some similar lowly part-time or short-term position.* Therefore, even though this section is short, pay attention to it. As an intern you don't have to *tell* someone you're good, you can prove it to them. An even greater advantage is that you can become invaluable by doing work no one else can do. Matt Grund's story is typical:

I got an internship through school, actually a lowly work-study position paying $6.50 an hour. I worked there part-time my whole second year on a specific project under the direction of another person. She left just before I graduated, so at that point I was the only one who knew anything about the project (plus I hid vital supplies around the office where only I could find them). Not surprisingly they made me an offer for full-time work. I decided that there was no way I could get that much responsibility in government or the other private places, so I took it.

If your school has a cooperative education program, check it out. Co-op programs bring the school and employers together to give students a mixture of education and on-the-job training. Compared with many internships, a student's co-op experience is formal and long-lasting, complete with a job contract and pay. The expectation is that the student will move after graduation to a full-time job with the firm he or she works with during school. At George Washington University, where there are co-op programs in engineering, business, and education, grad students must spend at least one semester working full-time on the job site. Marva Gumbs says, "Students love these programs because they get great experience and often move right into permanent jobs with their co-op firms."

• OTHER METHODS OF FINDING JOBS •

RESPONDING TO ADVERTISEMENTS

As I indicated above, responding to advertisements is not the optimum strategy, because (a) you are competing with hundreds of other people and (b) you're only competing on the basis of a résumé and cover letter. You don't get a chance to show your personality unless you make it to the interview round. Moreover, many advertised jobs will still go to people on the inside track; the employer may already have a candidate in mind before the position is posted, and the posting is done just to give the appearance of an unbiased search. For example, it is common for government job descriptions to be tailored expressly for the person they have in mind, so that his or her credentials fit exactly.

Nonetheless, you *can* get jobs by responding to advertisements. Bob Orndorff, the counselor at Georgetown, got his first job by mailing letters and résumés to jobs advertised all over the country. Bob says:

Even though the success rate on responding to ads isn't extremely high, people do get jobs this way, especially if they can orchestrate influence with excellent recommendations and personal contacts. Also, it's a cheap tactic—it only takes a little time and a few cents for the stamp.

Taking out your own advertisements. This is like wearing a sign saying that you're incompetent and don't know how to find a job. If you insist on seeing your name in print, take out a personal ad instead. Maybe you'll hit it off with someone and marry into the family firm.

Sending unsolicited résumés. If sending in résumés to personnel offices that have advertised is not a highly successful strategy, you can imagine that sending in unsolicited résumés "for your consideration" is a real waste of time. Richard Nelson Bolles cites a study showing that only one out of every 1,470 unsolicited résumés gets a response.

EMPLOYER USING UNSOLICITED RÉSUMÉS TO AMUSE CHILDREN—ONLY ONE OF MANY REASONS WHY THIS METHOD OF JOB HUNTING WON'T WORK

Some people with outstanding credentials may get interviews this way. One of my friends with an honors degree from Harvard did get three interviews for paralegal positions by sending unsolicited résumés. When she told me this story, for a minute I thought that all the experts were wrong, that you in fact can get jobs easily by doing "Dear Occupant" résumé mailings, but as I cross-examined her, I found out the truth. She only got interviews at firms where she had sent her résumé addressed personally to Harvard alumni.

Even if you are writing to a contact that you have reason to believe might hire you, you are better off couching your approach in terms of an informational interview—don't ask for a job. My friend Andy says:

It's a big mistake to apply for jobs that don't exist. Once you explicitly ask for a job, you invoke equal opportunity and human resources. I feel compelled by the spirit of equal opportunity to send any letters asking about jobs to personnel, where they are answered promptly and then locked in a large chest until Armageddon.

Career counselors. Career counselors can be vital for helping the lost and the spineless. If you can't make yourself get out of bed to go job hunting, having someone to give you structure can help.

Professional career counselors cost money—if you're paying by the hour expect to shell out at least $50 per. Therefore, use the ones in school while you can, as much as you can. Once you've found a counselor you like, see him or her regularly. You need a regular check-in to keep yourself motivated and to build a relationship with your counselor so that he or she really cares about your success.

Once you've graduated, most schools will let you use the counseling center as an alumnus, usually for a modest fee. If you move away from school, however, you've got problems. Although many schools do have reciprocal agreements to let each other's students scan job listings and use the career library, most do not provide counseling to students or alumni from other schools, so use your own counselors while you can.

If you do have to hire a counselor, I suggest you read Appendix C in *What Color Is Your Parachute?*, which sketches a sound strategy for identifying good counselors and getting your money's worth.

EMPLOYMENT OFFICES, HEADHUNTERS, AND JOB REGISTRIES

Employment offices vary dramatically in type and quality, from high-ticket, hand-holding firms for top executives to corner-of-the-wall fly-by-nights. A noninclusive list includes:

- *"Employer pays" employment agencies.* If they succeed in finding you a full-time job, the employer pays a percentage of your first year's salary to the agency. It can't hurt you to sign up with a couple, provided that they don't waste too much of your time, but be aware that these usually deal in low-level standard positions. "I'd like three clerk-typists and a stonemason, please." If you do sign on with one, read any application or contract with extreme care to make sure that you're not really signing up for a "job seeker pays" agency without knowing it.
- *"Job seeker pays" employment agencies.* You pay, usually a percentage of your first year's salary or a lump sum up front. Are you crazy? Don't even think about this. Also, be careful about misrepresentation. Lisa,

during the job search described above, found her way to an employment office, which was "up three flights of stairs, down a long hall, and in the back." She says:

They gave me a rush sales job, telling me that they could find me a job for sure. Then they shoved an application at me to sign. When I asked for time to read it, the woman told me, "You don't need to read it. It's our standard application." I read it anyway and discovered that it was a contract giving them 10 percent of my salary during the next year, even if the job I found had nothing to do with them. When I said I wouldn't sign it, they kicked me out.

• *"Temp" agencies*. The agency finds you temporary employment in exchange for a weekly cut from your employer. This is usually for secretarial type of work. However, don't turn up your nose. Not only can temping pay the grocery bills while you're hunting, but it has a big advantage over food stamps—namely, *it can lead to bigger things*. Tom Hall, with a master's in international relations, says:

My temp agency sent me to a presidential commission involved in foreign trade. I started off doing word processing. Then I started playing around with PageMaker doing graphics, and once they saw what I could do they started me working on their newsletter. Then I talked them into making me a permanent research assistant and I ended up researching articles on trade.

• *"Temp-to-Perm" agencies*. These are relatively new kids on the block. They focus on providing firms with low- to mid-range consultants: "We need someone who's familiar with D-Base 3." The agency hires you out as a temporary fill-in employee, but after a certain period, usually about three months, the employer can hire you full-time and the agency releases you from their contract. This can be great for both the organization and you. You each get a lengthy opportunity to peruse the merchandise before closing the deal.

• *Headhunters*. These people work on commission—usually the employer pays—to find someone to fill a specific job. They're mining high-grade ore here, highly employable people with lots of experience in a hot field. Don Brezinski says:

One of my friends has gotten his last two jobs from headhunters. They love him because he's in high-tech laboratory sales. They're always trying to recruit him away from his present jobs for something bigger and better, but headhunters aren't much use for the average person.

• *Job registries.* These just maintain listings of job seekers and/or jobs. If it doesn't cost much, it can't hurt to try. Again, I suggest you read *What Color Is Your Parachute?* for a good analysis and names of some sample registries. Bolles says:

So far as finding *jobs for people* is concerned, these clearinghouses and agencies, like employment agencies, really end up finding *people for jobs.* (Think about it!) Heart of gold though they may have, these agencies serve employers better than they serve the job hunter.

ON-CAMPUS RECRUITING

This won't help you in most fields. Jill Kirsten, director of the George Washington University career center, says:

On-campus recruiting only hires 10 percent of our students, primarily business, accounting, and engineering. This reflects the market— there are many more computing and business jobs than anything else.

• SALARY NEGOTIATION •

Most job-search books have a section on salary negotiation. This book has a short one because I've never been very good at negotiation myself, usually making do with whatever largess (or smalless) my bosses bestow. If you require an explanation of wily negotiation strategies, check out— surprise—*What Color Is Your Parachute?*, Chapter 6. The basic idea is that if you can figure out ahead of time by careful questioning what people in similar positions are paid at the organization, then you can ask for salary at the top end of that range.

Entry-level salaries in many fields are *low*, often unrealistically low for survival. Particularly if you are moving into an area with high costs of living, find out ahead of time how much money you will need for basics. If you're offered less than this, you may be able to use your budget figures as the basis for negotiation to a more realistic salary.

I have just one more piece of advice about salary: *it is much easier to get what you want when you're new.* This applies not only to salary per se but also to asking for that window office, secretarial support, or a new chair. It's much easier to get an extra couple of thousand when you start than it will be to get the same couple thousand a year later as a raise. And remember, if you don't ask, you don't get.

▪ RÉSUMÉS AND COVER LETTERS ▪

Résumés and cover letters make a team. The résumé tells your prospective employer what you can do that will be useful to him, and the cover letter helps to catch his attention, points out your interest in a specific job, and explains how your past experience, as presented in your résumé, fits you for this job.

YOUR RÉSUMÉ

The first thing you'll discover about résumés is that the experts disagree on both their importance and how they should be structured. The bottom line on résumés is that you'll need them whenever you apply for a job, if only to make the personnel office happy, so you might as well create the best résumés you can. Even if most people don't pay much attention to them, the person who hires you might.

Résumés for different types of jobs will have very different forms. A major distinction is between academic curricula vitae and résumés for nonacademic jobs. The curriculum vitae (CV), with its academic focus, puts education and teaching experience up front and is usually several pages or more long because it lists all the important publications—and often conference presentations—in the person's career. I've seen CVs with as many as twenty pages of publications, presentations, and awards. A traditional résumé, on the other hand, typically is no more than one or two pages, with a maximum of three for someone with a long career history.

Most nonacademic résumés fall into two general types, chronological and functional, or are hybrids of the two. A *chronological résumé* lists all the jobs you've had in reverse chronological order. It is useful for showing career development, including the amount of time between promotions. It works well for someone who has climbed straight, high, and fast. It could have the following entries:

SPECIAL ASSISTANT TO THE PRESIDENT. 1988–89.
Random Noise Corporation
269 Matadero Ave.
Palo Alto, California

Administrative support, including review of internal proposals, budget analysis, and speech writing. Developed and implemented new system of proposal review. Hired, managed, and trained team of three employees. Used knowledge of Japanese language to assist in high-level meetings with Japanese subsidiary.

ASSISTANT TO THE SPECIAL ASSISTANT TO
THE PRESIDENT. 1986–88.
Random Noise Corporation

Liaison with other departments in collecting budgetary information and internal proposals. Responsible for drafting external correspondence.

A *functional résumé* groups related skills together, regardless of when you acquired them. This is particularly useful for people like recent graduates, who may not have a long history of traditional employment in their career but do wish to highlight skills they have earned in a variety of settings. Thus, for example, if you handled the treasury of an amateur theatrical association, you could highlight this information by putting it under the heading "Financial Experience," when it might not show up at all in a traditional chronological résumé.

The best job-hunting book I've come across for explaining résumés is *Jobs for English Majors and Other Smart People,* by John Munschauer, which is also an excellent all-round guide for how the college-educated should handle their job search. It contains good examples of résumés and CVs and does an exceptional job of analyzing them line by line. There are also a number of books specifically on résumés, stuffed with examples. I suggest you go to your school library and sift through them. You can try *The Perfect Résumé,* by Tom Jackson, which takes a workbook approach, *Just Résumés,* by Kim Marino, or *Dynamite Résumés,* by Ronald Krannich and Caryl Rae Krannich (Ph.D.s!).

- *Address your audience.* Each résumé you give to someone should be individually tailored for the job you are applying for, or in the case of a purely informational interview, which does not involve a specific job, for the organization and the person who will read it. If the job is for a technical position, emphasize your technical experience. If it's for a managerial position, emphasize that.

To slant your résumé correctly for a specific job, you obviously have to know what the job is about. You can get information from the formal job description or from your contacts inside the organization. If you talk about the job in an informational or formal interview, afterward you can adjust your résumé accordingly before sending it with your thank-you letter.

- *Make sure your résumé emphasizes what you really want to do.* Take John's case. After five years as a manager, which he hated, he started looking for a job as a technical consultant. However, because he was used to thinking of himself as a manager, he organized his résumé in terms of his managerial experience. For example, he wrote about how on one project he hired and trained fourteen people, ensured continued funding for the project, and handled complicated project communications. When John asked a colleague to review his résumé, she said, "This résumé makes you look like the best manager in the world, and I'd hire you in a minute. But I wouldn't hire you as a technical person. There is nothing in here about technical expertise."
- *Make sure it doesn't contradict what you say in your cover letter or interview.* If you told the interviewer you're primarily interested in being a manager in product support, your résumé shouldn't say "sales." Leslie Graham, a manager in systems analysis, says:

I often get résumés that tell me about how great someone is at particular aspects of their job: they've written fifteen user's manuals, led fifteen training classes with thirty-seven people each, and won an award for a training manual. And I'm ready to hire the person because their résumé is exactly what I'm looking for. Then in the interview it turns out that they hate training classes and writing manuals, and that's why they're looking for a new job. Basically, the résumé lied and it wasted everyone's time.

- *Make your career history look coherent.* If you jumped around a lot from job to job, you can disguise this somewhat by using a functional résumé based on skills instead of chronology. If you are using a chronology, you can hide some gaps by choosing how you list the dates. For example, if you worked only a partial year in 1990, list the date you worked as "1990," not as "summer 1990."

You should also omit or downplay irrelevant career experiences. If you're looking for a job teaching history and you spent the previous summer working at the Dairy Queen, omit unless you can demonstrate just cause.

• *Avoid hyperbole and vagueness.* There are two schools of thought on this. The one I *don't* espouse, typified by Jeffrey Allen, author of *How to Turn an Interview into a Job*, tells you to avoid excessive detail in your résumé and instead to "use general phrases that will incite the interviewer to positive action—an invitation for an interview." He says to use phrases like "developed a series of," "consistently performed," and "was promoted to progressively responsible positions."

I can't say for sure whether or not this approach works with some employers, but I do know these empty phrases irritate me. They make me suspect the applicant has a weak background if he needs "action phrases" to impress me. They also insult the reader's intelligence. Your potential employer knows who wrote the résumé—*you*. Why should he be impressed just because you sing your own praises with words like "consistently performed at peak levels" or "developed a series of important innovations" (my phrases, not Jeffrey Allen's)? *I* espouse succinctness, clarity, and the straight facts. These are ultimately what an employer wants to know: What did you accomplish? What promotions did you receive? How rapidly did you receive them? How much money did you save? What publications or other products have you created? What awards or other official recognition have you received?

Try something concrete like:

After six months as a research assistant responsible for background research and fact checking of policy reports, was promoted to associate with a 25 percent raise. During the first year as an associate co-authored five case studies on recent changes in the political structures of African countries, two of which were reprinted by the journal *International Policy*. In addition . . .

Leslie Graham notes that after reading hundreds of résumés, the "objectives," listed at the top of each résumé, are the most irritating. They typically say something like:

Objective: to obtain a challenging position with a rapidly growing and dynamic firm in the field of software design where there is a need for motivated personnel with outstanding technical and organizational skills and a keen desire to improve productivity through good product planning.

Wouldn't this be refreshing instead?

> Objective: to obtain an overpaid and humdrum job with a moribund software company which needs lazy timeservers who will be so involved in petty bickering that the chance of getting a product out the door will be approximately zero.

Seriously, objectives may help, but state them simply. There's nothing wrong with saying:

> Objective: to work in a top-notch software design department where I can use my training in database design and analysis to help create programs that will please customers and bring in good profits.

• *Keep it tight*. Here is the "Summary of Experience" from a sample résumé in a recent job hunter's guide. It can be tightened by deleting the italicized words below:

> Seven years of experience in *performing a variety of* accounting and financial duties for several large companies in Georgia. Have served as troubleshooter *when necessary*, undertaken investigative and problem-solving assignments, and engaged in consulting department. *To avoid errors and difficulties*, have supervised the daily work of accounting personnel.

If you deleted the italicized sections, would the reader believe that the writer had performed only a single duty for seven years, troubleshot when unnecessary, and supervised accounting personnel in order to create errors and difficulties?

• *Get your résumé read by people you respect*. You need an honest, critical review because it is very difficult to objectively analyze your own résumé. Most school counseling centers will review your résumé (and cover letters) for you. Also, you can reapproach people with whom you've done an informational interview. Tell them that you're trying to tighten up your résumé and you'd value their advice. You can even get your résumé reviewed by the person you're trying to get a job from! One manager says:

> That's one of the advantages of an informational interview. If I'm approached by someone *before* they formally apply for a job, and I like them, then I can help them adapt their résumé so that it makes it through the personnel office. An applicant might have trouble because their résumé emphasizes the wrong things for the job that's

open, or the experience they list is inadequate. I can help them reemphasize or remind them that the computer analysis they did in their honors sociology project could qualify as experience.

Many people identify so strongly with their résumé—after all, it *is* their life—that they become peeved when people suggest changes. Try to take criticism objectively. If you get advice you don't agree with, make sure to ask for second opinions before disregarding it.

How to use your résumé

If you're responding to a job advertisement, you'll have to send in a letter and résumé to apply. If you're doing an informational interview, opinion differs on whether to send your résumé before the interview, hand it over during the interview, or send it afterward. My suggestion is that you do all three. Send one ahead of time so that the interviewer can use it to learn about you before you meet, bring one with you to the meeting in case he's lost the first, and send one afterward with your thank-you letter to be doubly safe. If you revise your résumé to reflect the meeting, so much the better.

Cover letters

The rules for writing a good cover letter are much the same as for writing a good résumé: speak to your audience, edit carefully for sense and form, keep it brief, and don't overdo the BS. *What Color Is Your Parachute?* won't help you much here, but, again, I strongly recommend *Jobs for English Majors and Other Smart People*. I do not recommend *Who's Hiring Who*, in which most of the sample letters try to sell too hard.

▪ COMPUTER HELP ▪

It's very time-consuming to create your own résumé format with a word processor, even if you use a word-processor résumé template, like those that come with Microsoft Word or Word Perfect. You save a huge amount of time by using a dedicated résumé program like Adams JobBank, Softkey's PFS Resume Pro, Davidson Perfect Resume, or WinWay Resume. They're all reasonably priced—under $50. All give you sample résumés to peruse and templates to type your information into. Once you've completed typing in your résumé information, you can change the complete layout of your résumé by clicking a button. Each click reformats everything, including fonts, centering, margins, location of dates or other attributes, so that you instantly change to the résumé style that suits you best. If you don't like one look for a particular job application, you can change to another in a second.

All the programs include some type of contact database to keep information on company names, addresses, and phone numbers, as well as data on company history, products, and notes on job interviews, phone calls, and other actions you plan to take on the job search. Of course, you could keep this information instead in a personal information manager (PIM) oriented toward contacts (see pages 127–34), like Sharkware, and a PIM would also let you schedule phone calls and other follow-up steps in your job search. That's where the résumé programs aren't very strong—most don't have a good scheduling function—so you probably want both a résumé program and a PIM.

You should also look for a résumé program that makes writing application cover letters and follow-up letters easy. Once you've finished the letter, programs such as Adams JobBank, Davidson Perfect Resume, and WinWay will instantly merge it with information from your job-contact database, filling in the employer's name, address, and other information. If you're engaged in a major job search, the letter-writing function could save you days.

The programs also give advice on how to job search and interview that ranges from useful to pretty lame (for example, don't smoke during your job interview). WinWay Resume and Adams JobBank have video interviews, where scary-looking bosses ask you hard questions. This sounds like a gimmick, but I found the interview realistic enough to make me nervous. Adams JobBank also gives you a CD-ROM with a searchable database of thousands of corporate profiles—if you're looking for a job in industry, this could be useful.

Of the four programs I looked at, none won for all-around best program—they've all got pretty big defects. PFS Resume Pro wins hands down for ease in making a résumé. It uses a "what you see is what you get" method, where you type your career information directly into the finished résumé. With the other three programs, you type data into a series of templates that the computer later processes into a résumé, so you're working somewhat blind. But PFS is weak in the job-contact database (there's a bug that doesn't give you enough room to type in a complete job announcement), and it doesn't have a quick way of generating follow-up letters by mail merging from the contact database. For ease in making follow-up letters, Adams JobBank is best, followed by Davidson Perfect Resume, and a weak showing by WinWay (it's got the capability to make quick letters, but it's tough to use). WinWay wins in the contact database department—Adams JobBank and Davidson Perfect Resume are even less comprehensive than PFS. If you've got the money, you might get PFS for the résumé and Adams JobBank for the letters.

CRUISING THE JOB HIGHWAY

The Internet is fast becoming the easiest way to find out about job listings. There are so many job-search sites out there, you'll be swamped once you start surfing. To start off, try WinWay's home page of links to other searchable job-posting databases (http://www.winway.com).

Stanford University's site has links to many, many other job sites: http://rescomp.stanford.edu/jobs/. For example, they list about twenty links to academic job postings, like the Private School Employment Network (http://www1.mhv.net/psen/).

For humor and class, try Emory University's Career Paradise site (http://www.emory.edu/CAREER/index.html). Another good site for would-be academics is the weekly posting of *The Chronicle of Higher Education* (http://chronicle.merit.edu/.ads/.links.html). See Appendix B for other job-search sites.

10 KEYS TO SUCCESS IN JOB HUNTING: • A REVIEW •

- *Choose your thesis or area of emphasis carefully*. Make sure that it will lead to a job you enjoy.
- *Start early*. Since it may take several months to a year to get a job, at the very least you should start looking this much before graduation. Ideally, plan for the job from the moment you start graduate school so you can make your grad school decisions accordingly.
- *Plan alternative routes*. Realize that circumstances change, so plan alternatives. For example, Mark Katz, a specialist on Soviet relations with the Third World at George Mason University, writes about how the changing political landscape has affected his career:

> I kind of sympathize with Castro and the other Third World radical leaders. I feel as if Gorbachev has cut me adrift just as he has them. And just as their future careers look bleak, so does mine.

At a minimum, if you are a doctoral student, plan routes leading to both academic and nonacademic careers.

- *Take charge.* Although you can get help, your career and your job search are in your hands. One counselor said:

  People want us to tell them, "Be here tomorrow for an interview at nine o'clock. Wear this. Do this." But it doesn't work that way. We can give them advice, but they've got to understand that job searching is a self-directed process that the students themselves are best able to do.

- *Get help.* Work *closely* with your school's counseling center. Also, use your graduate student support group to give advice and provide emotional support.
- *Don't lose heart.* Recognize that, except for those few annoying people who get jobs before they even leave school, finding a good job takes a long time and a lot of work.
- *Showing what you can do is better than telling.* People can judge your worth better through internships than interviews, and better through interviews than résumés and other written documents. Plan your strategy accordingly.
- *Make as many contacts as possible.*
- *Don't let your contacts dry up.* Once you've made contacts, cultivate them. Write, phone, visit, or send Christmas cards as appropriate.
- *Don't disdain an entry-level position.* Don Brezinski said:

  Grad students make a big mistake by thinking that the master's or Ph.D. means they've paid their dues. All it means is that they are now ready to pay their dues.

It's easier to get a job if you've already got one, and even a lowly position is a better springboard than no position at all.

A FINAL THOUGHT

If all else fails, try writing. As Jules Renard said: "Writing is the only profession in which one can make no money without being ridiculous."

APPENDIX A

. . . .

BUYING YOUR COMPUTER

AND SOFTWARE

. . . .

GIVEN HOW RAPIDLY HARDWARE AND SOFTWARE SYSTEMS ARE CHANGING, this book would soon go out of date if I tried to review specific systems in detail, so I mostly will take a general approach, explaining how different types of hard- and software can help you. Please note that I'm not a computer expert, merely an inquisitive amateur, so the advice below is my layman's opinion based on what works well for me mixed with advice from experts.

I apologize to Macintosh users. Because I'm only familiar with IBM-type machines, my comments focus on them. However, much of my general advice will still apply, and many of the software programs I mention have Macintosh versions.

Before you make major purchases, read some computer magazines for the general public such as *PC Magazine*, *Computer Shopper*, *Windows Magazine*, and, if applicable, *MacWorld*; and, spend some time at your university computer center—they often counsel students on computer purchases and offer discounts. One book that can give you a quick feel for available software programs is *Software: What's Hot! What's Not!* by Prima Publishing, Rocklin, CA (phone: 714 632-4400). It hasn't been updated since 1994, but even if its information is a little dated, it will still give you an excellent overview of different types of software programs.

Here are some pointers on buying computers:

- *Don't buy a dedicated word processor*. These are just glorified electric typewriters. For a little more money, you can get a real computer capable of running many types of programs.
- *Think twice before buying a laptop*. Think carefully about whether to

get a desktop or a laptop. Laptops cost about $1,000 more, they're more prone to break because they're not in metal cases and you're banging them around, the screens are smaller, hard drives are usually smaller, and you can't upgrade as easily. Plus, they're a lot easier to steal. I'd advise getting one only if you really need portability. If you do get one, make sure you get a model with long battery life and a full-sized keyboard, and avoid keyboards that have a function key, requiring you to push this extra key for many common commands. This will really slow you down during the editing process.

- *Check your university for deals.* Before you buy from a dealer, check whether your university supports certain computers and software. If you buy a system that is compatible with the university's and run into problems, the university's computer service is more likely to be able to help. They may also be able to arrange substantial discounts on hardware and software. The University of Michigan, for example, sells IBMs, Macintoshes, and Zeniths and associated software to students at substantially lower prices than you could get from a commercial dealer.

- *Check out reliability and service.* If you buy a national name brand, like Packard-Bell or Compaq, check out their current reputation, both for reliability and for service. Under warranty, some brands will have FedEx pick up your sick computer and deliver a replacement the next day, while others offer on-site service but neglect to tell you that it will take weeks for a service person to appear.

- *Be wary of generic.* You can often get more computer for the money by buying the house brand of a local company. Plus you can order the computer custom-made to your specifications (I had my retailer upgrade to higher-quality speakers and install an extra CD-ROM drive). But you need to be careful because quality can vary and even a guarantee of service won't help you if the company is dishonest or goes out of business. I bought my first computer from a local company that went out of business two weeks later. They'd built my computer with a defective motherboard, faulty memory, and a bad power supply that caught on fire, filling my room with smoke and cooking the hard drive. Joshua Pickering, a computer consultant who specializes in on-site service, says, "Unless you know a lot about computers, never, ever, ever consider buying a generic computer. Part of the price in paying for a name-brand computer is support. A mom-and-pop-type computer store cannot offer the same level of support that a major company can." On the other hand, a local company that does offer good in-house service may be much easier to deal with than a distant mega-company. The company that built my current generic computer has given me good service.

- *Consider mail order.* Some of the better computers made today are from mail-order vendors like Gateway 2000, Dell, and Micron. The pricing is better than similarly equipped computers in stores, but you make up some of the difference in shipping. You can find mail-order ads and research the relative merits of different components by reading magazines like *Computer Shopper* and *PC Magazine.*

• *Comparison-shop.* If you do buy commercially, comparison-shop and remember that in many computer stores the salespeople have authority to bargain, just as on the used-car lot. So find a low price in one store, then ask a second store if they can beat it, and then go back to the first and see if they will beat the second store's lowest price.

• *Don't scrimp on the modem.* Waiting for files to download across the Internet is slow enough anyway, without having your modem slow things down further, so upgrade yours if necessary. Make sure the speed is at least 28.8 baud (28,800 bits per second). With the proper software, a modem will give you the capability to send and receive faxes from your computer, link to other computers via the phone line, and send e-mail. Some upscale modems even have a voice synthesizer that can answer your phone.

• *Don't scrimp on RAM.* Make sure you've got enough RAM (random-access memory) to run today's big programs at top speed. RAM is temporary electronic storage where your computer keeps data while it is working with it. In the old days, about three years ago, eight megabytes of RAM was considered awesome, but now sixteen megs is the bare minimum you'll need to get the most out of Windows 95 and other monster programs. Ram prices change rapidly, and if you've already got a computer in need of a memory fix, now's the time to buy: it's now about $7 per megabyte, down from $50 a couple of years ago. According to Josh Pickering, "RAM requirements are only going to increase so if RAM prices are low when you buy your PC, upgrade to 32 MB or higher now."

• *Get a big hard drive.* The hard drive is a computer's main storage area where all data and files are saved and all programs are installed. Hard drives also have dropped in price and they've increased in size. A couple of years ago a good-sized drive was 250 megs, but today drives of 1.3 gigabytes (1,300 megs) are standard on mid- to high-end machines and 2-gigabyte machines are common. With today's bloated programs— Windows 95 alone needs 50 megs to install—you'll need a big drive.

• *Buy a CD-ROM drive.* You'll need at least one CD-ROM drive for running data-rich programs like Encyclopaedia Britannica. Also, many word processing, graphics, and other workhorse programs can now be purchased as CD-ROMs, and installing them is much easier from a CD-ROM than from diskettes.

One option most people don't think about is an extra CD-ROM drive. With two drives you can play music on one drive while accessing programs on the other. Or if you refer frequently to a reference CD like Encyclopaedia Britannica or Microsoft's Bookshelf, you can keep one loaded all the time, while keeping one CD for other uses. This will keep you from having to exchange CDs every time you want to look something up. Another option for those who frequently need to change back and forth between several CDs is a drive with a multiple CD changer, similar to those on an audio CD player.

With two drives it's important to make sure that the programs that control them—the drivers—do not conflict with each other. You'll be safest if you buy two identical CDs that use the same driver. Or you can avoid the problem altogether by looking for peripherals labeled "plug and play," which are designed to work without utilizing a driver.

• *Get a scanner.* You can get a cheap but effective black-and-white desktop scanner for around $300. Many people still see scanners as luxuries, but you should get one if you're doing a thesis or plan a career of research or teaching. With a scanner you can quickly scan paper documents and convert them into electronic word-processor documents. This means, for example, that you can convert to electronic form all the papers you collect as background material for your thesis. Then, when you write your thesis, you can use word searches to find particular passages in the documents, to check citations, or to cut and paste quotations into your thesis. By scanning, you can begin building an electronic library that can develop over your entire career.

The quality of the scan job will depend not only on the scanner but even more so on the optical character recognition (OCR) software that recognizes the scanned letters and translates them into word-processor characters. Unfortunately, all OCR software is not equal and programs differ greatly in their ability to recognize letters, particularly when the font is unusual or small, when the text is faint or smudged, or when the lines are not straight on the page. The more errors the OCR makes, the more time you'll spend cleaning up the scanned text with a spell checker. OmniPage Pro is the standard of excellence—it even does a good job with skewed text or text in multiple columns. Many scanners come with a cut-down version of OmniPage, and it doesn't cost much to upgrade.

• *Buy a laser printer.* Unless you need to print in color, avoid purchasing an inkjet printer, like HP DeskJet, and buy a laser printer. They're faster, cleaner, and you'll be glad you've got one when you're under deadline to crank out your three-hundred-page thesis. Many manufacturers, like Okidata and Brother, make good 600 dpi lasers for under $400.

- *Insure your computer.* Make sure you've got automobile and renter's or homeowner's insurance that covers your computer. Under many policies, you'll have to arrange for extra coverage.
- *Get backup capability.* Back up your data so you don't lose it if the hard drive fails. Most people don't know it, but the head inside is spinning at such high speed that it wears out quickly, and the average life of a hard drive is only a couple of years of continuous use (some drives will fail sooner, others last longer).

The old standby method of backup is to copy your data onto floppy disks as soon as you finish using your word processor or other application. This works pretty well if you're conscientious about backing up your data to a floppy, but even so, there's a big drawback. If your drive does give up the ghost and you need to replace it, it can take hours to recopy all your data from floppies to the new drive. Plus, it can take many more hours to reinstall all your programs and reconfigure them for your modem and other hardware.

Backup is much simpler if, instead of floppy disks, you buy a large-capacity backup drive capable of holding all the files in your system. One option is a tape drive, which functions similarly to a tape recorder and records your files on magnetic tape. But tape drives are so slow that it can take hours to back up your entire system. You can get around this problem by using the software to automatically run backups whenever you like, say every Wednesday at midnight, but tape drives still aren't nearly as fast or convenient as the Zip-type drives described below. Tape drives are most suitable for users with large computer systems loaded with lots of programs with complex configurations who would go through hell reinstalling and configuring all their programs. Because tape drives hold so much data (two or more gigabytes), you could restore all your data and programs exactly as they were originally configured, following a hard drive failure or other catastrophic data loss.

A faster option is to use an IOmega Zip drive or other Zip-type drive that uses special diskettes instead of tape. Josh says that "the Zip or other removable media drive is the best backup solution for most people. People should just get in the habit of saving word-processing documents and other files directly onto the drive." The Zip-type drives use cassettes that resemble standard 3.5-inch floppies but are larger and contain much more data—standard sizes are one hundred megabytes and one gigabyte. With hundred-megabyte cassettes, you can't back up your entire system, but you can back up a lot of files. With a one-gigabyte drive you could back up an entire moderate-sized system.

Zip-type drives currently cost twice as much or more than a tape drive, but the advantages make them worth it for many users. They copy data at close to the same rate as a hard drive, so backup is very fast. Zip-type drives function like hard drives and find data quickly, so copying a file from the drive onto your main hard drive takes only a few seconds. With a tape drive, you'd have to wait while the drive scrolls through yards of tape to find the program you want to copy, just as if you were searching for a song on an audio cassette.

Your Zip-type drive can double as your computer's extra hard drive—because a Zip disk can contain an entire software program, you can run the program off it, just as though you were running the program from your normal hard drive. This way, instead of cluttering up your hard drive with programs you only run occasionally, you can keep these programs installed and ready to go on Zip disks.

- *Use a surge protector*. Lightning strikes and strange fluctuations in the power and phone lines can fry your computer. Buy and use a surge protector that has modem protection; in addition to the power receptacles, there should be two small receptacles for your modem line in and out.
- *Protect your body*. Carpal tunnel syndrome can permanently incapacitate you, so be on the lookout for pain associated with computer use. Even relatively short periods of trauma can have severe effects. Although this is an extreme case, a doctor specializing in computer-associated injuries reported one patient who permanently lost most of the use of his hand after a week of playing his son's new Nintendo for four hours a night. Make sure you've set up your keyboard so that your wrists remain elevated and supported. You can buy a foam wrist pad for under $10 or strap-on wrist braces.

You can develop neck or back problems by staying for long periods in the "mouse position," bent forward with one hand extended. To avoid this, I use a trackball clipped to the side of my keyboard. Most people think trackballs are only for laptops, but if you clip one to the side of your full-sized keyboard you won't need to lean forward—you can use the keyboard and trackball in your lap. Make sure that you buy a trackball whose clip opens wide enough to fit the edge of the keyboard—some are made only for laptops and won't fit a full-sized keyboard. You can also cut down on fatigue by regularly changing the orientation of the mouse or trackball from left- to right-handed. Because I use a computer for long hours both at home and in the office, I use a right-handed trackball at home and a left-handed one at work, halving the exposure of each hand to injury.

Computer survival kit

Once you've purchased your computer, don't leave the store without these vital extras:

1. The monitor (often this is sold separately from the computer)
2. Surge protector with modem protection
3. Foam rubber wrist rest
4. Diskette and/or compact disc file box
5. Printer cable (if necessary)
6. Backup drive, either Zip-type or tape
7. One extra toner cartridge, plus paper for the printer
8. Two boxes of formatted, blank 3.5-inch high-density diskettes
9. Extra Zip (or other removable media) disks
10. Antivirus software

Basic software

There is now a vast array of software to choose from, everything from word processors to programs that plan your next vacation trip. The absolute minimum you'll need is a good word-processing program. I also strongly recommend one of the personal information managers (pages 127–34), which keep track of your appointments and addresses, and a bibliography program like EndNote (page 235). And you'll need a good Internet browser like Netscape or Microsoft's Internet Explorer. Other useful software includes presentation software (pages 256–59), like Harvard Graphics or Micrografx's ABC Graphics Suite, for making slides and other visual aids; résumé programs (pages 355–57) to help design your résumé and track job contacts; and language programs (page 375) to help you learn and translate foreign languages.

Below, I describe some basic software programs, while other helpful programs are described elsewhere in the book. See Appendix B for a list of software programs and manufacturers. In discussing software, I have tried to mention products with which I am personally familiar. For detailed comparisons of these programs with other software, read *Computer Shopper, PC Magazine*, etc., ask your retailer's advice, or befriend a lonely computer nerd.

• *Windows 95*. Windows 3.x (3.x signifies Windows 3.1 or its variants) will work fine for now with most programs you might buy, so if you've already got it there's no urgent need to upgrade to Windows 95 or one of its descendants. However, most programs are being redesigned for Windows 95, and it will be increasingly hard to find programs that run on 3.x. Most new computers come with Windows 95 pre-installed, although you can often get the option of choosing Windows 3.1. I'd opt for Windows 95.

Once I'd spent a couple weeks grumbling while getting used to Windows 95, I found I like it better than Windows 3.1. One of the great features is multi-tasking for programs designed for Windows 95. With multi-tasking, if one program is doing something that takes a long time, like processing a video file or downloading something from the Internet, you can let the program grind away while you work with another program. Windows 95 also makes it easier to do the dreaded task of installing and de-installing most new programs, although you might have problems with some of your old DOS games. In case you're hesitant about switching entirely to Windows 95, note that you'll still have the option of using your familiar old Program Manager and File Manager from Windows 3.1. Windows 95 also comes with the bonus of Internet Explorer, a good Internet browser (if you have an early version of Internet Explorer, you can download a free update from http://www.microsoft.com/windows).

Word processing programs and office suites. The present generation of word processing programs has much more advanced features than those of a few years ago. For example, WordPerfect 6.1 for Windows displays your document exactly as it will print out, including bold, underlined, or italicized text. The font is displayed in the type and size it will have in the printed document. Compared with the old days of WordPerfect 5.x for DOS, it's now easy to include foreign-language letters and other typographic characters and symbols. It's also much easier to make tables, columns, outlines, and use other advanced features. If you're still using a DOS version, upgrading is well worth it. Similar advanced features are found in Microsoft Word, Lotus WordPro, and other top-flight word processors. One great feature of Lotus WordPro is easy creation of file folder-like tabs that let you click and jump to different portions of a complex document.

One of the strongest reasons for using a Windows-based word-processing program is that it is easy to integrate with other Windows programs; for example, to insert a word-processor document into an e-mail message or drag a database table into a word-processor document. Such integration is easier than ever because word processors are now being packaged with other useful office software in "office suites." My favorite word processor, WordPerfect, for example, can now be bought as part of the Corel WordPerfect Suite that also contains QuatroPro (a spreadsheet), Corel Presentations (for making slides), Sidekick (a personal-information manager), and more. ClarisWorks has gone furthest in seamlessly integrating word processing, spreadsheet, database, graphics, and presentation capabilities in one easy-to-use program. Other office suites include Microsoft Office and the Lotus SmartSuite.

Most consumer-level computers come with some productivity software installed, which usually includes a word processor, spreadsheet, and presentation graphics. Usually these are "works-type" programs, such as Microsoft Works, Novell PerfectWorks, or ClarisWorks, which are scaled-down versions of programs sold in office suites. For example, Microsoft Works is the scaled-down version of Microsoft Office, which sells now for about $400. The best approach is to try what comes bundled with your computer and then upgrade to its office-suite counterpart if you need more power.

Whichever way you go, a suite has a big advantage—the package costs less than the individual programs purchased separately. But even more important, the separate pieces are tailored to work together. In the case of the Corel suite, for example, a spreadsheet table from QuatroPro can be dragged directly into a WordPerfect document. Like many programs, Corel WordPerfect Suite can be purchased at a special academic price for students. Be sure to check with the company about student discounts before buying any program retail.

- *Dictionaries and encyclopedias.* Any top-name word processor will come with a spell-check program, but often you need a dictionary, too, for looking up the meaning, derivation, or pronunciation of words. Microsoft Bookshelf is a great program that includes a complete American Heritage Dictionary, a thesaurus, a pretty good atlas, an almanac, and a computer-searchable dictionary of quotations, so you can find that perfect quote to head your thesis chapter. You can also buy the American Heritage dictionary separately from SoftKey, in a talking version for those who like to hear how words are pronounced.

Bookshelf stays running while you are in your word processor (whether Microsoft Word, WordPerfect, or another), and you can switch to it instantly from a menu that shows up at the top of your screen. Because of the amount of data contained in Bookshelf, you need a CD-ROM to run it. If you follow my advice and get two CD-ROM drives, you can keep

Bookshelf loaded in one CD and still have another free to play music CDs or run other programs.

Another Microsoft product is Encarta, a multimedia encyclopedia, which is only moderately useful as a research tool but a lot of fun—when you look up "avalanche," you get to see video footage of a thundering snowslide. If you're a serious encyclopediac, you can buy a single CD containing the entire Encyclopaedia Britannica. In this case, the computer version is truly better than the original, because within each article are hyper-links to related articles. This means that if you are reading about Napoleon and Corsica is mentioned, a single click of the mouse will take you to an article about Corsica, from where another click will take you to articles about Corsica's interactions with ancient Rome or its geologic history. The ability to follow linked articles as fast as you can click your mouse, plus the ability to search the entire encyclopedia at once for any subject, makes this an awesome research tool. The price is hefty, but there are discounts for students, and it's cheaper if you buy at the end of the year. A low-cost route is to access Encyclopaedia Britannica on the Internet—the current charge for unlimited access is $150 per year, but ask them about a student discount (see http://www.eb.com/ for a free test drive).

- *Spreadsheets.* Spreadsheets aren't just for accountants. Windows-based spreadsheets like QuatroPro, Lotus 1-2-3, or Excell are easy to use and make mundane numerical tasks much easier. For example, I use QuatroPro to divide up utilities and other household expenses for the monthly accounting with my housemates. It used to take me several hours to do these accounts by hand but takes only fifteen minutes using QuatroPro. If I make errors entering data, I can correct them, and QuatroPro gives me a new answer instantly. You can also use a spreadsheet to develop budgets for research proposals and to maintain and manipulate some types of research data. Recent versions of most spreadsheets allow you to analyze your data statistically with chi-square and other standard statistical tests. You can purchase spreadsheet programs separately or included in office suites. QuatroPro is part of Corel's WordPerfect Suite, Excell is part of Microsoft Office, Lotus 1-2-3 is part of the Lotus SmartSuite, and ClarisWorks contains a spreadsheet component.
- *Tools for your operating system.* There are many programs that offer software tools beyond what you get with your basic DOS or Windows operating system. PC Tools or Norton Desktop, for Windows 3.x or 95, for example, allows you to restore a file after you've deleted it (provided that it hasn't been written over), fix corrupted data files, move data away from failing portions of your hard drive, and duplicate a diskette with

one read (with Windows 3.1 you have to insert the original and copy diskette several times to complete a disk copy). If you're still using Windows 3.1, the PC Tools file manager for Windows 3.1 is much more powerful than the file manager that comes with Windows, making copying or moving files from one drive to another much easier. Either will allow you to create an emergency boot diskette so that you can restore your operating files and get your computer running even if your hard drive has been erased.

Both PC Tools and Norton Desktop also replace the clunky Windows 3.x Program Manager with a nice desktop with well-arranged icons, similar to what you get with Windows 95 or Macintosh. My favorite program to replace the 3.x Program Manager is the inexpensive but elegant Metz Task Manager. This program replaces icons with nice little buttons that you only have to click once, and it also supplies a few useful utilities, like a file finder that will scan your entire disk for the file that contains a specific word string. Contact Metz at http://www.metz.com/metz/. You can also get replacement desktops for Windows 95. For example, MicroHelp makes one called PowerDesk.

Another group of moderately priced programs allows you to diagnose and in some cases fix problems. These diagnostic programs are primarily for people who want to be able to understand and tweak their computers themselves. Some features, however, like emergency boot disks, crash protection, and change removal can be lifesaving even for the computer illiterate. Also, even if you don't know enough to fix the problem yourself, the results of a system check may help a technical support person figure out what's wrong.

Quarterdeck's WinProbe95 (also for Windows 3.1) focuses primarily on diagnosing the hardware components of your system, telling you what hardware is installed, and identifying conflicts and memory problems, and it fine-tunes your system to improve performance. One great feature is a tutorial that teaches you how to diagnose problems and how the components of your computer work.

Quarterdeck also makes FixIt, another Windows 95 program, which finds and fixes software conflicts and restores missing program files. For example, a common error in Windows 95 is that the connection is lost between a program and its shortcut on the Program menu—you click it and nothing happens. Or you might find that a contact management program, like Sharkware, loses its connection to the word processor it uses for mail merges. Or you might find one of the dreaded "system error caused by such and such a file" messages. FixIt can often identify these problems and restore the missing links. FixIt also has a change remover that monitors any changes that occur when you delete files or install or delete programs. This is a nice fail-safe feature even for the beginning computer user. If any of these actions cause problems, FixIt can undo the changes and return your system to its original state.

Both FixIt and WinProbe95 provide crash protection. They position themselves between the application you are running and your operating system, so that any error in the application does not crash the system. They can usually isolate the error even before the application crashes, giving you the option of saving your data and exiting the program before a crash causes you to lose the data. Like PC Tools and Norton Desktop, they also let you create an emergency boot disk containing your system's configuration so you can start your computer if it won't boot normally. CyberMedia's First Aid 95 Deluxe has some of the capabilities of the Quarterdeck programs, including crash protection and emergency disk creation. In addition, First Aid 95 comes with on-line Tech Support Yellow Pages that let you use the Internet to connect to software and hardware vendors in case you need to buy or download something to fix your computer.

• *"Expanding" your hard drive.* There are several programs that allow you to compress data so that you can fit more files onto your hard drive. One option is to select individual files or directories and compress them using a program like MicroHelp's Zip (most of these types of programs have "Zip" in the name). Depending on the type of data in the file, you may be able to squish them down to as much as half their previous size. When you want to use compressed files, you need to "unzip" them. With MicroHelp Zip this is a simple process of clicking on the file name in a screen that resembles the Windows 3.x file manager. Because you won't want to zip and unzip a file every time you use it, probably you'll use your Zip program only to archive your old word processor documents or other infrequently used files, or to cram more backup data on a floppy disk. You will also commonly find that downloaded software updates from Internet sites come zipped because zipped files travel more quickly across the Internet. To use the files once you download them, you'll have to unzip them.

Another option for those in search of more disk space are disk-compression programs like Stac Electronics' Stacker or Microsoft's DriveSpace. Unlike a Zip program, these programs compress all the data on your entire hard drive, and they do it automatically. Your programs will run normally, but you'll have much more apparent room on your drive. Reviews of Stacker and DriveSpace by *PC Magazine* show that performance depends on which operating system you're running. Under most systems, you're likely to get more compression—better than two to one—with Stacker, but Stacker can also make your machine run slower than DriveSpace, about 10 percent slower under Windows 95. DriveSpace has the additional benefit of coming free with Windows 95 or NT. Reviews say that both these programs work well, but they definitely introduce a new level of complexity and possible conflicts to your system setup, so they may be more appropriate for the advanced user. With the price of hard drives as low as they are now, you can probably save yourself the headache by just getting a new drive when you run out of space. You can read about these and other programs by checking out *PC Magazine OnLine* at http://www.pcmag.com or *APN TechReview* at http://www.apnpc.com.au.

A third approach is to use PowerQuest's PartitionMagic. Let's say you've bought the latest computer with a massive one-gigabyte hard drive. It's likely to come with all types of software preloaded on the single drive. With all this software crammed helter-skelter into a single huge drive, you've got a situation analogous to buying a big house without interior walls to divide up the living space. PartitionMagic lets you divide the hard drive into smaller, manageable sections, called "logical drives" (as compared to literal, physical hard drives), so that you can organize your software by grouping directories and putting them into different logical drives. With PartitionMagic you can build or remove these partitions after programs have already been installed (previously, you could only partition your physical drive prior to loading software).

But PartitionMagic gives you more than organization. By dividing your big drive into smaller partitions, the program packs files into the hard drive's space more efficiently and you save space. According to Power-Quest, if you do not partition your drive, you'll waste approximately 40 percent of your available 1 gigabyte, but if you divide it into partitions of less than 255 megabytes, you will waste only approximately 4 percent.

- *Memory management.* If you're in DOS or Windows 3.x and you frequently encounter the dreaded "out of memory" errors, you may solve the problem with a proprietary memory manager that improves on the performance of the memory manager that came with your operating system. For example, Quarterdeck's QEMM can improve programs run under Windows or DOS by increasing the amount of available conventional memory, which it does by moving some programs out of conventional memory to another area. The result is that you can run larger programs more quickly under Windows 3.x and DOS, and under Windows 3.x you may be able to keep more windows open at once. According to Quarterdeck technical support, you may not see much improvement in performance using a proprietary memory manager under Windows 95, unless you are using an older computer that uses drivers loaded into low memory.

- *Antivirus.* You are at risk from computer viruses if you exchange disk-ettes with other users or download files from the Internet. Although you can't get a virus just from exchanging e-mail, you could get one from an e-mail attachment if it's an executable file that you run. One of my friends was even contaminated by shrink-wrapped diskettes from a major software company. A virus can do anything from slowing down or crash-ing your system to wiping out your data. To protect yourself, you need at least one good antivirus program. Experts recommend that you use two or more programs, because no one program will catch all viruses, and each will catch some the others miss. You can purchase antivirus programs as a module of some utilities, like PC Tools, or as stand-alone products like Norton Antivirus and McAfee's VirusScan. With any antivirus, you need to get frequent updates to ensure that you have protection against the latest viruses—those pesty virus-makers are al-ways hatching something new—so figure in the cost of updates when buying the initial program. Many companies offer unlimited updates, which you can download off the Internet, for a set annual fee.

  Most antivirus programs monitor your system continuously for viruses, and they do this by running continuously in low memory as what are called "terminate and stay resident programs" (TSR). This constant vig-ilance comes at a price: they can conflict with other TSR programs, they take up some of the extremely limited space in low memory—which can result in "out of memory" errors—and you need to shut them off before installing a new program. All this is such a hassle that many people shut off their virus protection, leaving their computers vulnerable. McAfee's VirusScan in the Windows 95 or Windows 3.x version has beaten this problem by loading into high memory instead of running as a low-memory TSR. You can download McAfee off the Internet as shareware (http://www.mcafee.com/down/). You can find out a lot about viruses and antivirus programs by checking out the virus newsgroup at news:alt.comp.virus, or by contacting the home page of Henri Delger for information and free antivirus software at http://pages.prodigy.com/virushelp.

- *Cruising the Internet.* As a student, you'll probably get Internet access through your school, so you may not need to worry about paying for an account. If you should need to subscribe to a commercial service, note that prices and quality vary widely. Compuserve and some other well-known services charge you a monthly fee and then by the hour over some minimum. That's not much, but you can do better if you're just looking for no-frills e-mail and Internet access. For example, I use Erol's, which gives unlimited use for your monthly fee. With some no-frills services you'll have to obtain your own Internet browser—Netscape has been dominating the market, but Microsoft's Internet Explorer is giving them strong competition. If you purchase Windows 95 you can get Microsoft's Internet Explorer for free. For e-mail, you definitely want a full-featured, easy-to-use e-mail program like Eudora Pro because a weak program can make daily e-mail management very tiresome. You can download Eudora Light for free from http://eudora.com, which will suffice if you don't receive much mail, but upgrading to Adhere Pro will make mail handling much simpler.

- *Faxing.* You can also send and receive faxes with your computer's modem, viewing them on your screen or printing them with your printer. Most computers that come with a modem also come with bare-bones fax software, which may suffice if you don't need a lot of frills, but the free programs I've received were pretty bad. For those who want more capability and ease of use, you can try a program like Delrina's WinFax Pro or Datastorm's ProCommPlus. Because a fax is a picture and not a text document, you need to use OCR software, which comes with most dedicated fax programs, to convert the fax into a text document that can be edited on your word processor. This is a big advantage your computer has over a traditional fax machine, which does not give you the capability to electronically modify the paper fax. You can also use your fax program to create a word-processing document and send it out as a fax. If you need to send an exact facsimile—of a financial aid form, for example— you can use a scanner to input the document into your computer. If you haven't bought a scanner, another option is to use a dedicated fax machine to send faxes, and still receive them with your computer.
- *Exchanging data.* If you need to send a word-processing or other data file to a fellow researcher, one option is to attach it to an e-mail message and send it over the Internet. However, there are dedicated communications programs that let you send data more securely and rapidly. Datastorm's ProCommPlus, for example, lets you link two computers directly by modem so that you can exchange data without worrying that it will be pirated on the Internet. (ProCommPlus is a comprehensive communications package that gives you data transfer, fax capability, and an Internet browser.) You can also use ProCommPlus's scripting language to automate the data transfer, so if you wish to send your latest data every Thursday at midnight, ProCommPlus will do it automatically. ProCommPlus will also let you connect to electronic bulletin boards (BBS)

maintained by companies, so that you can find out about new products and download software updates. For example, it's common to find that a program you just bought won't work because your video driver (a computer program) is out of date. The easiest solution is usually to use ProCommPlus or another communications package to download a new driver from the BBS maintained by the video card manufacturer. This last use will become less and less important as more manufacturers develop Internet sites where you can find and download drivers.

Several programs, including Laplink for Windows 95 and Norton's pcAnywhere, allow you to access files or manipulate data in a remote computer. For example, if you are on a trip with your laptop, you can use Laplink to dial your desktop computer at home and read your e-mail. If you forget to bring a crucial document with you, you can call your home computer, edit the document remotely, and then download it into your laptop. Once you're back home, you can link the two computers and have Laplink synchronize files so that any changes you've made to a file are automatically updated in both computers.

- *Desktop publishers.* In the last decade, powerful but relatively user-friendly programs like Adobe's PageMaker and FrameMaker have made self-publishing easy. For example, with PageMaker you can take a research report or other word-processing document and lay it out as a quality professional report, complete with color photographs or other imported art. This can give professional gloss to unpublished research you submit with job applications or pass out at presentations. Compared to word processors, a desktop publisher makes it easier to handle tables, charts, columns, and other formatting. You can wrap text around photos or figures that you import from other programs. Students in fields like psychology, sociology, or business can use desktop publishers to design questionnaires and other research instruments. PageMaker has a built-in text editor that allows you to modify text while doing page layout; it allows you to switch back and forth easily between open documents; and it provides a scripting language that allows you to automate common tasks. For such a powerful program, PageMaker is quite easy to learn. If you want to get your feet wet with desktop publishing inexpensively, try Spinnaker's Easy Working for Windows Desktop Publisher, which costs roughly $30 and is easy to learn!
- *Graphics.* Graphics programs are much more powerful than they were ten years ago and contain so many features that it's impossible to do them justice in a small space. Take a look at the reviews in *Software: What's Hot! What's Not!* (Cheryl Currid & Company). You can use

these programs for graphic design, including logos and advertisements, and you can make charts and graphs, retouch scanned pictures and photographs, or create animation or original art using a variety of brush types and textures. For serious drawing, you can buy a pressure-sensitive pad with a stylus, which gives you much more control than a mouse does. Programs range in capability and price from modest, like CA-Cricket Paint, to high-powered programs like CorelDRAW!, which is the primary program I use. PaintShop Pro is a great program at only about $50.

CorelDRAW! is a graphics suite that contains several modules, including a drawing program (CorelDraw, without an exclamation point) that lets you manipulate text and draw and edit in color. You can lighten underexposed photos, edit out details you don't want, or colorize a black-and-white photo. The outputs can be incorporated into slide presentations (pages 256–59), or used in publication or any other application needing graphics work. Other good programs with similar capabilites are Micrografx's ABC Graphics Suite and the Fractal Design Painter.

• *Screen savers*. The most beautiful screen saver ever, by far, is Deep River's Fractal Sideshow, which works with either Windows 3.x or 95. (Order from Deep River Publishing, PO Box 9715-975, Portland, ME 04104, phone: 207 871-1684; http://www.deepriver.com/drp/catalog.htm.)

LANGUAGE SOFTWARE

CD-ROM software packages make language learning much easier. Compared to the torture of flash cards or languages tapes, even grammar drills can be fun with some of the better computer programs. Because different companies take different approaches to language learning and each student learns differently, you should probably get more than one program and use them to complement each other.

My favorite is the Learning Company's Learn to Speak series, which is well produced and offers you short movies, videos of native speakers, listening-comprehension tests, and lots of well-designed games. I've tried the Spanish version, and even drilling in vocabulary is fun. If you click on a vocabulary word, the computer speaks it, and if you click a button that says "hear in context," a Latin video babe or hunk appears and uses the word in a sentence. The Learning Company also publishes a great Vocabulary Builder CD, in some languages, which teaches you over two thousand words; it's packed with hundreds of photos and drawings of common objects and actions. In "learning mode," your computer will say that appropriate word aloud in Spanish as each picture comes on the screen. In test mode, the pictures act like flash cards and the computer keeps score of how many you type or say correctly (if your computer is equipped with a microphone, Learn to Speak will judge whether you say the word correctly). A bad answer, and you're rated a "tourist." They also publish Berlitz Think and Talk, containing elementary lessons in Spanish, French, Italian, or German. Given the choice between Learn to Speak and Berlitz, I'd go with Learn to Speak. I found it more fun, and it covers much more material.

Transparent Language also puts out a good series. They center their teaching on the written text of a story, which appears on the screen, read aloud by a disembodied voice (there's no video of the speaker, as there is in Learn to Speak). To help you follow along, the computer highlights whichever sentence in the story is being read, and the translation of the sentence appears below the story's text. With Transparent Language you get lots of practice in aural comprehension and relatively lengthy stories. As with Learn to Speak, there is an assortment of games that ask you to fill in blanks and unscramble sentences. Transparent Language also offers an add-on dictionary program that will give you more complete definitions of the words in your stories (I'm not sure you really need this) and a pretty feeble no-frills grammar program called GrammarPro!. If you like the Transparent Language series, you can buy additional CDs with more stories, including mysteries, modern fiction, and classics. Transparent Language is different enough from Learn to Speak that you wouldn't go wrong buying both programs and using them to complement each other.

I also strongly recommend Fairfield Language Technologies' Rosetta Stone series. Rosetta Stone consists of nonstop drills in which you're shown several photographs on a theme and have to choose the correct photograph in response to a spoken question in the language you're learning. For example, you might be shown different types of fire-fighting equipment and be asked to pick out the picture showing the hose. Rosetta Stone doesn't have some of the whistles and bells of the other programs—there isn't any video, for example—but it does a very good job of rapidly building vocabulary and the rudiments. My guess is that this program would do the best job of building your vocabulary and understanding of short conversational phrases.

I also reviewed BayWare's Power series (as in Power Spanish), which I found annoying. Apparently, they believe that learning a language is intrinsically boring, so they go nontraditional by putting together lots of hyperactive little games in a confusing learning structure. They also make the mistake of deemphasizing vocabulary learning, under the theory that you can pick that up as you go along.

For those who need to read journal articles or review Web pages in a foreign language you don't know well, there's help in the moderately priced ($129) PowerTranslator from Globalink. Although PowerTranslator won't do a perfect job, particularly on very complex sentences, colloquial, or metaphorical language, it will translate straightforward language well enough for you to get the gist. You can improve the capability of the program by adding to its basic dictionary. Try out a translation at their Web site: http://www.globalink.com.

APPENDIX B

■ ■ ■ ■ ■ ■ ■ ■ ■ ■ ■ ■

USEFUL INTERNET ADDRESSES

■ ■ ■ ■ ■ ■ ■ ■ ■ ■ ■ ■

- *Getting started on the Internet.* For a quick introduction to how to use the Internet, check out *The Big Dummy's Guide to the Internet*: http://www.cs.indiana.edu/docproject/bdgtti/

  Zen and the Art of the Internet: http://www.cs.indiana.edu/docproject/zen/

  or, for a more complete guide, *Internet Web Text*: http://www.december.com/web/text/
- *National Association of Graduate and Professional Students.* Find out about e-mail discussion lists and how to become politically active in fighting for graduate student rights, including how to lobby Congress not to cut financial aid. Take part in a survey designed to assess how exploited you are: http://nagps.varesearch.com/NAGPS
- *Links to grad school information.* The Catapult Job Web Home Page: Graduate and Professional School Guides will link you to lots of other sites with info on grad schools: http://www.jobweb.org/catapult/gguides.htm

  The commercial site, Link Library, maintained by Kaplan, has links to lots of other grad school sites: http://www.kaplan.com/library/
- *General grad school advice.* The document *What Every New Graduate Student at IUCS Should Know* has a good quick review of how to do well in graduate school: http://www.cs.indiana.edu/docproject/grad.stuff.html

  One topic is "How to Do Research at the MIT AI Lab," which, despite the name, has lots of good advice for students in any field. You can get there directly at http://www.cs.indiana.edu/mit.research.how.to.html
- *Grad school contacts.* This site contains a list of grad schools with the

offices to contact for information: http://saturn.uaamath.alaska.edu/
tartan/acm/gradschool.html

- *Application advice.* You can get good basic information on applying from
UCLA, including information about choosing a grad school, how the
application process works, and—most useful—an approximate schedule
of when to do what: http://www.lifesci.ucla.edu/bio/gsii.html

    Even more complete information is available from *A Guide for Pro-
spective Graduate School Candidates.* In addition to application strategies, this has information on financial aid and taking standardized tests:
http://www.jobtrak.com/gradschool__docs/gradschool.html

    You can also get a brief overview from *How to Apply to Graduate
School,* posted by the University of Texas Web Central: http://www.
utexas.edu/ogs/outreach/applyto/

- *Study tools.* For information on Encyclopaedia Britannica on-line, go to
http://www.eb.com/

    For information on Princeton Review study aids for the GRE: http:
//www.review.com/

- *Financial aid information.* The Grants in Graduate Study gopher site,
maintained by New York University, is a comprehensive directory of
graduate financial aid resources: gopher://cwis.nyu.edu:7011/00/Ad-
missions/GIGS/

    The Graduate School Guide site describes different types of financial
aid in detail and lists addresses for contacting grad schools: http://
www.schoolguides.com/

    Cornell University provides an index to numerous foreign and domestic
graduate fellowship opportunities: gopher://gopher.cornell.edu/11/.dirs/
GRFN

    The University of Texas offers lots of links to financial aid resources:
http://www.utexas.edu/depts/gradopp/resources/internet.html

    Find out about financial aid for minorities from: http://www.
finaid.org/finaid/focus/minority.html

    You can get information and links to other financial aid sites via the
Foundation Center: http://fdncenter.org/2index.html

- *Job search.* Try the WinWay home page for links to many searchable
job-posting databases: http://www.winway.com

    Stanford University's site has links to many, many other job sites:
http://rescomp.stanford.edu/jobs/

    For example, they list about twenty links to academic-job postings,
like the Private School Employment Network: http://www1.mhv.net/
psen/

    For future academics (there are nonacademic Ph.D.-type jobs, too),
try the weekly postings of *The Chronicle of Higher Education*: http://

chronicle.merit.edu/.ads/.links.html

Or try Job Listings in *Academia*, with links to over five hundred academic-job sites: http://volvo.gslis.utexas.edu/~acadres/jla.html

Academic Positions in Science (they've got nonscience positions, too): http://members.tripod.com/~academia/

The Academic Position Network: gopher://rodent.cis.umn.edu: 11111/

JobWeb, a job site for the overeducated, maintained by the National Association of Colleges and Employers at http://www.jobweb.org/

For humor and class, try Emory University's Career Paradise site at http://www.emory.edu/CAREER/index.html

Here are a few commercial sites with big searchable databases:

The Monster Board: http://www1.monster.com

CareerNet is a true monster: http://www.careers.org/

JobCenter Search: http://www.interbiznet.com/home/ibn/hunt/jol

The Internet Job Locator: http://www.joblocator.com/jobs/

CareerMosaic: http://www.service.com/cm/

BIBLIOGRAPHY

The following authors were referred to by name in this book.

Allen, Jeffrey G. *How to Turn an Interview into a Job* (New York: Simon & Schuster, 1983).

American Chemical Society. *Starting Salaries, 1991* (Washington, D.C.: American Chemical Society, 1991).

Appleson, Robert R. "Stronger Requirements and a New Alternative." In *The Master's Degree: Jack of All Trades*, edited by Joslyn L. Green (Denver: State Higher Education Executive Officers, 1987).

Armstrong, J. Scott. "Unintelligible Management Research and Academic Prestige." *Interfaces*, 1980, 10(2): 80–87.

Asher, Donald. *Graduate Admissions Essays: What Works, What Doesn't, and Why* (Berkeley, Calif.: Ten Speed Press, 1991).

Bauld, Harold J. *On Writing the College Application Essay: Secrets of a Former Ivy League Admissions Officer* (New York: Barnes & Noble, 1987).

Becker, Howard S. *Writing for Social Scientists: How to Start and Finish Your Thesis, Book, or Article* (Chicago: University of Chicago Press, 1986).

Berelson, Bernard. *Graduate Education in the United States* (New York: McGraw-Hill, 1960).

Bodian, Lester H. *Career Instrumentality of Degree Completion as a Factor in Doctoral Student Attrition.* Ph.D. thesis (Ann Arbor: University Microfilms International, 1987).

Bolles, Richard N. *The 1990 What Color Is Your Parachute?* (Berkeley, Calif.: Ten Speed Press, 1990).

Breneman, David W., and Ted I. K. Youn, eds. *Academic Labor Markets and Careers* (New York: Falmer Press, 1988).

Career Associates. *Career Choices for Students of Mathematics* (New York: Walker & Co., 1990).

Carter, Allan M. "The Academic Labor Market." In *Higher Education and the Labor Market*, edited by Margaret S. Gordon (New York: McGraw-Hill, 1974).

Carter, D. J., and R. Wilson, *Minorities in Higher Education, 1995–96* (Washington, D.C.: American Council on Education, 1996).

Cassidy, Daniel. *The Graduate Scholarship Book* (New York: Prentice Hall, 1990).

Columbia Books. *National Trade and Professional Associations* (Washington, D.C.: Columbia Books). Published annually.

Council of Graduate Schools. Reported in "Attracting Minority Graduate Students and Faculty in an Atmosphere of Increasing Competition," by Trevor L. Chandler. *CGS Communicator,* 1988, 21(5): 4–5.

Davis, Martha, Elizabeth Robbins Eshelman, and Matthew McKay. *The Relaxation and Stress Reduction Workbook* (Oakland: New Harbinger, 1990).

Doerr, Harriet. *Stones for Ibarra* (New York: Penguin, 1988).

Educational Testing Service. *GRE/CGS Directory of Graduate Programs* (Princeton: Educational Testing Service, 1991).

Endicott, Frank S. *The Endicott Report: Trends in the Employment of College and University Graduates in Business and Industry 1980* (Evanston: Placement Center, Northwestern University, 1980).

Feingold, S. Norman, and Glenda Ann Hansard-Winkler. *Where the Jobs Are: A Comprehensive Directory of 1200 Journals Listing Career Opportunities* (Garrett Park, Md.: Garrett Park Press, 1989).

Flam, Faye. "Still a 'Chilly Climate' for Women?" *Science,* 1991, 252: 1604–6.

Gale Research. *Directories in Print* (Detroit: Gale Research, 1990).

———. *Encyclopedia of Associations* (Detroit: Gale Research, 1990).

Glazer, Judith. *The Master's Degree: Tradition, Diversity, Innovation* (Washington, D.C.: Association for the Study of Higher Education, 1986).

Gorey, Edward. *Amphigorey* (New York: Paragon, 1979).

Green, Howard, and Robert Minton. *Beyond the Ivy Wall: 10 Essential Steps to Graduate School Admission* (Boston: Little, Brown, 1989).

Hall, Donald. *The Oxford Book of American Literary Anecdotes* (New York: Oxford University Press, 1981).

Hall, Roberta M., and Bernice R. Sandler. *The Classroom Climate: A Chilly One for Women?* (Washington, D.C.: Project on the Status and Education of Women, Association of American Colleges, 1991).

Halleck, Seymour. "Emotional Problems of the Graduate Student." In *Scholars in the Making,* edited by Joseph Katz and Rodney T. Hartnett (Cambridge: Ballinger Publications, 1976).

Hines, David. "Admissions Criteria for Ranking Master's-Level Applicants to Clinical Doctoral Programs." *Teaching of Psychology,* 1986, 13(2): 64–67.

Jackson, Tom. *The Perfect Résumé* (New York: Doubleday, 1981).

Katz, Mark N. "Gorbachev Ruined My Career." In Washington *Post*, January 6, 1991, "Outlook" section, p. 2.

Klein, Bernard. *Guide to American Directories* (Coral Springs, Fla.: B. Klein Publishers, 1989).

Krannich, Ronald L., and Caryl R. Krannich. *Dynamite Résumés: 101 Great Examples & Tips for Success* (Woodbridge, Va.: Impact Publications, 1992).

LaPidus, Jules B. "The Strain of Quality." In *The Master's Degree: Jack of All Trades*, edited by Joslyn L. Green (Denver: State Higher Education Executive Officers, 1987).

Lathrop, Richard. *Who's Hiring Who* (Berkeley, Calif.: Ten Speed Press, 1977).

Leider, Anne, and Robert Leider. *Don't Miss Out: The Ambitious Student's Guide to Financial Aid* (Alexandria, Va.: Octameron, 1996).

Long, Thomas J., John J. Convey, and Adele R. Chwalek. *Completing Dissertations in the Behavioral Sciences and Education: A Systematic Guide for Graduate Students* (San Francisco: Jossey-Bass, 1988).

Madsen, David. *Successful Dissertations and Theses* (San Francisco: Jossey-Bass, 1988).

Marino, Kim. *Just Résumés: 200 Powerful and Proven Successful Résumés to Get That Job* (New York: John Wiley & Sons, 1991).

Martin, Roy. *Writing and Defending a Thesis or Dissertation in Psychology and Education* (Springfield, Ill.: Charles C. Thomas, 1980).

May, Ernest R., and Dorothy G. Blaney. *Careers for Humanists* (New York: Academic Press, 1981).

McCuen, Jo Ray, and Anthony C. Winkler. *Rewriting Writing: A Rhetoric* (New York: Harcourt Brace Jovanovich, 1987).

Medley, H. Anthony. *Sweaty Palms: The Neglected Art of Being Interviewed* (Berkeley, Calif.: Ten Speed Press, 1984).

Munschauer, John L. *Jobs for English Majors and Other Smart People* (Princeton: Peterson's Guides, 1991).

National Business Employment Weekly (New York: *The Wall Street Journal*).

National Center for Education Statistics. *Profiles of Faculty in Higher Education Institutions, 1988* (Washington, D.C.: Office of Educational Research and Improvement, U.S. Department of Education, 1988).

———. *Institutional Policies and Practices Regarding Faculty in Higher Education* (Washington, D.C.: Office of Educational Research and Improvement, U.S. Department of Education, 1988).

———. *Student Financing of Graduate and First-Professional Education,*

1992–93 (Washington, D.C.: Office of Educational Research and Improvement, U.S. Dept of Education, 1995).

National Research Bureau. *Working Press of the Nation*, Volume 2: *Magazine and Editorial Directory* (Chicago: National Research Bureau, 1991).

National Research Council. *Summary Report 1994: Doctorate Recipients from United States Universities* (Washington, D.C.: National Academy Press, 1994).

Nelson, Robert L. "Special Problems of Graduate Students in the School of Arts and Sciences." In *Emotional Problems of the Students*, edited by Graham B. Blaine, Jr., and Charles C. McArthur (New York: Appleton-Century-Crofts, 1961).

Office of Educational Research and Improvement. *Bachelor's, Master's, and Doctor's Degrees Conferred, by Field, 1982–83*. Unpublished data cited in Glazer, *The Master's Degree*.

Oltman, Philip K., and Rodney T. Hartnett. *The Role of GRE General and Subject Test Scores in Graduate Program Admission* (Princeton: Educational Testing Service, 1984).

Peterson's Guides. *Peterson's Grants for Graduate Students* (Princeton: Peterson's Guides, 1991).

Sarnoff, Dorothy. *Make the Most of Your Best* (Garden City, N.Y.: Doubleday, 1981).

Sternberg, David. *How to Complete and Survive a Doctoral Dissertation* (New York: St. Martin's Press, 1981).

Stumpf, Stephen A., Elizabeth J. Austin, and Karen Hartman. "The Impact of Career Exploration and Interview Readiness on Interview Performance and Outcomes." *Journal of Vocational Behavior*, 1984, 24: 221–35.

Valdez, Ramiro. "First-Year Doctoral Students and Stress." *College Student Journal*, 1982, 16: 30–37.

van den Berghe, Pierre L. *Academic Gamesmanship* (New York: Abelard-Schuman, 1970).

Van Heuklom, Paul. Washington *Post*, October 12, 1991, p. A23.

Verba, Cynthia. *Graduate Guide to Grants* (Boston: Harvard University, 1992).

Wyman, Roger E., and Nancy A. Risser. *Humanities Ph.D.'s and Nonacademic Careers: A Guide for Faculty Advisers* (Evanston, Ill.: Committee on Institutional Cooperation, 1983).

INDEX